Lexical Categories

For decades, generative lingu
verbs, nouns, and adjectives
presenting simple and substantive syntactic definitions of these three lexical
categories. Mark C. Baker claims that the various superficial differences found
in particular languages have a single underlying source which can be used to
give better characterizations of these "parts of speech." These new definitions
are supported by data from languages from every continent, including English,
Italian, Japanese, Edo, Mohawk, Chichewa, Quechua, Choctaw, Nahuatl,
Mapuche, and several Austronesian and Australian languages. Baker argues
for a formal, syntax-oriented, and universal approach to the parts of speech,
as opposed to the functionalist, semantic, and relativist approaches that have
dominated the few previous works on this subject. This book will be welcomed
by researchers and students of linguistics and by related cognitive scientists of
language.

MARK C. BAKER is Professor of Linguistics and Chair of the Department of
Linguistics at Rutgers University and a member of the Center for Cognitive
Science. He is the author of *Incorporation: a theory of grammatical function changing* (1988), *The polysynthesis parameter* (1996), and *The atoms of
language: the mind's hidden rules of grammar* (2001), as well as of numer-
ous articles in journals such as *Linguistic Inquiry* and *Natural Language and
Lingustic Theory*.

In this series

CAMBRIDGE STUDIES IN LINGUISTICS
General Editors: P. AUSTIN, J. BRESNAN, B. COMRIE,
W. DRESSLER, C. J. EWEN, R. LASS, D. LIGHTFOOT,
I. ROBERTS, S. ROMAINE, N. V. SMITH

LEXICAL CATEGORIES

Verbs, Nouns, and Adjectives

MARK C. BAKER

Rutgers University

CAMBRIDGE
UNIVERSITY PRESS

PUBLISHED BY THE PRESS SYNDICATE OF THE UNIVERSITY OF CAMBRIDGE
The Pitt Building, Trumpington Street, Cambridge, United Kingdom

CAMBRIDGE UNIVERSITY PRESS
The Edinburgh Building, Cambridge CB2 2RU, UK
40 West 20th Street, New York, NY 10011-4211, USA
477 Williamstown Road, Port Melbourne, VIC 3207, Australia
Ruiz de Alarcón 13, 28014 Madrid, Spain
Dock House, The Waterfront, Cape Town 8001, South Africa

http://www.cambridge.org

First published 2003

Printed in the United Kingdom at the University Press, Cambridge

Typeface Times 10/13 pt   *System* LATEX 2_ε [TB]

A catalogue record for this book is available from the British Library

Library of Congress Cataloguing in Publication data

Baker, Mark C.
Lexical categories: verbs, nouns, and adjectives / Mark C. Baker.
    p.   cm. – (Cambridge studies in linguistics)
Includes bibliographical references and index.
ISBN 0 521 80638 0 (hardback) – ISBN 0 521 00110 2 (paperback)
1. Parts of speech.   2. Grammar, comparative and general – noun.
3. Grammar, comparative and general – verb.   4. Grammar, comparative and
general – adjective.   5. Grammar, comparative and general – grammatical
categories.   I. Title.   II. Series.
P270 .B35   2002
415 – dc21   2002067074

ISBN 0 521 80638 0 hardback
ISBN 0 521 00110 2 paperback

To the memories of John S. Baker (1934–1968)

Gary Clay (1940–2001)

and Kenneth Hale (1934–2001).

I wish our earthly father figures could be a little more eternal.

Contents

Acknowledgements

To all the excellent reasons that I give my students for finishing their research projects as promptly as possible, I will henceforth add this: that you have a better chance of remembering all the people who deserve your thanks. This project was begun years ago, in a different country, when I had a different job title and different neighbors, and I doubt that anyone I have been in contact with during my transitions over the past eight years has failed to make some kind of impact on this work for the better. But rather than giving into my fears of forgetting and simply erecting a monument to "the unknown linguist," I gratefully acknowledge the help of those that happen to be currently represented in my still-active neurons. I hope that the others can recognize themselves in the gaps.

Financial support came first from the Social Sciences and Humanities Research Council of Canada and FCAR of Quebec, and more recently from Rutgers University.

Among individuals, I give pride of place to those who have shared their knowledge of their native languages with me with so much generosity, patience, and insight: Uyi Stewart (Edo), Grace Curotte and Frank and Carolee Jacobs (Mohawk), Sam Mchombo (Chichewa), Kasangati Kinyalolo (Kilega), and Ahmadu Kawu (Nupe). I would have little to work with if it were not for them.

Next, I thank my former colleagues at McGill University, who were instrumental in my taking up this project and in its first phase of development, especially Lisa Travis, Nigel Duffield, Uyi Stewart, Mika Kizu, Hironobu Hosoi, Ileana Paul, Asya Pereltsvaig, Mikael Vinka, and (from the greater Montreal community) Claire Lefebvre.

I also thank my current colleagues at Rutgers University, who helped me bring this project to completion and remove some of its faults, especially Veneeta Dayal, Roger Schwarzschild, Ken Safir, Jane Grimshaw, Alex Zepter, and Natalia Kariaeva. Two cohorts of Advanced Syntax Seminar students also made many useful suggestions, pushed me with good questions, and uncovered relevant data.

xii *Acknowledgements*

I thank the following people for reading significant chunks of the manuscript and giving me the benefit of their comments: Veneeta Dayal, Heidi Harley, Henry Davis, Hagit Borer, and five anonymous reviewers for Cambridge University Press. These people had different perspectives that complemented each other in wonderful ways and have helped to make this a better rounded and more knowledgeable book than it otherwise would have been.

In a special category of his own is Paul Pietroski, my official link to the world of philosophy. I also thank Lila Gleitman, Susan Carey, and others I have met through the Rutgers Center for Cognitive Sciences for discussions relevant particularly to chapter 5 of this book.

I have had two opportunities to present this research in an extended fashion away from my home university of the time: once at the 1999 LSA summer institute at the University of Illinois Urbana-Champaign; and once in a mini-course at the University of Comahue, General Roca, Argentina. These affected my views of what I was doing in profound ways, in part by putting me in contact with generous and energetic experts on other languages, including David Weber (Quechua), Jerrold Sadock (Greenlandic), Pascual Masullo, and Lucia Golluscio (Mapuche). I also thank Ken Hale for help with Nahuatl data. Without these people, I might literally have come to the opposite conclusions. For help on a more theoretical level, I thank many other participants in these forums, notably David Pesetsky and Joseph Aoun.

I have had opportunities to present parts of this work in many other contexts, including conferences and colloquia around the world. Here is where I am in the gravest danger of forgetting people, so I will name audiences only: the 9th International Morphology Meeting in Vienna, the 1996 NELS meeting in Montreal, the 1996 ESCOL meeting in St. John, New Brunswick, and colloquium audiences at MIT, University of Massachusetts Amherst, University of Connecticut, UCLA, University of Bergen, University of Tromsø, Nanzan University, and others. Members of these audiences contributed valuable suggestions, some of which are acknowledged at specific points in the text.

On a more general level, I thank my family, Linda, Kate, Nicholas, and Julia, for supporting me in many ways, keeping my body and soul in relative health, and showing flexibility in what counts as a vacation day or a Saturday morning activity.

Finally, I thank the God of historic Christianity, Father, Son, and Holy Spirit, not only for supplying the resources to attempt this project but also for the resources to draw each breath along the way.

Abbreviations

Agreement morphemes in Mohawk and other languages are glossed with a complex symbol consisting of three parts. The first is an indication of the person (1, 2, 3) or gender (M [masculine], F [feminine], N [neuter], Z [zoic], or a number indicating a noun class). The second is an indication of number (s [singular], d [dual], p [plural]; the latter two can be further specified as in [inclusive] or ex [exclusive]). The third is an indication of which grammatical function the morpheme cross-references (S [subject], O [object], P [possessor], A [absolutive], E [ergative]). When two agreement factors are expressed with a single portmanteau morpheme, their features are separated with a slash. Thus "MsS/1pinO" would indicate a masculine singular subject agreement together with a first person plural inclusive object agreement.

Other abbreviations used in the glosses of morphemes are as follows. Readers should consult the original sources for more on what these categories amount to in particular languages. When I could do so with relative confidence, I have changed the abbreviations used in the original source so that the glosses of the examples in this book would be more internally consistent.

ABS	absolutive case
ACC	accusative case
ADV	adverb
AFF	inflectional affix (especially on As in Japanese)
AN	adjectival noun (Japanese)
APPL	applicative
ART	article
ASP	aspect
ASSOC	associative
BEN	benefactive
CAUS	causative
CIS	cislocative
CL	classifier

COMP	complementizer
COP	copula
DAT	dative case
DEM	demonstrative
DESID	desiderative
DET	determiner
DIR	directional
DUP	duplicative
DYN	dynamic tense (Abaza)
ERG	ergative case
FACT	factual mood (Mohawk)
FEM	feminine gender
FOC	focus particle
FUT	future
FV	final vowel (Bantu)
GEN	genitive case
HAB	habitual
HSY	hearsay
IMPER	imperative
IMPF	imperfective aspect
INCEP	inceptive
INCH	inchoative
INCL	inclusive
INDEF	indefinite
INDIC	indicative
INF	infinitive
INSTR	instrumental
INTEROG	interrogative
INV	inverse
LK	linker
LOC	locative
MASC	masculine gender
NCL	noun class prefix
NE	prenominal particle (Mohawk)
NEG	negative
NEUT	neuter gender
NOM	nominative case
NOML	nominalizer
NSF	noun suffix

PART	partitive
PASS	passive
PAST	past
PERF	perfect or perfective
PL, PLUR	plural
POSS	possessive
PRED	predicative functional head
PRES	present
PRT	particle
PUNC	punctual
REAL	realis
RED	reduplication
REL	relative marker
SE	reflexive clitic (Italian)
SG	singular
STAT	stative aspect
SUBJN	subjunctive mood
TNS	tense
TOP	topic
TRAN	transitive
TRANS	translocative
VALID	validator (Quechua)
VBZR	verbalizer
VEG	vegetable gender (Jingulu)

The following are abbreviations of linguistic terms: names of principles, grammatical categories, theoretical frameworks, and the like:

Ag	agent theta-role
AP	adjective phrase
Arb	arbitrary interpretation
C	complementizer
CSR	canonical structural realization
D, Det	determiner
ECP	empty category principle
Go	goal theta-role
HMC	head movement constraint
LFG	lexical-functional grammar
LVC	light verb construction

NLC	noun licensing condition
NP	noun phrase
P&P	principles and parameters theory
PHMG	proper head movement generalization
PP	prepositional or postpositional phrase
RPC	reference-predication constraint
SM	subject-matter theta-role
Spec, XP	specifier of XP
SVC	serial verb construction
T	tense
Th	theme theta-role
UTAH	uniformity of theta-assignment hypothesis
VP	verb phrase

1 The problem of the lexical categories

1.1 A theoretical lacuna

It is ironic that the first thing one learns can be the last thing one understands. The division of words into distinct categories or "parts of speech" is one of the oldest linguistic discoveries, with a continuous tradition going back at least to the *Téchnē grammatikē* of Dionysius Thrax (*c.* 100 BC) (Robins 1989: 39). Dionysius recognized that some words (*ónoma*, alias nouns) inflected for case, whereas others (*rhēma*, alias verbs) inflected for tense and person. This morphological distinction was correlated with the fact that the nouns signified "concrete or abstract entities" and the verbs signified "an activity or process performed or undergone." The historical precedence of this linguistic insight is often recapitulated in contemporary education: often when students enter their first linguistics class, one of the few things they know about grammar is that some words are nouns, others are verbs, and others are adjectives. Linguistics classes teach them many fascinating things that go far beyond these basic category distinctions. But when those classes are all over, students often know little more about what it means to be a noun, verb, or adjective than they did at first, or indeed than Dionysius did. At least that was true of my education, and of the way that I learned to educate others.

For many years, most of what the Principles and Parameters (P&P) tradition of Generative Syntax has had to say about the lexical categories is that they are distinguished by having different values for the two binary distinctive features $+/-$N and $+/-$V in the following way (Chomsky 1970).[1]

---

[1] Chomsky (1970) did not, in fact, include adpositions in his feature system at first. The gap was filled in by Jackendoff (1977), in light of his influential view (which I argue against in the appendix) that prepositions constitute a fourth lexical category.

More recent sources that use essentially this feature system include Stowell (1981), Fukui and Speas (1986), and Abney (1987). Fukui's innovation was to extend Chomsky's feature system from the lexical categories to the functional ones. Abney's goal is similar, except that he suppresses the feature $+/-$verbal, making it difficult to account for the difference between nouns and adjectives or between verbs and prepositions in languages where these are distinct. See section 1.3 below for Jackendoff's (1977) alternative system and others related to it.

(1)   a +N, −V = noun
         b −N, +V = verb
         c +N, +V = adjective
         d −N, −V = adposition (preposition and postposition)

But this theory is widely recognized to have almost no content in practice. The feature system is not well integrated into the framework as a whole, in that there are few or no principles that refer to these features or their values.[2] Indeed, it would go against the grain of the Minimalist trend in linguistic theory (Chomsky 1995) to introduce extrinsic conditions that depend on these features. All the features do is flag that there are (at least in English) four distinct lexical categories. Since 4 is 2^2, two independent binary features are enough to distinguish the four categories, but there is no compelling support for the particular way that they are cross-classified in (1). By parallelism with the use of distinctive features in generative phonology, one would expect the features to define natural classes of words that have similar distributions and linguistic behaviors. But of the six possible pairs of lexical categories, only two pairs do not constitute a natural class according to (1): {Noun, Verb} and {Adjective, Adposition}. Yet these pairs do, in fact, have syntactic similarities that might be construed as showing that they constitute a natural class. For example, both APs and PPs can be appended to a transitive clause to express the goal or result of the action, but NPs and VPs cannot:

(2)   a John pounded the metal flat.   (AP)
         b John threw the ball into the barrel.   (PP)
         c *John pounded the metal a sword.   (NP)
         d *John polished the table shine.   (VP)

In the same way, only adjectives and adpositions can modify nouns (*the man in the garden* and *the man responsible*) and only they can be preceded by measure phrases (*It is three yards long* and *He went three yards into the water*). All told, there is probably as much evidence that adjective and adposition form a natural class, as there is that noun and adposition do. The feature system in (1) is thus more or less arbitrary. Stuurman (1985: ch. 4) and Déchaine (1993: sec. 2.2) show that syntactic evidence can be found in favor of any logically possible claim that two particular lexical categories constitute a natural class.

---

[2] At one point, case theory was an exception to this. In the early 1980s, it was common to say that the −N categories could assign case, whereas the +N categories received case (Stowell 1981). That is not the current view however; rather, Ns and As license genitive case, which happens to be spelled out as *of* in English (Chomsky 1986b).

Stuurman goes on to conclude that the idea of decomposing syntactic categories into complexes of features is bankrupt.

Related to this is the fact that generative linguistics has been preoccupied with explaining the similarities that hold across the lexical categories, and has had little to say about their differences. X-bar theory, a central component of the theory (at least until recently), clearly had this goal. Chomsky (1970) introduced X-bar theory precisely to account for the observation that nouns take the same range of complements and form the same types of phrases as verbs do. From then till now, the job of X-bar theory has been to account for the sameness of the various categories, but not for their differences. This is also true of the extensive research on functional categories over the last two decades. A common theme in this work, as initiated by Abney (1987), has been to account for the structural parallels between clauses and nominals – for example, the similarity of complementizers and case markers, of tense and determiners, and of aspect and number. Much important insight has come from these two research thrusts. But when one is steeped in these lines of work, it is easy to forget that the various lexical categories also differ from one another, and the theory has almost nothing to say about these differences. In most contexts, one cannot swap a verb for a noun or an adjective and preserve grammaticality, and X-bar theory and the theory of functional categories by themselves can never tell us why. The time thus seems ripe to attend to the differences among the lexical categories for a while.

1.2   Unanswerable typological questions concerning categories

A serious consequence of the underdevelopment of this aspect of syntactic theory is that it leaves us ill equipped to do typology. The literature contains many claims that one language has a different stock of lexical categories from another. In many cases, these claims have caused controversy within the descriptive traditions of the language families in question. Since there is no substantive generative theory of lexical categories, we have no way to assess these claims or resolve these controversies. Nor do we make interesting predictions about what the consequences of having a different set of basic categories would be for the grammar of a language as a whole. Therefore, we cannot tell whether or not there is any significant parameterization in this aspect of language.

To illustrate this crucial issue in more detail, let us consider the actual and potential controversies that arise when trying to individuate the lexical categories in the Mohawk language. For example, does Mohawk have adjectives? The traditional Iroquoianist answer is a unanimous no; Mohawk has only stative verbs, some of which are naturally translated as adjectives in English. The primary evidence for this is that putative adjectives take the same agreement prefixes and some of the same tense/aspect suffixes as uncontroversial intransitive verbs:

(3)   a *ka*-hútsi   compare: t-a'-*ka*-yá't-ʌ'-ne'
           NsS-black   CIS-FACT-NsS-body-fall-PUNC
           'it is black'   'it (e.g. a cat) fell'
        b *ra*-hútsi   compare: t-a-*ha*-yá't-ʌ'-ne'
           MsS-black   CIS-FACT-MsS-body-fall-PUNC
           'he is black'   'he fell' (*ra* → *ha* when not word-initial)
        c ka-rák-ʌ   compare: t-yo-ya't-ʌ'-ʌ
           NsS-white-STAT   CIS-NsO-body-fall-STAT
           'it is white'   'it has fallen'
        d ka-hutsí-(Ø)-*hne'* compare: t-yo-ya't-ʌ'-ʌ-*hne'*
           NsS-black-   CIS-NsO-body-fall-STAT-PAST
           (STAT)-PAST
           'it was black'   'it had fallen'

The tradition of considering inflectional evidence of this kind as central to judgments about category membership goes all the way back to Dionysius's *Téchnē*, and has been influential throughout the history of linguistics in the West (Robins 1989).

Putative adjectives are also like intransitive verbs in another way: they both allow noun incorporation, a process by which the head noun of an argument of the verb appears attached to the verb root to form a kind of compound (Mithun 1984; Baker 1996b):

(4)   a Ka-wis-a-hútsi   thíkʌ.
           NsS-glass-Ø-black   that
           'That glass is black'
        b T-a'-ka-wís-ʌ'-ne'   thíkʌ.
           CIS-FACT-NsS-glass-fall-PUNC   that
           'That glass fell.'

This seems to corroborate the claim that words like *hutsi* 'black' are verbs in Mohawk.

Nevertheless, if "adjectives" are verbs in Mohawk, then they must be identified as a subclass that has some special properties. Adjectival roots cannot, for example, appear in the punctual or habitual aspects, but only in the stative aspect:

(5)   a *wa'-ká-rak-e'   compare: t-a'-ka-yá't-ʌ'-ne'
          FACT-NsS-white-PUNC   CIS-FACT-NsS-body-fall-PUNC
          'it whited'   'it fell'
       b *ká-rak-s   compare: t-ka-yá't-ʌ'-s
          NsS-white-HAB   CIS-NsS-body-fall-HAB
          'it whites'   'it falls'

This restricted paradigm does not follow simply from the semantic stativity of words like *rakʌ* '(be) white' because transitive stative predicates like *nuhwe'* 'like' can easily appear in all three aspects. Even when both "adjectives" and verbs appear in the stative aspect, there are differences. Eventive verbs in stative aspect always show what looks like object agreement with their sole argument (see Ormston [1993] for an analysis consist with Baker [1996b]). In contrast, adjectival verbs in stative aspect often show subject agreement with their sole argument:

(6)   a *ka*-rak-ʌ   (*yo-rak-v* NsO-white-STAT)
          NsS-white-STAT
          'it is white'
       b te-*yo*-hri'-u
          DUP-NsS-shatter-STAT
          'it has/is shattered'

A more subtle difference between "adjectives" and (other) intransitive verbs is that only "adjectives" permit a kind of possessor raising. When a noun is incorporated into a word like *rak* 'white', that word can bear an animate object agreement marker that is understood as expressing the possessor of the incorporated noun (see (7a)). Comparable eventive verbs allow simple noun incorporation, but they do not allow a similar animate object agreement marker, as shown in (7b) (Baker 1996b: ch. 8.4).

(7)   a *Ro*-nuhs-a-rák-ʌ   ne Shawátis.
          MsO-house-Ø-white-STAT NE John
          'John's house is white.'
       b *Sak wa'-t-*ho*-wis-á-hri'-ne'.
          Jim FACT-DUP-*MsO*-glass-Ø-break-PUNC
          'Jim's glass broke.'

The unanswerable question, then, is this: do these differences justify positing a separate category of adjectives in Mohawk after all? Or do we continue to say that Mohawk has only verbs, but concede that there are two subtypes of verbs, intransitive stative verbs and other verbs? Generative syntactic theory gives no leverage on these questions, precisely because there are no principles of the theory that mention verbs but not adjectives or vice versa. Therefore, the choice we make has no repercussions and makes no predictions. In essence, the decision comes down to a matter of taste or terminology (Schachter 1985).

Similar issues arise concerning whether Mohawk has a distinct category of adposition. Some Iroquoianists have argued that it does; others say that the putative adpositions are really stative verbs or derivational noun suffixes. The best candidates are four bound morphemes that have locative meanings: *-'ke/-hne* 'at,' *-ku* 'in,' *-oku* 'under,' and *-akta* 'near.' (8) shows the results of combining these elements with four representative nouns of Mohawk:

(8)	'bed'	'box'	'table'	'car'
Ø	ka-nákt-a'	o-'neróhkw-a'	atekhwára	ká-'sere-'
'at'	ka-nakt-á-'ke	o-'nerohkw-á-'ke	atekhwará-hne*	ka-'sere-ht-á-'ke
'in'	ka-nákt-a-ku	o-'neróhkw-a-ku	atekhwara-tsher-á-ku	ka-'seré-ht-a-ku
'under'	ka-nakt-óku	o-'nerohkw-óku	atekhwara-tsher-óku	ka-'sere-ht-óku
'near'	ka-nakt-ákta	o-'nerohkw-ákta	atekhwara-tsher-ákta	ka-'sere-ht-ákta

The attraction of saying that these locative morphemes are stative verbs comes from the combinations in (8) having some of the same morphological peculiarities as noun incorporation into verbs. Nouns that are historically derived from verbs must be augmented by a "nominalizer" morpheme when they are incorporated into a verb. Thus, *-tsher* is added to *atekhwara* 'table' in (9a), *-ht* is added to *'sere* 'car' in (9b), and nothing is added (9c).

(9)   a Λ-k-atekhwara-*tsher*-úni-'
         FUT-1sS-table-NOML-make-PUNC
         'I will make a table.'
    b wa'-ke-'sere-*ht*-óhare-'
         FACT-1sS-car-NOML-wash-PUNC
         'I washed the car.'
    c wa'-ke-'nerohkw-a-hninu-'
         FACT-1sS-box-Ø-buy-PUNC
         'I bought a box.'

The examples in (8) show that the same lexically idiosyncratic augments appear when combining the locative elements with the nouns. Furthermore, when the incorporated noun (plus augment, if any) ends in a consonant and the verb root begins in a consonant, a special joiner vowel /a/ is inserted between the two (e.g. (9c)); (8) shows that this rule also applies to locative elements. These idiosyncrasies do not take place when other, clearly derivational suffixes are added to nouns.

Locative elements differ from stative verbs and derivational suffixes in other respects however. For example, the inflectional prefix on the noun (usually *ka-* or *o-*) is lost when it is incorporated into a verb (see (9)), but not when it is combined with a locative element, as shown in (8). (10) shows that even a possessive prefix can show up on a noun-plus-locative form.

(10)   Shawátis   *rao-*'seré-ht-a-ku
        John   MsP-car-NOML-Ø-in
        'in John's car'

This prefix *rao-* is phonologically distinct from any prefix that appears on true verbs.

Nouns that combine with locative elements also acquire new distributional possibilities. Nouns in Mohawk must normally be linked with a pronominal/agreement prefix on some verbal element in the clause. Thus (11b) is ungrammatical, in contrast with (11c). However, (11a) shows that this requirement does not hold of a noun plus a locative element.

(11)   a ThíkΛ o-nut-á-'ke   yó-hskats   ne okwire'-shú'a.
          that   NsO-hill-Ø-at NsO-be.pretty NE tree-PLUR
          'On that hill, the trees are pretty.'
        b *ThíkΛ onúta',   yó-hskats   ne okwire'-shú'a.
          That   hill   NsO-be.pretty   NE tree-PLUR
          'As for that hill, the trees are pretty.'
        c ThíkΛ   onúta' yó-hskats.
          That   hill   NsO-be.pretty
          'That hill is pretty.'

This difference in syntactic distribution is unexpected if the locative elements are merely derivational morphemes that form nouns from nouns.

Overall, then, nouns with the locative endings are not exactly like stative verbs, or simple nouns, or any other class of expressions in Mohawk. Again, the question arises whether these facts are enough to justify positing a distinct category of adposition for Mohawk. And again syntactic theory gives us little help in answering the question.

Finally, we can ask whether there is a category distinction between nouns and verbs in Mohawk. Most of the Iroquoianist literature says that there is, but there are potential grounds for doubting this, and Sasse (1988) argues against a distinction. Like verbs (and adjectives, if those are distinct), nouns can be used as the main predicate of a clause, as shown in (12).

(12)   a Ka-núhs-a'   thíkʌ o-'nerohkw-a'-kʌha.
        NsS-house-NSF that   NsO-box-NSF-former
        'That old box is a house.' (a child's play house, or a street person's shelter)
        b Ka-rák-ʌ   thíkʌ o-'neróhkw-a'.
        NsS-white-STAT that   NsO-box-NSF
        'That box is white.'

There are also inflectional similarities between nouns and other categories. Potential evidence for the standard view that nouns are a distinct category is the fact that no tense/aspect marker can be attached to nouns, not even the stative:

(13)   a *wa'-ká-nuhs-*e*'   punctual 'it housed'
        b *ka-núhs-*ha*'   habitual 'it always houses'
        c *(y)o-núhs-*u*   stative 'it is a house'
        d *o-khwarí-(Ø)-*hne*'   past 'it was a bear.'

Furthermore, the pronominal/agreement prefixes that attach to nouns are slightly different from the ones that attach to (adjectives and) verbs, as shown in (14).

(14)   a *ka*-núhs-a'   compare: *ka*-rák-ʌ
          NsS-house-NSF   NsS-white-STAT
          '(it is a) house'   'it is white'
        b *ó*-wis-e'   compare: *yo*-hnír-u
          NsO-glass-NSF   NsO-hard-STAT
          '(it is a) glass'   'it is hard'
        c *rao*-núhs-a'   compare: *ro*-nuhs-a-rák-ʌ
          MsP-house-NSF   MsO-house-Ø-white-STAT
          '(it is) his house'   'his house is white'

The prefixes that appear on nouns are not *very* different from the prefixes that attach on verbs, however. The nominal prefixes are cognates of the verbal ones: they can be analyzed as having the same underlying form, the noun prefixes being derived from the verb prefixes by morphophonological rules that delete initial glides (as in (14b)) and that create diphthongs out of some simple vowels (as in (14c)).

There are also more subtle parallelisms between the prefixes on nouns and the prefixes on verbs. An unaccusative verb (a verb that takes only an internal, theme argument) takes a prefix that expresses the person–number–gender properties of its subject; typically the form is a "subject" agreement prefix ((15b)), although some verbs are lexically marked as taking "object" agreement. In a similar way, a noun takes a prefix that expresses the person–number–gender properties of its referent, typically with a "subject" agreement (15b), but sometimes with an "object" agreement instead, depending on the particular noun root. A goal or affected object argument can also be added to almost any verb; this is always expressed as an "object" prefix (15a). In the same way, most nouns can take a possessor, and this too is expressed with the relevant "object" prefix ((15a)).

(15)   a *akó*-wis-e'   compare: t-a'-*akó*-hs-ʌ'-s-e'.
          FsP-glass-NSF   CIS-FACT-FsO-Ø-fall-BEN-PUNC
          'her glass'   'it fell on her; she dropped it'
       b *ra*-ksá'-a   compare: t-a-*ha*-yá't-ʌ'-ne'.
          MsS-child-NSF   CIS-FACT-MsS-body-fall-PUNC
          'boy'   'he fell'
       c **shako*-ksá'-a   compare: *t-a-*shako*-yá't-ʌ'-s-e'.
          MsS/FsO-child-NSF   CIS-FACT-MsS/FsO-body-fall-BEN-PUNC
          'her boy'   'he fell on her; she dropped him'

Given these generalizations, one would think that nouns and unaccusative verbs should also be able to bear explicitly transitive agreement prefixes, with the subject factor of the prefix expressing the referent of the noun or the theme of the verb, and the object factor expressing the possessor of the noun or the affected object of the verb. But this is not so: transitive prefixes are impossible on both nouns and unaccusative verbs, as shown in (15c). There is a rather striking overall parallel between the inflection of nouns and the inflection of unaccusative verbs in Mohawk, with the referent of the noun being analogous to the theme of the verb, and the possessor of the noun being analogous to the goal/affected object of the verb. This parallelism led me to propose that nouns in Mohawk form the same kinds of syntactic structures as unaccusative verbs (Baker 1996b: ch. 6). One could then take this one step further, and claim that nouns actually *are* unaccusative verbs. In this view (roughly that of Sasse 1988) there would be no distinction between the two categories in Mohawk syntax, but only at a superficial level of morphophonology.

This radical conclusion would be premature, however, since there are also differences between nouns and unaccusative verbs. As mentioned above, an important property of unaccusative verbs (including "adjectives") in Mohawk is that they allow their theme argument to be incorporated. In contrast, the referent argument of a noun can never be incorporated into the noun, as shown in (16).

(16)   a *Ka-'nerohkw-a-núhs-a'   (thíkʌ).   (compare (12a))
NsS-box-Ø-house-NSF   that
'That box is a house.'
b Ka-'nerohkw-a-rák-ʌ   (thíkʌ)
NsS-box-Ø-white-STAT   that
'That box is white.'

In Baker (1996b), I had no explanation for this difference between nouns and unaccusative verbs. Yet it does not seem to be an accidental difference; there are quite a few languages that allow noun incorporation into verbs (Mithun 1984), but no known languages that allow noun incorporation into nouns. Such a difference should ideally follow from a proper understanding of what it is to be a noun as opposed to a verb. It does not, however, follow from a theory that merely says that nouns are +N, −V and verbs are +V, −N. Nor does this theory give any firm basis for deciding whether nouns are a distinct class of heads from verbs in Mohawk or not.

I have lingered over the lexical category system of Mohawk because I believe that the issues it raises are entirely typical of those presented by other languages. Many languages are said not to distinguish certain adjectives from stative in-transitive verbs, including other Native American languages (Choctaw, Slave, Mojave, Hopi, etc.) and some African languages (such as Edo and Yoruba) (Dixon 1982; Schachter 1985). Other languages are said not to distinguish adjectives from nouns, including Quechua, Nahuatl, Greenlandic Eskimo, and various Australian languages (Dixon 1982; Schachter 1985). But even in these languages writers of dictionaries and grammars are often led to distinguish "adjectival nouns" from other nouns or "adjectival verbs" from other verbs because of some subtle phenomena. There is also a great deal of uncertainty across languages over what counts as an adposition as opposed to a noun suffix or dependent verb form. Even the existence of a noun–verb contrast is controversial in a few language families, most notoriously the Wakashan and Salish families of the Pacific Northwest and some Austronesian languages (Schachter 1985). These controversies typically hinge on disagreements about what importance to assign to different kinds of evidence, such as inflectional paradigms, derivational possibilities, syntactic distribution, and semantically oriented factors. The general problem of distinguishing categories from subcategories in a prin-cipled way has been observed by typologists like Schachter (1985: 5–6) and Croft (1991), among others. Since generative theory offers no decisive way to resolve these questions, we are left not knowing whether there is significant crosslinguistic variation in this respect or not, and if so what its repercussions are. This is a fault that I wish to remedy.

1.3 Categories in other linguistic traditions

Before embarking on a large-scale effort to fill this theoretical gap in the Chomskian framework, it is worth briefly surveying other approaches to see if they have already resolved these issues in a satisfactory way. If so, it could be a waste of time to develop a theory from scratch; the sensible thing to do would be to switch to another theory, or at least to co-opt some of its ideas. A quick survey suggests, however, that other approaches are not substantially ahead of the P&P tradition in this respect.

While he accepts the same theoretical presuppositions as Chomsky (1970), Jackendoff (1977: 31–32) proposes the alternative breakdown of the lexical categories into binary distinctive features given in (17).

(17)   a Nouns are +subj, −obj
        b Verbs are +subj, +obj
        c Adjectives are −subj, −obj
        d Adpositions are −subj, +obj

This system gives somewhat different natural classes of categories from Chomsky's original system; noun and verb form a natural class for Jackendoff but not for Chomsky, and so do adjective and adposition. Jackendoff asserts that these natural classes are the most useful ones internal to the assumptions of his (now-dated) theory. Jackendoff's features +/−subj and +/−obj, however, have no more actual syntactic content than Chomsky's +/−V, +/−N, their more evocative names notwithstanding. The feature +/−subj was chosen because verbal constructions and nominal constructions can both have subjects in English (the pre-nominal genitive, in the case of NP), whereas adjectives and prepositions do not. In the same way, the feature +/−obj invokes the fact that verbs and prepositions can be followed by a bare NP object, whereas nouns and adjectives in English cannot be. Jackendoff explicitly states, however, that these are merely heuristic labels, not to be taken too seriously. He realizes that his observations are not crosslinguistically robust: French nouns, for example, do not take English-like subjects (*Jean livre 'John('s) book', versus *le livre de Jean* 'the book of John'), and some Dutch adjectives can take NP complements. Even in English, a noun need not take a subject, and when it does not have one it does not thereby become an adjective. Similarly, not all verbs take an object, and those that do not are still not adjectives. Jackendoff's feature system is therefore not really any better than Chomsky's for our purposes. Nor are the natural classes of categories defined by (17) detectably more useful for syntactic theory than those defined in (1) (Stuurman 1985: ch. 4). Whereas I will agree with Jackendoff that whether a category takes a subject is a crucial defining feature, I think it is a mistake to try to make the second distinction also in terms of grammatical functions or argument structure. What is needed is a truly orthogonal second dimension to the analysis.

Déchaine (1993) argues for a system of lexical (and functional) categories that has the same topology as Jackendoff's, in that it makes noun and verb a natural class opposed to adjective and adposition. She draws the distinction in terms of a feature $+/-$referential, rather than $+/-$subject, however. Thus questions about whether nouns truly have subjects (and whether adjectives do not) are not problematic for her. In saying that nouns and verbs are both +referential, she wants to capture the fact that nominal projections denote things with the help of a determiner and verbal projections denote propositions with the help of a tense. Adjectives and adpositions, in contrast, are $-$referential. As such, they form modifiers rather than primary projections, and they do not have associated functional categories. Déchaine's system is, perhaps, the best that one can use with more or less arbitrary distinctive features. But it does not escape the problems that beset all such frameworks: the problem that no simple assignment of feature values leads naturally to an explanation of the various syntactic properties of a given category.

Hale and Keyser (1993; 1997) also assume the same gross topology of lexical categories as does Jackendoff. Their primary concern is not to explicate the nature of the lexical categories themselves but to use the lexical categories to explicate theta theory. They claim that verbs and prepositions take complements, and nouns and adjectives do not; this is like Jackendoff's $+/-$obj feature. They also claim that adjectives and prepositions form predicates, requiring a subject, whereas nouns and verbs do not. This is the exact opposite of Jackendoff's $+/-$subj feature. (The reversal is not as shocking as it might seem, however, because Jackendoff and Hale and Keyser have different senses of "subject" in mind: for Jackendoff, the subject of a given category is inside a projection of that category, whereas for Hale and Keyser it is outside the projection.) However, lexical categories have these properties only at the abstract level of lexical syntax in their system. Matters are significantly different in the more directly observable level of syntax proper, where verb is the prototypical predicative category, and nouns and adjectives can also take complements. Hale and Keyser's work was one of the motivating inspirations for my taking up this topic, and one of my concerns will be to adapt their insightful analysis of the differences between denominal verbs and deadjectival verbs. However, I seek a version in which the fundamental properties attributed to the lexical categories are true at the level of the normal syntax, and this will lead me to some of the opposite conclusions.

Somewhat farther afield are the alternative generative approaches, such as Lexical Functional Grammar (LFG), and Generalized Phrase Structure Grammar. Although these depart from mainline Chomskian assumptions in some important respects, they have not put forward a distinctive view of the lexical categories. Bresnan (1982: 294–95, 301) endorses Jackendoff's basic idea and takes it up into LFG. She is more serious about having the feature value +subj correspond to instances of a category that are predicated of something than Jackendoff was. But the disadvantage of this is that every lexical category can have the + value of this feature. The result is that the two features +/−subject and +/−object do not define four syntactic categories in a systematic way. Pollard and Sag (1994: 22–23), in contrast, seem less optimistic about the value of decomposing the lexical categories into more primitive features, despite their overall commitment to a feature-based theory. They simply list noun, verb, adjective, and preposition as four possible values of their "part of speech" feature. This feature is independent of the subcategorization features associated with the head, and indeed of all the features that do most of the syntactic work (see also Sag and Wasow [1999]).

Within Relational Grammar, Carol Rosen (1997) and Donna Gerdts have explored the idea that nouns and adjectives are syntactically similar to unaccusative verbs. This claim is very similar to my (1996b: ch. 6) analysis of nouns in Mohawk. Like that view, theirs captures some significant-looking parallels, but leaves unexplained the differences that force us to say that nouns are not *literally* a subclass of unaccusative verbs.

The standard formal semantics literature also leaves someone interested in the differences among lexical categories unsatisfied. The baseline assumption within this tradition is that nouns like *dog*, adjectives like *tall*, and intransitive verbs like *walk* all start out as one-place predicates that denote sets and are of type <e, t>. This is explicit in Siegel's (1980) work on the adjective, for example; see also Heim and Kratzer (1998: 62–63) for a recent discussion. Just as in Chomskian theory, the preoccupation has been to capture the similarities among the various categories – notably that they can all be used as predicates in matrix sentences or small clause environments. Differences between the categories are blithely assumed to be syntactic or morphological in nature. (Larson and Segal [1995] are somewhat unusual in including an explicit discussion of what makes the lexical categories different. They appeal to some lesser known distinctions in the philosophical semantic literature, particularly Geach [1962] and Gupta [1980]. Also relevant is Chierchia's [1998] claim that nouns can start out being of type <e>, rather than <e, t>. I will follow up these leads in chapter 3.)

In contrast to the generativists, functionalist linguists have had questions about the nature of the lexical categories and crosslinguistic variation in category systems quite high on their research agendas. Many leading functionalists have discussed the matter at some length, including Dixon (1982), Hopper and Thompson (1984), Givon (1984: ch. 3), Langacker (1987), Croft (1991), and others. While I am not able to discuss all these works in detail, some overall trends can be identified. The characteristic leading ideas of the functionalist views are that the lexical categories are prototype notions with fuzzy boundaries and that they are grounded in semantic and/or pragmatic distinctions. Hopper and Thompson (1984) and Givón (1984: ch. 3) argue that the different categories typically differ in the temporal properties of the things that they refer to: verbs denote events, which are dynamic, short-term states of affairs; adjectives denote states or properties, which are typically medium-length states of affairs; nouns denote things, which are long-term states of affairs. The emphasis is somewhat different for Croft (1991), Hengeveld (1992), and Bhat (1994). These authors distinguish the categories in terms of their prototypical functions in an act of communication: nouns are words that are typically used to refer; verbs are typically used to predicate; adjectives are typically used to modify. (Langacker [1987] blends aspects of both these two views: he distinguishes nouns from adjectives and verbs in that only the latter are intrinsically relational [i.e. predicative], whereas he distinguishes verbs from adjectives and nouns in that they tend to denote a process that develops over time.) The word "typically" is crucial here. Nouns *can* be used as predicates in predicate nominal constructions, and verbs *can* be used to refer to events in gerund constructions. These are not the prototypical uses of those words, however, and extra morphological or syntactic marking often accompanies them in their nontypical usage (see especially Croft [1991: ch. 2]). As a result, these functionalist approaches are not vulnerable to the discovery of simple counterexamples in the way that Jackendoff's, Hale and Keyser's, or Bresnan's theories are.

These functionalist approaches undoubtedly contain important grains of truth, and the functionalist-typologists have collected valuable material on what these issues look like across languages. Important landmarks are: Dixon (1982), who called early attention to the issue of variation in category systems; Bhat (1994), who gives a more recent and comprehensive overview of the issues; Wetzer's (1996) and Stassen's (1997) closely related works, which have collected a large range of relevant material. I make frequent use of these authors' empirical material and typological generalizations. Moreover, my leading intuition about nouns and verbs (but not adjectives) is very similar to Croft's, Hengeveld's, and Bhat's – that nouns are somehow inherently suited to referring and verbs are inherently predicative, other uses requiring the support of additional morphosyntactic structure.

These debts and commonalities notwithstanding, I believe that there are significant advantages to working out these intuitions within a more deductive, generative-style framework. I take it that a crisper, more formal theory of the lexical categories would be inherently desirable if one could be produced that was adequately grounded in empirical fact. The very feature that insulates functionalist approaches from easy counterexamples (its use of prototypes) also prevents them from making sharp predictions about the morphosyntax of the lexical categories. A generative approach might support a richer deductive structure, much as one can build a taller building on rock than on sand. Perhaps then linguistic theory could get farther beyond the familiar insights of traditional grammar than has been possible so far. Since we do not know that such a theory is impossible, it is worth trying to develop one. I also refer interested readers to Newmeyer (1998: ch. 4) for a detailed discussion of the functionalist approach to categories that shows how an informed formalist can remain unconvinced by it.[3]

Another concern is what functionalist approaches imply about the nontypical members of a category, beyond the fact that they can exist. *Eat* is a prototypical instance of the category verb because it describes a process of limited duration, whereas *hunger* is a less typical instance of a verb. This judgment about prototypicality fits well with the fact that *hunger* is related to the more common adjective *hungry*, but there is no adjective equivalent to *eat* in English or other languages. This is all well and good, but it says little about why the syntaxes

---

[3] Newmeyer also makes the useful point that much of the gradation observable in which notions are expressed by words of which category can be attributed to the learning process, rather than to the theory of the categories *per se*. Learning is a pragmatic matter concerning language use on anyone's view. I touch on these matters, and the related question of why certain concepts tend to be lexicalized with words of a given category, in chapter 5. I also give a brief critique of notionally based theories of the lexical categories there.

Let me also add a comment on functionalists' attempts to find language-external grounding for the lexical categories. Croft (1991: chs. 2,3), for example, tries to explain the tripartite distinction between nouns, verbs, and adjectives in terms of semantic distinctions between things, actions, and properties, and the pragmatic distinctions between referring, predicating, and modifying. As for the semantics, I am not sure that there is a language/mind-independent ontological difference between things, events and properties – at least not one that maps neatly into the lexical categories. As for the pragmatics, I wonder why there are precisely these three pragmatic functions, no more and no less. These "external groundings" look like different labels for the language-internal noun/verb/adjective distinctions to me.

of *hunger* and *hungry* are so different, even though they express essentially the same property. *Hungry* differs from *hunger* in requiring a copula ((18a)), in being able to modify a noun directly ((18b)), in not bearing past tense morphology ((18c)), in being compatible with degree expressions ((18d)), and in being usable as a resultative secondary predicate ((18e)).

(18)   a Chris hungers.   versus   Chris *(is) hungry.
        b a hungry person   versus   *a hunger person
        c Chris hungered.   versus   *Chris (was) hungried.
        d Chris is as hungry as Pat. versus   *Chris as hungers as Pat.
        e ?The vet told them that they must walk their dog hungry each night. versus
           *The vet told them that they must walk their dog hunger each night.

In all these respects, *hungry* is identical to more prototypical adjectives like *small*, and *hunger* is identical to more prototypical verbs like *eat*. If one is interested in why this particular cluster of discrete consequences results from which lexical category a particular word happens to be in, a prototype theory is unlikely to hold the answer. Nor does the answer seem to lie in the nature of the eventuality being described, since *hungry* and *hunger* are a very close minimal pair in this regard. This seems to be a job for a relatively autonomous theory of grammar.

My view also differs rather sharply from the functionalist views of Croft, Hengeveld, and Bhat when it comes to adjectives. These authors all claim that it is the basic nature of adjectives to be modifiers, whereas I do not. I develop the idea that all one needs to say about adjectives is that they are not inherently predicative (like verbs) or inherently referential (like nouns). That they make good modifiers can be derived as a theorem from this, as shown in chapter 4.

This section is obviously not a full-scale comparison or critique of the theoretical approaches mentioned. Comparing frameworks built on different foundations is a much more subtle and tricky process. These remarks are intended only to situate my project in the larger context of the field, and to give preliminary justification for approaching the topic in a particular way – from an integrated formal perspective that emphasizes the differences among the lexical categories rather than (only) their similarities. Indeed, the task of full-scale comparison is in a sense premature, given that there is not yet a credible P&P theory worth comparing. My primary goal in this work is to provide such a theory. I draw some comparisons on specific points in passing in the chapters that follow, wherever that seems feasible and appropriate. Fuller cross-framework comparison, however, will have to wait for another occasion, after it can be judged to what extent my generative approach is successful in its own terms.

1.4 Goals, methods, and outline of the current work

1.4.1 Goals

My goal then is to provide a theory of the distinctions among the lexical categories within a formal generative approach to language, thereby redeeming the long-standing promissory note known as $+/-$N and $+/-$V. Such a theory should provide a unified account of the range of grammatical environments in which one lexical category can be used but not another, and of differences in the internal structure of words and phrases headed by the various lexical categories. The theory should also shed light on typological and parametric issues, providing a principled way of resolving controversies about the category inventories of particular languages. By doing so, it will lead to an answer to the larger question of whether languages differ significantly in their lexical category systems.

One sign of a successful theory is that it should apply to both "familiar" and "exotic" languages with roughly equal ease and insight. To that end, I develop and test my hypotheses with three sources of data in mind. Much data will come from English, the Romance languages, and (to a lesser extent) Japanese – languages that are spoken natively by many linguists and that have been studied extensively from a generative point of view. A roughly equal amount of data will come from three less-known languages that I have been able to study intensively with consistent access to native speakers: the Amerindian language Mohawk, the Nigerian language Edo, and (to a lesser extent) the Bantu language Chichewa. Finally, the book will be sprinkled with examples from other languages taken from secondary sources that seem clear and helpful, supplemented in some cases by communication with people who know those languages. Using this third source of information is more feasible for this project than for many others, because the lexical categories are familiar from traditional grammar and basic to grammatical systems; therefore, some information on this topic is available in virtually all grammars. By keeping these three sources of information in balance, I hope to avoid the dangers of both superficiality and parochiality. I do not attempt to construct a large and balanced sample of languages to test my ideas, the way that Hengeveld (1992), Wetzer (1996), and Stassen (1997) have, but where possible I test my ideas against generalizations that they have discovered, and use their lists to identify other languages worth looking into.

Another sign of a successful theory is that it should explain both elementary phenomena and subtle, sophisticated ones. For this reason, I try to account for surprising contrasts among the lexical categories that occur in the corners of particular languages. At the same time, I also try to account for contrasts between the lexical categories that are so familiar that it is easy to forget that they do not have a good theoretical explanation. For example, a subtle distinction between verbs and other categories that emerges from the literature on unaccusativity is that intransitive verbs can be unaccusative, but comparable nouns and adjectives cannot. Burzio (1986) showed that some verbs allow their sole argument to be expressed by the partitive clitic *ne*, but comparable nouns and adjectives do not:

(19)   a Se ne   rompono molti.   (verb)
           SE of.them break   many   (Burzio 1986; Cinque 1990)
           'Many of them broke.'
        b *Ne   sono buoni pochi (dei suoi articoli).   (adjective)
           of.them are good few   (of his articles)   (Cinque 1990: 7)
           'Few of them (his articles) are good.'
        c ?*Ne   sono professori molti.   (noun)
           of.them are   professors many   (Mario Fadda, personal communication)
           'Many of them (people who wear glasses) are professors.'

I seek to explain this rather obscure fact in terms that also explain the obvious fact that predicative nouns and adjectives need copulas in English main clauses, whereas verbs do not:

(20)   a John ran.
        b John *(was) happy.
        c John *(was) a fool.

As for the noun–adjective distinction, Kayne (1984a: 139) notices that even though a genitive noun phrase and a nationality adjective can both express the agent in a derived nominalization ((21a,b)), only the genitive noun phrase can bind a reflexive anaphor ((21c) versus (21d)).

(21)   a Albania's resistance
        b the Albanian resistance
        c Albania's destruction of itself
        d *the Albanian destruction of itself

I seek to explain this subtle contrast in terms that also explain the obvious fact that bare nouns can appear in subject positions, but bare adjectives and verbs cannot:

(22)   a Water frightens me.
        b *Poor frightens me.
        c *Sing frightens me.

Functionalists' approaches rarely seem to get beyond the simplest data, whereas generative approaches often seem obsessed by the most baroque details; I hope to be responsive to both.

I will fail in these goals, of course, to varying degrees. But that is no excuse for not having the right goals.

1.4.2 Background theoretical assumptions

The lexical categories are a topic that spans many of the traditional divisions of linguistics, including inflectional morphology, derivational morphology, syntax, and semantics. I intend not to worry much about these distinctions, but to seek accounts of the differences among the categories that show up in all four domains in a unified way. With respect to the morphology–syntax boundary, this is a principled view: I believe that many aspects of morphology can in fact be attributed to head movement and other syntactic processes (Baker 1988c; Baker 1988a; Baker 1988b; Halle and Marantz 1993; Halle and Marantz 1994; Baker 1996b). With respect to the syntax–semantics boundary, this is more a view of convenience. For important parts of my theory, I present both a semantic intuition and a syntactic principle or representational device that expresses that intuition, leaving open questions about which of these is primary. On the one hand, it could be that the semantics is primary, and the syntactic principles and representations are notational conveniences that can be eliminated from the theory. On the other hand, it could be that the syntactic representations are primary, and the semantic effects emerge from them as we try to make use of the peculiar cognitive representations we find in our heads. Or both could be basic in their own domains, coexisting in a kind of natural, near-homomorphic relationship. I will not much concern myself with which of these views is ultimately correct. It will, however, be obvious that I am primarily a syntactician by training and temperament. Therefore, while I take ideas from the semantic literature at some points, I concentrate on those aspects of the problem that have a syntactic side to them, and expect my proposals to be judged by those criteria first. Beyond this general style of doing things, chapter 5 contains a discussion of what my research into the lexical categories seems to imply for questions about how syntax, morphology, semantics, and the lexicon relate to one another.

Next, a word about framework labels. I have chosen to present this research as an instance of the Principles and Parameters framework, even though that label is not used as often as the historically prior Government-Binding or the subsequent Minimalism. This is intended not only to express a quixotic longing for a measure of the historical continuity and cumulativeness of "normal science," but as the most neutral label for an inquiry that is broadly Chomskian in its concerns and background assumptions. In practice, for much of what I say the details of the framework are not particularly important, precisely because the topic at hand is one that no stage of Chomskian linguistics has had much to say about. Thus, the issues that arise are largely independent of those that characterize the different stages of the theory. Much of the distinctive technology of Minimalism, for example, centers on the role of features of various kinds in triggering movement, but the whole topic of movement is largely orthogonal to my inquiry, overlapping it only in one particular area (section 3.5). These innovations are thus of little relevance to this book. Given this, it seems reasonable to take the most generic label available, trying to achieve a kind of linguistic lingua franca. I do not intend this as a rejection of recent Minimalist ideas. On the contrary, I will have considerable use for the Bare Phrase Structure aspect of Chomsky (1995: sec. 4.3) in what follows, with its de-emphasis on X-bar theory. A tacit effect of this is that I often do not distinguish very carefully between (say) a noun and the noun phrase it heads, the difference between the two category types being of no theoretical significance within Bare Phrase Structure assumptions. This facet of the theory comes into its own particularly in chapter 4, where I explain the various contexts in which adjectives can appear. In that sense, this work is Minimalist. The least Minimalist-looking feature of my discussion will be the use of referential indices on nouns and noun phrases, in violation of Chomsky's (1995: 211) guideline of inclusiveness. But I take this to be relatively insignificant in practice. My proposals can be recast in the same way as the binding theory has been – as a particular notation that expresses aspects of the interpretation of syntactic structures at the interface with the conceptual intentional system. Those who are purer Minimalists than I are invited to interpret it as such.

Beyond these general hints, I will not lead the reader through a systematic outline of the theoretical background I assume here. Rather, I will try to use linguistic notions that have a relatively broad currency, emphasizing their intuitive content. I also explain more particular theoretical notions as they come up along the way.

1.4.3   Outline of leading ideas
Finally, I will outline the leading ideas of this work, and how they are distributed over the chapters that follow. Chapter 2 concentrates on the properties of verbs that set them apart from the other lexical categories. The basic idea is that only verbs are true predicates, with the power to license a specifier, which they typically theta-mark. In contrast, nouns and adjectives need help from

a functional category Pred in order to do this. This is the indirect cause of predicative nouns and adjectives' needing a copular element in many languages ((20)), as well as the fact that only the arguments of verbs can undergo certain movement processes ((19)), among many other things. Chapter 3 focuses on the distinctive properties of nouns. The main idea in this chapter is that only nouns can bear a referential index, because only they have "criteria of identity" in the sense of Geach (1962) and Gupta (1980). This means that only they can bind anaphors ((21)), traces of various kinds, and the theta-roles of verbs ((22)), among other things. Chapter 4 turns to adjectives, arguing that all one needs to say is that they are neither nouns nor verbs. In contrast to theories that attribute a particular modificational character to adjectives (Croft 1991; Hengeveld 1992; Bhat 1994), I hold that adjective is essentially the "default" category. It appears in a nonnatural class of environments where neither a noun nor a verb would do, including the attributive modification position, the complement of a degree head, resultative secondary predicate position, and adverbial positions. In the appendix, I argue that adpositions are not part of the system of lexical categories at all; rather, incorporation patterns show them to be functional heads that create adjuncts of various kinds. The resulting theory thus compares with the standard one as follows:

(23)   *Chomskian*   *My proposal*
        Noun is $+N, -V$ Noun is $+N = $ 'has a referential index'
        Verb is $-N, +V$ Verb is $+V = $ 'has a specifier'
        Adjective is $+N, +V$ Adjective is $-N, -V$
        Preposition is $-N, -V$ Preposition is part of a different system (functional).

For the core categories of noun and verb, my proposal gives substance to the features $+N$ and $+V$, so that important principles of the theory make use of them. For the more marginal categories of adjective and preposition, there are significant revisions as to where they fit into the overall picture.

Each main chapter closes by applying the theory to typological questions, investigating languages that have been claimed not to have the category being studied in that chapter. In each case, a close look at the data through the magnifying glass of my theory yields the rather surprising result that there is much less variation in lexical category systems than has usually been thought. Most languages – probably all – turn out to have the same three-way distinction between nouns, verbs, and adjectives falling out along reasonably familiar lines, once various confounding factors (such as the presence of functional categories) are properly controlled for.

Chapter 5 concludes the study by considering exactly what kinds of linguistic entities have a categorial nature, and how lexical category phenomena shed light on the overall architecture of the human language faculty. It also proposes an answer to the question of why languages do not differ in their stocks of lexical categories in terms of the fact that conceptual development precedes linguistic development and provides the grounding for its very first stages.

2 *Verbs as licensers of subjects*

2.1 Introduction

What is the essential property that makes verbs behave differently from nouns and adjectives in morphology and syntax? This question is perhaps the easiest place to begin, because there is an obvious starting-point in the widespread recognition that verbs are the quintessential predicates. They are inherently unsaturated expressions that hold of something else, and thus the nucleus around which sentences are typically built. Many linguists of different schools have recognized the significance of this. Among the formalists, Jackendoff (1977) partially defines verbs with the feature "+subject" (although this does not distinguish them from nouns, in his view). Among the functionalists, Croft (1991) identifies predication as the pragmatic function that provides the external motivation for the category verb. I argue for the precise version of this intuition stated in (1).

(1)   X is a verb if and only if X is a lexical category and X has a specifier.

The discussion will unfold as follows. I begin by explaining why (1) is a plausible way of distinguishing verbs from other categories, and why it is more promising than some of the obvious alternatives (section 2.2). Next I explore (1)'s implication that predicate nouns and adjectives, unlike verbs, must be supported by a functional head I call Pred in order for the clause to have a subject (section 2.3), showing that this functional head is seen overtly in some languages (section 2.4). Even in languages where Pred is not realized phonologically – perhaps the majority – its presence can be detected by morphological tests; Pred frequently prevents categories other than verbs from combining with tense/aspect morphology (section 2.5) or causative morphemes (section 2.6), for example. I then turn to more purely syntactic matters, showing how the presence of a specifier makes VPs more likely to be head-final than other projections (section 2.7). It also accounts for the fact that certain verbs behave like unaccusative predicates, in contrast to corresponding adjectives and nouns, which behave like unergative predicates in many languages (section 2.8). Throughout the chapter it becomes clear that the combination of an adjective and a Pred is equivalent in many respects to a verb; section 2.9 capitalizes on this, arguing that verbs are derived by conflating an adjective into a Pred, adapting a view of Hale and Keyser (1993). Finally, section 2.10 faces the typological question of whether the category of verb as defined in (1) is attested in all human languages or not. I argue that it is.

2.2   Initial motivations

To see the significance of (1), we can consider it in the context of the phrase-structure properties of other categories. Almost any category can combine with a complement. In the Bare Phrase Structure terms of Chomsky (1995: ch. 4), this means simply that a member of any category can combine with a phrase to create a new phrase of which it is a head. (2) gives a range of examples:

(2)   a eat [some spinach]   (verb)
       b pieces [of cake]   (noun)
       c fond [of swimming]   (adjective)
       d under [the table]   (preposition)
       e will/to [eat some spinach]   (tense)
       f the [piece of cake]   (determiner)
       g too [fond of swimming]   (degree)
       h that [Kate ate spinach]   (complementizer)

This is a general characteristic of syntax that does not distinguish one category from another.[1] However, the ability to head a constituent that contains a second phrase – a specifier as well as a complement – is much more restricted. Among the functional categories, only some members of each category can do this. The finite tenses of English can have a specifier, for example, but nonfinite *to* cannot, as shown in (3a). Similarly, the genitive determiner *'s* can have a specifier, but the articles *the* and *a* cannot ((3b)). The null complementizer can have an interrogative specifier, but *that* and *for* cannot ((3c)). The degree word *too* can have an amount expression as its specifier, but the degree word *so* cannot ((3d)).

---

[1] Not every instance of a particular category always takes a complement, of course; many particular nouns and adjectives, and some prepositions and determiners usually appear without complements. There might be entire categories like "interjection" that never take a complement, but their syntactic significance is marginal.

(3)   a I predict [Kate *will* eat spinach]   (tenses)
          I prefer [(*Kate) *to* eat spinach]
        b I saw [Julia-*'s* picture of Paris]   (determiners)
          I saw [(*Julia) *the/a* picture of Paris]
        c I wonder [when Ø Julia went to Paris]   (complementizers)
          I think [(*when) *that* Julia went to Paris]
        d Nicholas is [two inches *too* tall]   (degrees)
          Nicholas is [(*two inches) *so* tall]

Whether an item takes a specifier or not is thus an important characterizing feature for the functional categories. (1) claims that this property subdivides the lexical categories too. Those lexical categories that take a specifier are verbs; those that do not are nouns and adjectives.

The way a verb comes to have a specifier is somewhat different from the way most functional categories do, however. Tenses and complementizers acquire their specifiers by movement: some constituent contained inside their complement moves to become the specifier of the phrase. This is not the case for verbs. Rather, the specifier of a verb usually comes from direct combination with some other phrase that is constructed independently.[2] In Chomsky's terms, verbs typically get specifiers from "External Merge," whereas tenses and complementizers get specifiers by "Internal Merge." (I leave open where the possessive DP in Spec, DP and the measure phrase in Spec, DegreeP come from.) In practice, this means that verbs usually assign a thematic role to the phrase that is their specifier. Following Chomsky's (1995: ch. 4) adaptation of Hale and Keyser (1993), I assume that there are two domains in which this happens (see also Bowers [1993] and others). A verb that takes an AP or PP complement assigns a theme role to its specifier:

(4)   a I made [$_{VP}$ John [come to the party]]   (*John* is theme of *come*)
        b I made [$_{VP}$ the box [break open]]   (*the box* is theme of *break*)

A verb that takes an NP complement assigns an agent role to its specifier:

(5)   I made [$_{VP}$ Chris [dance a jig]]   (*Chris* is agent of *dance*)

A verb can also take a VP complement, in which case it again assigns an agent role to its specifier. The head of the lower VP almost always combines with the head of the higher VP, deriving a surface representation with only one spelled-out verb:

---

[2] Raising verbs and auxiliary verbs are exceptions to this; they get their specifiers by NP-movement, in more or less the same way that finite tense does. I return to this below.

(6)   a I made [$_{VP}$ Chris bring$_i$ [$_{VP}$ John [V$_i$ to the party]]]   (*Chris* is agent of

bring, break)

b I made [$_{VP}$ Chris break$_i$ [$_{VP}$ the box [V$_i$ open]]]

I assume that examples in which a single verb appears to take two complements are always to be analyzed this way, as consisting of two verbal projections that take one complement each, following Kayne (1984a), Larson (1988), and Hale and Keyser (1993). Using Chomsky's (1995: ch. 4) terminology, we can call the higher verbal position in structures like (6) v (in lower case), and the lower position V (in upper case). Both, however, qualify as verbs, as long as they have lexical content, given the definition in (1).

The structures in (4)–(6) also exist without an overt NP, AP, or PP complement to the V:

(7)   a I made [John [come –]]
        b I made [the box [break –]]
        c I made [Chris [dance –]]
        d I made [Chris bring$_i$ [John [V$_i$ –]]]

Like Hale and Keyser, I assume that the verbs have a covert complement in these cases, so that the theme and agent arguments are still in specifier positions; see section 2.9 for discussion of just what this covert complement is.

Hale and Keyser (1993) actually make a somewhat stronger claim: they say that these phrase-structural configurations are the only ones in which NPs that bear theme and agent roles can be found. I adopt a slightly weakened version of their view, given in (8).

(8)   Agent and theme roles can only be assigned to specifier positions.

This is a subpart of the Uniformity of Theta Role Assignment Hypothesis (UTAH) of Baker (1988a), which Hale and Keyser seek to derive. (8) is weaker than Hale and Keyser's view, because for me it is a correspondence, whereas for them it is a definition; the agent role simply *is* the [__ V VP] configuration, they believe, and the theme role *is* the [__ V AP/PP] configuration. (In this, they were presumably inspired by Jackendoff's [1976; 1983] view that thematic roles are designated positions in a conceptual structure.) The definitional view seems too strong, however. Taken literally, I do not see how Hale and Keyser's theory can say anything about the various semantic entailments that characterize agents and themes (see, for example, Dowty [1991]). Thus, reduction of thematic role to syntactic position seems impossible for much the same reason that it seems impossible to reduce the qualia of green to particular neural firings. Systematic correspondence between the two is the most we can aspire to for now.

Nevertheless, (8) is still strong enough to have consequences: taken together with (1), it implies that simple nouns and adjectives can never assign agent or theme thematic roles – an implication I return to in section 2.9.

It is tempting to try to combine (1) and (8), and make it the defining property of verbs that they assign agent and theme theta-roles.[3] This would be a mistake, however. First, if these particular thematic roles were built into the definition, one would have to be sure one could distinguish them from other thematic roles in a reliable way. This is a notoriously difficult enterprise, the thematic roles having clear central instances but fuzzy boundaries. More importantly, there are a few verbs that do not assign any thematic role to their specifier. Verbs like *seem* and *appear* are the clearest case; perhaps weather predicates are another. But even though these verbs have no thematic role to assign to a specifier, they must still have a specifier, in the form of the pleonastic pronoun *it*:

(9)   a I made [*(it) seem/appear that I was happy]
        b Sowing the clouds made [*(it) rain/snow]

(Here as above I use examples in which the projection of the verb being studied is in its bare infinitive form, as the complement of a verb like *make*. This helps to ensure that the requirement of having a subject is a property of the verb itself, not caused by the presence of a finite tense.) This may seem like a peculiarity of English, since many languages do not require an overt pronoun with these verbs. However, this is simply because many languages never require overt pronouns, often because the person/number/gender features of the pronoun are adequately expressed in the verbal morphology, as in Spanish, Italian, and Mohawk. Not surprisingly, the required subject of the verb shows up not as a pleonastic pronoun, but as a pleonastic subject agreement in these languages:

(10)   *(*Yo*)-kʌnór-u.   compare: *Yo*-yó't-e'.   (Mohawk)
        NsO-rain-S T A T   NsO-work-I M P F
        'It is raining.'   'She/it is working.'

Every language I know of that shows visible agreement with third person neuter subjects uses that agreement also with weather verbs. (9) and (10) show that being a verb is fundamentally a syntactic matter, as expressed in (1), not a semantic matter of denoting the type of event that has a particular kind of participant (an agent and/or a theme). Functional theorists such as Croft (1991) would say that these verbs are nonprototypical instances of the category verb.

---

[3] I stated my theory this way in earlier versions of this work (Baker 1996c; Baker and Stewart 1996).

Nevertheless, they clearly are verbs, and as such a specifier is indispensable. (1) is thus the definition of a verb, not part of the prototype for a verb, I claim.

Auxiliary verbs also illustrate this same point. These are verbs that do not assign any thematic roles, but express only aspectual information, such as the progressive or the perfect:

(11)   a The box broke open.
        b The box has broken open.
        c The box is breaking open.

The nominal *the box* is thematically related only to the verb *break* in these examples, and semantically the aspect has scope over the entire eventuality, including the subject. Therefore, on purely semantic grounds, one might expect the structures in (12).

(12)   a has [$_{VP}$ the box [broken open]]
        b is [$_{VP}$ the box [breaking open]]

But this is not what we find on the surface. *Have* and *is* are (nonprototypical) verbs, and as such they must have a specifier. In this case, they acquire one, not by theta-role assignment, nor by pleonastic insertion, but by NP-movement:[4]

(13)   a [$_{VP}$ the box$_i$ has [$_{VP}$ t$_i$ [broken open]]]
        b [$_{VP}$ the box$_i$ is [$_{VP}$ t$_i$ [breaking open]]]

Again, this is not a peculiarity of English. In Baker (2002), I report that the semantically plausible Aux–Subject–Verb–Object order in (12) is not found in any SVO language, based on the data from 530 languages summarized in Julien (2000). Orders like (12) are found in the Celtic languages, but these are crucially VSO languages, where there is independent evidence that all verbs (not just auxiliaries) move to the left of their subjects.

---

[4] Minimalists might think that the NP-movements in (13) are triggered not by the auxiliaries, but by the "EPP" feature of the Tense node (Chomsky 1995). However, auxiliaries seem to trigger movement even in the absence of a tense node. The examples in (i) are somewhat unnatural for semantic reasons, but they are vastly better than the alternatives in (ii).

(i)   ?I made the box be breaking open.
        ?I made the box have broken open.
(ii)   *I made be the box breaking open.
        *I made have the box broken open.

Sportiche's (1988) stranded quantifier test for movement also suggests that the subject moves into the specifier position of the second auxiliary on its way to become the specifier of tense and the first auxiliary:

(iii)   It is disconcerting [for the boxes$_i$ to t$_i$ have [all t$_i$] been t$_i$ breaking].

See also Zepter (2001) for word order evidence that auxiliary verbs have specifiers in German.

Taking (1) to be the definition of a verb clearly commits me to the existence of null pronominal subjects in nonfinite clauses like the following:[5]

(14)   a [PRO helping/to help oneself to an extra donut] is considered rude
        b John hurt his finger [(while) PRO washing himself]
        c Mary called me [(in order) PRO to exonerate herself]
        d Mary persuaded me [PRO to help myself to a donut]
        e Mary prevented me [from PRO cutting myself with the knife]
        f [PRO having cut himself with a knife] John rushed to the hospital
        g [PRO beaten and bruised] John slunk home to lick his wounds

But this claim is hardly novel in the P&P tradition, which believes in these elements for independent reasons (see Chomsky [1981] and many others). The phonetically null subject provides the necessary local antecedent for the *self-*reflexives in these examples, for instance.

Chomsky (1981) in fact argues from examples like (15) that understood subjects are always structurally present with nonfinite verbs but not with nouns.

(15)   a John promised Mary [– to wash *herself/himself in the stream]
        b John told Mary [– some embarrassing stories about himself/herself]

The anaphoric object in the embedded clause of (15a) can only refer to John, not to Mary. This is because there must be a null subject in the embedded clause, which is bound by the matrix subject. Since this null subject is the closest possible antecedent for the anaphor, it must be the actual antecedent. (15b) is roughly parallel to (15a) in certain semantic/pragmatic respects: if John is telling the stories, then they must be his stories; he is the agent or owner of the stories. One might thus consider positing a control relationship also in (15b), which would relate the matrix subject to a null PRO functioning as the possessor of the NP. But if this were the case, then the anaphor in (15b) should only be interpretable as referring to John, as in (15a). This is not correct: the anaphor in (15b) can refer to either of the matrix clause participants. Chomsky's conclusion is that there is no covert subject in the noun phrase *stories about himself*, although there is one in the verbal clause *to wash himself*. This fits

---

[5] It is possible within my theory to avoid positing a PRO in simple subject-control cases like (i):

(i)   John wants/tried/came [(PRO?) to eat spinach].

These structures are precisely those that often undergo restructuring in languages of the world (Rizzi 1982), so that *wanna eat* acts like a single complex verb. PRO can be avoided in these examples by saying that *want* and *eat* are two heads of what is essentially a single verb phrase. Then the single NP *John* could count as the specifier of both verbs, satisfying (1) with no empty category. (An analysis like this is presented for 'go to' constructions in Mohawk in Baker [1996b: sec 8.3].)

beautifully with (1). Alternative explanations for this class of phenomena exist, of course, and I will not debate their relative advantages here. I simply intend this invocation of the Chomskian theory of empty categories and control to show that examples like (14) and (15a) do not falsify (1), and may even support it.[6]

The most challenging aspect of defending (1) is not to show that all verbs have specifiers, but to show that the other lexical categories cannot have them. Nouns and adjectives certainly can appear without specifiers, as seen in (16).

(16)   a *Water* is refreshing.   (specifierless N)
        b *Cold* water is refreshing.   (specifierless A)

But they can also be used predicatively, in which case they seem to take subjects just as much as verbs do. I illustrated the subject-taking properties of various verbs in English by embedding them under the causative verb *make*, because *make* selects a bare VP complement (I assume), with no obvious functional head. Thus, in this context we can be relatively certain that it is the verb that requires a subject, not tense or some other functional head. But NPs and APs can also be embedded under *make*, in which case they too are preceded by a subject:

(17)   a The chemist took a hydrogen and oxygen mixture and made [#(it) water].
        b Then she put the water into the refrigerator to make [*(it) cold].

Predicate nominal and adjectival constructions can even be used to describe essentially the same eventualities as verbs do in some cases:

(18)   a Chris hungers.   (verb)
        b Chris is hungry.   (adjective)

(19)   a The metal doorknob shines in the light.   (verb)
        b The metal doorknob is shiny.   (adjective)

(20)   a That arrow spins around.   (verb)
        b That arrow is a spinner.   (noun)

(21)   a Mary skis whenever she can.   (verb)
        b Mary is an avid skier.   (noun)

There is no clear difference in the quality of the theta-role that the subject bears in these examples. If the subjects of the verbs are themes, then it is reasonable to say that the subjects of the adjectives and nouns are also themes (or perhaps

---

[6] Essentially the same distinction is found in Reinhart and Reuland's (1993) binding theory, although it is cast in different terms since for them reflexivity is about predicates, not noun phrases. For them, the contrast between (15a) and (15b) stems from the fact that *wash* is a verb, and therefore a predicate marked as reflexive by *self*, whereas *stories* is a noun, and therefore not a predicate. Their correlation between lexical category and predicatehood is equivalent to (1).

agent, in the case of (21b)). Even if a thematic difference could be teased out, it is not likely to be one that one would feel good about building a theory of category differences around.[7]

That these subjects all have the same thematic role does not, however, imply that the thematic role is assigned in exactly the same way. There are differences to capture, as well as similarities. Nouns and adjectives in many languages need help in order to be main clause predicates; they must appear in construction with a copular verb like *be*:

(22)   a Chris hungers.
        b Chris *(is) hungry.
        c Chris *(is) a skier.

This is often interpreted as a superficial and language-particular fact, induced by tense morphology affixing only to verbs in English (unlike Abaza) and by tense needing to be expressed in all matrix clauses in English (unlike Russian and Hebrew). But I want to put forward a stronger interpretation of these facts, claiming that the frequent need for a copular element to appear with predicate adjectives and nouns but not verbs is a reflection of the fact that the structures in (22b,c) are more complex. Nouns and adjectives are never predicates in and of themselves; they can only count as predicates in a derivative sense, by being part of a more articulated structure. More specifically, I argue that the subject in sentences like (22b,c) originates outside the NP/AP, as the specifier of a silent functional category I call Pred.

Prima-facie evidence that there is a structural distinction between (22a) and (22b,c) comes from unaccusativity diagnostics such as *ne*-cliticization in Italian. The inverted subject of certain intransitive verbs can have a genitive or partitive *ne*-clitic extracted from it, as shown in (23a). In this respect, the subjects of these verbs are like the objects of ordinary transitive verbs (Belletti and Rizzi 1981; Burzio 1986). *Ne* cannot, however, be extracted from the inverted subjects of comparable adjectives and nouns ((22b,c)).

(23)   a Se ne   rompono molti.   (Burzio 1986)
          SE of.them break   many
          'Many of them broke.'

---

[7] It is standard to say that the subjects of predicate adjectives receive a theme role, by parallel with morphologically related verbs, although occasionally other terms have been used (e.g. "attribute" in Pesetsky [1982]). For predicate nouns, the thematic role of the subject is often called R, if it is called anything at all, following Williams (1981). However, the parallelism between the R of nouns and the theme role of adjectives and unaccusative verbs has been noticed and sometimes expressed theoretically (Baker 1996b: ch. 6; Rosen 1997).

b *Ne   sono buoni pochi (dei suoi articoli).   (Cinque 1990: 7)
of.them are   good few   (of his   articles)
'Few of them (his articles) are good.'

c ?*Ne   sono professori molti.   (Mario Fadda, personal communication)
of.them are   professors many (e.g. of people who wear glasses)
'Many of them (people who wear glasses) are professors.'

This subtle contrast between verbs and other categories has no obvious connection to the superficial inflectional properties of verbs, but it does suggest that there is a structural difference between verbs and predicate nouns/adjectives. A theory that starts with the assumption that only verbs take subjects directly gives us immediate leverage on this paradigm. I fill in the particulars of such a theory in the next section, and discuss in detail how it relates to a variety of unaccusativity diagnostics in section 2.8.

Before going on, I want briefly to compare (1) to two other common intuitions about what it is to be a verb. A widespread belief in the functionalist literature is that verbs are those words that refer to "events." Events are distinguished from "things" (the referents of nouns) and "properties" (the referents of adjectives) in that they are relatively transitory. Typical events last for only a short time and then are gone, in contrast to things and their properties, which tend to persist through time. This is central to the notion of verb found in Givón (1984: ch. 3) and Langacker (1987); it also plays an important role in Hopper and Thompson (1984) and Croft (1991). I do not consider this intuition nearly as promising as the view that verbs always have specifiers. The sentences in (24), for example, describe states of affairs that are as long lasting as one can imagine (at least according to some theologies).

(24)   a God exists.
        b God loves Abraham and Sarah.
        c God sustains the universe.
        d The square root of four equals two.

In contrast, the following examples use predicate nouns and adjectives as ephemeral as many events: (25a) is allowed to be true for at most seven minutes at a time in many bridge tournaments, and New Jersey drivers are unsettled if (25b) persists even one minute.

(25)   a Chris is the declarer.   (the person responsible for playing the hand)
        b The traffic light is red.

These examples do not refute the functionalists, since their statements are intended to be true of the prototypical verb as opposed to the prototypical noun or adjective. They would say that the examples in (24) and (25) do not contain prototypical uses of the categories in question. But these examples make the idea look less promising, particularly within a generative framework that requires definitions and wants premises that it can deduce consequences from. And I do not believe that examples like (24) are all that marginal. *Exist*, *sustain*, and *equal* may not be prototypical verbs, but so far as I know it is normal across languages for these states of affairs to be expressed using a verb. Nonprototypical verbs can express long-lasting states of affairs, but they still must have subjects. Therefore having a subject is a more essential property of being a verb, I claim.

Vaguely related to these functionalist ideas is the tradition in Davidsonian semantics of saying that verbs are sortal predicates of events. On this view, the logical form of a sentence like (26a) is roughly (26b) (Davidson 1967; Parsons 1990; Pietroski 1998).

(26)   a Booth shot Lincoln with this gun.
         b ∃x (shooting(e) & agent(e, Booth) & theme(e, Lincoln) & with(e, this gun))

This invites the view that perhaps all and only verbs are predicates of events in this sense. But in order to flesh this out, one would need to specify exactly what counts as an event in this view. If one takes a narrow view of events, then examples like (24) and (25) pose the same problem for formal semanticists as for functionalists: it is difficult to separate the states of affairs that verbs are predicates from those that nouns and adjectives are predicates of in a language-independent way. In practice, most semanticists go the other direction and take a very broad view of events. They thus attribute the same kind of "e" positions to nouns and adjectives that they do to verbs (Higginbotham 1985; Parsons 1990: ch. 10; Larson and Segal 1995: sec. 12.4). This allows them to develop a consistent semantics, but it means that the bearing of an e-type role cannot be the defining difference between verbs and other categories. Kratzer (1989) and Diesing (1992) represent the most notable attempt to get some syntactic mileage out of attributing e-roles to some lexical heads but not others. For them, the presence of an e-role distinguishes stage-level (temporary) predicates from individual-level (permanent) predicates, a distinction that has certain syntactic and semantic ramifications. There is, however, no simple correlation between the stage-level/individual-level distinction and the lexical category distinctions. Adjectives can be stage-level (*Firemen are available*) or individual-level (*Firemen are altruistic*) by all accounts. It is often said that nouns cannot be stage-level predicates (Rapoport [1991], for instance), but examples like (25a) tell against this; also a person can by law be president of the United States for at most eight years out of a life of at least forty-three years. The most one could say is that verbs are always stage-level predicates, and (24a,d) makes me unsure of even this very partial correlation.

I conclude that (1) is the most promising way to define the category verb in universally valid, syntactically significant terms. The rest of this chapter is devoted to fleshing out this proposal, and showing how various language-particular differences between verbs and other categories can be explained in terms of it. I return briefly to the relationship of my syntactic definition of verb to pragmatic and notional characterizations in chapter 5.

2.3   The distribution of Pred

I begin filling in the details of my analysis by taking a closer look at the claim that there is an additional piece of structure in sentences like (27b) and (27c) as compared to (27a). This structure allows nouns and adjectives to be used predicatively, even though they do not take specifiers inherently.

(27)   a Chris hungers.
        b Chris *(is) hungry.
        c Chris *(is) a teacher.

This proposal can be seen as a novel blend of two proposals already present in the literature. The standard generative theory for years has been that verbs, nouns, and adjectives can all theta-mark a subject generated in the specifier of their maximal projection, as shown in (28).

(28)   a [−TNS [$_{VP}$ Chris [$_{V'}$ hunger]]]
        b [−be+TNS ... [$_{AP}$ Chris [$_{A'}$ hungry]]]
        c [−be+TNS ... [$_{NP}$ Chris [$_{N'}$ teacher]]]

In matrix clauses, the subject raises out of its theta-position to become the subject of the clause as a whole, whereas a verb like *make* selects the VP, AP, or NP "small clause" directly. This is the subjects-across-categories theory of small clauses from Stowell (1983) and much subsequent work. This theory dovetails nicely with the formal semantics view that intransitive verbs, simple adjectives, and common nouns are all one-place predicates, of type <e, t>.

Bowers (1993) develops an alternative to this view. He argues that no category can assign a theta-role to its specifier position; rather each category must be supported by a functional head called Pred (for Predication). Pred heads a maximal projection PredP, and the "subject" of the lexical category is generated as the specifier of this phrase, as in (29).

(29)   a [– TENSE [PredP Chris ØPred [VP sing]]]
         b [– be+TENSE ... [PredP Chris ØPred [AP hungry]]]
         c [– be+TENSE ... [PredP Chris ØPred [NP teacher]]]

For verbs, Bowers' Pred is very similar to the elements others have proposed to license the "external arguments" of verbs, such as the voice head of Kratzer (1996) and the v of Chomsky (1995: ch. 4). The distinctive feature of Bowers' proposal is that this element is generalized across the categories: As and Ns also need this functional head in order to take a subject. Bowers' syntactic research converges with semantic proposals by Chierchia (1985) and Chierchia and Turner (1988), who claim that lexical categories correspond not to predicates but to a special kind of property *qua* individual. These individuals do correspond in a systematic way to predicates/propositional functions, however. As a result, they can be made into predicates by an "up" operator that Chierchia symbolizes as $^\cup$. Bowers takes the semantics of Pred to this operator:

(30)   ØPred' $= ^\cup$ (the function from individuals to propositional functions)

Bowers' theory is like the standard theory in that it emphasizes the similarities of predication structures across categories; it simply does so in a different way. One can do more justice to the differences among categories by combining the views, taking the standard view for verbs and the Chierchia/Bowers proposal for comparable adjectives and nouns. I claim that the basic structures for sentences like (27) are roughly as in (31) (details about the tense node and the position of the auxiliary are suppressed).

(31)

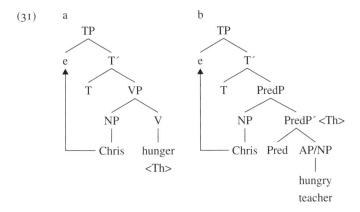

In (31a), *Chris* is the subject of the verb, and an internal argument in the sense that it is generated inside the maximal projection of the verb. In contrast, *Chris* is not the subject or internal argument of the adjective or noun in (31b); it is not technically an argument of the noun or adjective at all. That a clause built around a stative verb can be semantically equivalent to one built around an adjective is ensured by the definition of the "up" operator; it is an axiom of Chierchia's system that every property exists as both an individual and as a propositional function. In my syntactic terms, this means any simple property can in principle be realized as either an adjective or a verb (or both). It follows that stative verbs are semantically equivalent to adjectives plus Pred. The primary difference is in the syntactic packaging, not the lexical semantics. (Of course, people are biased as to which properties they prefer to associate with verbs, and which with adjectives or nouns. This can be attributed to learning theory via the notion of Canonical Structural Realizations; see Newmeyer [1998] and chapter 5 for discussion.)

It is important to realize that, given Chierchia's semantics, it is not really the Pred that theta-marks the subject of a nominal or adjectival predicate. Rather, Pred takes an NP or AP and makes a theta-marking category out of it. To express this, I put the <Th[eme]> argument structure annotation on the Pred′ node in (31b), rather than under Pred°. One consequence of this is that I need not say that all subjects of nonverbal predication get exactly the same theta-role. The precise theta-role is a function of the lexical meaning of the A/N, not just the meaning of Pred. Perhaps the subject of some behavioral adjectives or *–er* nominals should be considered agents rather than themes (e.g. *Chris is being difficult on purpose*, *Pat is an avid skier*). I am not sure if this is correct in fact, but the possibility exists within the system. More dramatically, the lexical semantics of some APs and NPs is such that Pred does not activate a theta-role for them, even though it does make them into predicates. The specifier of PredP is then filled with a pleonastic *it*, parallel to what we saw with verbs that lack an agent or theme theta-role:

(32)   a the announcement makes [$_{PredP}$ *it* Pred [$_{AP}$ likely [that prices will go down]]]
        b I consider [$_{PredP}$ *it* Pred [$_{NP}$ a cinch [that Chris will win]]]

The general parallelism between Pred+AP and VP thus extends to raising adjectives and raising verbs. These issues are exactly the same as those that arise with the v/Voice node in Chomsky's and Kratzer's treatment of external arguments. The v has the power to create an outer theta-role such as agent for a VP that otherwise would not have one, but it cannot create this theta-role for absolutely any verb (there is no transitive version of *arrive*, for example) and the exact flavor of the theta-role that is created can vary (it can be agent, experiencer, or causer). These matters are a function of the semantic value of the VP as well as that of the v.

My proposal can be tested against the evidence that Bowers gives in favor of all categories co-occurring with Pred heads. The structural differences between his theory and mine are actually quite narrow. I agree with Bowers that the agent argument of a transitive verb is not assigned in the minimal VP, but rather in the specifier of a higher head (see (6)), and Bowers agrees that that the theme argument of transitive verbs is assigned to the specifier of VP. Bowers adopts the same structure for unaccusative verbs, except that their Pred does not assign a theta-role, but the theme subject of V moves through its specifier position as shown in (33b) (Bowers 1993: 617).

Considering unaccusativity diagnostics will lead me to adopt the same structure (section 2.8).

(33)   a [Chris TENSE ... [PredP/vP t ØPred/v [VP sandwich eat]]]
        b [Chris TENSE ... [PredP/vP t Øpred/v [VP t fall]]]

Bowers' structures and mine thus differ primarily in the label of the head that introduces the agent: for Bowers, it is Pred, a functional category identical to one found with predicate nouns and adjectives; for me, it is v, a lexical head, distinct from anything found in nonverbal predication.

Because the overall geometry of most clauses is the same in the two theories, much of the evidence that Bowers presents in favor of his theory does not distinguish it from my proposal. For example, Bowers discusses the fact, originally pointed out by Maling (1976), that "objects" can be followed by floating quantifiers if and only if they are followed by a predicative category. This predicative category can be an N, A, or V:

(34)   a We consider the men all fools/crazy.   (Bowers 1993: 618)
        b We made the children all cry.
        c *We saw the men all.

For Bowers, the *all* in both (34a) and (34b) appears adjoined to the subject of predication in Spec, PredP and is left behind when that NP raises into the domain of *consider* or *make* for accusative case licensing. But this does not distinguish the two theories. I can just as well say that *all* is stranded in Spec, PredP in (34a) and in Spec, vP in (34b). For this type of argument, the topology of the clause is what matters, not the exact character of the heads.

Some of Bowers' arguments do, however, hinge on the identity of the specifier-licensing head, and here our theories do make different predictions. Bowers claims that his theory accounts in a very straightforward way for the fact that predicative expressions can be conjoined, even when they seem to belong to different lexical categories, as shown in (35).

(35)   a I consider John crazy and a fool.
        b I consider John$_i$ [$_{PredP}$ t$_i$ ØPred [$_{AP}$ crazy]] and [$_{PredP}$ t$_i$ ØPred [$_{NP}$ a fool]]

Bowers give this sentence the analysis in (35b), in which it is actually two PredPs that are conjoined. The subjects of these PredPs are then raised out to an accusative case position associated with the verb *consider* in Across the Board fashion. (35a) thus reduces to a simple case of conjunction of like categories. This analysis also carries over straightforwardly to my theory. What Bowers does not notice is that similar sentences that conjoin an adjective or a noun with a verb are very bad:[8]

(36)   a *Eating poisoned food made Chris sick and die.
        b *A hard blow to the head made Chris fall and an invalid.

Any category of predicate can be the complement of a causative verb (*The poison made Chris sick; The poison made Chris die*), but nevertheless verbs cannot be conjoined with nonverbs. Bowers' theory predicts that these sentences should be possible under the analysis in (37a).

(37)   a poison made him$_i$ [$_{PredP}$ t$_i$ ØPred [$_{AP}$ sick]] and [$_{PredP}$ t$_i$ ØPred [$_{VP}$ t$_i$ die]]
        b poison made him$_i$ [$_{PredP}$ t$_i$ ØPred [$_{AP}$ sick]] and [$_{vP}$ t$_i$ v [$_{VP}$ t$_i$ die]]

In contrast, my proposal implies that (36a,b) involve conjoining a PredP with a vP. This can be properly ruled out by the ban against coordinating unlike categories. The verbs in (36) are unaccusative, but similar structures are also ruled out when the verb is transitive or unergative:

(38)   a *Sitting in the hot sun made Chris thirsty and drink a can of soda.
        b *Winning the game made Chris champion of the chess club and celebrate.

We find here a sharp distinction between predicative NPs and APs on the one hand and VPs on the other hand, just as my theory expects.

    Another argument that Bowers gives for the presence of PredP in verbal sentences comes from the distribution of adverbs. He claims that VP-final adverbs like *perfectly* attach to VP proper, whereas manner adverbs like *quickly*,

---

[8] Here I switch from *consider* to *make*, which is also a small-clause selecting verb, but unlike *consider* it can take bare VP/vP complements as well as AP and NP small clauses. Notice that it is possible to conjoin a stative predicate and an eventive predicate under *make*, as long as both are headed by a verb, as shown in (i) (I thank Natalia Kariaeva for this example). This shows that (36) and (38) are not ruled out by a simple semantic condition to the effect that the aspectual qualities of the two conjuncts must match.

(i)   The incident made Mary hate John and ask for a divorce.

which can come before or after the VP, attach higher, to PredP. Adverb licensing is a complex topic, and I will not try to evaluate the correctness of this proposal; for now, it suffices to say that the analysis is compatible with my theory as well, with the amendment that manner adverbs adjoin to vP, not PredP. This change is not completely trivial, however. Since Bowers holds that the Pred that appears with transitive verbs is the same as the one that dominates predicate nouns and adjectives, his theory expects that manner adverbs should appear in this second environment as well. This does not seem right:[9]

(39)   a Mary confidently played the violin. (Bowers 1993: 606)
        b ??Mary was confidently a violinist   (cf. Mary was a confident violinist.)

On my theory, the adverb *confidently* is attached to vP in (39a). Since there is no vP (but only a PredP) in (39b), there is no automatic expectation that the adverb should be able to appear there. Again, the facts suggest that the structure of verbal clauses is significantly different from the structure of nonverbal predication.

2.4   Copular particles

If the structures of predication presented in (31) are correct, then we would expect to find overt manifestations of the Pred head in some languages. Bowers (1993) believes that Pred in English is phonologically null, so its distribution cannot easily be observed. But that is presumably an accidental fact about English. It is common for a functional category to be silent in some languages but rare for it to be silent in all languages. If overt Preds can be found, we should be able to observe that they appear with nouns and adjectives but not verbs. In this section, I argue that such elements do exist in quite a few languages, including Edo and Chichewa.

The English copular verb *be* has roughly the distribution expected of a Pred, coming before an adjective or noun predicate in a matrix clause, but not before a verb (see (27)). There are, however, good reasons not to adopt this analysis. First, no form of *be* appears with predicate nouns and adjectives in untensed small clause contexts, as shown again in (40).

---

[9] I do not include an example with an adjective, because it is hard to tell whether the adverb is attached to PredP (which is the construction of interest) or modifies the adjective directly inside AP. An example like *?Chris is quickly jealous* is not too bad, but it is hard to tell if its structure is *Chris is [t quickly Pred [$_{AP}$ jealous]]* or (as I suspect) *Chris is [t Pred [$_{AP}$ quickly jealous]]*. This complication does not arise with predicate nominals, since adverbs cannot appear in NP/DP.

(40)   a The poisoned food made Chris sick/an invalid.
         b I consider Chris intelligent/a genius.
         c With Chris sick/an invalid, the rest of the family was forced to work harder.

If *be* were performing the theta-role creating function of a Pred, then it should be required also in these contexts, or the subject of predication would have no theta-role. Conversely, *be* appears with participial verbs, even though as verbs they should have no problem theta-marking a subject:

(41)   a Chris *(is) dying.
         b The vase *(was) broken by Pat.

The presence of *be* in (41) seems closely related to its presence in (40). This range of data implies that the copula in English is not involved primarily in the dynamics of theta-role assignment, but rather appears when the lexical head of the clause cannot bear finite tense and agreement morphology. Moreover, there is evidence in the literature that *be* and its cousins in other Western European languages is syntactically like a raising verb, and hence thematically inert (Burzio 1986; Rizzi 1986b: 81–85).

But what is wrong for one language can be right for another. The Nigerian language Edo does have copular particles with exactly the distribution expected for Pred. When Edo Ns and As are used as main clause predicates, they must appear as the complement of a copular element – *yé* for adjectives or *rè* for nouns (Omoruyi 1986; Agheyisi 1990). No comparable element is required for verbs:

(42)   a Èmèrí   mòsé.
           Mary   be.beautiful$_V$
           'Mary is beautiful.'
         b Èmèrí   *(yé)   mòsèmòsè
           Mary   PRED   beautiful$_A$
           'Mary is beautiful.'
         c Úyì *(rè)   òkhaèmwèn.
           Uyi PRED   chief$_N$
           'Uyi is a chief.'

(Notice that many adjectives are morphologically related to nearly synonymous stative verbs in Edo. The adjectival form differs from the verb in having a level tone pattern rather than a low–high tone pattern. Adjectives may also undergo intensive reduplication.) Unlike English, however, *yé* and *rè* are never used as auxiliaries in the verbal system of Edo:

(43)   Òzó *(yé/rè)   sò.
         Ozo PRED   shout
         'Ozo is shouting.'

Edo does use preverbal auxiliary elements; present progressive, for example, is indicated by the auxiliary *ghá* (*Ózò ghá sò* 'Ozo is shouting'). But the verbal aux-iliaries are completely distinct from the copulas used with predicate As and Ns.

It is even more significant that predicative APs and NPs in Edo require *yé* and *rè* even when they are embedded under suitable matrix verbs. Edo has a causative verb *ya* 'make' that takes bare VP complements of various kinds, as shown in (44).

(44) a Íyé   mwèn ó   yá   mwèn lé èvbàré nè íràn.
         mother my   she made.PAST me.ACC cook food   for them
         'It's my mother that made me cook food for them.'
      b Íyé   mwèn ò   yà   mwén lé èvbàré nè íràn.
         mother my   she make.HAB   me.ACC cook food   for them
         'It's my mother that makes me cook for them.'

The embedded verb in (44a,b) does not change its tone, which is how past versus nonpast tense inflection is realized in Edo. Also, the subject of the embedded verb is the accusative case form of the first person singular pronoun, not the nominative form *i*. The *ya* construction in Edo is very similar in both these respects to *make* causatives in English, suggesting that *ya* too selects a "small clause" with no Infl-type functional element. The complement of *ya* can perfectly well be headed by a stative verb, as shown in (45).

(45) a Úyì yá   èmátòn pèrhé.
         Uyi made metal be.flat$_V$
         'Uyi made the metal be flat.'
      b Ò yá   òwá   bàá.
         it made house be.red
         'It made the house red.'

However, these examples become completely ungrammatical when the stative verb is replaced with an adjective:

(46) a *Úyì yá   èmátòn pèrhè.
         Uyi made metal flat$_A$
         'Uyi made the metal flat.'
      b *Ò yá   égógó wòrò
         it made bell long
         'It made the bell long.'

This is exactly what we expect if adjectives cannot assign a theta-role to a specifier apart from the Pred *yé*. The postverbal NPs are left un-theta-marked, and the sentences are ruled out by the theta criterion. A nominal small clause is also impossible as the complement of *yá* without *rè*:

(47)   *Òzó yá   Úyì òkhaèmwèn.
        Ozo made Uyi chief
        'Ozo made Uyi a chief.'

These sentences improve dramatically when the copular particle is included in the complement:[10]

(48)   Úyì yá [PredP èmátòn ?(dòó) yé [AP pèrhè]]   (contrast (46a))
        Uyi make   metal INCEP be   flat
        'Uyi made the metal to be flat.'

(47) can be similarly improved by adding *rè*. Thus, *yé* and *rè* are not used as category neutral auxiliaries, but are essential to using adjectives and nouns predicatively in all contexts. I conclude that these are genuine, phonologically overt instances of the category Pred.

Further evidence that *yé* is a Pred head in Edo and not a mere auxiliary comes from the distribution of a floating quantifier-like element *tòbórè* 'him/herself' (plural form: *tòbíràn* 'themselves'). Sportiche (1988) argues that floated quantifiers like *all* in English are elements that are left behind when the NPs they were adjoined to move to some higher position. For example, in raising constructions a floated quantifier can appear stranded in the embedded subject position, as shown in (49a).

(49)   a the birds$_i$ seem [$_{VP}$ [all t$_i$] to have left]
        b the birds$_i$ will [$_{VP}$ [all t$_i$] fly South by November]

Floated quantifiers can also follow the tense particle in sentences like (49b); Sportiche interprets this as evidence for the VP-internal subject hypothesis, that subjects originate in a position lower than Spec, TP, and move there for case reasons. Stewart (2001) shows that *tòbórè* in Edo has a very similar distribution, and can be accounted for under the same analysis. Edo does not have clear raising constructions, but *tòbórè* appears stranded before the embedded subject position in control infinitives; it also can appear after tense particles and other auxiliaries:

(50)   a Òzó hìá   tòbórè   dún!mwún ìyán.
        Ozo tried himself pound   yam.
        Ozo tried to pound the yam by himself (and succeeded).'

---

[10] See Baker and Stewart (1996) for additional examples and more discussion of the *ya* construction. (48) is only fully grammatical if the inceptive particle *dòó* is present as well as *yé*. I have not investigated this element with any care, but it does not seem to be a verb, nor to have anything to do with theta-role assignment. It seems to be added for aspectual reasons.

b Òzó_i ghá [_{vP} t_i tòbọ́rè dùnmwún ìyán]
   Ozo will   by.self pound   yam
   'Ozo will pound the yams by himself.'

Given this background, the claim that Edo *yé* is a Pred predicts that a floated *tòbórè* should be able to appear before *yé* (specifiers coming before heads in a head-medial language like Edo), but not between *yé* and the adjective. This prediction is exactly correct:

(51)   Òzó_i [PredP t_i (tòbọ́rè) yé [AP   (*tòbórè) mòsèmòsè]].
        Ozo   by.self PRED   by.self   beautiful
        'Ozo alone is beautiful.'

Edo contrasts sharply with English in this respect, since floated quantifiers easily come between the copula and a predicate adjective or noun in English (*The babies are all beautiful/geniuses*). This shows that subjects cannot be generated internal to AP in Edo; rather their lowest position is higher than *yé*. This is strong support for the view that adjectives are not theta-markers, and *yé* is responsible for introducing the thematic subject. Parallel facts hold for the nominal copula *rè*.

    Part of the claim that *yé* and *rè* are heads of category Pred in Edo is that they are functional items, not true verbs. The distinction between lexical and functional is not always a crisp one, unfortunately, but there is plenty of superficial evidence for this distinction in Edo. First, monosyllabic verbs vary in tone to show the past–nonpast distinction (see *ya* in (44) for an example), whereas *yé* has an invariant high tone:

(52)   *Òzó yè mòsè.
        Ozo   be beautiful
        'Ozo is (now/always) beautiful.'

Also, *yé* cannot be nominalized (*ùyémwèn*) or undergo predicate cleft, as true verbs in Edo typically can (see Stewart [2001] on the Edo predicate cleft).

(53)   *Ù-yé-mwèn   ọ́ré Òzó yé mòsèmòsè.
        NOML-be-NOML FOC Ozo be beautiful
        'It's being that Ozo is beautiful.'

Finally, *yé* plus an adjective cannot appear in a serial verb construction, as one would expect if *yé* were a stative verb (see Stewart [2001] also for the Edo serial verb construction shown in (54b)):

(54)   a *Òzó gbé èmátòn yé   pèrhè.
          Ozo beat metal   PRED flat_A
          'Ozo beat the metal, causing it to be flat.'

b Òzó gbé èmátòn pèrhé.
Ozo beat metal   be.flat$_V$
'Ozo beat the metal, causing it to be flat.'

Yé thus lacks the salient morphological and distributional properties of verbs, even though it has similar thematic properties. This supports the view that it is not a true verb, but rather a functional head. Parallel arguments can be constructed for *rè*, the particle that introduces predicate nominals. (In section 3.8 I return to the topic of why some languages like Edo use different copulas for nominal and adjectival predication.)

Another language that has a phonologically overt Pred is Chichewa (Bantu). The Chichewa particle *ndì* shows up before predicate nominals and adjectives, but not verbs (my data on predication in Chichewa come from Sam Mchombo [personal communication]):

(55)   a M-kango ndì   w-a   u-kali.
         3-lion   PRED 3-ASSOC 3-fierce
         'The lion is fierce.'
       b M-kango ndì   m-lenje.
         3-lion   PRED 1-hunter
         'The lion is a hunter.'

Like Edo *yé*, this element is morphologically defective in ways that suggest it is a functional head, not a true verb: it does not end in the "final vowel" *–a*, and it does not bear tense or subject agreement morphology. To attribute a property in something other than present tense, one needs to use the verbal copula *li* (in the past) or *khala* 'sit, stay' (in the future).

(56)   Sam a-na-li   mphunzitsi ku   Malawi, koma tsopano ndi
         Sam 3sS-PAST-be teacher   LOC Malawi but   now   PRED
         mphunzitsi ku   Calif.
         teacher   LOC Calif.
         'Sam used to be a teacher in Malawi, but now he is a teacher in California.'

These items are more like regular verbs, taking the usual subject agreement prefixes and tense markers. Another sign that *ndi* is not a verb is the fact that it cannot undergo verb incorporation, to combine a causative morpheme, contrasting in this respect with *khala*:

(57)   Mbidzi zi-na-khal-its-a   (*zi-na-ndi-its-a)   mkango
         Zebras 1oS-PAST-sit-CAUS-FV   1oS-PAST-PRED- CAUS-FV   3-lion
         w-a   u-kali.
         3-ASSOC 3-fierce
         'The zebras made the lion (be/become) fierce.'

Also, *ndi* is not used as an auxiliary in the verbal system (as far as I know). Its distribution is thus the same as *yé/rè* in Edo, except that there is no morphological distinction between the Pred used with Ns and the one used with As in Chichewa.[11] Notice that in Chichewa it is not at all plausible to say that *ndi* is inserted for morphological reasons, such as to support tense, since *ndi* cannot in fact bear these inflections; that is the job of *li* and *khala*. Nevertheless, it is still required in sentences like (55), and my proposal explains why.

To the Eurocentric observer, these nonverbal copular elements may seem rather exotic, since almost all of the European languages have verbal copulas that are not direct manifestations of Pred.[12] The same is true of familiar adjoining languages like Arabic and Hebrew. But Europe is a rather small and linguistically homogeneous place. Recent typological research shows that these nonverbal copulas are not particularly rare. Stassen's (1997: 77–91) 410-language survey found nonverbal copulas all over the world. Overt Preds seems to be the norm for languages throughout Africa, including not only Niger–Congo languages but also such languages as Hausa, Kanuri, Gude, Mande, Somali, and Berber. Some non-African languages with overt Preds (mentioned also by

---

[11] The other way to test my hypothesis is to see whether Pred is required under causative verbs in Chichewa. In fact, an overt copula is needed, but it must be *khala* 'sit' rather than *ndi*:

(i) Mbidzi zi-na-chit-its-a   kuti m-kango *(u-khal-e)   w-a   u-kali.
     Zebras 10S-PAST-do-CAUS-FV that 3-lion   3-stay-SUBJN 3-ASSOC 3-fierce
     'The zebras made the lion (be) fierce.'

This follows from the fact that the periphrastic causative verb in Chichewa selects a subjunctive complement, not a tenseless one, and *ndi* cannot bear the necessary mood morphology.

Two analyses are possible for the verbal copulas *li* and *khala* in Chichewa: they could be thematically inert auxiliary verbs dominating a null Pred, like *be* in English, or they could be true verbs that take an AP/NP complement and assign a theme theta-role to the subject. On the latter view, they would be identical to Pred, except for being classified as lexical categories rather than functional. I tentatively assume that this second view is the correct one, but this is not crucial.

[12] One Indo-European language that might have overt instances of Pred is Irish. NPs in Irish can be the predicate of a tenseless small clause if and only if they are preceded by the particle *ina* (Chung and McCloskey 1987: 179, 180 n.4):

(i) ...agus é   *('na) dhíodóir
     and   him PRED a.lawyer
     'while he was a lawyer'

Chung and McCloskey conjecture that *ina* is an "Agr-particle serving the function of morphologically marking the NP as predicative rather than referential." This suggestion makes perfect sense within my framework if *ina* is an overt Pred. In matrix clauses, the verbal copula *tá* 'be' is used, but it is in addition to *ina*, not in place of it:

(ii) Tá   sé *(ina) dhlíodóir.
     be.PRES he PRED lawyer
     'He is a lawyer.'

This example has an English-like auxiliary copula that bears tense and an Edo-like Pred, both appearing overtly in the same clause, as one would expect to be possible.

Irish has a variety of other copular constructions as well, which warrant closer study from my perspective. For example, there is a nonverbal copula *is* that appears with predicate nominals and (especially in Old Irish) adjectives (Carnie 1995). I tentatively take this to be a portmanteau form, realizing both Pred and tense.

Wetzer [1996]) are: (from Asia) Parji, Chinese, Vietnamese; (from Oceania) Niuean, Samoan; (from New Guinea) Awtuw, Agtu; (from North America), Chemehuevi, Wappo, Popoloc; (from South America) Canela-Kraho, Chacabo, and Paumari. (58) gives examples from two of these.

(58)   a Miytiy *po*   wokək (rame).   (Awtuw [Feldman 1986: 136, 138])
        Miytiy PRED tall   man
        'Miytiy is (a) tall (man).'
        b 'O   le   f•ma'i l=o='u   tam•.   (Samoan [Mosel and
                                                            Hovdhaugen 1992]
        PRED ART doctor ART-POSS-1s father
        'My father is a doctor.'

It is thus not at all rare for the Pred head that my theory is based on to show up overtly, even though this does not usually happen in the most familiar languages.

2.5   Inflection for tense

My proposal is that verbs take subjects directly and nouns and adjectives do not, as a universal definition of these categories. Thus, Pred is present with predicate nouns and predicate adjectives in all languages, not just in languages like Edo and Chichewa where it is visible. This structural fact can then be used to give indirect explanations for other distinctive characteristics of verbs, I claim.

Perhaps the most obvious difference between verbs and other lexical categories is that in many languages only verbs can be inflected for tense and related notions, such as aspect and mood. This is clearly true in English, which has *walked*, *walks*, and *walking* but not *catted*, *cats*, *catting*, or *bigged*, *bigs*, *bigging*. This is supposedly why one needs a verbal copula in nonverbal predications in English. The same restriction on tense morphology holds in many other languages. For example, bare nouns and adjectives can be used as predicates in Arabic, but only with a default present tense interpretation. Past or future tense predications cannot be made by attaching the relevant morphemes directly to the noun or adjective; rather a copular verb must be inserted to bear the relevant morphology.

(59)   a Omar mṛiḍ/muʕəllim   (Arabic [Benmanmoun 2000: 8])
        Omar sick/teacher
        'Omar is sick/a teacher.'
        b Omar kan mṛiḍ /muʕəllim
        Omar was sick/teacher
        'Omar was sick/a teacher.'

This is a very common situation in languages of the world; other examples of the type include Imbabura Quechua (Cole 1985: 67–68) and Mojave (Munro 1976: 48–50).

(60) a Juan-ka   mayistru-mi   (ka-rka).   (Imbabura Quechua)
         Juan-TOP teacher-VALID be-PAST/3
         'Juan is (was) a teacher.'
      b ʔinyep hamakha:v-č   (ido-pč-m).   (Mojave)
         me   Mojave-SUBJ be-TNS-TNS
         'I'm a Mojave.'

Exactly which tenses, aspects, and subject agreement categories require auxiliaries and which do not varies somewhat from language to language, although
it is usually the less-marked categories of present tense and third person subject
that are most likely to omit the auxiliary. Hengeveld (1992), Wetzer (1996), and
Stassen (1997) give extensive discussion of the range of attested possibilities.

These facts relate to one of the oldest definitions of verb in the history of
linguistics: for the Ancient Greeks, verbs were a part of speech without case inflection, but that inflected for tense, person, and number (Robins 1989: 39). This
characterization has been prominent in the Western study of language ever since.
This morphocentric view is not great as a universal definition, because languages
vary significantly in their inflectional systems. In some languages, tense can attach even to nouns and adjectives (e.g. Turkish and Abaza, see below); in other
languages, not even verbs are inflected for tense (e.g. Yoruba, Nupe). Nevertheless, there are valid implicational universals at work here. Wetzer (1996)
shows that nouns and adjectives agree with their subject in person only if the
verbs in the language regularly bear such agreement. Both Wetzer (1996) and
Stassen (1997) argue at length that languages in which a past–nonpast distinction is marked obligatorily by affixes on verbs do not treat nominal and
adjectival predicates like verbs morphosyntactically; they refer to this as the
tense parameter. There is thus a large residue of the ancient view of verbs that
should follow naturally from the true definition.

On the surface of things, it seems easy to sketch a functionalist account of why
this difference should hold. Verbs typically denote transitory events that hold
only for a brief period (Givón 1984: ch. 3). It is therefore natural for speakers to
locate those events in time with an indication of tense or related notions. Since
predicate nominals and adjectives tend to indicate more permanent states of
affairs, it is less important to locate them in time; they are likely to hold at most
times. But I have already questioned the accuracy and utility of making this
the fundamental distinction between verbs and other categories (section 2.2).
And indeed in all of the languages cited above it is perfectly natural to put a
nonverbal predication in a past or future tense; it just requires an auxiliary to
do so. Why not then attach the relevant affix directly to the noun or adjective?

The first step toward explaining this is to make some background assumptions
explicit. The usual P&P assumption is that tense is generated as a separate node

in the syntax–an idea that has its origins in Chomsky's (1957) classic analysis of the English auxiliary system. More specifically, tense counts as the head of the clause, and takes the lexical predication as its complement. Now if a particular tense is specified as being an affix (like past in English, as opposed to future), it will attract another head to itself so it can attach to that head morphologically.[13] The question, then, is why in many languages this host must be a verb and not a noun or adjective.

Most P&P-style theories are content to stipulate this. They say either that tense attracts something with a +verb feature, or that it is specified as being an affix that attaches only to verbs (see, for example, Benmanmoun [2000] for an otherwise successful analysis of Arabic along these lines). But within such a theory there is no formal reason why the tenses of a language could not be specified as +noun instead, thereby affixing to predicate nominals but needing an auxiliary with verbs – a scenario that never happens. I must do better than this, because my goal is to eliminate the arbitrary category features like +verb from the syntax and related morphology.

To see how this can be done, consider the structures of Arabic examples like (59a,b) within my theory. There must be a null Pred dominating the NP or AP that creates a thematic role for the subject. The PredP that it heads could be the immediate complement of tense, giving the structure in (61b). Alternatively, PredP could be the complement of an auxiliary verb, which is itself the complement of tense, as in (61c). By contrast, an ordinary verbal projection will be embedded directly under tense, because it needs no Pred in order to take a subject, as in (61a).

(61)   a   b

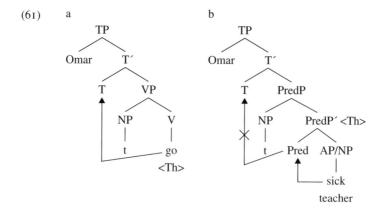

---

[13] Here I assume a "building" theory of the morphology – syntax interface, like that of Baker (1988a), rather than a "checking" theory like that of Chomsky (1995) (see Baker [2002]). The basic idea can, however, be stated in either framework.

c

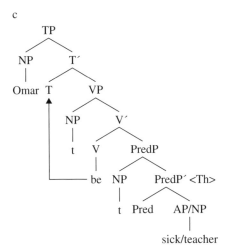

If T in these stuctures is not an affix, then no attraction takes place. Under these conditions (61b) is well formed, resulting in sentences like (59a). (Benmamoun [2000] gives a variety of independent arguments that present tense does not attract a head in Arabic, although other tenses do.) (61a) is also well formed under these conditions. The (61c) structure with an auxiliary, however, will be marked or ungrammatical: it is blocked by (61b), which has the same interpretation with less syntactic structure (cf. Chomsky's [1991] notion of economy of representation).

Consider now what happens when tense is an affix, as past tense is in Arabic and the other languages considered above. Then it will attract a lexical head, causing it to undergo head movement so that the affix has a host to attach to. For the verbal structure in (61a) this creates no problem: the head of the complement of T is a lexical root, and there is nothing to prevent it from moving to the T node. In (61b), however, the only lexical root that tense could attract is more deeply embedded: the PredP intervenes between it and T. I claim that this Pred blocks the attraction of the noun or adjective by T, causing the structure to crash. There are two derivations to consider. First, the noun or adjective cannot move directly to tense skipping over Pred; that derivation violates the Head Movement Constraint of Travis (1984), Baker (1988a), and Chomsky (1986a):

(62)   The Head Movement Constraint (HMC)
        A word-level category X can move to adjoin to another word-level category
        Y only if the phrase headed by X is immediately dominated by a projection
        of Y.

The more promising derivation is the one indicated in (61b), in which the N or A adjoins to Pred and then moves on to T. The result of moving N or A to Pred is, however, a complex Pred, not an N or A. This derivation thus results in T attaching not to a lexical head, but to a functional head that contains a lexical one. I take this to be a violation of tense's basic morphological requirement, which can be stated as follows:[14]

(63)   (In certain languages, certain) tenses must attach to a lexical category.

This constraint is motivated by the fact that tense affixes cannot attach to the overt independent Preds of Edo, Chichewa, Awtuw, or Samoan, as we saw in the previous section. The morphological structure created by this kind of head movement is technically no different.

In contrast, the structure in (61c) is grammatical when tense is an affix. In this case, tense can satisfy (63) by attracting the verbal auxiliary head immediately below it. This time the extra structure that includes the auxiliary is not blocked by anything simpler, given the ungrammaticality of (61b). The result is examples like (59b) in Arabic.

In this way, I replicate the successes of earlier theories without directly stipulating that tense has a privileged relationship to verbs as opposed to nouns or adjectives. The familiar observation that tense often attaches only to verbs is not a basic defining property of the category. Rather, it follows indirectly from the fundamental theta-role assigning difference between verbs and nonverbs, which forces additional structure to be present in nonverbal predications, making it more difficult for tense to find a lexical host. Note also that it is not important that the functional head in question be precisely tense; it could just as well be an aspect node, a mood node, or a subject agreement node (if that is different from tense). It is not the label of the node that is essential, but its configuration. This analysis thus generalizes to the full range of functional heads that have scope over a clause.

It is also possible for a language to have the nonverbal predication structure in (61b), but no auxiliary that is suitable to make the structure in (61c). In such

---

[14] In section 2.9 I open up the possibility of another kind of derivation from this underlying structure, one in which the A combines with Pred by *conflation*, where this is understood as incorporation prior to lexical insertion. The result of this kind of movement will not be a Pred or an A but a V, which can be attracted to tense. This grammatical derivation does not produce a language that looks like Arabic, but rather a language in which the verb–adjective distinction seems to be neutralized.

While the account given in the text covers Arabic and similar languages directly, English requires one to say a little more. First, *be* in English is required even in the present tense, so **Chris a teacher* is not a possible matrix clause. This can be explained by saying that even the present tense of English is an affix. Harder to explain is the fact that *be* is needed even under independent tense particles like *will* (*Chris will *(be) a teacher*). Perhaps *will* in English selects some other functional head which is itself an affix, therefore necessitating the presence of a verb form it can attach to.

a language, nonverbal sentences would be possible only in unmarked/present tense. Mohawk is an example:[15]

(64) a Uwári akó-skar-e'   ne Sak.
         Mary FsP-friend-NSF NE Sak
         'Sak is Mary's boyfriend.'
       b Áthere' ne thi.   (Deering and Delisle 1976: 129)
         basket NE that
         'That's a basket.'

This is a common variant of the Arabic situation; other such languages include Mapuche and Cree.

Recall, however, that tense/mood/aspect/agreement marking does not distinguish verbs from other categories in all languages. If a language has no tense affixes at all, tense inflection *per se* obviously does not distinguish one category from another; Yoruba and Nupe are cases in point. There are also languages like Abaza, in which tense and agreement morphology attaches to nouns and adjectives as well as to verbs.

(65) a Awəy d̦-s-č̌ʷəməɣ-b.   (O'Herin 1995: 123)
         she   3s-1sS-hate-STAT/PRES
         'I hate her.'
       b Awəy d-mgʷadəw-b.   (O'Herin 1995: 131)
         she   3s-pregnant-STAT/PRES
         'She is pregnant.'
       c Y-aba   də-ɉʲmaxč̌ʲa-b.   (O'Herin 1995: 127)
         3sM-father 3s-goatherd-STAT/PRES
         'His father is a goatherd.'

Salish and Wakashan languages also fit this description (see section 3.9), as does the Uralic language Nenets (Wetzer 1996) and the Mayan language Tzutujil (Daley 1985). Such languages can be accounted for by saying that their tenses are less fussy than the tenses of languages like Arabic: they can attach to any host, lexical or functional:

(66)   (In certain languages,) tenses may attach to any word-level category.

---

[15] Another way to analyze the Mohawk case would be to say that Mohawk does not require a tense projection to be present in matrix clauses. This would have the advantage of not positing a Ø present tense for nonverbal sentences when no Ø allomorph of the tense/aspect node can be observed in verbal sentences. Stassen (1997) claims that copula-less nonverbal predications are attested in many languages in which tense is always an overt affix on verbs; he cites Sinhalese, Alabama, Burmese, and various languages of Australia and New Guinea. I would need more detailed information about what range of tense interpretations the verbless sentences in these languages can have in order to determine which of these two possibilities is correct for each language.

In such a language, the derivation in (61b) in which a noun or adjective moves through Pred to tense is legitimate. This is the source of (65b,c).[16]

The difference between (63) and (66) clearly comes down to a morphological property of the particular tense morphemes themselves. As such, it can vary not only from language to language, but even from tense to tense within a particular language. Turkish is a case in point (Wetzer 1996). Four tense categories (present, past, conditional, and inferential) attach directly to nouns and adjectives as well as to verbs in this language, whereas the others (continuative, aorist, future, necessitive, and optative) need a verbal copula when they co-occur with nouns or adjectives. Thus, the past tense in Turkish looks like Abaza and the future tense in Turkish looks like Arabic:

(67)   a in-di-m   versus   gel-ecek-sin
           descend-PAST-IsS   come-FUT-2sS
           'I descended'   'you will come'
        b zengin-di-m   versus   zengin *(ol)-acak-sin
           rich-PAST-IsS   rich   be-FUT-2sS
           'I was rich'   'you will be rich'
        c bahçivan-di-m   versus   öğretmen *(ol)-acak-Ø.
           gardener-PAST-IsS   teacher   be-FUT-3sS
           'I am a gardener'   's/he will be a teacher'

My theory thus allows room for a certain amount of crosslinguistic variation in how tense is realized, which is an advantage over an approach that defines verbs in terms of tense and related inflections. However, I take it that tense cannot specify which lexical category it attaches to. This derives an implicational universal: tenses and related elements attach to nouns and adjectives in a given language only if they also attach to verbs. This follows from the fact that verbs are structurally closer to tense than predicative nouns and adjectives by virtue of taking subjects directly. Therefore, verbs are the easiest lexical category for tense to attach to. That this morphological universal holds is not big news, but the fact that it can be explained by an independently motivated syntactic definition of verb is a significant result.

---

[16] A few languages have distinct tense markers that attach to different lexical categories. In Japanese, for example, present tense is expressed by *–ru* on verb roots (*tabe-ru* 'eat-PRES') but by *–i* on (one class of) adjectives (*aka-i* 'red-PRES'); see section 4.6.1 for examples and references. I take this to be an ordinary case of morphologically conditioned allomorphy, to be handled as in Halle and Marantz (1993). The adjective adjoins to Pred, which adjoins to tense. Pred in the context of an adjective like *aka* 'red' is spelled out as Ø; T[+present] is spelled out as *–i* in the environment of Ø and as *–ru* otherwise. See Nishiyama (1999) for details.

2.6   Morphological causatives

In addition to their characteristic inflections, verbs also take dedicated derivational morphology in many languages. For example, many languages have
causative morphemes that attach productively to verb roots, but not to nouns
or adjectives. This is true even though there is no intrinsic semantic reason
why only the kinds of eventualities denoted by verbs can be caused. On the
contrary, there is no similar category restriction on the periphrastic causatives
formed with *make* in English. To the extent that these verbal derivations are
formed in the syntax, I want to explain this restriction too from the basic fact
that only verbs take subjects directly, without relying on features like $+/-$V
or $+/-$N either in the morphological subcategorizations of the affixes or in
the "attractor features" of higher heads. This can be accomplished using very
similar reasoning to that in the previous section.

Consider languages in which causation is expressed not (only) by an independent verb, but by a causative affix. There is a long tradition of deriving such
constructions from an underlying source like (68a) by way of a process of head
movement/incorporation (Baker 1988a).

(68)   a The hot sun made [VP Chris hunger]
        b The hot sun hunger$_i$-made [VP Chris t$_i$]

Li (1990) observes the important fact that this kind of head movement cannot take a lexical category (such as verb or adjective) and move it through a
functional category before attaching it to another lexical category such as the
causative verb. As in Baker (1996b), I refer to "Li's Generalization" with the
more mnemonic name the Proper Head Movement Generalization:

(69)   The Proper Head Movement Generalization (PHMG).
        A lexical head A cannot move to a functional head B and then to a lexical
        head C.

The most obvious reflex of this condition is that verbs must be incorporated into
the causative head without any of the tense, aspect, or agreement morphology
that they otherwise usually bear (see Li [1990] for data). The PHMG combines
with the theory defended here to predict that no morphological causative should
be possible from structures like (70).

(70)   a The hot sun made [PredP Chris Pred [AP hunger]]
        b The accident made [PredP Chis Pred [NP (an) invalid]]

There are several conceivable derivations, all of which are ruled out. First, the adjective or noun could move through the Pred head on its way to the causative morpheme; this is ruled out by the PHMG. Alternatively, the adjective or noun could skip over Pred on its way to the causative morpheme; this violates the HMC stated back in (62):

(71)   a *The hot sun hungry$_i$-made [$_{PredP}$ Chris Pred($+t_i$) [$_{AP}$ t_i]]
         b *The accident invalid$_i$-made [$_{PredP}$ Chis Pred($+t_i$) [$_{NP}$ t_i]].

Finally, the Pred could be omitted altogether. Then the incorporation of the adjective or noun would be possible in principle, but there would be no theta-role assigned to the subject of the adjective or noun. The structure then would be ruled out by the theta criterion, on a par with (46) and (47) in Edo. I thus derive the prediction that whereas a periphrastic causative construction can appear to be category-neutral, selecting either VP, AP, or NP small clauses, a morphological causative construction cannot be category-neutral, suffixing to V, A, or N with equal ease.

This prediction is supported by data from a wide range of languages. (72)–(74) show three languages that are known to have causative morphemes that attach productively to verbs, as shown in the (a) examples. In none of these languages can the same morpheme attach to an adjectival root or a nominal root, as shown in the (b) and (c) examples.

(72)   a Mwana a-ku-d-ets-a   zovala.   (Chichewa [Bantu])
           1.child 3sS-PRES-be.dirty$_V$-CAUS-FV clothes.   (Alsina and Mchombo
                                                               1991)
           'The child is making the clothes be dirty.'
         b *Mbidzi zi-na-kali-its-a   m-kango.
            10.zebras 10S-PAST-fierce$_A$-CAUS-FV 3-lion
            'The zebras made the lion fierce.'
                                                    (Bresnan and Mchombo 1995:
                                                     242, n. 58)
         c *Mbidzi   zi-na-fumu-(i)ts-a   m-kango.
            10.zebras   10S-PAST-chief$_N$-CAUS-FV 3-lion
            'The zebras made the lion a chief.'   (cf. Bresnan and Mchombo
                                                      1995: 242, n. 58)

(73)   a Noqa-ta puñu-chi-ma-n.   (Huallaga Quechua)
           I-ACC   sleep$_V$-CAUS-1O-3S   (Weber 1989: 161)
           'It makes me sleep.'
         b *Chakra-:-ta   hatun-chi-pa:-ma-sha.   (Weber 1989: 166)
            field-1P-ACC big$_A$-CAUS-BEN-1O-3/PERF
            'He enlarged my field for me.'
         c *Juan Jose-ta   wamra-chi-n.   (compare with (76b))
            Juan Jose-ACC child-CAUS-3S
            'Juan made Jose a (his) child.'

(74)   a John-ga   Mary-o   ik-(s)ase-ta.   (Japanese)
          John-NOM   Mary-ACC   goV-CAUS-PAST
          'John made Mary go.'
        b *Taroo-ga   heya-o   hiro-sase-ta.[17]
          Taro-NOM   room-ACC   wideA-CAUS-PAST
          'Taro widened the room.'
        c *Hanako-ga   Taroo-o   sensei-sase-ta.
          Hanako-NOM   Taro-ACC   teacherN-CAUS-PAST
          'Hanako made Taro a teacher.'

The same generalization holds in Amharic (Mengistu Amberber, personal communication), Kannada (Sridhar 1990: 276), Yimas (Foley 1991), Greenlandic (Fortescue 1984), and other languages. Mohawk seems not to have adjectives (but see section 4.6.3) so that case does not arise, but it is clear that the causative affix – *st/-ht* that attaches to verbs (including "adjectival" ones) does not attach also to nouns:

(75)   a Wa-shakó-ye-ht-e'.   (Mohawk)
          FACT-MsS/FsO-wake.up-CAUS-PUNC
          'He woke her up.'
        b *Wa'-e-ristoser-a-ht-e'.
          FACT-FsS-butter-Ø-CAUS-PUNC
          'She made it into butter (i.e. by stirring the cream too hard).'

This is not to say that languages cannot have morphological causatives that are derived from nouns or adjectives. Huallaga Quechua, for example, has such derivations. But a distinct causative affix must be used in these cases: -*cha* rather than the -*chi* seen in (73a).

(76)   a llañu-cha: (David Weber, personal communication)
          thin-make
          'to make X thin (e.g. yarn, when spinning)'
        b wamra-cha:
          child-make
          'to make X one's child; to adopt X'

-*Cha*, on the other hand, cannot attach to verb roots, so one would not have *puñu-cha 'put to sleep.' English also has derivations similar to Quechua –*cha*, although not to Quechua –*chi*; it has a series of morphemes that attach to nouns

---

[17] This Japanese example becomes grammatical if the suffixed form *hiro-sase-ta* is replaced by the sequence of words *hiro-ku shi-ta* 'wide do-past' (Mihoko Zushi and Koichi Nishitani, personal communications). Here there is no incorporation of the adjective into the causative verb, and hence no violation of the PHMG. The example is thus correctly predicted to be possible.

or adjectives but not verbs to give a causative verb, the most productive of which
is *–ize*:

(77)   a The government legalized eating spinach. (made it legal)
        b The university modernized its curriculum. (made it modern)
        c The lab technician finally crystallized the salt solution.   (made it into
                                                                        crystals)
        d The high temperature and pressure fossilized the animal's bones.
                                                                (made them fossils)
        e *The magician appearized the genie.   (made it appear)
        f *The lab technician dissolvized the salt in water.   (made it dissolve)

Quechua *–cha* and English *–ize* thus have essentially the opposite attachment
properties as Chichewa *-its*, Quechua *-chi*, or Japanese *-sase*.

    My theory does not predict that it is impossible to derive causative verbs from
adjectives and nouns; it only predicts that what is needed to form causatives
from the nonverbal categories is significantly different from what is needed
to form causatives from verbs. Therefore, a single lexical item cannot readily
do both. I have assumed that *make* in English and its affixal counterparts in
Chichewa and Japanese are two-place predicates that take a causer as one argument and a state- or event-denoting phrase as the other. This second argument
is usually a VP, but it can also be a PredP if incorporation is not triggered.
If incorporation is triggered, however, then PredP cannot appear, and there is
no theta-marker for the causee. In contrast, causative morphemes that attach
preferentially to nouns and adjectives can be analyzed as three-place predicates.
They select an agent NP x, a theme NP y, and a property-denoting AP/NP z, with
the meaning that x causes y to have property z. They thus appear in structures
like (78a).

(78)   a [$_{vP}$ Juan v [$_{VP}$ Jose *–cha* [$_{NP}$ child]]]
        b [$_{vP}$ it v [$_{VP}$ me *-cha* [$_{VP}$ sleep]]]

Here the theme *Jose* is theta-marked by the V *–cha*, and the noun *wamra*
'child' can readily incorporate into *–cha*, there being no intervening head to
block the movement. The complex head *wamra+cha* then raises to v to derive
the final structure. An example with an AP complement of *–cha* would work
the same way. (In fact, the derivation is more productive and semantically
transparent when the complement is an adjective than when it is a noun, a fact
I return to in sections 3.8 and 3.9. See also chapter 5 for a different analysis
of *–ize* derivations in English.)

    If one tried to combine a VP projection with a morpheme that has the lexical
properties described above, however, serious theta-theoretic problems arise.
The minimally different structure (78b) is ruled out because the verb root *puñu*

'sleep' fails to assign its theta-role to a suitable category inside its maximal projection. This problem could be solved by generating an additional NP like 'baby' inside VP, giving something that would mean approximately 'It causes me to have the property of the baby sleeping.' Although this structure is thematically complete, it would be bad because the second NP 'baby' would overtax the case licensing powers of the causative morpheme. It is probably also semantically ill formed, because 'baby sleep' cannot be mapped onto a property that can be predicated of *me* by Chierchia's "up" operator. Nor can one say that the causative morpheme is an obligatory control predicate that induces a referential dependency between its object and the covert subject of its complement, because it is not a control-inducer in (78a). A lexical item with these lexical properties is thus well adapted to causativizing adjectives and nouns, but not verbs. Because the theta-role assigning properties of verbs are significantly different from those of nouns and adjectives, a single morpheme with well-defined thematic properties of its own is not flexible enough to causativize both.

How striking are these results? A critic can legitimately say "not very." The prediction cannot be interpreted as an absolute prohibition against the causative of an adjective ever resembling the causative of a verb, because we cannot rule out the possibility that two affixes are accidentally homophonous, even though they have different lexical properties. After all *bank* (the side of a river) and *bank* (the financial institution) sound exactly the same in English, even though their lexical semantic properties are completely different. Such a case of accidental homophony seems to have arisen in the Imbabura dialect of Quechua, according to Cole (1985). This dialect has lost the usual Quechua affix *–cha*, and *–chi* appears on verbs, nouns, and adjectives (although less productively on the latter).[18] Such cases blunt the sharpness of almost all morphological generalizations. On the other hand, these patterns will look more striking if it turns out that most of the world's periphrastic causative constructions are like *make* in English in being able to take any kind of predication structure as a complement. Then the fact that incorporation-triggering causatives are almost always fussy about category distinctions will stand out by contrast, to the credit of the theory that explains it. Unfortunately, I do not know any general surveys of the properties of periphrastic causatives that speak to this issue.

---

[18] Another possible counterexample that has been brought to my attention is Hebrew, where the hiCCiC pattern that combines with adjectival roots (Borer 1991) is also a productive causativizer of verb roots. It may be significant that the deadjectival forms are not inherently causative, but can be used as inchoatives as well. Hebrew morphology is also more difficult to interpret because of its nonconcatenative character. (I thank the participants at the 1997 meeting of the Israel Association of Theoretical Linguistics at Bar Ilan University for discussion of this point.)

Apart from questions about the strength of the typological generalization, how readers will feel about this analysis will depend on how content they are with arbitrary morphological and syntactic selection. If one does not mind stipulating that one particular affix attaches only to verbs and another attaches only to nouns and adjectives, then the facts surveyed here can easily be described without my theory. There are explanatory issues, however. If the morphological selection were stated in terms of the standard features $+/-$V and $+/-$N, then one would expect to find causative affixes that subcategorize for a $+$V root, and therefore attach to both adjectives and verbs but not to nouns, just as there are affixes like *–ize* and *-cha* that attach to $+$N roots (i.e. nouns and adjectives). Yet this seems rare at best, and one should explain why. And one should always ask deeper questions: what is it about the category or feature "verb" that makes causative affixes care so much about it? What is the link between the fact that verbs can combine with only one kind of causative morpheme and the other distinctive properties of verbs? My theory is able to answer these sorts of questions by deducing apparent differences in morphological subcategorization from more basic differences in syntactic structure.

The analysis I have given for causative morphemes generalizes in a straightforward way to other affixes that are verbal heads underlyingly. Any head that selects a "propositional" complement and triggers incorporation should attach only to verbs, for the reasons discussed. A likely further case in point is suffixal benefactive applicative markers. In Baker (1996b: ch. 9), I analyze these as verbs that have a three-place argument structure similar to *give*. An example like 'cook-APPL Y food' has the underlying structure 'X gave Y [$_{VP}$ cook food].' As predicted, the Chichewa benefactive morpheme *-ir-* attaches to all major classes of verbs in Chichewa, but not to adjectives (Bresnan and Mchombo 1995: 242, n. 58; Sam Mchombo, personal communication).

(79)   a Alenje   a-ku-lúk-ir-a   pa-mchenga.
          2-hunters 2S-PRES-weave-APPL-FV on-sand
          'The hunters are weaving on the beach.'
        b *M-kango u-na-kali-(i)r-a   mbidzi / m'nkhalango.
          3-lion   3S-PAST-fierce-APPL-FV zebras / in-jungle
          'The lion is fierce for the zebras/in the jungle.'

The prediction can also be tested with desiderative affixes, which are bound forms meaning 'want.' For example, the Japanese desiderative suffix *–tai* can attach to verbs (*tabe-tai* '(I) want to eat (it)') but not to predicate nouns or adjectives (**sensei-tai* '(I) want to be a teacher'; **utsukushi-tai* '(I) want to be beautiful'), as expected. A particularly interesting case is *naya* in Quechua. Unlike the causative affix *–chi* in most Quechua languages, *-naya* can attach to either verb roots or noun roots (Cole 1985; Muysken 1988), although it is less productive on nouns. At first this looks like a counterexample to my proposal, but a closer look at what the derived forms mean vindicates the analysis. The examples in (80) appear to be typical (Cole 1985: 181–82).

(80) a Nuka-ta miku-naya-n
       I-ACC   eat-DESID-3S
       'I want to eat.'
    b Nuka-ta yaku-naya-n
       I-ACC   woman-DESID-3S
       'I want a woman (sexual desire, viewed as vulgar).'

Although (80a) and (80b) have parallel grammatical structures, they are not parallel in what they mean. 'Want' in (80a) is interpreted as a control predicate: it means 'I want that I eat,' with the haver of the desire being the same as the agent of the desired event. There is no similar control in (80b); indeed, the incorporated noun is not understood predicatively at all. The sentence does not mean 'I want to be a woman' (say, via a sex-change operation), but rather 'I want a woman,' with 'woman' functioning as an argument. This usage does not have a Pred dominating 'woman,' so head movement is not blocked, and (80b) is grammatical. My theory explains why this form cannot have the predicative reading as well. The three imaginable structures are sketched in (81), with the third one predictably ruled out.

(81) a $[I_k$ -want $[_{VP}$ PRO$_k$ eat$]]$ Verb incorp. possible (=(80a))
    b $[I_k$ -want $[_{NP}$ woman$]]$ Noun incorp. possible (=(80b))
    c *$[I_k$ -want $[_{PredP}$ PRO$_k$ Pred $[_{NP}$ woman$]]]$ Noun incorp. blocked by Pred

The simple device of stipulating what categories an affix can attach to is inadequate here, since *-naya* can attach to both Ns and Vs. The difference is that the incorporated V must be understood as a predicate of the surface subject, whereas the incorporated N cannot be. This supports the claim that verbs are inherently predicates, but nouns (and adjectives) are not.[19]

---

[19] Another topic that is worthy of study in this connection is nominalization – derivational affixes that change verbs or verbal projections into nouns or nominal projections. I hope that this inquiry into the nature of verbs, adjectives, and nouns will lead (me) to a better understanding of the complexities of nominalizations and gerund constructions, but this area is enormously rich and complex, so apart from some remarks in chapter 5 I leave this topic for a separate study. See Baker and Stewart (1996) for some evidence from nominalizations in Edo that supports my basic thesis that verbs can assign a theme role to a specifier, but adjectives cannot.

2.7   Word order differences

I turn now from the morphological and morphosyntactic traits of verbs to the purely syntactic topic of word order. It is well known since Greenberg (1963) that most languages with fixed word order have a consistent direction of headedness: either all major phrases are head-initial, or all are head-final. In English, for example, nouns, verbs, and adjectives all come before their complements (*eat* your spinach, *branches* of the tree, *fond* of cribbage), whereas in Japanese the corresponding heads all come after their complements. There are, however, a non-negligible number of languages that have mixed word orders. Zepter (2001) investigates such languages, and observes that verbs stand out as having different word order from other phrases. She argues for the following implicational universal:

(82)   Only languages with head-final VP show non-uniform head/complement orders across different phrasal categories.

German is Zepter's paradigm example of this generalization, in which noun phrases and adjective phrases are head-initial but verbs are phrase-final:

(83)   a [DP das [NP Zimmer [PP im hinteren Teil des Schlosses]]]   (NP)
            the   room   in back   part the castle
        b [DegP sehr [AP stolz [PP auf meinen Vater]]]   (AP)
            very   proud   on my   father
        c ... [CP daß die Tante_i [VP t_i [DP dem Gärtner] hilft]   (VP)
            that the aunt   the   gardener helps

These examples also show that most functional categories are also head-initial in German, including the complementizer *daß*, the various determiners, and the adpositions. Persian is another language Zepter cites as having this pattern:

(84)   a taxrib-e   doshman-hâ   (NP-initial)
          destruction-EZ enemy-PLUR
          'the destruction of the enemy'
        b bâ   simâ   (PP-initial)
          with Sima
        c Man ketâb-o   mi-xun-am   (VP-final)
          I   book-the PRES-read-1sS
          'I read the book.'

How then does Zepter's word order generalization relate to the more universal and fundamental fact that verbs are the only lexical category that take specifiers?

Zepter derives the generalization in (82) from my basic proposal about categories in an interesting and plausible way, making use of optimality theoretic reasoning. The requirement that heads come first in their phrases clearly out-ranks the requirement that heads come last in their phrases in languages like German and Persian. This accounts for the head-initiality of most phrases in these languages, including noun phrases. Verbs, however, face an additional challenger for initial position, because they alone of the lexical categories take specifiers. Specifiers also want to come first in their phrases, and this require-ment takes precedence over the need for heads to come first in both English and German. In addition to these familiar word order principles, Zepter adds the principle in (85).

(85)   A head should be at an edge of its maximal projection.

(85) crucially does not specify which edge of the projection a head must appear at; it is different in this respect from the usual head-first/head-last conditions. In German and Persian these constraints are prioritized as follows:[20]

(86)   a A specifier is at the left edge of its phrase.
        b A head is at the edge of its phrase.
        c A head is as far to the left as possible in its phrase.
        d A head is as far to the right as possible in its phrase.

Verb phrases always have specifiers, and this specifier (which may be an empty category, such as trace or PRO) comes leftmost by (86a). The verb therefore cannot be at the left edge of VP, so it appears at the right edge of VP instead, with (86b) overriding (86c). VPs are thus head-final in German and Persian. NP and PP do not have specifiers, so (86a) does not apply to them. (86b) and (86c) can then both be fully satisfied by putting the head at the left edge of the phrase. This configuration violates only (86d), the lowest-ranked constraint in this system.

  In contrast to German and Persian, uniformly head-initial languages like English are those in which (86c) is ranked above (86b). As a result, verbs never follow their complements in English. Uniformly head-final languages like Japanese are those in which (86d) is ranked above (86c). (86b) has little effect in this kind of language. It never causes verb phrases to be head-initial in an otherwise head-final language, because specifiers always want to be initial, there being no opposite of (86a) in Zepter's system. Therefore specifiers never compete with verbs for phrase-final position, forcing them to claim phrase-initial position as a consolation prize. As a result, there can be no

[20] Zepter's typology also contains another factor, which accounts for the fact that tense/infl is head-initial in German and the African languages Vata and Gbadi (but not Persian). I omit this factor from my discussion because it is in practice relevant only to functional categories.

such language as "Reverse German" or "Reverse Persian." This completes the theoretical derivation of the generalization in (82).

Overall, Zepter (2001) succeeds in giving a relatively restrictive typology of word order systems that makes room for mixed word order languages like German and Persian without allowing every imaginable combination of word orders. Verbs stand out as being special with respect to word order in these mixed languages. This fact can be simply explained in terms of the most basic property of verbs – the fact that they alone of the lexical categories have a specifier.

2.8   Unaccusativity diagnostics

While it has not previously been said that verbs differ from the other lexical categories in *whether* they assign a theme theta-role, there is a body of literature claiming that verbs differ from other categories in *how* they assign the theme theta-role. In particular, it has been said that verbs assign a theme theta-role to an *internal* argument (one that is inside the smallest projections of the verb) whereas corresponding adjectives and nouns assign this role to an *external* argument (one that is outside at least the smaller projections of the head, and perhaps outside the entire maximal projection). As a result, the theme-subject of a verb may behave like the direct object of a transitive clause in certain respects, but the theme-subject of a noun or adjective does not. Morphosyntactic phenomena that reveal a similarity between transitive objects and the sole argument of certain intransitive verbs are known as unaccusativity diagnostics (Levin and Rappaport-Hovav 1995). In this section, I show that these category-sensitive effects can be explained by my theory, with the difference between internal- and external-theta-role assignment recast as the difference between theta-role assignment by a lexical head and theta-role assignment in the specifier of the functional head Pred. The details of how this works out depend on the language-specific properties of the particular unaccusativity diagnostic. I focus on four cases that I take to be representative of a general phenomenon: *ne*-cliticization in Italian, noun incorporation in Mohawk, possessive datives in Hebrew, and floated quantifiers in Japanese. Parts of this section are necessarily more technical than much of the rest of this work, for which I ask the reader's indulgence.

2.8.1   Italian

I begin with Italian, a language in which unaccusativity has been studied intensively. Perhaps the most famous unaccusativity diagnostic of all is *ne*-cliticization in Italian (Belletti and Rizzi 1981; Burzio 1986). *Ne*-cliticization is the phenomenon in which the genitive case complement of a noun or the nominal head of a quantified expression is replaced by the clitic *ne* 'of it, of them,' which is then attracted to the tensed verb of the clause. This can apply to the object of a transitive verb:

(87)   Giovanni ne   inviterà   molti – .   (Burzio 1986: 23)
        Giovanni of.them   will.invite many
        'Giovanni will invite many of them.

With intransitive verbs, a distinction appears. The subject of such verbs can always come after the verb in Italian, in superficially the same position as direct objects. If the verb takes an agentive subject, *ne*-cliticization is not possible as shown in (88a); this shows the same ungrammaticality as *ne*-cliticization of the subject of a transitive verb, shown in (88b).

(88)   a *Ne   telefoneranno molti.   (Burzio 1986: 22)
          of.them will.telephone many
          'Many of them will call.'
        b *Ne   esamineranno il caso molti.
          of.them will.examine the case many
          'Many of them will examine the case.'

Ne-cliticization is possible, however, from the postverbal subject of a passive verb ((89a)) or an anticausative verb ((89b)), just as it is with the object of the corresponding transitive verb. *Ne*-cliticization is also possible with certain intransitive verbs (the unaccusatives) that are thematically similar to passives and anticausatives, even though they do not have transitive versions ((89c)).

(89)   a Ne   sarebbero riconosciute molti (di vittime).   (Burzio 1986)
          of-them would.be recognized many (of victims)
          'Many of them (the victims) would be recognized.'
        b Se ne   rompono molti.
          SE of-them break   many
          'Many of them break.'
        c Ne   arriveranno molti.
          of.them will.arrive many
          'Many of them will arrive.'

Ne-cliticization also reveals a distinction among the lexical categories. *Ne* cannot express the subject of an adjective derived from a comparable verb root, even when the thematic role of the subject seems to be the same (Burzio 1986; Cinque 1990). Thus (89a,b) contrast minimally with (90a,b).

(90)   a *Ne   sarebbero sconosciute molti (di vittime).   (Burzio 1986)
           of.them would.be unknown_A many (of victims)
           'Many of them (the victims) would be unknown.'
        b *Ne   sono spezzati due (di   rami),   purtroppo. (Cinque 1990: 33)
           of.them are   broken_A two (of branches) unfortunately
           'Two of them (the branches) are broken, unfortunately.'

This is not a peculiarity of one particular method of deriving adjectives, such as adjectival passive formation. Cinque (1990) shows that other classes of adjectives derived from verbs also do not allow *ne*-cliticization, including adjectives derived by -*bile* 'able':

(91)   *Ne   sono confermabili poche (di notizie).
         of.them are   confirmable few   (of news.items).
         'Few of them (the news items) are confirmable.'

Even most morphologically simple adjectives show this same resistance to *ne*-cliticization:

(92)   *Ne   sono buoni pochi (dei suoi articoli).   (Cinque 1990: 7)
         of.them are   good few   (of his   articles)
         'Few of them (his articles) are good.'

(A relatively small and semantically homogeneous class of modal and epistemic adjectives are exceptions to this; see (94) below.) Finally, while this has not been discussed in the literature, the subjects of predicate nominals pattern with adjectives rather than with unaccusative verbs in these respects. They too are unable to launch a *ne*-clitic:

(93)   ?*Ne   sono professori molti. (Mario Fadda, personal communication)
          of.them are   professors many
          'Many of them (e.g. people who wear glasses) are professors.'

Apparently, the theme argument of an intransitive verb acts in certain ways like a direct object, whereas the theme arguments of comparable adjectives and nouns do not. This shows that whether a particular predicate is categorized as an adjective or a verb has grammatical consequences that go well beyond its inflectional and derivational morphology.

The few discussions of this issue in the P&P literature have been inadequately general. For example, Levin and Rappaport (1986) argue that the "externalization" of the theme arguments of adjectives is an automatic consequence of the fact that an adjective must have an external argument in order to be usable in the syntax, as either a predicate or an attributive modifier. This claim turns out to be factually false. Cinque (1990) shows that there is a small class of adjectives in Italian whose arguments are not external. With these, *ne*-cliticization is possible:

(94)   Ne   sono probabli ben   poche (di dimissioni).
       of.them are likely   really few   of resignations
       'Few of them (resignations) are really likely.'

(Sentences like this also show that the ones in (90)–(93) are not ruled out for some trivial morphological reason, like *ne* being unable to attach to an adjective or noun.) Raising adjectives like *likely* in English are another case in point. Hence, it cannot be true that adjectives need an external argument *by definition*.

In place of Levin and Rappaport's suggestion, Cinque (1990) proposes that adjectives derived from verbs cannot take internal arguments because the adjectival suffix intervenes structurally between the verb root and its attempted internal argument. This explanation is also suspect, for several reasons. First, nouns derived from unaccusative verbs remain unaccusative (Giorgi and Longobardi 1991), even though the morphemes that derive such nouns are at least as robust as the morphemes that derive adjectives. Second, Cinque's proposal says nothing about the fact that many simple adjectives in Italian are also "unergative"; his suggestion applies to (90) and (91) but not to (92). This seems like a missed generalization.

Others have more or less given up on this problem in one way or another. Pesetsky (1982) assumes without argument that the theta-role assigned by adjectives is different from the one assigned by verbs (he calls it "attribute"), while Borer (1991) abandons the UTAH-like idea that similar theta-roles should be assigned in similar structural configurations.

Looking at the full range of Italian facts, it seems too strong to say that all adjectives must have external arguments, and too weak to say that only derived adjectives must have them. Rather, the correct empirical generalization is a thematic one:

(95)   a The theme argument of a verb is an internal argument.
        b The theme argument of an adjective or noun is an external argument.

(95) correctly captures the facts, as long as the NP in Cinque's example (96) does not count as a theme – and there is no good reason to say that it should.

My theory happens to yield the generalization in (95) almost immediately. Notice first that the notion "external argument," originally from Williams (1981), is a suspect one in current generative theory. Since the advent of the VP-internal subject hypothesis in the late 1980s, it has become common to analyze many external arguments as internal arguments that have been raised by NP-movement to a position outside the maximal projection of the theta-marking head. In addition, some instances of so-called external arguments can be analyzed as not being arguments of the relevant head at all. Marantz (1984) and Kratzer (1996) take this view of agent NPs: the reason agents are found outside the basic VP is that they are not strictly speaking arguments of the verb at all. Rather they are introduced into the clause by a higher head that Kratzer calls Voice and Chomsky (1995) calls v. My proposal is that the same thing is true of theme arguments with respect to adjectives and nouns: the theme is not, strictly speaking, an argument of the adjective or noun at all. Therefore, if it appears anywhere, it must be outside the maximal projection of the adjective or noun. In contrast, the theme NP is an argument of a comparable verb; hence it must be inside the VP, because all true arguments are internal.

This provides a structural basis for explaining the contrast between *ne*-cliticization in verbal clauses and nonverbal clauses in Italian. Let us assume that *ne* is a head-like element generated together with the associated quantifier in the normal argument position, which moves to attach to the inflected verb or auxiliary (Belletti and Rizzi 1981). Then the structure of (92) would be (96a), whereas the structure of (89b) would be (96b). (Example (96b) abstracts away from the verb movement to tense that is found in Italian [Pollock 1989], and (96a) leaves open the exact origin of *be* in nonverbal sentences.)

(96)   a   b

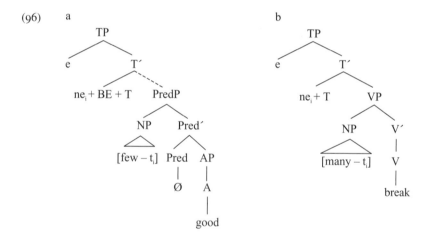

These representations differ in a theoretically significant way: the subject of the verb 'break' originates in the specifier of VP, a lexical category, whereas the subject of 'good' originates in the specifier of PredP, an uninflected functional category. It is generally harder to move something from a functional phrase than from a lexical one. Such movements risk violating the Empty Category Principle (ECP) – a principle originally proposed by Chomsky (1981) to explain the fact that it is harder to question subjects (in Spec, TP, a functional category) than direct objects (in VP, a lexical category).

The ECP needs to be stated with some care in order to achieve the desired effect. We need to distinguish direct objects and the subjects of unaccusative verbs (which are generated in Spec, VP) from both the subjects of transitive verbs and unergative verbs (in Spec, vP) and the subjects of nonverbal predicates (in Spec, PredP). The former allow *ne*-cliticization and the latter do not. I cannot simply invoke the specifier-complement distinction, because all of these nominals are in specifier positions in my theory, as in many post-Larson (1988) theories. I cannot simply invoke the lexical-functional distinction, because this makes the cut in the wrong place, grouping Spec, vP with Spec, VP rather than with Spec, PredP. In order to see what condition preserves the intent of the original ECP within current views about phrase structure, consider the structure of a clause with a transitive verb, such as (88b), given in (97).

(97)

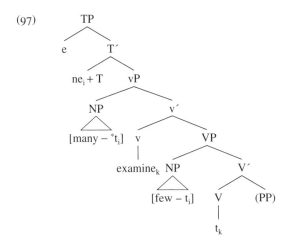

Here the V element incorporates into v to create the transitive verb 'examine'. We know that a *ne*-clitic can move out of the lower Spec, but not out of the higher one. The obvious difference between the two positions is that the lower specifier position is c-commanded by a lexical head, whereas the higher one is not. I therefore state the ECP as follows:

(98)   Empty Category Principle:[21]
         If Y is a trace of movement (other than NP movement), Y is licensed if and
         only if there is an X^0 level category Z such that Z c-commands Y, Y is in the
         minimal domain of Z and Z is lexical.

---

[21] The following notions are presupposed in this statement of the ECP:
    X is in the minimal domain of Y if and only if X is inside the maximal projection YP of Y
    and there is no maximal projection ZP that properly contains X but not Y or a trace bound by Y
    (cf. Chomsky [1993: 12–14]).

[Few t] satisfies this condition in (97), with Z = 'examine', but [many t] does not. Even if 'examine' moves on to tense, as happens in Italian, the resulting head is a complex tense node. This is not a lexical category, and hence not a potential licenser of the trace.

Examples with a trace in the subject position of a nonverbal predication are ruled out in a similar way. Even if there were some higher head which Pred could move to so that it c-commanded its subject, the derived head still would not be lexical. (The sole argument of a modal or epistemic adjective, in contrast, starts out as the complement of the adjective. A trace inside it is then licensed by the adjective in accordance with (98), explaining the grammaticality of (94).)

Finally, traces in the subject of an unaccusative verb are licensed in the same way as those in the object of a transitive verb, as long as we say that there can be a non-theta-marking v position in these structures which the V moves to and therefore c-commands the theme (as in Bowers [1993], and others). I thus revise the simplified structure in (96b) to (99).

(99)

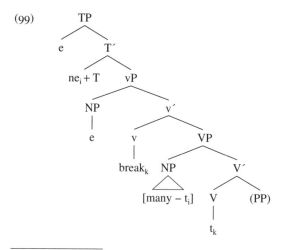

X c-commands Y if and only if the smallest phrase that properly contains X also contains Y (Reinhart 1983; Chomsky 1986a). Note that I am crucially using c-command rather than m-command here.

This formulation in (98) exempts NP-traces (the traces of movement to an A-position for purposes of checking Case) from the ECP. This is necessary because NPs can move to Spec, TP to license their Case from Spec, VP, Spec, vP, or Spec, PredP. There are precedents for this exemption; see, for example den Dikken (1995: 8–11). Chomsky (1986a: sec. 11) does not exempt NP-movement from the ECP *per se*, but does introduce extra devices to accommodate it.

The Minimalist Program has been wary of the ECP because it traditionally involves a notion of government that does not reduce to primitive phrase structural relations (Chomsky 1995). The formulation in (98) avoids this conceptual concern. I am not immediately concerned with the status of the ECP in current theory, whether it is a basic principle, a corollary of a more general condition, or an epiphenomenon. My primary concern is to show that my theory of the verb – nonverb contrast allows these facts to be related to other, more familiar ones.

Although there is no thematic subject in the specifier of vP in (99), I must claim that some kind of specifier is there, in accordance with (1). For English, where the unaccusative subject consistently raises to Spec, TP, we can say that Spec vP contains a trace of this subject (Bowers 1993). Italian allows the unaccusative subject to stay in situ, inside VP (Burzio 1986; Belletti 1988). In this language, it is normal to assume that there is a null expletive in Spec, TP at S-structure. I assume that this expletive is originally inserted in Spec, vP and then raises to Spec, TP, again leaving a trace in Spec, vP.[22] In this way, then, we can explain the fact that verbal predicates are unaccusative but corresponding nonverbal predicates are not.

Cinque (1990) discusses a number of other unaccusativity diagnostics in Italian in addition to *ne*-cliticization. Most of these reveal the same contrast between unaccusative verbs on the one hand and ordinary adjectives on the other. They include extraction from sentential subjects, anaphor binding of the subject by a dative NP, long-distance binding by the subject, movement of null CP operators, and complementizer selection. I believe that Cinque's explanations for all these contrasts can be carried over into my framework, making crucial use of the structural distinction between (96a) and (96b)/(99). If so, then all of this material counts as indirect support for my basic claim that adjectives (and nouns) need the help of a functional category, Pred, in order to have a specifier, whereas verbs do not. Rather than going through each of Cinque's cases in detail, however, I prefer to go on to unaccusativity diagnostics in other languages.

I also omit full discussion of a similar unaccusativity diagnostic that is found in distantly related Russian, as described by Pesetsky (1982). Direct object NPs that are normally marked with accusative case in Russian can be marked with genitive case when they are within the scope of negation; this is known as the genitive of negation. The subjects of nonagentive unaccusative verbs can also be marked with genitive case in these circumstances, but the subjects of thematically similar adjectives and nouns cannot be. Pesetsky analyzes these genitive noun phrases as a kind of quantifier that must undergo movement at the level of Logical Form. This movement leaves a trace that is subject to the ECP, which is licensed in the case of unaccusative verbs, but not for predicate nouns and adjectives. This then provides further evidence in favor of my theory. Since the logic of the situation is so similar to that of *ne*-cliticization

---

[22] This proposal works smoothly if there is an expletive *pro* in subject position in Italian, as most P&P theories of the 1980s and early 1990s assumed. It is not so clear if this analysis is compatible with Alexiadou and Anagnostopoulou's (1998) proposal that the subject-requiring (EPP) feature of T is satisfied by the agreement on the verb in pro-drop languages like Italian. I leave closer exploration of the interactions between these two theories for future research.

in Italian, I do not repeat Pesetsky's examples or the details of the analysis here. Rather, I press on to consider unaccusativity phenomena in some non-Indo-European languages, because only they can confirm that these ideas are truly universal.

2.8.2   *Mohawk*

The most famous unaccusativity diagnostic in Mohawk is noun incorporation (NI). For predicates that are uncontroversially verbal, there is a very close correspondence between the arguments that can be incorporated in Mohawk and the arguments that can launch *ne*-clitics in Italian (Baker 1988a: ch. 3). Direct objects of transitive verbs can be incorporated, as can subjects of unaccusative and anticausativized verbs, but subjects of transitive verbs, subjects of unergative verbs, dative objects, and objects of prepositions cannot be incorporated (see also Baker [1996b: ch. 7] for examples, references, and discussion). (100) contrasts an unaccusative verb, which allows incorporation of its subject, with an unergative verb, which does not.

(100)   a Wa'-ka-wír-ʌ'-ne'.
            FACT-NsS-baby-fall-PUNC
            'The baby fell.'
        b *Wa'-t-ka-wir-ahsʌ'’tho-'.
            FACT-DUP-NsS-baby-cry-PUNC
            'The baby cried.'

These parallels can be explained in a unified way under the assumption that noun incorporation and *ne*-cliticization are both syntactic movement processes (Baker 1988: ch. 3).

There is, however, a sharp difference between the two languages when it comes to words like 'good.' Recall from chapter 1 that such words appear to be verbal, rather than adjectival in Mohawk. There is a good deal of morphological evidence for this: no copular verb ever appears with such predicates, they bear tense and person agreement morphemes (see chapter 1), and they can take the same causative and benefactive suffixes as unaccusative verbs (Baker 1996b) (contrast this with (72)-(74) from Chichewa, Quechua, and Japanese). The structure of a sentence like (101a) is therefore presumably the one in (99) rather than the one for true adjectives in (96a). The head noun of the stative verb's argument can then move to adjoin to the verb, leaving behind a trace that satisfies the ECP. This movement creates sentences like (101b) and (101c).

(101)   a Ka-rak-ʌ́-(hne')   thíkʌ o-'neróhkw-a'
            NsS-be.white-STAT-(PAST)   that NsO-box-NSF
            'That box is (was) white.'
         b Ka-'nerohkw-a-rák-ʌ   (thíkʌ).
            NsS-box-Ø-be.white-STAT   that
            'That box is white.'
         c Ka-nuhs-íyo   (thíkʌ).
            NsS-house-be.good   that
            'That house is good.'

The structure of (101b) is (102), prior to the verb combining with tense:

(102)   [$_e$ Tense [$_{vP}$ e box$_i$+be.white$_k$ [$_{VP}$ [that t$_i$] t$_k$]]]

Mohawk "adjectives" also behave like unaccusative verbs in several other respects, which can be analyzed in essentially the same way.[23]

In contrast, roots like *nuhs* 'house' are nouns in Mohawk, not verbs. In morphological terms, this class of words cannot bear tense or true person agreement (although they do have a dummy third-person prefix), and they cannot combine with causative or benefactive morphemes (see (75b)). There is thus no sign of a mismatch between the category systems of Mohawk and Italian in this domain. My theory says that these nouns cannot assign thematic roles apart from a Pred head. I thus correctly predict that noun incorporation into a predicate nominal is impossible in Mohawk. (103b) is bad for essentially the same reason as the *ne*-cliticization in (93) is bad in Italian.

(103)   a Ka-núhs-a'   thíkʌ o-'nerohkw-a'-kʌ́ ha. (predicate nominal)
            NsS-house-NSF   that   NsO-box-NSF-former
            'That old box is a house.'   (i.e. a child's play house, or a street person's
                                              shelter)
         b *Ka-'nerohkw-a-núhs-a'   (thíkʌ). (incorporation into pred nom'l)
            NsS-box-Ø-house-NSF   that
            'That box is a house.'
         c *[PredP [that t$_i$] Pred [NP box$_i$+house]]

---

[23] The fact that predicates like 'white' and 'good' can have a morphological causative in Mohawk is evidence not only that they are verbs, but that they are unaccusative verbs, because unergatives cannot be causativized morphologically in Mohawk (Baker 1996b: 351–52). These predicates can be incorporated into the benefactive applicative morpheme, and when this happens the resulting clause is defective in its agreement properties in the same way that benefactives of unaccusatives are (Baker 1996b: 436; cf. 196–97). Finally, these verbs allow a particular kind of quantifier float that is otherwise allowed with unaccusative verbs and the objects of transitive verbs, but not with unergative verbs (Baker 1996b: 155–56).

   In section 4.6.3 I will reexamine this issue, claiming that there is some evidence that Mohawk roots like *rak* 'white' and *iyo* 'good' are inherently adjectival in their subatomic structure, even though they must become verbs in the course of the derivation.

The trace of the noun in (103c) is not in the structural relationship with a lexical head that the ECP requires. It is not even c-commanded by its antecedent, given that NI targets the lexical head rather than the tense node and nouns do not move to tense in Mohawk.

We thus have a straightforward account of the difference between verbal and nonverbal categories in Mohawk with respect to incorporation. The comparison between Mohawk and Italian demonstrates elegantly that the inherent category of a particular item has a large impact on its syntax. *Iyo* 'good' acts like an unaccusative predicate because it is a verb, whereas *buoni* 'good' acts like an unergative predicate because it is an adjective, even though their intuitive lexical semantics is the same. This is excellent support for a syntax-centered conception of the lexical category distinctions, rather than one rooted in lexical semantics or pragmatics (see chapter 5).

2.8.3   Hebrew

Hebrew also has an unaccusativity diagnostic that shows verb–nonverb contrasts. The overall logic of the case is very similar, but its inner workings are somewhat different because the diagnostic does not involve movement.

Borer and Grodzinsky (1986) (B&G) observe that when a dative expression in Hebrew is found with a transitive verb, it can be interpreted as the possessor of the direct object, but not as the possessor of the subject. In light of such facts, they propose the following condition:

(104)   Possessive dative must c-command the possessed NP or its trace. (B&G: 198)

Since c-commanding the trace left behind by moving an NP is equivalent to c-commanding the NP itself, a dative expression can be interpreted as the possessor of the subject if the verb is unaccusative, but not if it is unergative:

(105)   a Ha-maftexot naflu li.   (B&G: 184)
            the-keys   fell   to.me
            'My keys fell.'
         b *Ha-po'alim 'avdu   li.   (B&G: 182)
            the-workers   worked to.me
            'My workers worked.'

Dative expressions found with simple adjectives and nouns cannot be understood as the possessor of the subject, however:

(106)   a Ha-simla hayta   lebana (*li). (Hagit Borer, personal communication)
          the-dress be.PAST white (to.me)
          'The (*my) dress was white.'
      b Ha-naheq-et hayta   xola (*le-Rina). (Hagit Borer, personal
          the-driver   be.PAST sick (to Rina)   communication)
          'The (*Rina's) driver was sick.'
      c Ha-naheq-et hayta   rofa   (*le-Rina). (Ron Artstein, personal
          the-driver   be.PAST doctor (to Rina)   communication)
          'The (*Rina's) driver used to be a doctor.'

Nonverbal categories thus behave like unergative predicates rather than unaccusative ones in this respect, as we have come to expect. Just as in Italian, minimal pairs can be constructed that contrast verbal passives with adjectival passives: the verbal passive allows a possessor interpretation for the dative element, but the adjectival passive does not, even though the theta-role assigned seems to be the same (B&G: 192–94).

(107)   a Ha-matana hunxa   (li)   betox kufsa   (verbal passive)
          the-present place-PASS to.me inside a.box
          'The (my) present was placed inside a box.'
      b Ha-matana hayta munaxat (*li)   betox kufsa   (adjectival passive)
          the-present was   placed$_A$ to.me inside a.box
          'The (*my) present was placed inside a box.'

(Note that the verbal and adjectival passives are morphologically distinct in Hebrew, unlike English and Italian.) Conversely, verbs derived from adjectives by an inchoative derivation do allow the possessor interpretation of the dative element (Borer 1991):

(108)   Ha-naheq-et xalta   le-Rina. (Ron Artstein, personal communication)
       the-driver   became.sick to Rina
       'Rina's driver got sick.'

This range of facts also follows readily from my proposal. One only has to make the additional assumption that the Hebrew dative expression is always generated inside the lexical projection – VP, AP, or NP, as the case may be. The relevant structures are:

(109)   a The keys$_i$ Tense [$_{VP}$ t$_i$ fall$_k$ [$_{VP}$ t$_i$ t$_k$ to-me]]
      b The driver$_i$ be+Tense [$_{PredP}$ t$_i$ Pred [$_{AP/NP}$ sick/doctor to-Rina]]

There is NP movement to the surface subject position in both structures (through Spec, vP, in (109a)). In the verbal structure the dative phrase following the verb is contained in the same phrase (VP) as the trace, satisfying condition (104). (The dative expression does not technically c-command the theme in this structure, but does m-command it [Chomsky 1986a]. I take the switch from c-command to m-command to be a minor change, preserving the intent of B&G's original condition within a system that uses binary branching.) In the adjectival or nominal structure, however, the dative phrase is not contained in the same phrase as the trace, since the theme role is not assigned until the PredP level. (104) thus correctly rules out a possessive interpretation for (106) or (107b).

2.8.4   *Japanese*

The last case of this type I discuss is Japanese (with special thanks to Mika Kizu, Hiro Hosoi, and Miwako Uesaka for help with the facts discussed in this section). The best-known unaccusativity diagnostic in this language concerns the distribution of floating quantifiers, a test originally due to Miyagawa (1989). Miyagawa's leading idea is similar to B&G's: a floating quantifier must be in a mutual c-command relationship with the NP that it is understood as quantifying over or with a trace of that NP. Such quantifiers can therefore be used to probe where a given NP was generated prior to movement. Suppose that a floated quantifier is unambiguously inside the basic VP, as shown by the fact that it comes between a PP or VP-adverb and the verb. Quantifiers in this position can be associated with the subject of an unaccusative verb ((110a)), but not with the subject of an unergative verb ((110b)), as expected.

(110)   a *Doa-ga*   kono kagi de   *2-tu*   aita.   (Miyagawa 1989: 662)
          door-NOM this   key with 2-CL   opened.
          'Two doors opened with this key.'
        b ?*Gakusei-ga*   zibun no   kane   de   *5-nin* denwa-sita.
          Students-NOM self   GEN money with 5-CL   telephoned
          'Five students telephoned using their own money.'

The subject of the unaccusative verb binds a trace inside the VP, which is in the necessary local configuration with the floated quantifier, as shown in (111a). In contrast, the subject of the unergative verb binds no trace within VP, but only one in Spec, vP. Therefore the floated quantifier does not c-command any member of the chain of the subject in (111b) and cannot be interpreted as quantifying over it. (See the next section for discussion of the representation of unergative clauses.)

(111)

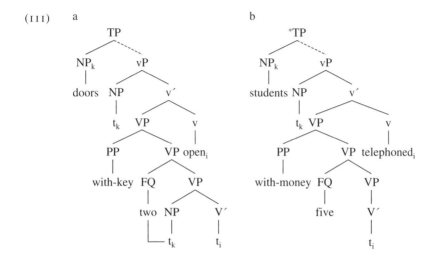

What happens when the predicate in one of these structures is an adjective (or noun) rather than a verb? The answer is that the structure is ungrammatical, as shown in (112a); this sentence is comparable to the unergative sentence in (110b), rather than the unaccusative one in (110a). (112b) shows that when the adjective is used as the complement of a verb like *nat-ta* 'became', the stranded quantifier is fine again.

(112) a *Kodomo-ga*   (*eeyoo-busoku-de) *san-nin*   yowa-katta.
          Children-NOM malnutrition-from   three-CL weak-PAST
          'Three children were weak from malnutrition.'
       b *Kodomo-ga*   eeyoo-busoku-de *san-nin*   yowa-ku nat-ta.
          Children-NOM malnutrition-from three-CL weak   become-PAST
          'Three children became weak from malnutrition.'

These patterns also follow from my basic structural hypothesis, together with the assumption that *de* phrases in Japanese (and other, similar items) are generated inside the projection of a lexical head (VP or AP). In (112a), the *de* phrase cannot be a dependent of PredP, but only of AP, and from this position the quantifier does not c-command the theta-position of the subject:

(113)

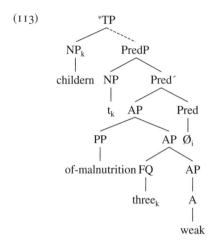

In (112b), the *de* phrase can be generated in the VP headed by the unaccusative verb 'become'. This VP also contains the floated quantifier and the theta-position of the subject, so the structure is fine.

Similar contrasts can be found from other unaccusativity diagnostics in Japanese, such as the possibility of nominative *ga*- drop, and the possibility of making compounds with deverbal and deadjectival nouns.

2.8.5   Conclusion

Overall, my claim that the subject of unaccusative verbs has a different syntactic status from the subject of predicate nouns and adjectives has considerable crosslinguistic support. This proposal accounts in a unified way for differences between nonagentive verbs and other, thematically comparable lexical categories with respect to a variety of unaccusativity diagnostics. I close this phase of the discussion with a historical note. In their early work on unaccusativity, Perlmutter and Postal (1984) included at the head of their list of predicates that are unaccusative crosslinguistically "predicates expressed by adjectives in English." In making this statement, they seem to have had in mind evidence from agreement in languages like Lakhota and Choctaw (on the latter, see Davies [1986]). In both of these languages, however, the predicates in question are verbs on the surface, as in Mohawk. In languages that have a category of adjectives that is clearly distinct from verbs, adjectives do not behave like unaccusatives. One thus has to attach a strange-sounding rider to Perlmutter and Postal's original generalization: predicates expressed by adjectives in English are unaccusative *unless they happen to actually be adjectives*. In standard generative theories, which treat the various lexical categories in a uniform manner, this exemption looks peculiar, to say the least. But it makes good sense in the context of my fundamental claim that verbs are the only lexical category that can license their own specifier.

2.9   Adjectives in the decomposition of verbs

Cinque (1990) and Borer (1991) point out that these differences in how verbs and adjectives assign theta-roles pose a serious theoretical problem for the Lexicalist Hypothesis of Chomsky (1970) and for the idea that theta-roles are always assigned in the same structural position (the UTAH of Baker [1988a]). The successes of my proposal here also seem to come at the expense of these important ideas. At a minimum, the UTAH must be weakened so that the proper syntactic configuration for the assignment of the theme theta-role is relativized to the lexical categories, with adjectives and nouns using a different configuration from verbs – or so it appears. In this section, I argue that there is nevertheless a way to maintain the core of the UTAH, which involves dynamically deriving all verbs from adjectives in the syntax. (Readers who are not so interested in these relatively abstract concerns can skip this section without much damaging their understanding of my overall theory.)

It is important to realize that verbs and adjectives are quite similar in how they assign theta-roles other than theme. This implies that a significant residue of the UTAH must be maintained in any case. Adjectives in English and Italian can take as complements goal-like phrases marked by *to* or its equivalent in other languages, and *of*-phrases, shown in (114) and (115), respectively.

(114)   a He is [AP generous to his students].
         b Gianni è [AP riconoscente a chiqunque aiuta i propri amici].   (Italian)
           Gianni is   grateful   to whoever   helps his own friends.
                                                          (Cinque 1990: 18)

(115)   a Chris is [AP certain of this]
         b Gianni è [AP sicuro di questo]   (Italian)
           Gianni is   sure   of this.

There is no standard term for the theta-role that *of*-phrases bear; I tentatively refer to it as *subject-matter* (compare Pesetsky [1995: 55–60]). I assume that the clausal complements of Cinque-type adjectives such as *likely* and *clear* also bear this subject-matter role (see (94)). Proof that these *of* and *to*-phrases are within the AP comes from the fact that they are carried along with the adjective when it is fronted by *wh*-movement (*How certain of his intentions are you?*

I wonder how generous to his students John is).[24] What is significant for the UTAH is that verbs can also select goal-phrases and subject-matter phrases, in addition to the characteristically verbal arguments of agent and theme. Overall, then, the arguments that an adjective can take are a proper subset of the arguments that a verb can take. The simplest adjectives are, of course, those that take no argument; these correspond to ordinary verbs that take only agent and/or theme arguments:

(116)   a The door is open.   (adjective: no argument)
         b The door opened.   (verb: theme)
         c Chris opened the door.   (verb: theme and agent)

Adjectives that take goal arguments correspond to verbs that can take goal arguments together with an agent and/or a theme:

(117)   a Chris is generous to the students.   (adjective: goal argument)
            Chris is loyal to the king.
         b Chris went to China.   (verb: theme and goal)
            Chris walked to the park.   (verb: agent and goal)
            Pat sent Chris to the store.   (verb: agent, theme, and goal)

Adjectives that take subject-matter arguments correspond to verbs that take subject-matter arguments as well as agents and/or themes:

(118)   a Chris is certain of this.   (adjective: subject-matter)
            It is likely/clear that John will win.
         b Chris spoke of love and duty.   (verb: agent and subject-matter)
            I suddenly realized that John will win.   (verb: theme and subject-matter)
            I persuaded Chris of my innocence.   (verb: agent, theme, and subject-
                                                  matter)

Finally, some adjectives take both goal and subject-matter arguments, as in (119a). (119b) shows that both goals and subject-matters can sometimes appear with verbs too, along with the distinctively verbal theta-roles.

(119)   a It is clear to me that Chris will win.   (adjective: goal and subject-matter)
            It is obvious to everybody that Chris will win.
         b I talked to Chris and Pat about their child.   (verb: agent, goal, subject-
                                                            matter ...)
         c I spoke only three words to Chris and Pat about their child.   (... and theme)

---

[24] Nothing much hinges on these *to-* and *of*-phrases being complements of A as opposed to adjuncts attached to AP, however. In the appendix, I argue that all putative PP complements are really adjuncts. All that matters for this section is that each phrase type that appears in AP also appears in VP, regardless of the exact nature of its position.

When one stops to think about it, the fact that the possible arguments of an adjective are a proper subset of the possible arguments of a verb is a bit surprising. It could have been otherwise. If one adhered strictly to the original ideas behind X-bar theory and the Lexicalist Hypothesis, one would expect adjectives and verbs to have exactly the same range of arguments, contrary to fact. Alternatively, if one foregrounded the important categorial distinction between verbs and adjectives, one might expect adjectives and verbs to select arguments with quite different, even non-overlapping, theta-roles. The result that the arguments of adjectives are a subset of the arguments of a verb calls for a different kind of approach. I suggest that it points to a decompositional approach, in which an AP is contained inside each VP underlyingly. VPs are really APs plus something. More specifically, they are APs plus two operators, one that adds theme arguments and one that adds agent arguments.

That there is a syntactically distinct element responsible for adding agent arguments is now a fairly standard view, in the wake of Hale and Keyser (1993), Chomsky (1995), and Kratzer (1996). I have mentioned several times the idea that transitive clauses contain a v head that dominates VP, and the transitive verb is the result of combining the V head with this v. Thus, I have assumed throughout neo-Larsonian structures like the one in (120).

(120)

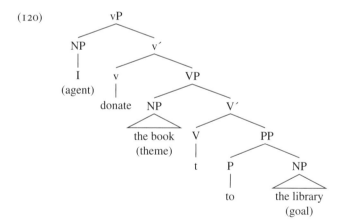

This structure is motivated in large part by the convergence of two distinct research thrusts. Research into lexical semantics has led to the conclusion that many transitive verbs decompose semantically into some kind of CAUSE operator plus another predicate that characterizes the event or state that is caused (Dowty 1979; Parsons 1990). Following broadly Jackendovian lines (Jackendoff 1976; Jackendoff 1983), the thematic role agent (or, more generally, causer) can be defined as the first argument of this CAUSE operator. The theme, however, is not a direct argument of CAUSE; rather it is a proper subpart of the event or state that constitutes the second argument of CAUSE. It is tempting, then, to identify the v in (120) with this CAUSE element and the V with the result-expressing predicate. (120) then also explains the familiar fact that (abstracting away from passive) agent phrases c-command theme phrases and therefore have syntactic and semantic prominence over them in most languages, perhaps all. (121) illustrates this asymmetry for English with a standard range of prominence-sensitive phenomena.

(121)   a The student insulted the professor.
         b No student insulted any professor.
            (compare: *Any student insulted no professor.)
         c Every female student insulted her linguistics professor.
            (compare: ?*Her favorite student insulted every linguistics professor.)
         d Which student insulted which professor?
            (compare: *Which professor did which student insult?)

In (121b), the negatively quantified agent licenses a polarity form of the theme, but the reverse dependency is bad. In (121c), the universally quantified agent creates a bound interpretation of the pronoun contained in the theme; again the opposite dependency is ruled out (Reinhart 1976; Reinhart 1983). In (121d), the interrogative agent takes clause-initial position rather than the interrogative theme (the Superiority Condition of Chomsky [1973]). Facts like these establish clearly that agent phrases c-command theme phrases (apart from passive). This seems to be a projection into the syntax of the lexical semantic asymmetry between causers and themes just described – the fact that the agent is a direct argument of CAUSE, the outermost layer of the semantic decomposition of a verb like *insult*, but the theme is not. One can well imagine a theory in which the compositional semantic relations implicit in the meaning of a verb did not project into the syntax, but the fundamental asymmetries in (121) (together with elementary facts about word order and phrase structure) suggest that in natural languages they do.

My proposal in this section is that this same reasoning should be applied to the theme argument as well. Just as many transitive verbs can be semantically decomposed into CAUSE plus what is in effect an unaccusative verb, so unaccusative verbs can be decomposed into a BE operator plus what is in effect an adjective. My use Chierchia's (1985) semantic theory ensures that this is possible, because a propositional function (a verb) can always be seen as the result of applying the "up" operator to a property *qua* individual (i.e. an adjective) (see section 2.3). Indeed, this is nothing more than a modern version of a very old idea that goes back to Aristotle and was adopted by the Port Royal grammarians of the seventeenth century, according to which all verbs "signify affirmation" and are derived from the copular verb *be* plus an adjective-like participle (Robins 1989: 138). Like CAUSE, this BE operator takes two arguments: an entity-denoting first argument and a property-denoting second argument. BE maps these two arguments onto the state of the entity having the property (at a particular time). The theme theta-role can be defined as the first argument of BE, again roughly following Jackendoff (1976, 1983). The second, property-denoting argument may be simple, or it may have internal structure, containing a goal or subject-matter argument that helps to specify the property in question. Thus, a fuller lexical decomposition of a verb like *donated* would be [x CAUSE [y BE [DONATED to z]]].

Pursuing this analogy between agents and themes further, I suggest that just as CAUSE projects into the syntax as a v head distinct from V, so BE projects into the syntax as a V head, distinct from an AP which expresses the property. Thus, the structure in (120) is refined as in (122).

(122)

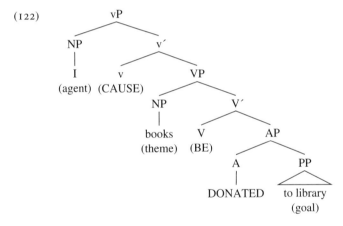

The surface verb *donate* is derived by combining the A, V, and v into a single item, in a way that I return to below. Just as the decomposition of a transitive verb into v and V predicts that agents asymmetrically c-command themes, so this further decomposition into V and A predicts that themes asymmetrically c-command the AP-internal constituents goal and subject-matter. This is correct (abstracting away from dative shift), as shown by Larson (1988).[25] (123) gives data parallel to (121) showing that the theme argument has prominence over a goal argument; (124) shows the same for themes and subject-matter arguments.

---

[25] Dative shift, of course, reverses the prominence relation between the theme and the goal (Larson 1988). The existence (and in some languages the necessity) of dative shift has led to controversy about which is higher on the thematic hierarchy, theme or goal, and this is directly related to the

(123)   a I donated my old issues of Lingua to the department library.
      b I will donate no book to any library.   (negative polarity)
        (compare: *I will donate any book to no library.)
      c I will donate every first edition in my collection to the estate of its author.
        (compare: ??I will donate his original manuscript to each author.)
                                   (bound anaphora)
      d What will you donate to which library?   (superiority)
        (compare: ??Which library will you donate what to?)

(124)   a I convinced Kate of my good intentions.
      b You will convince no one of any of your views.   (negative polarity)
        (compare: *You will convince anyone of none of your views.)
      c I convinced every amnesiac of his former identity.
        (compare: *I convinced its original proponent of every theory.)
                            (bound variable anaphora)
      d Who did you convince of what?   (superiority)
        (compare: *What did you convince whom of?)

The parallelism between the two phases of predicate decomposition is thus quite complete.

This line of analysis provides a very straightforward account of the generalization about argument structures that we were trying to explain. The curious fact was that the range of argument-like phrases that appear with adjectives is a proper subset of the range of argument-like phrases that appear with verbs. This now makes perfect sense: since all verb phrases in fact contain an adjective phrase underlyingly, it automatically follows that the kinds of phrases that are licensed inside an AP can also be found inside a verb phrase.[26] The converse, however, is not true: verb phrases contain arguments that APs cannot – in particular, the agents introduced by v and the themes introduced by V.

This analysis also automatically recaptures the UTAH. The problem for the UTAH was that verbs and adjectives seem to assign the theme theta-role in

---

    question of which version is base-generated and which (if either) is derived. I think there is good evidence that double object constructions are derived from an underlying structure like the one in (122) by something like NP-movement, but the evidence cannot be reviewed here. See Baker (1996a) and Baker (1997) for discussion.

[26] While this generalization is true of argument-like phrases, there are comparative phrases that seem to appear in APs but not in semantically similar verb phrases, as shown in (i).

    (i)   a I am (as) hungry as a horse.
          b I am hungrier than Chris.
          c ??I hunger as a horse.
          d *I hunger than Chris.

    These *as*-phrases and *than*-phrases are not really syntactic dependents of the A *hungry*, but rather of the degree heads *as* and *–er* (cf. section 4.3 for more on degrees). These degrees are functional heads, and as such they block the movement of A into V by the HMC and PHMG. Therefore sentences like (ic, d) cannot be formed.

different ways, verbs assigning it inside VP and adjectives assigning it outside AP. (122) dissolves this concern: the theme theta-role is always assigned in the same syntactic configuration as the Specifier of a BE/Pred head, which takes an AP as its complement. (Compare Hale and Keyser [1993], who define theme as an NP in the specifier of a VP that has an AP [or PP] complement.) Therefore I henceforth adopt the view that transitive verbs always decompose syntactically into something like [x CAUSE . . . [y BE [ADJECTIVE (to/of z)]]] (see Baker [2001b] for some further discussion).[27]

This proposal also solves a technical problem that comes from combining Bare Phrase Structure theory (Chomsky 1995: ch. 4) with my leading ideas that verbs always have a specifier ((1)) and that the theme theta-role can only be assigned to a specifier position ((8)). According to Bare Phrase Structure, a phrase cannot have a specifier unless it also has a complement. This is a simple matter of definition: a complement is defined as a phrase that merges with a head and a specifier is any other phrase that merges with the unit formed by that first merger (Chomsky 1995: 245). The problem is that ordinary transitive sentences like *Julia ate a fish* seem to have a theme but no other complement of V. How then can *a fish* be a specifier? (122) resolves this tension by saying that theme-selecting Vs always have an abstract AP complement.

It follows directly from my definition of theme that a theme can never be an immediate constituent of AP; APs are simply too small a chunk of linguistic representation to contain a theme.[28] This result was already anticipated in (8), which along with (1) implies that there could not be a theme (or an agent) in AP (or NP). We have already seen some empirical evidence that this is true from adjectival passives and *-able* forms in section 2.8, but the prediction should be

---

[27] There is a long-standing tradition, largely rooted in Dowty (1979), of giving such a decomposition to accomplishment verbs, while treating stative verbs and perhaps activity verbs as semantically simple. However, there is linguistic evidence against treating any transitive verb as simple. For example, Davis and Dermidache (2000) claim that all transitive verbs in Salish are built from monadic (unaccusative) roots, even stative ones. Similarly, Pylkkänen (1997) shows that stative psychological verbs must be decomposed in Finnish.

It is tempting to think of the process of adjectival passivization that we have seen in passing in English, Italian, and Hebrew as a derivational process by which the adjectival element implicit in a verb is picked out and allowed to stand on its own. There are empirical obstacles that this view would have to face, however. The most obvious one comes from verbs that are transparently related to adjectives, such as *open* or *clear*. In such cases, there is a clear semantic difference between the simple adjective (*the table is clear*) and the adjectival passive (*the table is cleared*). The adjectival passive implies that there was an event of clearing the table at some earlier time, whereas the simple adjective is consistent with the possibility that the table has always been clear. This suggests that the relationship between adjectival passives and the adjectival elements present in the decomposition of verbs is (or can be) less direct.

[28] A theme can, of course, appear inside an AP when the A takes a clause as its goal or subject-matter argument. For example, in *Chris is [AP eager to read the book], the book* is a theme – but it is the theme of the verb *read*, not of the adjective *eager*.

perfectly general, holding even for derived adjectives that do not have a passive-like interpretation. Adjectives derived by the affix *–ive* provide an interesting test. When these adjectives are used predicatively, their subject corresponds thematically to the agentive subject of the related verb, not to the theme. One might therefore think that a theme argument could be the complement of A in just this case, because it is not called on to be the subject. In fact, this is impossible, just as I predict. Adjectives in *-ive* can perfectly well contain goal-like arguments, as shown in (125).

(125) a Chris is submissive to the king.   (Chris submits to the king.)
       b Chris is responsive to questions.   (Chris responds to questions.)
       c Chris is attentive to his patients.   (Chris attends to his patients.)

But they cannot in general have a theme-like complement, corresponding to the direct object of the transitive verb:[29]

(126) a Chris is destructive (*of/??to books).
       b Chris is decisive (*of this kind of issue).
       c Chris is elusive (*of the police).
       d Mark is productive (*of good ideas).
       e Chris is creative (*of new genres).
       f This proposal is corrective (*of the situation).
       g The novel is descriptive (*of life in England).
       h Chris is disruptive (??of the class).
       i This result is negative (*of/??to the hypothesis).
       j Chris is permissive (??of this kind of behavior).

---

[29] There are a nontrivial number of exceptions to this generalization; (i) gives a sample.

(i)   a Chris is attractive to women. (cf. Chris attracts women.)
          Chris is abusive to pets.
       b Chris is protective of her ideas (cf. Chris protects her ideas.)
          Chris is supportive of my proposal.
          This is representative of her ideas.
          Chris is critical of the new trend in linguistics.

My suggestion about such examples is that they arise in borderline cases, in which a certain participant of the event being described can plausibly be categorized as either a theme or some other thematic role. The implication of my theory for such cases is that the choice is lost in the adjectival version of the word: the participant in question can only be treated as a goal or subject matter, not as a theme. This is consistent with the fact that sometimes the preposition that appears with the complement is *to*, rather than *of*, as in (ia). This happens systematically with psychological predicates, where the internal argument can be considered a goal/experiencer rather than a theme. In a parallel way, I would like to say that the *of*s found in (ib) are not the default *of* found in English derived nominals, but rather one of English's semantically significant *of*s – either the *of* that introduces subject-matter phrases, or partitive *of*, or the source-like *of* found in *I deprived him of water*.

k This material is reflective (?of infrared radiation).
l This reward is excessive (*of my expectations).
m Chris is imaginative (*of new ways to catch mice).

Some of these examples are taken from Sproat (1985), one of the few generative discussions of *-ive* adjectives. Sproat concludes that it is a lexical idiosyncrasy of *-ive* that it does not inherit the internal arguments of its base verb; *-ive* happens not to be a "functor category" in the terminology of Di Sciullo and Williams (1987). But the data in (125) show that this is not only stipulative, but false; it is only the theme argument of the verb that can not be inherited by the *-ive* adjective. These facts constitute a puzzle for Chomsky (1970)-style assumptions about X-bar theory and derivation, in which it is assumed that the argument structures of morphologically related words are the same, all things being equal. The theory proposed here, in contrast, explains this gap, drawing a deep connection between the facts in (126) and the better known fact that themes are externalized in adjectival passives. Both are manifestations of the simple truth that the theme role cannot be assigned inside AP, by definition.

There are still some loose ends to tie up. The first concerns how the proposal that verbs contain an adjectival element applies to intransitive verbs. I assume that the representation of unaccusative verbs is exactly the same as the one for transitives given in (122), except that instead of CAUSE they contain a v that does not theta-mark, as discussed in the preceding section. For eventive unaccusative verbs, this v might be thought of as a syntactic expression of Dowty's (1979) BECOME operator. As for unergative verbs, there are two ways that they could fit into the system. They could also contain a covert A, but one for which BE does not create a theta-role, similar to Cinque-adjectives like *likely*. This would give the underlying representation in (127).

(127)

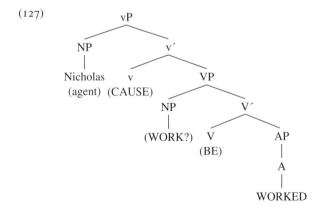

The alternative is that unergative verbs could consist of just a v with an NP complement (rather than a VP or AP complement), where the N is a "cognate object," as proposed by Hale and Keyser (1993) (see (5) and (7c)). Either way, the lexical verb would be derived by combining the A or N head into v. A theoretical problem with (127) is that it contains a VP with no obvious specifier. This could be solved either by saying that the position is filled by an often-silent cognate object (borrowing this from Hale and Keyser's view), or by saying that the problematic node is destroyed by the conflation of v into V. Assuming that the problem can be handled in one of these ways, (127) has the advantage of maximizing the similarities between transitive, unaccusative, and unergative verbs. It implies that one does not have to sharply distinguish the representation of transitive *eat* from that of intransitive *eat* or from its purely unergative near-synonym *dine*. It also helps in explaining the behavior of some unaccusativity diagnostics. For instance, unergative verbs seem to have a lower VP or AP projection that can contain a dative expression in Hebrew and instrumental PPs and floated quantifiers in Japanese (see (111b)). Therefore, I tentatively prefer structure (127) to Hale and Keyser's for most examples, although I leave the question somewhat open.

The last point to clarify is exactly how surface verbs are derived from adjectives plus a Pred/BE head. I assume that this comes about by a process of conflation, in approximately the sense of Hale and Keyser (1993). (They take the term from Talmy [1985], but give it a specific theoretical construal.) Within P&P-style theories, conflation is taken to be closely related to incorporation (i.e. head movement), but there are at least two ways to work this out. Hale and Keyser's own proposal is that conflation is incorporation in the lexicon, a derivational cycle prior to the syntax proper. Chomsky (1995) and others have taken the alternative position that there is no essential difference between conflation and incorporation; both are head movement in the normal syntax. I will blend elements of these two positions, viewing conflation as incorporation in the syntax but prior to the insertion of vocabulary items.

There have been many debates about whether lexical items are inserted at the beginning of the syntax or at the end. Suppose that we leave the insertion point open, so that the insertion of a vocabulary item can take place at any point in the derivation as long as the language has an item that can realize the particular collection of syntactic formatives in question. Then derivations can go as follows. First, an adjective can be merged with its goal and/or subject-matter arguments (if any) to create an AP. At this point, an adjective root could be inserted, if the language has one. Then the AP is merged with a Pred, and the combination is merged with a theme argument (if one is sanctioned by the lexical meaning of the AP). At this point Pred can be spelled out as an appropriate vocabulary item: *ye* in Edo, *ndi* in Chichewa, Ø in English and the derivation proceeds. This is summarized in (128). (When vocabulary insertion happens for the NP and PP is irrelevant.)

(128)   a A
        b [$_{AP}$ A (PP)]   merge
        c [$_{AP}$ fond/hungry (PP)]   vocabulary insertion
        d [$_{PredP}$ Pred [$_{AP}$ fond/hungry (PP)]]   merge
        e [$_{PredP}$ Ø/ye [$_{AP}$ fond/hungry (PP)]]   vocabulary insertion
        f [$_{PredP}$ NP Ø/ye [$_{AP}$ fond/hungry (PP)]]   merge
        . . .
        g [NP$_i$ be$_k$+Tense [$_{AuxP}$ t$_i$ t$_k$ [$_{PredP}$ t$_i$ Ø/ye [$_{AP}$ fond/hungry (PP)]]]]]
        end result: Chris is hungry; Chris is fond of spinach;
                       Òzó yé zùròzùrò. (Edo, 'Ozo be foolish')

Alternatively, suppose that no vocabulary item was inserted for the adjective or Pred along the way. Head movement could apply, adjoining A to Pred. This obeys the normal restrictions on movement, including the HMC and the PHMG. The A+Pred combination can then be spelled out as a verb root, if the language has a suitable root available. This gives a derivation like (129).

(129)   a A
        b [$_{AP}$ A (NP)]   merge
        c [$_{PredP}$ Pred [$_{AP}$ A (NP)]]   merge
        d [$_{PredP}$ A$_i$ +Pred [$_{AP}$ t$_i$ (NP)]]   move
        e [$_{VP}$ like/hunger [$_{AP}$ t$_i$ (NP)]]   vocabulary insertion
        f [$_{VP}$ NP like/hunger [$_{AP}$ t$_i$ (NP)]] merge
        . . .
        g [NP$_k$ Tense [$_{VP}$ t$_k$ like/hunger [$_{AP}$ t (NP)]]]
        end results: Chris hungers; Chris likes spinach;
                    Òzó zùrò. (Edo, 'Ozo foolishes')

The question of Pred's status with respect to the functional/lexical distinction now arises more crucially. In fact, it has a somewhat intermediate status. On the one hand, Pred is like a functional category in that it has no rich, distinctive lexical semantics associated with it. It is also a closed class category: each language has only a small number of Preds, probably no more than one or two. On the other hand, Pred is like a lexical category in that it licenses a noun phrase by theta-role assignment (or by calling for an expletive). This is something that prototypical functional categories like tense and complementizer cannot do. It seems reasonable then to say that Pred is a functional category in and of itself, because it lacks encyclopedic content. If, however, it acquires encyclopedic content by a process of conflation, it automatically becomes a lexical category.

When A and Pred are lexicalized separately as in (128), the ECP will not permit most traces in the Spec of PredP, giving the results discussed in section 2.8. Also, if some higher element such as tense or a causative morpheme attracts a head, it will not have access to A because of the intervening Pred; this gives the results in sections 2.5 and 2.6. But if A conflates with Pred so that the two are lexicalized together, as in (129), then the resulting head counts as lexical. Since the head has a specifier, it is a verb by definition. If the derived lexical head raises on to v, traces in its specifier will pass the ECP, there will be nothing to block a higher T or causative V from attracting it, and so on. In this way, the results of the previous sections can be preserved in a system in which verbs are derived from adjectives in the syntax.[30]

The view sketched here makes the very strong claim that all languages have adjectives of a sort in underlying representations. Languages might differ in their class of vocabulary items; in extreme cases, conflation of A into Pred might become effectively obligatory because there are no vocabulary items that can realize A and Pred individually. Such a language would have only verbs on the surface. Mohawk seems to be such a language, as mentioned at various points in this chapter. But the logic of the account says that even languages like Mohawk must have abstract adjectives as basic building blocks of the clause prior to vocabulary insertion. I return to some evidence that supports this claim in section 4.6.3

2.10   Are there languages without verbs?

In the light of this extended inquiry into the nature of verbs, I can meaningfully pose the first major typological question: is the category of verb universal? We now have a precise notion of what a verb is and of how the morphosyntax of verbs is shaped by their basic nature. Therefore we can imagine in detail what a language without verbs would be like. We can also compare the imagined language to descriptions of actual languages, to assess whether such languages actually exist.

The literature generally assumes that the category of verb is universal. Indeed, the cases of category-neutralization that have been suggested generally work in favor of the verb. Many languages are said to have no adjective–verb distinction, and the neutralized category is always taken to be a verb, not an

---

[30] The other category that one would expect these considerations to apply to is Voice/v, the head that licenses agent theta-roles. Perhaps this too is inherently functional, but I assume that it always conflates with the head of its VP complement, creating a lexical category (a verb).

adjective. Mohawk and Choctaw are languages of this type, which I discuss at the end of chapter 4. A few languages have been said to have no noun–verb distinction, including the Wakashan languages, the Salish languages, and some Austronesian languages. In these cases, linguists are shier about identifying the sole existing category as being either nominal or verbal. The roots in question are, however, thought to be intrinsically predicative, particularly in Salish; thus, they are more like my conception of a verb than like my conception of a noun. I discuss these languages at the end of chapter 3, once the idea of what a noun is is in place. A language without verbs is thus the typological variation that one is least likely to find, judging by the existing literature.

It is not at all inconceivable that a human language could exist without a lexical category of verb, however. One probably could not have a natural human language without agents, themes, and predications. The creation of these is not, however, the exclusive privilege of verbs in my theory; functional categories can do this too. Pred is a functional category that takes an AP or NP complement and assigns a theme role to its specifier, and v (alias voice) is a functional category that assigns an agent role to its specifier. A language could have transitive and intransitive clauses without having lexical verbs by using a small number of these functional items either separately or in combination. Such a language would be just like English on my analysis, except that A (and N) would never conflate into Pred or v to create lexical verbs. In such a language, the A (or N) would appear as uninflected root in construction with a small number of functional heads that determine what arguments are present. These heads would probably be described as auxiliaries of some kind.

There are certainly languages with constructions that fit this description. Usually these are called *light verb constructions* (LVCs) in the literature. Typical examples of LVCs are given in (130) from Urdu (Barker 1967: 145).

(130) a Mə̃y   khəRa hū.
          I   stand   be
          'I stand, am standing.'
       b Mə̃y   ys   pətthər ko   kəhRa   kərūga.
          I   this stone   ACC stand   make-FUT
          'I will stand this stone up.'

The adjective *khəRa* 'standing' combines with one of two auxiliaries to give the equivalent of a verbal sentence in English. Whether the auxiliary is 'be' or 'make' determines the argument structure of the complex, quite apart from the inherent properties of the head. It is not unreasonable to say that these

constructions are the result of the A not conflating into Pred and v, which are
then spelled out as 'be' or 'make,' respectively. Such constructions are common
in Urdu, although the language has ordinary verb constructions as well. It is not
inconceivable that there could be a language that has no lexical verbs, but only
LVCs similar to (130).[31]

The most serious candidate that I have found for a verbless language is the
Australian language Jingulu, as described by Pensalfini (1997). Nevertheless,
I argue that even this language does have verbs, thereby lending support to the
belief that all languages do.

Jingulu has exactly three verbal items that can inflect for agreement and
(suppletively) for tense; Pensalfini glosses them as 'come', 'go,' and 'do/be.' A
simple example with one of these words is (131a). If one wants to say anything
other than 'come', 'go,' or 'do', one must combine a bare root that has lexical
semantic content with one of these three items, which then functions as an
auxiliary, bearing the tense and agreement of the clause ((131b)).

(131)   a Ya-angku.
            3s-will.come
            'He will come.'
         b Jirrkiji-mindu-wa.
            run-1dS.INCL-will.go
            'You and me will run off.'

While the inflected auxiliary is strictly obligatory, Pensalfini shows that the
lexical root can occasionally be omitted when it is recoverable from discourse,
as in (132).

(132)   Ajuwara manyan nya-nu?   Ngindi-mbili nga-nu.
         where   sleep   2sS-did   DEM-LOC   1sS-did
         'Where did you sleep?'   'I did [it] there.'

In rare cases, roots can appear separated from the inflected auxiliary by some
other constituent:

(133)   Ambaya ngaya   nga-nu Warranganku-mbili.
         speak   1s.NOM   1s-did Beetaloo-LOC
         'I spoke about Beetaloo.'

---

[31] The Indo-Iranian LVCs are a better illustration of what I have in mind than the Japanese kind,
which have been much discussed since Grimshaw and Mester (1988). The reason is that the
arguments present in the clause are clearly a function of which particular "light verb" is used
in Indo-Iranian. This is different from Japanese, where the light verb is always *suru*, and the
number of arguments seems to be set by the nonverbal lexical head.

(132) and (133) together show that these auxiliaries are not affixes that are morphologically attached to the verb root. Pensalfini also shows that the same lexical
root can often co-occur with various auxiliaries, each combination producing a
somewhat different semantic effect. (134) and (135) give some examples of this.

(134)   a Ngaba-nga-ju karnarinymi.
           hold-1sS-do   spear
           'I have a spear.'
      b Ngaba-nga-rriyi   karnarinymi
           hold-1sS-will.go spear
           'I will take a spear.'
      c Ngaba-jiyimi karnarinymi.
           hold-come   spear
           'He's bringing a spear.'

(135)   a Ngaruk baka-nga-rriyi
           dive   1sg-will-go
           'I'll dive down.'
      b Ngaruk baka-ngayi arduku
           dive   1sg-will.do carefully
           'I'll submerge (something) carefully.'

On the basis of this range of data, Pensalfini argues that the three "auxiliaries" are the only true verbs in Jingulu, and that they do all the theta-marking
of nominal arguments. That explains why they are always required, and nothing
else is. In contrast, the roots have no distinctively verbal features, either inflectional or theta-theoretic. They are optionally adjoined to the clause to increase
its semantic content without much affecting its syntax. This description sounds
very much like what we expect a language that has no lexical verbs but only
adjectives to look like.

There are, however, reasons not to accept this analysis. The first is particular to my framework, and does not necessarily apply to Pensalfini's original
hypothesis. For me, a lexical category that has no theta-role to assign to a specifier (and no referential index) is an adjective, by definition. Therefore, roots
like *ngaba* 'hold' and *ngaruk* 'dive' must be adjectival within my theory. The
problem is that Jingulu has another class of words, syntactically distinct from
these "verbal" roots, that wants that label. These true adjectives differ from the
verbal roots in several ways: (i) they can be predicated of subjects without a
verbal auxiliary; (ii) they can form complex nominals without relativization;
(iii) they agree in gender with an associated noun; and (iv) clauses that contain
them have relatively strict subject–predicate word order. These properties of
true adjectives are shown in (136).

(136)   a Miring-mi bardakurru-mi   (Pensalfini 1997: 138)
           gum-VEG   good-VEG
           'Gum is good.'
     b Jami-na   diman-a-rni   laja-ardu ngamul-u lanb-u.
       that-MASC horse-MASC-ERG carry-go big-NEUT load-NEUT
       'That horse is carrying a big load.'

(136a) shows a predicative adjective construction, featuring fixed subject – predicate order and no verbal auxiliary. The adjective also bears the "vegetative" suffix *–mi* in agreement with the gender of its subject; this affix that is never borne by verbal roots. (136b) contains an instance of direct attributive modification between an adjective and a noun, the adjective again agreeing with the noun in gender. These are quite normal properties for adjectives to have. (Property (iv), for example, suggests that predicative adjectives are in construction with a null Pred. This would mean that a trace is not licensed in the subject position, reducing the range of empty categories that can appear there and fixing the word order. Property (ii) is discussed in depth in section 4.2.) The verbal roots seen in (134) and (135) have none of these properties. Therefore on theory internal grounds the "verbal roots" cannot be collapsed with adjectives, and must be analyzed as a different category. The only alternative would be to say that Jingulu has no verbs but two subclasses of adjective that have almost no properties in common – an odd move that would gain nothing.

If verbal roots are truly verbs, then they must theta-mark specifiers after all. Two pieces of evidence in favor of this can be gleaned from Pensalfini's discussion. The first is that verbal roots in the absence of auxiliaries can be derived to form nouns in ways that imply that they have an argument structure. Some examples are (Pensalfini 1997: 145–46):

(137)   a darr-ajka;   dabil-ajka-rni
        eat-NOML(Th)   hold-NOML(Th)-NSF
        'what one eats, food'   'what one holds, handle'
     b Ngany-ajkal-irni;   ngirrm-ajkal-a   murdika-rna
        sing-NOML(Ag)-FEM   fix-NOML(Ag)-MASC car-DAT
        'singer'   'fixer of cars, mechanic'

The affix *–ajka* derives patient nominals that refer to the theme of the action named by the root. In contrast, the affix *–ajkal* derives agentive nominals that refer to the doer of the action named by the root. The existence of these systematic derivations strongly suggests that the verbal roots themselves have agent and patient arguments to start with; these then can be picked up in different ways by the different kinds of nominalization (which may be syntactic; cf. chapter 5).

Even more importantly, another look at examples like (134) shows that using different auxiliaries in combination with a given verbal root does not necessarily give alternative argument structures. If the auxiliaries really spell out various combinations of the functional heads Pred and v that do the theta-marking, then one would expect different choices of auxiliary to give systematically different arrays of arguments, as in Urdu. This is not the case in (134); rather, sentences with the root *ngaba* 'hold' are transitive with all three auxiliaries. This strongly suggests that the root is the real theta-marker here, determining how many arguments are present and what their thematic interpretation is. The three inflected verbs can instead be analyzed as thematically inert verbal auxiliaries, like those found in periphrastic tenses in Indo-European languages, rather than as light verbs. The element of meaning that they add to the clause generally has less to do with thematic role assignment than with the directional properties of the event: the use of 'go' indicates motion away from the point of reference; the use of 'come' indicates motion toward the point of reference; and the use of 'do' is unmarked for direction. 'Do' in particular has an extremely wide range of uses, appearing in clauses of any argument structure. (134a) and (135b) show 'do' in transitive clauses; (138a) and (138b) show it with an unaccusative-type verb; (138c) shows it with an unergative verb; and (138d) shows it with a ditransitive verb.

(138)   a Burluburlubi-wurru-ju dardu jamana juliji burluburluba-ju.
          float-3pS-do   many that   bird float-do
          'Many birds are floating.'   (Pensalfini 1997: 333)
        b Nyamba wawa boorn-nga-marra   Warranganku-mbili.
          DEM   child born-1sS-do.PAST Beetaloo-LOC
          'I was born at Beetaloo.'   (Pensalfini 1997: 334)
        c Nganya-ju.
          sing-do
          'He's singing.'   (Pensalfini 1997: 140)
        d Ngunya-nga-nu wurraku ngima-rni babirdimi-rni nginda-baja-rna
          give-1sS-did   3p.ACC that-FOC yam-FOC   that-PL-DAT
          wawa-la-rna.
          child-PL-DAT
          'I gave this yam to the children.'   (Pensalfini 1997: 205)

Comparing (134) with (138), it seems clear that the root determines the number and flavor of the theta-roles and not the inflected auxiliary – which means that the root counts as a true verb.

Even Jingulu, then, has a lexical category of verbs. While one can imagine that a language might not have verbs within my theory, I have failed to find an actual language that instantiates this possibility. Now that we know precisely what a verb is – a lexical category that takes a specifier, and the only one that can assign agent and theme roles – we can see that all known languages have instances of that category. This raises the intriguing question of why all actual human languages are like this. But before facing this question on the edge of linguistic inquiry, we need to achieve a similar level of understanding of the other lexical categories, noun and adjective – and learn that they too are found in all languages.

3 *Nouns as bearers of a referential index*

3.1   What is special about nouns?

I turn now to consideration of what sets nouns apart from verbs and adjectives. Using phrase structure and theta-role assignment to distinguish verbs from nouns and adjectives builds on relatively familiar techniques; syntacticians are accustomed to specifying the theta-grid of a lexical item and to having this grid determine the syntactic structure that the word appears in. The basic principles that regulate theta-role assignment are also very familiar. Working from this model, some generative linguists have attempted to define all of the syntactic categories in terms of their characteristic argument structures and/or the grammatical functions that they take (Jackendoff 1977; Bresnan 1982; Hale and Keyser 1993). But there is little evidence that this is the right approach. Simple nouns do not differ from adjectives in these respects: the phrase structure and theta-role assignment dynamics of *John is a fool* are essentially identical to those of *John is foolish*, for example, even though *fool* is a noun and *foolish* an adjective. As a result, we saw in the last chapter that both nouns and adjectives need a copular particle in order to be used predicatively, both tend not to take tense morphology, both need a different causativizer than verbs do, and both act like unergative predicates. Nouns apparently differ from adjectives and verbs not in their argument structures, but along some other dimension altogether. Finding that dimension requires some theoretical inventiveness.

The leading idea of my account is the following claim, which exists in both a semantic guise and a syntactic guise:

(1)   a Semantic version: nouns and only nouns have *criteria of identity*, whereby
            they can serve as standards of sameness.
          b Syntactic version: X is a noun if and only if X is a lexical category and X
            bears a *referential index*, expressed as an ordered pair of integers.

The semantic version of (1) comes from Geach (1962) and Gupta (1980) by way of Larson and Segal (1995). The idea in a nutshell is that only common nouns have a component of meaning that makes it legitimate to ask whether some X is the same (whatever) as Y. This lexical semantic property is the precondition that makes nouns particularly suited to the job of referring, since it is fundamental to reference to be able to keep designating the same entity over and over again (Wiggins 1980: ch. 1). My theory thus shares a point of similarity with Hopper and Thompson's (1984) intuition that nouns indicate "discourse manipulable participants" – i.e. they are uniquely suited to reference-tracking. This idea also bears a more general similarity to the widespread intuition that nouns are inherently associated with the function of reference (see, for example, Croft [1991]).[1] However, I claim that the special referential powers of a noun are an easy corollary of their fundamental nature as stated in (1), not the fundamental nature itself. This has some important advantages when we come to account for uses of nouns and their projections that are not referential, such as in quantificational expressions (see (3)) and as predicate nominals.

The syntactic corollary of a noun's criterion of identity is, I claim, a *referential index*. Because nouns can refer, they are the natural bearers of this syntactic annotation, and certain grammatical conditions regulate its distribution in the syntax. I use the following two conditions in particular:

(2)   a The second member of the index of a noun must be identical to an index of its sister (theta-role assignment) or to the index of a dependent element that it c-commands (chain-formation).
       b No syntactic node can both license a specifier and bear a referential index.

(2a) (which I will call the *Noun Licensing Condition* [NLC]) is a generalization of that half of the theta criterion that says that NPs must receive theta-roles (see also the Extended Coherence Condition of Bresnan and Mchombo [1987]). (2b) says in essence that nothing can be both a verb and a noun simultaneously. It ensures that there are three kinds of lexical categories defined by my system, rather than four. It is conceptually related to the logical point that no category can both refer and be a predicate, made by Geach (1962) and others.

There is a substantial history to the idea of giving nouns and their projections referential indices; such indices were used in the formulations of the binding theory in Chomsky (1980; 1981), for example. In more recent Minimalist work, Chomsky (1995) has proposed that indices should be eliminated from syntactic

---

[1] Déchaine's (1993) system of categories sounds similar to this, inasmuch as she says that +referential is one of the features that define the category noun. The parallel is not as close as it seems, however, because Déchaine holds that verbs are also +referential. This feature thus does not distinguish the two categories for Déchaine the way it does for me. Déchaine says that verbs are +referential, because they refer to events; I say that TP and CP can refer in this sense, but VP on its own cannot (see section 3.4).

representations. My use of referential indices is intended to invoke aspects of the older P&P tradition, but they are not exactly the same as those previous elements. The obvious formal difference is that I conceive of the referential index as an ordered pair of integers, rather than as a single integer, as in most previous work. The reasons for this will become clear when I explain in more detail the criterion of identity and how it relates to the referential index in the next section. It does not actually matter to my theory whether these indices are present throughout the computation of a linguistic structure. A legitimate alternative would be that these indices are added at the conceptual-intentional interface, just beyond LF. The substance of my theory can thus be made consistent with Chomsky's (1995) view that indices are not part of the linguistic representation proper. I nevertheless include indices freely in my syntactic representations, because I do not know any compelling reason to say they are not there and because it makes the representations more explicit. I leave the exact status of these indices at the different stages of linguistic computation open for further conceptual reflection and empirical research.[2]

A major interest of Geach and Gupta in introducing the criterion of identity was to explain why only common nouns can be the restrictors for quantifiers like *each*, *every*, *some*, and *no*. This is shown in (3); note that the nouns do not refer here.

(3)   a No [NP letter(s)] arrived today.
           No [NP wine] is served during Lent.
        b *No [AP rude] is tolerated here.
        c *No [VP pay(ing) parking fees] is pleasant.

In a similar way, only NPs can appear with articles that mark distinctions like definite versus indefinite and specific versus nonspecific – a generalization that is crosslinguistically robust.

(4)   a I admire the governor/the Africans/the wine Chris makes.
        b I pounded the metal (*the) flat.
        c I saw the boy (*the) cry/crying.

Numerals and other expressions of cardinality, including morphological marking for singular and plural, are also restricted to noun environments. I discuss

---

[2] An anonymous reviewer suggests that the use of indices in syntactic representations might be consistent with Chomsky's inclusiveness condition if the indices are already present in the lexical representations of the nouns. Unfortunately, this will not do: the *capacity* to have an index is implicit in the lexical entry of each noun, but the particular index associated with each token of a noun will in general be different. This allows different tokens of the same common noun to refer to different individuals of the same kind, as in *My dog{i,k} chased another dog{n,m}*.

the basic notion of a criterion of identity in more detail in section 3.2, along with how it accounts for categorial differences in number marking; I then extend the analysis to determiners and quantifiers in section 3.3.

Another characteristic property of nouns is that they can be the antecedents of pronouns, reflexives, and traces. The most elegant demonstration of this distinction comes from comparing genitive NP subjects with adjectives of nationality inside derived nominals. In some cases, the genitive NP and the adjective seem almost synonymous, as in *Albania's resistance* and *the Albanian resistance*. In spite of this similarity, the genitive NP can license a reflexive pronoun as the complement to the noun, but the nationality adjective cannot (Kayne 1984a):

(5)   a Albania's destruction of itself grieved the expatriate community.
       b *The Albanian destruction of itself grieved the expatriate community.
          (cf. The Albanian self-destruction ...)

The genitive NP can also be understood as the theme of the event referred to by the nominalization, whereas this is usually impossible for the corresponding nationality adjective, as shown in (6). This contrast can be subsumed to one in (5) if one assumes that there is a trace in the canonical theme position, and that only the NP can bind this trace:

(6)   a Albania's destruction t by Italy grieved the expatriate community.
       b *The Albanian destruction t by Italy grieved the expatriate community.

More generally, NPs can provide the antecedents for pronouns in discourse, whereas this is at best very marginal for APs and VPs. This class of facts is the most transparent consequence of the claim in (1b) that nouns and their projections are the only lexical categories that bear a referential index; hence they are the only categories that can be antecedents in binding theory and that can form certain kinds of movement chains.[3] I defend this empirical generalization and show how it ultimately traces back to the criterion of identity in section 3.4 for anaphora and in section 3.5 for movement.

Nouns are also special in that they (and their projections) constitute the canonical argument phrases. As a result, they occupy the core argument positions of

---

[3] Certain functional categories are like NP in bearing a referential index, including not only DP, but also CP and perhaps TP. Hence these categories can also take part in movement, anaphora, and the other phenomena that I describe as being NP-specific. This is parallel to the fact that certain functional categories are like V in licensing a specifier (Pred, v/Voice). See the appendix for more on the parallelism between lexical categories and functional categories in these respects.

the clause, including subject, direct object, and object of a preposition, whereas APs and VPs cannot, as shown in (7).

(7)   a A mistake/errors in judgment/slander led to Chris's downfall.
       b *Proud led to Chris's downfall.   (compare: Pride$_N$ led . . .)
       c *Boast$_V$ led to Chris's downfall.   (compare: Boasting$_N$ led . . .)

In section 3.6, I argue that this difference reduces to the difference in (5) by combining the idea that only nouns have a criterion of identity with Williams' (1989) view that theta-roles are intrinsically anaphors.

Section 3.7 explores two more subtle consequences of (1), together with the condition in (2a) that anything that has a referential index must be coindexed with something else in the structure. I claim that this explains the fact that NPs adjoined to a clause must correspond to a pronoun or gap internal to the clause, whereas adjuncts of other categories need not:

(8)   a *Women, life is difficult.
       b Women, their life is difficult.
       c For women, life is difficult.

It is also notable that NPs cannot count as clauses on their own; rather they must at a minimum be introduced as the arguments of some almost-meaningless existential verb in language after language ((9)). This too is a consequence of the condition in (2a), I will claim.

(9)   a *A dragon. It terrorized the countryside, eating cattle and . . .
       b Once there was a dragon. It terrorized the countryside, eating cattle and . . .

Perhaps the most curious difference between nouns and other categories arises in connection with the material on conflation considered in section 2.9. Nouns are just like adjectives in that they can be used as predicates as long as there is a supporting Pred or linking verb that licenses a specifier. Such predicate nominals can appear on the surface as the complement of a stative copula, as the complement of an inchoative verb like 'become,' or as the complement of a causative verb. (10) shows this range of examples in English; (11) gives similar data for Imbabura Quechua (Cole 1985: 67, 179).

(10)   a John is a man.   (compare: John is hungry.)
       b John became a man.   (compare: The sky became clear.)
       c The battle made John a man.   (compare: The wind made the sky clear.)

(11)   a Juan-ka   mayistru-mi   (ka-rka).   (cf. Wasi-ka   yuraj-mi   ka-rka.)
          Juan-TOP teacher-VALID be-PAST.3S   house-TOP   white-VALID   be-PAST.3S
          'Juan is/was a teacher.'   'The house was white.'

b Libru tuku-rka.
   Book become-PAST.3S
   'It became a book.'

Adjectives can also conflate with Pred to derive stative verbs. When this sub-structure is further embedded under inchoative and/or causative operators, the result can be a change of state verb or a causative verb. Predicative nouns, in contrast, typically do not conflate with Pred to form verbs, as shown in (12) and (13) (Cole 1985: 179–80).

(12)   a *John mans.   (compare: John hungers.)
       b *John manned.   (compare: The sky cleared.)
       c *The battle manned John. (compare: The wind cleared the sky.)

(13)   a *Libru-ya-rka.   (compare: Jatun-ya-rka.)
          book-become-PAST.3S   big-become-PAST.3S
          'It became a book.'   'He became big.'
       b *libru-chi-rka-ni   (compare: ali-chi-rka-ni.)
          book-CAUS-PAST-1S   good-CAUS-PAST-1S
          'I made it into a book.'   'I caused it to become good;
                                             I repaired it.'

Nouns can be converted into verbs, of course, but the meaning that results is systematically different from the meaning one gets from verbalizing an adjective (see Hale and Keyser [1993]). The verb *clear* means simply 'to become clear,' but the verb *man* means nothing like 'to become a man'; rather it means 'to endow something with a suitable crew or operators,' as in *Man the torpedoes!* Causative and inchoative derivations from nouns are not entirely ruled out; to *knight* someone is roughly to make them become a knight, for example. But the ability to verbalize easily is a recurrent difference between adjectives and nouns, showing up even in languages that otherwise have little evidence of a noun–adjective distinction (see Heath [1984] on Nunggubuyu as well as Cole [1985] on Imbabura Quechua). In section 3.8, I consider the structure of predicate nominals more closely, and derive their relative inability to verbalize from condition (2b).

Finally, once we know what a noun is and what the grammatical consequences of being one are, we can evaluate typological questions concerning the universality of this lexical category. In section 3.9, I consider claims that nouns are nondistinct from adjectives in various languages (Australian languages, Quechua, Nahuatl, Greenlandic), and claims that nouns are nondistinct from verbs in a few languages (Salish, Wakashan, Austronesian). In each case, there is good evidence for a separate class of nouns, once one knows where to look for it.

3.2 The criterion of identity

Since (1) is the defining property of nouns in my theory, I must start by explaining it in more detail, beginning with what is meant by a "criterion of identity."

The idea that common nouns differ from other categories in having a criterion of identity comes from the logic literature, specifically Geach (1962) and Gupta (1980).[4] According to these authors, common nouns are like intransitive verbs and adjectives in that they all have a "criterion of application." Thus, knowing what *dog* means helps us to know which things are dogs, just as knowing what *soft* means helps us to know which things are soft and knowing what *cry* means helps us to know which things are crying. This criterion of application is what formal semanticists often model by saying that all of these elements denote sets, and are of type $<e, t>$. However, Geach and Gupta claim that common nouns have something more. In addition to determining which things fall under a certain concept, they also set standards by which one can judge whether two things are the same or not. This is their criterion of identity.

Geach illustrates this point by observing that the frame "X is the same ___ as Y" is meaningful if and only if the blank is filled by a noun. (14) shows that any type of noun can be used in this frame, including singular count nouns, plural nouns, mass nouns, and abstract nouns.

(14)   a That is the same man as you saw yesterday.
           b Those are the same women as we saw last night.
           c That is the same water as was in the cup this morning.
           d The French want to have the same liberty as the Americans have.

Adjectives and verbs (or verb phrases) are uniformly terrible in this environment:

(15)   a #That is the same long as this.
           b #She is the same intelligent as he is.
           c #I saw Julia the same sing as Mary did.
           d #I watched Nicholas the same perform a stunt as Kate performed.

One can, of course, say that the examples in (15) are ruled out on syntactic grounds, since *the* is a determiner, *same* is an adjective, and only nouns fit into the syntactic environment [Det A___]. On this view, the deviance of phrases like

---

[4] I became aware of this work from the endorsement in Larson and Segal (1995) – one of the few introductory formalist works that discuss seriously the issue of what makes the various lexical categories different from one another.

    In the following discussion, I gloss over certain philosophical complexities about what it is to have a concept and how it relates to knowing a word so as not to confuse the main point.

the same intelligent would be no different from the deviance of **a miserable jealous*. But Geach and Gupta are trying to use these examples to point to a deeper truth, claiming that the inability of adjectives to occur with determining expressions (including *the same*) stems from the fact that adjectives have no criterion of identity. The claim is that the sentences in (15) are not merely ungrammatical, but incoherent. While this distinction can be a subtle one, I believe it is correct. There are ungrammatical sentences that are perfectly interpretable, where native speakers know exactly what they would mean if they were well formed; a famous example is Chomsky's (1957) **The child seems sleeping*. The examples in (15) do not have this flavor; they are semantically uninterpretable as well as ungrammatical.[5]

Gupta (1980: 23) adds the significant observation that different common nouns can have different criteria of identity. For him, this explains the invalidity of the following argument:

(16)   a Every passenger is a person.
        b National Airlines served at least 2 million passengers in 1975.
        c *Not*: National Airlines served at least 2 million persons in 1975.

(16a) is presumably true, so there is no relevant difference between the criteria of application of *passenger* and *person* in this context. However, if Mary takes a National Airlines flight on 13 September 1975, and another on 22 November 1975, she is the same person on the two occasions, but she is not the same passenger from the point of view of the airline's record keeping, reported in (16b). Even though the same entities on the airplane are both passengers and people, the way of deciding whether X is the same person as Y is different from the way of deciding whether X is the same passenger as Y. Therefore, the criteria of identity of the two words are different. When counting passengers one can count Mary at least twice, but when counting persons one should count her only once. The airline thus served more passengers than people, and (16c) cannot be deduced from (16a) and (16b).

---

[5] Ken Safir (personal communication) points out that (ia) is possible, in which *the same* seems to be equating two VPs. However, I believe that (ia) has the same structure as (ib), where *the same* is composed with a noun that has a (rather broad) criterion of identity.

(i)   a Mary tore up her application form, and John did the same.

       b Mary tore up her application form, and John did the same thing.

English often makes up for the fact that VPs cannot enter into anaphora by using the generic verb *do* with a pronominal direct object, as in *Mary tore up her application and John did it / so too* and *What did Mary do?* (i) is part of the same pattern.

Another example that illustrates Gupta's point is (17), in the context of a father and his children who build toy castles out of the wooden blocks in a block set.

(17)   a That is a castle.
         b That is a block set.
         c That is the same block set as the one that was there this morning.
         d That is the same castle as the one that was there this morning.

In this case, the same entity is both a (toy) castle and a block set; it satisfies the criterion of application of both nouns. Thus, (17a) and (17b) are both true. One cannot, however, infer (17d) from these statements plus (17c). If the same pieces of wood are present on both occasions but they have been completely rearranged, then it is the same block set as it was, but it is not the same castle. On the other hand, if the blocks of the castle were replaced one by one with blocks from another set, preserving the design, one might say that it is the same castle as was there this morning, but it is not the same block set. Thus, common nouns provide standards of sameness by which we can judge whether X is the same as Y. Different nouns can provide different standards of sameness, and words of other categories do not provide such a standard at all. I take this to be the fundamental property that distinguishes common nouns from the other categories.[6]

---

[6] Wiggins (1980: ch. 1) argues against a metaphysical interpretation of Geach's observations, in which paradigms like (17) are interpreted as showing that there is no absolute notion of identity. Wiggins demonstrates that there is a fundamental tension between this view and Leibnitz's Law that identicals have all the same properties. Motivated by this, Wiggins claims that the demonstratives in examples like (17a) and (17b) actually denote different things, albeit things that exist in the same time and place and are made up of the same matter. He also claims that the *is* in (17b) does not express a relationship of identity, but rather a relationship of material composition, comparable to the locution *is made of*.

One can accept Wiggins' metaphysical point about absolute identity, while still holding that Geach and Gupta observed something important about natural language. Natural languages seem systematically apathetic toward the distinctions that Wiggins is led to draw. Common nouns have a uniform grammar, even though Wiggins distinguishes those that express true substances from those that denote titles, roles, stages, etc. Similarly, I do not know any language that systematically uses different copulas in sentences like (17a,b). As for the possibility that (17) is simply an equivocation based on the demonstratives denoting different things, notice that the two predicates can be conjoined with a single demonstrative as subject:

(i)   That is the same block set but is not the same castle as was here this morning.

So even if metaphysically there are two things present in the same space of the family room floor, natural language need not record the difference. Overall, natural language is not as concerned with strict numerical identity as it is with the equivalence classes defined by common nouns. (I thank Paul Pietroski for pointing out Wiggins' work to me, and for helpful discussion of it.)

If these logical/semantic observations are on the right track, then we can ask how this is expressed in syntactic representation (if at all). I propose that nouns' having criteria of identity corresponds to nouns' being the only lexical category that bears a referential index. I conceive of this index as an ordered pair of integers, giving syntactic representations of the form $X_{\{j,k\}}$. This representation corresponds semantically to the interpretation 'j is the same X as k,' or in symbolic terms *same(X)(j,k)*. Whenever X is a noun the expression is meaningful, given Geach's observation, but for other choices of X it is ill formed.[7] This gives the following axioms:

(18) a $N\{i, k\} = i$ is the same N as k is (same(N) (i, k))
      b For all i, $N\{i, i\}$ (reflexivity: for all i, i is the same N as i)
      c $N\{i, k\}$ iff $N\{k, i\}$ (symmetry: i is the same N as k iff k is the same N as i)
      d $N\{i, k\}$ and $N\{k, n\} \rightarrow N\{i, n\}$ (transitivity: if i is the same N as k and k is the same N as n, then i is the same N as n)

(18a) expresses the semantic value expressed by this notation. (18b,c,d) make it explicit that common nouns correspond to *equivalence relations* in the mathematical sense. Equivalence relations are a generalization of the core notion of equality; they are two-place relations that have the properties of symmetry, reflexivity, and transitivity, as expressed in (18b,c,d). This suitably expresses the intuition that common nouns set different standards of sameness.

I further assume that each use of a full noun in a syntactic structure introduces a new integer into that structure, expressed by the first member of the ordered pair. The second integer of the pair, in contrast, must be shared with something else in the syntactic structure (cf. (2a)). These assumptions recall the practice of Discourse Representation Theory (DRT) (Kamp and Reyle 1993), in which every noun is seen as introducing a new discourse referent. Coreference is

---

[7] For the use of indices on pronouns, determiners, CPs and other nonlexical projections, see sections 3.3 and 3.4 below. Proper nouns also bear referential indices. They probably do not have distinctive criteria of identity, but rather inherit the criterion of identity from some common noun they are related to. For example, *John* and all other names for people depend on the criterion of identity of *person*. See Geach (1962) and Gupta (1980) for some discussion of this matter.

(18a) says in essence that nouns are fundamentally two–place predicates. This could also be modeled by giving them a theta-grid with two positions, comparable to that normally associated with a transitive verb. However, these theta-roles would not be assigned to argument positions, the way the theta-roles of a verb are. More generally, the syntax treats the "arguments" of a dyadic verb very differently from the understood "arguments" of a noun. For this contingent reason, I use a different representational device for the two, which are then subject to different syntactic principles. Interestingly, nouns always correspond to equivalence relations, whereas verbs typically do not, with the special exceptions of *equal* in mathematical language, and perhaps the *be* of identity statements. (There are symmetrical predicates like *resemble*, but even these do not express true equivalence relations. It is odd to say that *John resembles himself*, and *John resembles Chris* together with *Chris resembles Sue* does not imply *John resembles Sue*.)

expressed in DRT not by associating two NPs with the same discourse referent directly, but rather by equating the discourse referent of the second NP with the one introduced by the first NP in a separate condition. The DRT method is illustrated in (19b), in contrast to the more familiar P&P style of indexing in (19a).

(19) a I bought a pot$_i$ and a basket$_k$. The pot$_i$ is heavy. (traditional P&P index)
b I bought a pot$_i$ and a basket$_k$. The pot$_n$ is heavy, n = i. (DRT style)
c I bought a pot$_{\{i,k\}}$ and a basket$_{\{l,m\}}$. The pot$_{\{n,i\}}$ is heavy. (my notation)

The DRT approach may seem a bit clumsy and redundant, but they have reasons for doing it this way (which I will not review). The indexing style I use is compared to the others in (19c). It combines aspects of both (19a) and (19b). Like (19a), the relationship between the two NPs is captured entirely within the indices of those two NPs, with no need for an extra predicate. Like (19b), the second token of *pot* in (19c) introduces something new to the representation, the integer n. Also like (19b), the referent of n is equated to the referent of i, the integer introduced by the first token of *pot*, by virtue of being contained in the same index. (19c) also makes explicit the fact that the referent of i and the referent of n are equivalent *according to the standard of pothood*, as opposed to some other standard. In this, it contrasts with the DRT-style representation in (19b), which assumes an absolute notion of equality. Following up on Geach's and Gupta's idea, natural language is not built around a single notion of exact numerical equality, but each common noun comes with its own standard of equality by which its coreference relations can be judged. Like (19b), the indexing style in (19c) might seem clumsy and richer than is required, compared to the more Spartan style in (19a). It is true that (19c) says little more than (19a) does, precisely because nouns correspond to equivalence relations. The integers i, k, and n necessarily all have the same reference in (19c) by transitivity ((18d)), so it seems one might just as well use only i, as in (19a). This simpler indexing style would indeed be adequate for most purposes, and readers are invited mentally to reduce my ordered pairs to a simple integer if they like. But given that the bearing of a referential index is underwritten by the lexical semantic property of having a criterion of identity in my view, and since identity is inherently a two-place relation, I assume that pair-indices ultimately make more sense conceptually. In point of fact, most P&P theoreticians who are really serious about indices and how they are interpreted end up opting for an indexing system that is richer than a single index. This enables them to capture subtle but important differences between (say) dependent readings of pronouns versus "accidental" coreference readings, versus disjoint reference readings (Lasnik 1989; Fiengo and May 1994).

There will also be occasional benefits to the richer representation even for my restricted interests, such as in the analysis of predicate nominals given in section 3.8.

This fundamental difference between nouns and other lexical categories immediately explains one of the salient morphological distinctives of nouns, the fact that nouns often inflect for number (singular versus plural and sometimes dual). Geach and Gupta both point out that the criterion of identity associated with nouns is what allows them to be used for counting (this observation goes back to Frege's *The Foundations of Arithmetic*; see also Wiggins [1980: 43–44]). An essential precondition for counting a group of things is the ability to distinguish which of those things are the same. In order to count a group of dogs, I must not count the same dog twice. Therefore, I must know if X (the one I am focusing on now) is the same dog as Y (the one I just counted). In other words, I must use *dog*'s criterion of identity. The importance of criteria of identity is underscored by castle-made-of-blocks examples like (17). Suppose that someone points to what is on the family room floor and asks "how many?" The correct answer depends crucially on which common noun one has in mind. All three of the following could simultaneously be true of what is on the floor:

(20)   a One. (That is one block set.)
        b Three. (That is three castles.)
        c One hundred. (That is one hundred blocks.)

Since nouns support counting, it is not surprising that some of them can appear with plural morphology and other morphosyntactic expressions of cardinality in English and many other languages:[8]

(21)   a The dog died.
        b The (five) dogs died.

---

[8] Of course, number morphology (and numerals) is not possible with all nouns in English and similar languages, only with the count nouns. Mass nouns also have a criterion of identity, however, and there is a generalization of these ideas that applies to them. Water, for example, cannot be counted, but it can be measured. Like counting, measuring depends on a criterion of identity: one must not measure the same water twice; therefore, one must be able to recognize when X is the same water as Y. This rarely shows up in the inflection on the noun, but a syntactic reflex of this is that mass nouns co-occur with measure phrases, whereas comparable adjectives and verbs do not. The paradigm in (i) illustrates within the mass domain the same fundamental contrast between nouns and adjectives that (22) illustrates within the count domain.

(i)   a The soup contains salt.
       b The soup is salty.
       c The soup contains two cups of salt.
       d *The soup is two cups (of) salty.

(Some adjectives also allow a kind of measure phrase, as in *Thumbelina is six inches tall*, but I assume this is a distinct phenomenon, related to the degree argument discussed in section 4.3.)

In contrast to nouns, adjectives and verbs do not have criteria of identity; thus, they do not support counting. I can think of what is on the family room floor in (17) as being brown, but this thought does not give me a way of counting it, of deciding whether there is one or three or one hundred. As a result, adjectives and verbs cannot be inherent bearers of singular, dual, or plural morphology. This seems to be correct. Superficially, (22a) and (22b) mean close to the same thing, but (22b) uses a noun to express the idea and (22a) uses an adjective. With the noun comes a criterion of identity, and it can be meaningfully pluralized, as shown in (22c). The adjective, however, does not give a way of individuating Chris's afflictions, and it cannot be pluralized, as shown in (22d).

(22) a Chris is sick.
      b Chris has a disease.
      c Chris has (two) diseases.
      d *Chris is (two) sicks.

(23) presents a similar comparison between verbs and nouns. The simple verb *nap* is almost synonymous with the periphrastic construction *take a nap*. However, the noun in the latter construction can be plural (and otherwise counted), but the simple verb cannot be:

(23) a Chris will nap this afternoon.
      b Chris will take a nap this afternoon.
      c Chris will take (two) naps this afternoon.
      d *Chris will (two) naps this afternoon.

This explains the typological generalization that if only one category bears number morphology, it will be nouns (see Givón [1984: ch 3]; and Croft [1991: 79, 83]).

When number morphology does appear on verbs and adjectives, it is usually in a derivative sense, as the result of morphosyntactic agreement / concord with a noun projection that bears number marking inherently. (24) gives elementary examples of this kind of agreement in number in Spanish:

(24) a el perro rojo   'the red dog'
      b los perros rojos   'the red(s) dogs'
      c el perro come.   'the dog is eating.'
      d Los perros comen.   'the dogs are eating.'

This kind of agreement is found in many Indo-European languages, Semitic languages, the Bantu languages, some Australian languages (e.g. Nunggubuyu [Heath 1984]), some New Guinean languages (e.g. Yimas [Foley 1991], Arapesh [Aronoff 1994: ch. 4]), and others. That adjectives and verbs often pick up number specification from nearby nouns in this way only reinforces the fact that they themselves are not intrinsically specified for number.

One does occasionally find similar-looking number-like morphology on both nominal constructions and verbal constructions where it is not the result of an agreement rule. (25) illustrates a case of this kind in Mohawk.

(25)   a Ka-nuhs-a-hútsi   thíkʌ.
           NsS-house-Ø-black this
           'This is a black house.'
        b Ro-natar-úni   ne Sak.
           MsO-bread-make.STAT NE Sak
           'Sak has made bread.'
        c Ka-nuhs-a-hútsi-*s*   thíkʌ.
           NsS-house-Ø-black-HAB   this
           'These are black houses.'
        d Ra-natar-úni-*s*   ne Sak.
           MsS-bread-make-HAB NE Sak
           'Sak makes bread; Sak is a baker.'

(25a) is a type of predicate nominal construction. (Here I anticipate the reanalysis of this construction to be given in section 4.6.3, rather than my preliminary analysis of chapters 1 and 2 where stative predicates like *hutsi* are purely verbal.) (25b) gives a comparable example in which the predicate is a verb with an incorporated object. Both of these predicates can take the suffix –*s*, traditionally called the habitual, as shown in (25c) and (25d). In (25c), this suffix has the effect of pluralizing the predicate nominal. In (25d), it has the effect of saying that bread-baking is a characteristic habit of the subject. Now if something is a habit of Sak's, it usually means that Sak does that action more than once. This makes it tempting to see –*s* as being a kind of plural marker in (25d), just as it is in (25c); in (25c), it expresses a plurality of things and in (25d) it expresses a plurality of events. If that were the whole story concerning these forms, it would go against my analysis of nouns as being the only bearers of a criterion of identity. It is significant, however, that the expected contrast between nouns and verbs appears when a numeral expression is added, as shown in (26).

(26)   a Wisk ni-ka-nuhs-ake   ka-nuhs-a-hutsi-s.
           five   PART-NsS-house-PLUR NsS-house-Ø-black-HAB
           'There are five black houses.'
        b *Wisk ni-yo-yʌt-u   ra-natar-uni-s   ne   Sak.
           five   PART-NsO-lie-STAT MsS-bread-make-HAB NE Sak
           'Sak makes / made bread five times.'

When *–s* combines with a predicate nominal, the result can easily co-occur with a numeral construction, as in (26a); the numeral expresses the cardinality of the plurality of houses, as one would expect. If *–s* on verbs simply indicated a plurality of events, one would expect that it could also combine with a numeral construction, and the numeral would express the cardinality of the plurality of events. But this is impossible, as shown in (26b). This subtle contrast is exactly what we expect on the view that nouns have a criterion of identity that supports cardinality expressions but verbs do not. (25d) turns out not to be as similar to (25c) as one might have thought at first glance: it is not really the plural of a VP, but rather a true habitual.[9] The generalization that nonnominal words cannot take intrinsic plural morphology is thus supported even in Mohawk once one looks beneath the surface.[10]

3.3   Occurrence with quantifiers and determiners

That nouns have a criterion of identity, and thus make possible individuation, counting, and measuring, also accounts for the special relationship they have to quantifiers and determiners, as was recognized by Geach (1962) and Gupta (1980) in their original discussions of the notion.

[9] I tentatively assume that the habitual on verbs in Mohawk is a kind of universal/generic quantifier over events; see Baker and Travis (1998) for details. On this view, the ungrammaticality of (26b) is comparable to the ungrammaticality of adding a cardinality predicate to a universal quantification, like *five every book* in English.

One can, of course, count events in English, but I take it to be significant that this always involves a dummy noun; one says (ib), rather than (ia).

(i)   a *Chris knocked on the door four/fourly.
       b Chris knocked on the door four times/on four occasions.

Here the noun *time* or *occasion* provides the criterion of identity that makes enumeration possible, a factor that cannot come directly from the verb in (ia). (This implies that *twice* is a suppletive form of *two times*, *once* is a suppletive form of *one time*, and so on, as seems reasonable.) See section 4.5 for the role that noun heads play in making adverbial modification possible in a more general context.

[10] Another characteristic morphosyntactic property of nouns in some languages is that they inherently bear gender, in contrast to adjectives and verbs which only show gender by agreement with a gender-bearing noun. This is true in roughly the same range of languages as those that show agreement with nouns in number: Indo-European, Semitic, Bantu, Australian, and New Guinean languages. Since gender is similar to number in this respect, it would be nice if a similar analysis could be given for it. Although this seems plausible, it is harder to argue that gender distinctions are logically dependent on the presence of a criterion of identity, because gender often has little or no semantic content. Perhaps part of having a criterion of identity is having the ability to classify things within the folk taxonomy of the language, and gender is part of this folk-taxonomic system in languages that have it. As and Vs do not classify the things that fall under their criteria of application in this sense, so they do not bear gender in their own right.

For some discussion of case morphology, see section 3.6 and the appendix.

Those quantifiers in English that form a constituent with an XP and are in complementary distribution with the articles *the* and *a* can be taken to be heads of category Determiner (D). Such heads can merge with an NP complement, but not with an AP or VP complement:

(27)   a No/some/many/most/every [$_{NP}$ dog(s)] barked.
        No/some/much/most [$_{NP}$ wine] is drunk during Lent.
        b *No/some/much/many/most/every [$_{AP}$ rude] is tolerated here.
        c *No/some/much/many/most/every [$_{VP}$ pay(ing) parking fees] is pleasant.

In syntactic terms, it is common to say that Ds select an NP complement. My goal, however, is to eliminate arbitrary uses of categorial features from the theory. An NP is simply a lexical category that has a criterion of identity and a referential index, given the conjecture in (1). The substantive question is why quantifiers need a complement that has these particular features.

A semantic explanation is available that is implicit in the very term *quantifier*. Quantifiers express quantities, and the notion of a quantity depends on the notion of counting or measuring. The grammatical quantificational schematas in (27a) are interpreted by evaluating how many (or how much) of that which meets the description of the NP also satisfies the description of the rest of the clause with the NP removed. *Most dogs barked*, for example, is true if more than 50 percent of the things that are dogs are things that bark. *No dog barks* is true if none of the things that are dogs are things that bark. *Every dog barks* is true if 100 percent of the things that are dogs bark, and so on. These matters can only be decided if there is a way of counting the things in question (or measuring, in the case of mass nouns). The criterion of identity of the NP complement of the determiner provides this. As a result, the structures in (27a) are good. APs and VPs, in contrast, have no criterion of identity. They thus do not provide a basis for the counting/measuring that is required in evaluating a quantificational schema. There is no way of comparing the quantities of that which is rude and that which is tolerated here in (27b), so the sentences are semantically deviant (and similarly for (27c)). That quantifiers form phrases with NPs rather than other categories can thus be seen as a semantic necessity rather than a stipulated fact of syntactic selection once nouns are defined as in (1).[11]

---

[11] Quantifiers show up in natural languages not only as determiners with NP complements, but also as adverbs of quantification that are adjoined to sentences as a whole. Thus, the following sentences are nearly equivalent, and both involve a kind of quantification (Heim 1982).

  (i)   *Most* cats that fall from a fifth story window survive.
  (ii)   If a cat falls from a fifth story window, it *usually* survives.

To the extent that adverbs of quantification like *usually* bind indefinite noun phrases, the lexical content of those NPs can provide a way of individuating the cases to be evaluated in (ii), just

This reasoning can be extended to account for the fact that the articles *the* and *a* in English take only NP complements, as shown by the contrasts in (28) and (29).

(28)   a John has the / an illness.   (NP)
        b *John is the / a sick.   (AP)
(29)   a I made John sing the / a song.   (NP)
        b *I made John the / a sing.   (VP)

Similar effects are found with articles in other languages. (30) shows that predicate nominals (like other nominals) can be marked for definiteness in Edo, but predicate adjectives and verb phrases cannot be:

(30)   a Úyì ọ̀ré né!né ọ̀khaẹ̀mwẹ̀n.
        Uyi be the   chief
        'Uyi is the chief.'
        b Né!né òkpìá yé (*né) mòsèmòsè.
        the   man is the   beautiful
        'The man is beautiful (has the same beauty we were discussing?)'
        c Úyì *(né) dẹ́ àkhé.
        Uyi the   buy pot
        'Uyi bought a pot (was the agent of the pot-buying we discussed?)'

There are different views about exactly what articles are semantically correct, but for any of the major contenders a criterion of identity is easily seen to be necessary. The Russellian tradition takes *a* and *the* to be quantifiers: *a* is an ordinary existential quantifier, and *the* is an existential quantifier with uniqueness/maximality requirements added. On this view, (28) and (29) are simply two more instances of the paradigm in (27). For example, one can only decide that John has the unique / maximal disease if one knows how to individuate diseases and can judge whether John has the same disease as the one we know about from the context. The lexical properties of the noun *disease* support this judgment, but those of the adjective *sick* do not. In the same way, there can be a unique song in a particular situation, but one cannot determine this for *sing*.

The alternative approach to the articles is to say that they have no inherent quantificational force, but mark a pragmatic distinction, as in the File Change Semantics of Heim (1982) and the Discourse Representation Theory of Kamp (1981). On this view, the definite determiner indicates that the referent of the noun is presupposed to be familiar from the prior discourse (or the speech

---

as in (i). In other examples, these adverbs can be understood as linking whole clauses, and clauses are nonlexical projections that also bear a referential index (see section 3.4). Finally, the adverbial affix *–ly* itself counts as a nominal element, with its own criterion of identity; see Déchaine and Tremblay (1996) and section 4.5 below.

context) and the indefinite determiner is presupposed to be novel. Heim states
these conditions directly on indices: the index of a definite NP must be the same
as the index of some previous NP, whereas the index of an indefinite NP must be
different from those of all previous NPs. Any such novelty / familiarity condition
clearly presupposes a notion of sameness, and we have seen that there is no
single linguistic standard of sameness that can be deployed across the board.
Rather a particular standard of sameness – a criterion of identity – must be
provided. The obvious source of this criterion of identity is the complement of
the determiner, which therefore must be nominal, by the definition in (1). This
can be made explicit by giving the definite and indefinite determiners the crude
glosses in (31).

(31)   a *the N{i, k}* = "k is presupposed to be the same N as some index already
            known from the context."
        b *a N{i, k)* = "k is not presupposed to be the same N as any index already
            known from the context."

This view also explains the contrasts in (28) and (29). An expression like *the
disease* translates into 'i that is the same disease as k,' but *the sick* gives 'i that
is the same sick as k,' which is undefined. The contrast between *the song* and
the sing would be similar. It is their criteria of identity that makes it possible
for nouns to track the sameness and difference of things over a discourse. As a
result, nouns are inherently suited to the task of reference tracking, and therefore
to reference itself (compare Hopper and Thompson [1984] and Croft [1991]).

   On my view, then, determiners are functional heads that for semantic reasons
must take a complement that has a referential index and that (I assume) passes
that referential index on to the DP as a whole. This view stands in opposition
to the received wisdom of much of the field, which is that NPs are essentially
predicative categories, and determiners are needed to make them into something
that can refer and can function as an argument. On this alternative perspective,
NPs do not bear referential indices, although determiners and/or DPs might.
This is the most common view in formal semantic treatments, and Longobardi
(1994) has made influential use of it in the syntax literature. Longobardi's view
is based on the fact that (most) nominals must appear with a determiner in order
to be used as an argument in English and the Romance languages. In contrast,
NPs need not be embedded in DPs when they are used predicatively, or when
they are used outside the context of a clause in vocative expressions and curses
(Longobardi 1994: 612).

(32)   a Ho   incontrato *(un/il) grande amico di Maria ieri.
          I-have met   a/the   great   friend of Maria yesterday
        b Gianni è tenente/   amico di Maria.
          Gianni is lieutenant/ friend of Maria
        c Tenente, esegua l'ordine!
          lieutenant perform the-command
        d Maledetto tenente!
          damn   lieutenant

Singular count nouns in English show the same behavior, except that an indefinite article is required in the English equivalent of (32b). Longobardi thus concludes that "a 'nominal expression' is an argument only if it is introduced by a category D" (1994: 620).

Attractive as this paradigm is in Italian and French, it is not very robust crosslinguistically. Many languages – probably the majority – allow at least some nouns to be used as arguments even without an overt determiner. Even in English, this is possible with plural count nouns and mass nouns (*I saw trees/grass in the park*). Longobardi is aware of this, of course; he covers these cases by assuming that they are DPs with a null D head, the D position being filled by movement of the N at LF. But he has no direct evidence for this invisible LF movement in English; it is motivated purely by the attractiveness of the parallelism it creates with the Romance languages. Other languages allow even singular count nouns to be used without an overt determiner, as in the following example from Edo:[12]

(33)   Íkóróbá vuọ́n ghá nọ́}nọ́.
        bucket fill ASP drip
        'The bucket filled up and started to drip.'

Many languages have no overt determiners at all, including Chinese, Japanese, the Slavic languages (Chierchia 1998), Hindi (Dayal 2001), Mohawk (Baker 1995; Baker 1996b), and Chichewa. The presumption that null determiners are ubiquitous in all these languages seems undermotivated and artificial.

In some of these languages, it is possible to construct syntactic arguments to show that no determiner is present. Mohawk, for instance, allows the head of its object noun phrase to be incorporated into the verb, where the incorporation

---

[12] Note that the bare singular count noun here is in the subject position. Edo and the other languages mentioned are thus not like Italian, in which bare nouns are allowed only as direct objects, suggesting that they have a phonologically null determiner that is only licensed when it is properly governed by a verb (Longobardi 1994; Chierchia 1998).

is commonly analyzed as head movement in the syntax. A simple example is given in (34).

(34)   Wa'-ke-nakt-a-hnínu-'.   (Í-k-ehr-e'   tsi Uwári ʌ-ye-núhwe'-ne'.)
       FACT-1sS-bed-Ø-buy-PUNC Ø-1sS-think-IMPF that Mary FUT-FsS-like-PUNC
       'I bought a/the bed. (I think that Mary will like it.)'

Two rough syntactic structures for this example are given in (35), one using the Longobardian assumption that null determiners are generated with every NP used as an argument ((35a)) and one without a DP projection ((35b)). (Details concerning the exact initial positions of the subject, object, and verb are suppressed here; see section 2.9 for my exact assumptions about this.)

(35)   a Longobardian, with DP   b Without DP

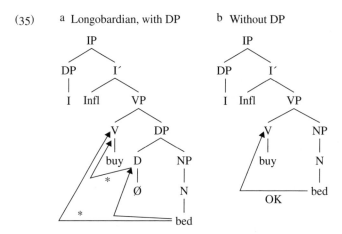

If the object can be generated as a bare NP, as in (35b), the incorporation is entirely straightforward. The null determiner in (35a), in contrast, creates problems. It intervenes between the initial position of the noun and its target position, threatening to disrupt the strict locality that head movement requires. Skipping over the null D to incorporate directly into the verb violates the Head Movement Constraint (Travis 1984; Chomsky 1986a; Baker 1988a). Moving through the determiner position on the way to V, on the other hand, violates the Proper Head Movement Generalization that head movement cannot proceed from a lexical head to a functional head and then back to a lexical head (Li 1990). Thus, no incorporation should be possible from the structure in (35a).[13] Since

---

[13] This argument might be circumvented by tinkering with the formulation of the principles involved. For example, the PHMG could be formulated to say that movement cannot pass through a functional head to a lexical one *unless the functional head lacks phonological content*, or the

noun incorporation is possible, the structure in (35b) must be permitted in Mohawk. This means that the structure is compatible with Universal Grammar, and there is no compelling reason not to take the simplest analysis of more common examples like (33) in Edo as well. Moreover, both the incorporated noun in Mohawk and the bare NP subject in Edo can introduce discourse referents, providing the antecedent for a subsequent pronoun (see (34)). Hence nouns and their projections have a referential index even in the absence of a DP projection.

Chierchia (1998) also argues against a universalist interpretation of Longobardi's constraint on semantic grounds. He picks up on the fact (noted also by Longobardi) that the apparently bare noun phrases of most languages have a restricted range of interpretations. They can always be interpreted as generics or as indefinites with narrowest scope. In addition, they can be understood as definite NPs in languages that do not have a definite article. What seems to be impossible crosslinguistically is interpreting a bare noun phrase as an indefinite that takes wide scope with respect to operators like negation and adverbs. This restriction is not expected if phonologically null but otherwise normal determiners are commonplace; there is no obvious reason why a null determiner could not have the semantic value of *a* or *some* in English. Instead, Chierchia develops an analysis in which nouns in some languages are fundamentally of type <e>, referring to kinds. Such nouns can be used as arguments without a DP projection. Their generic interpretation comes for free, and the "narrow scope indefinite" readings are the result of certain semantic manipulations that take place when an individual- or stage-level verb is applied to a kind-level argument, in the spirit of Carlson (1977) (Chierchia [1998: 364] calls this "Derived Kind Predication"). The definite interpretation can arise as a spontaneous type-/sort-shift in languages where this is not blocked by the presence of a lexicalized definite determiner. None of these manipulations can, however, give a wide-scope indefinite reading. Chierchia thus proposes the following parameter (1998: 400):

(36)   The Nominal Mapping Parameter: N → [+ / −arg, + / −pred]
        a N is +arg, −pred: Chinese
        b N is +arg, +pred: Germanic (with articles), Slavic (without articles)
        c N is −arg, +pred: French, Italian (with a null determiner)

HMC could be stated as saying that head movement cannot skip over a functional head *that has phonological content*. But unless they emerge naturally from a more principled understanding of the constraints involved, these adjustments are not very attractive. They violate the fundamental research strategy that phonologically empty elements should have the same syntax as overt ones, all things being equal.

Chierchia's semantic arguments converge with my syntactic argument in an attractive way. Incorporated objects in Mohawk are known not to have a null determiner for syntactic reasons, and they have precisely the range of readings that bare NP arguments are predicted to have in Chierchia's system. They can be definite or narrow scope indefinites, but they cannot be wide-scope indefinites, as shown in (37) (see also Mithun [1984]).

(37)   Yah te-wake-nakt-a-hninu.
        not NEG-1sO-bed-Ø-buy.STAT
        'I didn't buy the bed.' *or*
        'I did not buy a(ny) bed.'   (Not ($\exists$x [bed x] (I bought x)))
        Not: 'There is a bed that I didn't buy' (*$\exists$x [bed x] (not (I bought x)))

Similarly *Ì má dé ágá* ('I did-not buy chair') means only 'I didn't buy any chair' in Edo.

While I agree with Chierchia that nouns can be of argumental rather than predicate type (<e> rather than <e,t>), I take this one step farther and say that nouns are always inherently argumental as a matter of Universal Grammar. In this respect, I out-Chierchia Chierchia and reject the Nominal Mapping Parameter as such. Chierchia uses the distinction between argumental and predicative to model the distinction between languages that have a count/mass distinction in their nominal syntax and languages that do not. In contrast, I want to use it to capture the distinction between nouns/adjectives and verbs. The positive case for using the distinction in my way was presented in chapter 2. The negative case for not using it in Chierchia's way is that the distinction between count and mass nouns seems to be universal – or if it can be neutralized at all the neutralization does not correlate with the possibility of having determinerless noun phrases in the way Chierchia predicts. According to Chierchia, the consequences of a language having inherently nonpredicative nouns are those in (38).

(38)   a Generalized bare arguments
        b The extension of all nouns is mass
        c No (ordinary) plural morphology
        d Generalized classifier system

Chinese and Japanese are Chierchia's paradigm examples of this type of language. Edo and Mohawk are like Chinese and Japanese in allowing nouns of all kinds to appear without determiners in all syntactic positions ((38a)). However, both clearly have a count/mass distinction. (39) illustrates this for Edo.

(39) a Ávbé èbé / *àmẹ̀n dè-lé.
    PLUR leaf / water fall-PLUR
    'The leaves / *waters fell.'
  b Òzó dẹ̀-lẹ́ àkhé / *àmẹ̀n.
    Ozo buy-PLUR pot / water
    'Ozo bought pots / *water(s).'
  c Òzó miẹ́n àkhé èvá / *àmẹ̀n èvá.
    Ozo find pot two water two
    'Ozo found two pots / *two waters.'

Edo has a plural marker *ávbé* that appears with count nouns but not mass nouns, as in (39a) (it is a pre-nominal particle rather than an affix, but this should not make any difference). Edo also has a suffix that goes on verbs to mark that their object is plural (Stewart 1997); this is natural with count nouns as objects but not with mass nouns ((39b)). Finally, Edo expresses numerical constructions by directly juxtaposing a numeral with the count noun head, without the use of a classifier ((39c)). Very similar arguments can be given for Mohawk. (See also Cheng and Sybesma [1999] for evidence that there is a count / mass distinction even in Chinese.) Chierchia's parametric cluster in (38) is thus not well supported, and I am free to use the idea that nouns are inherently nonpredicative for languages with a count/mass distinction as well.

What about those instances in which nouns really must appear with determiners in argument position, as singular count nouns must in English and all nouns must in Romance languages? Should we explain this by saying that such nouns are inherently predicates, as Chierchia does? I believe not. The most important argument against this is that there is no evidence that these nouns can be predicates in other environments. In section 2.8 we saw evidence that nouns in Italian can only be predicates if they are transformed into such by the presence of a functional category Pred; as a result, nouns require a copular verb to bear tense, and they do not behave like unaccusative predicates. The same is true for English count nouns. If Chierchia's approach were correct, we would expect to find a language in which mass nouns need to be introduced by Pred when used as predicates, but count nouns do not. But no such language has been attested in this literature, nor do I know of any plausible cases. It is also notable that many determiners in languages like English can appear with both count nouns and mass nouns. This is somewhat awkward for a theory in which the two are of fundamentally different semantic types, but it is to be expected on my theory in which all nouns are inherently of type <e>. Of course

I can perfectly well accept (40) as a parameter defining the Romance languages (and presumably others, including the Salish languages).

(40)   In some languages, Ns cannot appear directly in argument position; they must be embedded in DPs.

But I deny that this shows anything deep about the semantic types of nouns in the languages in question (as for Chierchia), much less about the nature of nouns universally (as for Longobardi). (40) is a mere fact, no more remarkable than the fact that complementizers are required for clausal embedding in some languages (e.g. Romance) but not others (e.g. English), a fact that otherwise tells us little about the internal structure of clauses in the language. Reading too much significance into (40) does more syntactic and semantic harm than good, I claim.

All this means that I must, of course, say that the exact semantics of the determiners is systematically different from the semantics associated with them in the standard account. On my account, they would be functions from type <e> to the Generalized Quantifier type <<e, t>, t>, rather than functions from <e, t> to <<e, t> t>. But this is not a problem; Chierchia (1998: 353) observes that it is "completely trivial" to redefine determiners in this way. I thus take (41) to be the basis for the universal syntax and semantics of NPs.

(41)   a Common nouns: type <e>, intrinsically denote kinds.
        b Definite determiners: Functions from <e> to <e>, perform a sort shift from a kind to the maximal instantiation of that kind in context. (This sort shift comes for free in languages where it is not blocked by the existence of a definite determiner.)
        c Pred: Chierchia's "up" operator; maps kind-denoting Ns (type <e>) to predicates (<e, t>).
        d Quantificational determiners: "Lift," various functions from kinds (<e>) to Generalized Quantifiers (<<e, t> t>).

The sort shift in (41b) can come for free, without the help of a syntactically present functional category, but the more radical type shifts in (41c) and (41d) cannot. The range of possible noun-type meanings is the same as in the standard account; the only difference is which are basic and which are derived. This arrangement seems optimal for the study of syntax and the syntax–semantics interface.

If the determiners really selected for predicates, as the standard view would have it, then one might expect that the copular particle Pred would have to appear between the determiner and the noun in languages in which it is overt, such as Edo. But this is of course false:

(42)   a Úyì *(rè)   òkhaèmwèn.
        Uyi PRED chief
        'Uyi is a chief.'
     b Né!né (*rè)   òkhaèmwèn rré.
     c the   PRED chief   came
        'The chief came.'

Copular particles are never needed to join a determiner to its noun phrase.[14] Moreover, the view that determiners map predicates onto generalized quantifiers has no explanation for the fact that determiners can combine with common noun phrases but not verb phrases and adjective phrases, which also denote predicates in the standard view. All these facts fall into place more simply if determiners take expressions of type <e> as their complements, and all nouns are inherently of this type. This fits with my overarching claim that determiners select something that already has a criterion of identity and a referential index, rather than creating those features themselves.[15]

---

[14] In some languages, classifiers are needed to join (certain) quantifiers to the nouns they quantify over. This plays an important role in Chierchia's discussion. Such classifiers probably do not have the function of making the nouns into predicates so that they can compose with a determiner, however. First, the classifiers are usually historically nouns themselves, not some kind of verbal element. This makes them an odd choice for service as a predicate-former. Second, the classifiers typically form a constituent with the quantifier, not with the head noun, giving [[quantifier classifier] noun], not [quantifier [classifier noun]]. Finally, the classifiers are never used in forming predicate nominals. In the Mayan languages, at any rate, the classifier is probably best treated as a kind of agreement morpheme that appears on the quantifier, similar to the way that determiners agree with their noun complement in gender in many languages (see Aissen [1987] for relevant data from Tzotzil).

[15] Longobardi (1994: 620–21) makes an interesting observation concerning conjunction that he interprets as showing that the locus of referentiality in a DP is the determiner, not the noun. If two NPs are conjoined under a single determiner then the DP is understood as designating a single individual. In contrast, if the second conjunct has a determiner of its own, then the expression is understood as designating two distinct individuals:

(i)   a La mia segretaria e   tua   collaboratrice sta/*stanno uscendo.
           the my secretary   and your   collaborator   is/are   going.out.
        b La mia segretaria e   la tua collaboratrice stanno/*sta uscendo.
           the my secretary   and the your collaborator   are/is   going.out.

Thus, the number of understood referents matches the number of determiners, not the number of noun phrases.
   My theory can perfectly well represent this difference as follows (the possessive adjectives are omitted, for simplicity).

(ii)   a $[_{DP\{i,k\}}$ La $[_{NP\{i,k\}}$ secretary] and $[_{NP\{i,k\}}$ collaborator]]
        b $[_{DP\{i+n,k+m\}}$ la $[_{NP\{i,k\}}$ secretary]] and $[_{DP\{n,m\}}$ la $[_{NP\{n,m\}}$ collaborator]].

The two DPs that are coordinated in (iib) have distinct indices, as is normal for two nominals with different lexical content. The conjunction then sums these two indices to form a plural index {i+n, k+m} for the nominal expression as a whole, in what we may take to be the usual way. In (iia) the two NP conjuncts have the same referential index, which then becomes the index of the whole NP. This marked treatment of the indices is forced by the fact that *la* in

Before going on, there are superficial counterexamples to my claim that determiners can take NP but not VP or AP complements that must be considered. English allows bare adjectives to follow *the* in examples like the following:

(43)   a I envy the rich.
        b The proud annoy me.
        c The meek will inherit the earth.

In English this is very limited; DPs like those in (43) are generally possible only when referring generically to a whole class. *The rich* in (43a) means 'rich people in general,' for example. Many other languages allow the equivalent of *the*+A more freely, in situations where English uses the dummy noun *one*. Italian is like this (Longobardi 1994; Chierchia 1998), as is Edo:

(44)   Ì ghá dẹ́ né pèrhẹ̀.
        I will buy the flat
        'I will buy the flat one (a chair).'

Other languages allow inflected verbs to appear embedded under the definite determiner, forming what is often described as a headless or internally headed relative clause. The following are typical examples from Mohawk (Baker 1996b: sec. 4.3.2):

(45)   a Wa-shakoti-yéna-'   ótya'ke ne <u>wa-shakoti-'shʌ′ni-'</u>.
           FACT-MpS / 3pO-hold-PUNC some   NE fact-MsS / 3pO-defeat-PUNC
           'They held some of the ones that they defeated (in battle).'

Italian is a singular form of the determiner, the complement of which must have a singular index. This account generalizes to English expressions like *a friend and a neighbor stopped by* (two people) versus *A friend and neighbor stopped by* (only one person). These facts thus fall within the bounds of what can be handled within my system. To what degree this account counts as a principled explanation must await a closer analysis of how the syntax of conjunction meshes with my theory of indices and categories. Longobardi's effect also needs to be studied with plural determiners and determiners that are not marked for number, where the facts become quite complex.

I also put aside examples like *an alleged communist* and *a fake gun*. The special property of these examples is that it does not follow from someone being an alleged communist that they are a communist. Perhaps these must be treated as internally complex common nouns, in which a referential index is associated with the A+N combination, but not with the noun head itself. The issue could perhaps be clarified by studying how the criterion of identity of these A+N combinations relates to the criterion of identity of the noun it is built from. (For example, does *alleged communist* have the same criterion of identity as *communist*? My guess is probably not.) This very special type of adjective might truly be a function from one common noun meaning into a new one, as in Siegel (1980).

b Sak ra-núhwe'-s   ne   <u>khey-uny-ʌ'ni</u>   anúwarore.
    Sak MsS-like-HAB   NE   IsS/FsO-make-BEN/STAT   hat
    'Sak likes the hat that I made for her.'

These counterexamples are only apparent, however. I argue that there is a phono-logically null noun or noun phrase in all such cases, which makes them perfectly consistent with my analysis. The null noun provides the criterion of identity (and hence the referential index) that the determiner requires.

    This proposal is not very radical, and most generative linguists would prob-ably agree with it. For the D+Adj constructions in (43) and (44), the common assumption is that there is a null noun that heads the complement of the D to which the adjective adjoins as an attributive modifier (see again Longobardi [1994] and Chierchia [1998]). The structure is thus (46b), rather than the apparently simpler (46a).[16]

(46)   a *[$_{DP}$ the [$_{AP}$ rich]]
         b [$_{DP}$ the [$_{NP}$ rich$_A$ [$_{NP}$ Ø]]]

Evidence that supports (46b) over (46a) comes from the fact that the adjectival projection in these constructions is subject to the well-known (if not well-understood) restrictions that apply to attributive adjectives in general. First, clearly attributive adjectives cannot take complements, and neither can bare adjectives following *the*:

(47)   a I am tired of listening to proud (*of their accomplishments) people.
         b I am tired of listening to the proud (?*of their accomplishments).

The same is true in Edo, for those (very few) adjectives that can take com-plements at all. Second, clearly attributive adjectives cannot appear with true

---

[16] Wojdak (2001) argues for (46a) over (46b) in Wakashan by pointing out that it is bad for more than one adjective to follow the determiner in the absence of a noun. Her observation is also valid for English: one can say *I despise proud rich people*, but not **I despise the proud rich*. I have no explanation for this intriguing fact.

    A third logical possibility is that the adjectival roots *rich*, *proud*, and *meek* in (43) have been converted into nouns by a presyntactic process of zero-derivation. Then the syntactic structure would be the unproblematic one of [$_{DP}$ the [$_{NP}$ rich]]. However, words like *proud* do not acquire the morphological, syntactic or semantic properties of (other) nouns in English. For example, they cannot have a singular count meaning (**A proud just walked in*), they cannot take the plural suffix (**The prouds annoy me*), and they cannot appear without the definite determiner (**Proud annoy me*). Similarly, *pèrhè* 'flat' in (44) does not have the morphosyntactic properties of a noun in Edo: it does not begin with a vowel, as all (other) nouns do in the language; the determiner has a different shape, appearing as *né* rather than the reduplicated form *né!né* found before nouns; and it too cannot appear without this definite determiner (**Ì ghá dé pèrhè* 'I will buy (a) flat (one)'). Thus, there is good evidence that the head is still adjectival in (43) and (44).

degree heads like *so*, *too*, *as*, and *how*, and neither can bare adjectives following *the*:

(48)   a I don't like (??too) proud (*to associate with others) people.
       b I don't like the (??too) proud (*to associate with others) –.

Third, some adjectives cannot be used in attributive positions at all (or only with a large shift in meaning); these adjectives also sound bad as bare heads following *the*:

(49)   a *At the meeting, *the present people* voted to go on strike. (OK: *the people present*)
       b *At department meetings, *the present* try to assign all the work to the absent.

These patterns are expected, if the structure is as in (46b), but not if it is (46a). ((49b) also shows that the structure [the Ø A(P)] is not possible in English; apparently *the* cannot come immediately before Ø in English, perhaps for phonological reasons[17].) Fourth, in languages that show agreement between attributive adjectives and modified nouns, such as Italian and Chichewa, the adjective in a D+Adj construction typically shows agreement in gender and number with an understood noun phrase. This is expected if the structure is one of attributive modification, as in (46b), but not in (46a), in which the AP is not syntactically linked to any gender-bearing NP.

The structure in (46b) also gives a principled way of talking about the fact that the definite determiner is required in these constructions, originally proposed by Longobardi (1994).

(50)   a The meek will inherit the earth.
       b *Meek will inherit the earth.
       c *A meek will inherit the earth.

---

[17] The generalization that *the* cannot come immediately before Ø in English accounts for its distribution with nonadjectival modifiers as well, as shown by contrast between (i) and (ii).

(i)   a [The responsible Ø] should be promoted.   (AP)
       b The needs of [the many Ø] outweigh the needs of [the few Ø].   (QP)
       c [The dying Ø] should be attended to first.   (VP?)

(ii)   a *[The Ø responsible for successful new products] should be promoted.   (AP)
       b *[The Ø in the city] often look down on [the Ø in the country].   (PP)
       c *[The Ø getting As on the tests] needn't do the homework.   (VP?)
       d *[The Ø that are dying] should be cared for first.   (CP)

When I say that this constraint may be phonological in nature, I have in mind a possible connection to the well-known fact that English auxiliaries cannot contract with the subject when they come before a null VP (*Sue bought a book, and I will/ *I'll Ø too*). Like auxiliaries, *the* in English is phonologically a clitic, so it is not surprising that it should obey similar restrictions. (I thank Norvin Richards for raising the question of the ungrammaticality of (iib).)

d *These meek will inherit the earth.
e *No meek will fail to inherit the earth.

The structure in (46b) contains a null head. Such null heads are subject to strict licensing and identification requirements (the Empty Category Principle of Chomsky [1981] and subsequent work). The definite determiner plausibly plays this licensing function in languages like English, Italian, and Edo. In contrast, the analysis in (46a) does not posit any null structure, so the licensing conditions on null items cannot be used to explain why a particular determiner should be required. (A fuller explanation, of course, would say something about why definite articles make particularly good licensers of $\emptyset_N$; so far, most accounts have just stipulated this [Chierchia 1998: 395].)

I conclude that expressions like *the proud* and similar constructions in other languages are not true counterexamples to the claim that determiners take only NP arguments. On the contrary, assuming that the determiner must be followed by an NP even when none is apparent plays an essential role in explaining a range of subtle facts. It forces the language learner to infer the presence of a null noun head in all Det+Adj constructions, accounting for the ungrammaticality of examples like (47)–(49). The criterion of identity that the determiner requires in these constructions comes either from reconstructing a common noun recovered from a discourse antecedent into the Ø position, as in Edo's (44), or by filling in a generic common noun like *people*, as in the English examples.[18]

Similar considerations apply to putative instances of a verbal projection being embedded directly under a determiner, such as the Mohawk example repeated in (51a).

(51) a Wa-shakoti-yéna-' ótya'ke ne wa-shakoti-'shʌ'ni-'.
          FACT-MpS/3pO-hold-PUNC some NE FACT-MsS/3pO-defeat-PUNC
          'They held some of the ones that they defeated (in battle).'
      b *[$_{DP}$ the [$_{VP}$ *pro* defeat *pro*]]
      c [$_{DP}$ the [$_{CP}$ Op$_i$ C [$_{IP}$ *pro* defeat t$_i$]]]

---

[18] The account of *the proud* given in the text probably does not extend to the use of *the*+A in superlatives in English (e.g. *Chris is the tallest*). Unlike *the proud*, these expressions have the distribution of APs, not NPs: they are possible as resultative predicates (*I pounded this piece of metal the flattest*) and are not completely comfortable in subject and object positions (*??The tallest won the election*). Also, it is reasonably acceptable for the superlative adjective to have a complement: *Chris is the proudest of the children's accomplishments*. Thus, the structure is probably not [$_{DP}$ the [$_{NP}$ tallest [$_{NP}$ Ø]]], but rather [$_{DegP}$ the [$_{AP}$ tallest]] (agreeing with Corver (1997: 123, n. 4)), with *the* acting as a degree head (see section 4.3). The homophony of this degree element with the definite determiner is then semi-accidental (there is no comparable use of *né(né)* in Edo, for example).

My (unremarkable) claim is that such examples do not have the simple structure in (51b), but the more articulated structure in (51c). In (51c), an inherently nominal null operator is generated in one of the argument positions associated with the verb and then undergoes *wh*-movement to gain scope over the CP as a whole. This operator then provides the referential index that the determiner requires. Baker (1996b: sec. 4.3.2) gives detailed arguments that this kind of operator movement takes place in Mohawk. I will not repeat the crucial data here, but only summarize the main arguments:

(52)   a The operator can originate in any argument position of the relative clause.
b The operator can undergo successive cyclic movement.
c The operator cannot escape from an island internal to the relative clause.
d The operator can induce pied piping of a possessed noun.
e Only one operator can appear at the top of each relative clause.
f The operator sometimes shows up overtly as a *wh*-expression (*tsi nikayv*, parallel to *ka nikayv* 'which').

In short, there is just as much reason to say that determiner + verb constructions in Mohawk involve operator movement as there is to say that relative clauses in English do. The only significant difference between the languages is that relative clauses without an overt noun phrase head that binds the operator are common in Mohawk but not in English. This difference has no bearing on my theoretical point: either *pro* is present as the head of the relative clause in Mohawk (but not English), or the null operator itself is sufficient. Either way, there is a nominal source for the referential index required by the determiner. (The criterion of identity of the null operator that undergirds this index is probably relatively trivial in this case: it is the same as *person/who* or *thing/what* in English, depending on animacy.)

These considerations seem to extend to determiner + verb / clause constructions in other languages as well. For example, Williamson (1987) gives evidence that the "internal head" of the relative clause in (53) from Lakhota undergoes movement at LF to adjoin to the relative clause as a whole.

(53)   a [DP [S Mary [owįža wą] kage] ki] he   opewathų.   (Overt structure)
Mary quilt   a   make the DEM I-buy
'I bought the quilt that Mary made.'
b [DP [S Mary t kağe] [owįža wą] ki]   he   opewathų.   (LF)
Mary   make quilt   a   the DEM I-buy

Similarly, Watanabe (1991) argues for operator movement in internally headed relative clauses in Japanese.[19] Thus, none of these cases seriously threatens the

[19] Reinhart (1987) and others have analyzed internally headed relative clauses of the Lakhota kind as involving the unselective binding of an NP *in situ* by the determiner that selects the clause

generalization that quantifiers and determiners semantically require a complement that has a criterion of identity, and hence is nominal rather than verbal or
adjectival.[20]

3.4   Nouns in binding and anaphora

My task now is to go on and show how nouns' having a criterion of identity and
a referential index can explain differences between nouns and other categories
that go beyond those that originally caught Geach's and Gupta's attention.
Toward this end, I turn to a cluster of facts that concern the special role of NPs
in anaphora, binding, and movement – the domains in which the presence of a
referential index is most obviously relevant. My claim is that since only nouns
and their projections bear these indices, they alone can enter into relationships
of coreference and binding. The next section then extends this result to certain
kinds of movement relationships.

The most elegant demonstration that noun projections play a special role in
anaphora comes from comparing the genitive NP subject of a nominalization
with a nationality adjective that modifies the derived noun. These two structures can be nearly synonymous, as shown by the minimal pair in (54a) and
(54b).

(54)   a As a former citizen of Rome, Italy$_{\{j,k\}}$'s invasion of Albania distressed me.
        b As a former citizen of Rome, the Italian invasion of Albania distressed me.
        c ... It$_{\{j\}}$ should have known better.

as a whole, with no operator movement required. Such an analysis is also compatible with the
essence of my theory, because the internal head bound by the determiner can be seen as providing
the necessary criterion of identity.

[20] One might also expect to find a pattern in which an element that occurs in construction with nouns
as a marker of definiteness also occurs in construction with verbal projections, but with verbs
it marks not definiteness but some other (possibly related) notion that is compatible with verb
meanings. This would be the equivalent in the definiteness domain of the situation involving
number marking described in section 3.2 (see (26) from Mohawk). A possible case in point
is *O* in Fongbe as described by Lefebvre (1998). This particle can follow a noun as a definite
determiner as in (i), or it can follow a VP/clause as in (ii).

(i)   N Dú àsÓn Ó.
       I eat crab the
       'I ate the crab (in question/that we know of).'
(ii)   Súnù Ó gbà   mÓtò Dé Ó.
       man the destroy car   a   the?
       'Actually / as expected, the man has destroyed a car.'

The clause-final *O* in (ii) does not seem to express a second reference to an event already present
in the discourse context, as one might expect if it were truly a definite determiner for clauses.
Rather, it seems to add some kind of adverbial sense, which (depending on its scope) Lefebvre
renders as 'actually' or 'as expected.' This fits my general prediction. Unfortunately, the exact
semantic value of this second use of *O* is not clear enough to me to permit further speculation.

This near-synonymy notwithstanding, a difference appears when these sentences are followed by a sentence with a pronoun, such as (54c). If (54c) follows (54a), the pronoun is easily construed as referring to Italy; however, this construal is much less natural when (54c) follows (54b). This supports the claim that APs are not good antecedents for pronouns in discourse. The contrast becomes sharper if the subsequent pronoun is a reflexive form; in this case the example with a nationality adjective is completely unacceptable, whereas the one with the genitive noun phrase is still fine (Kayne 1984a):

(55)   a Albania$_{\{j,k\}}$'s destruction of itself$_{\{j\}}$ grieved the expatriate community.
         b *The Albanian destruction of itself$_{\{j\}}$ grieved the expatriate community.
         c The Albanian self-destruction grieved the expatriate community.

This contrast is clearer because reflexives are required to have a syntactic antecedent within a local domain, whereas pronouns can often be understood as referring to something that is inferable from the general context. (The relative acceptability of (55c), where the reflexive sense is achieved by compounding rather than by using an anaphoric NP, drives home the point that (55b) is not bad because there is nothing for it to mean. See Giorgi and Longobardi [1991: 126] for replication of this contrast with several kinds of anaphors in Italian.) Nor does it help to use a pronoun that is c-commanded by the agent-expressing phrase; an adjective cannot count as an antecedent for a pronoun even when there is c-command.[21]

(56)   a Italy$_{\{j,k\}}$'s announcement that it$_{\{j\}}$ would invade Albania caused a stir.
         b ??The Italian announcement that it$_{\{j\}}$ would invade Albania caused a stir.

Examples like these ((55) in particular) were first pointed out by Kayne (1984a: 139). Kayne concludes from them that an adjective cannot bind an NP because the two differ in syntactic category. As a theoretical condition, this statement is "incomplete and rather unprincipled" within the terms of the standard theory, as Giorgi and Longobardi (1991: 126) acknowledge. In contrast, Kayne's generalization emerges very naturally from my theory of categories, in which the defining difference between adjectives and nouns is that only the latter

---

[21] This contrast could be sharpened by using potential antecedents that are inherently quantificational, because then the pronoun interpreted as a variable must truly be syntactically bound (Reinhart 1983). Clearly a quantificational genitive NP can bind a c-commanded pronoun, as in (ia). It is less clear if there are quantificational equivalents of nationality adjectives, but (ib) is a possible case. A bound reading of the c-commanded pronoun is certainly impossible, as expected.

(i)   a Each country's$_{\{j,k\}}$ announcement that it$_{\{j\}}$ would ban nuclear testing caused a celebration.
         b *The universal announcement that it$_{\{j\}}$ would ban nuclear testing caused a celebration.

can bear a referential index. The binding of anaphors and pronouns requires that they be c-commanded by and coindexed with their antecedent (Chomsky 1981). An AP might be able to c-command an anaphor or a pronoun, but it certainly cannot be coindexed with one, because AP cannot bear an index. (56b) thus cannot have the intended interpretation as a function of sentence grammar, and (55b) is ruled out entirely. If we assume that the referential index of a phrase also provides a readily accessible antecedent in discourse for a pronoun even when there is no c-command (Kamp and Reyle 1993; Fiengo and May 1994), then this reasoning applies also to the somewhat fuzzier contrast in (54).

This effect can be traced back from the referential index to the criterion of identity that underlies it as the most basic difference between nouns and adjectives. Coindexing is a grammatical expression that corresponds to a semantic relationship of intended coreference between (say) a pronoun and something else in the discourse (see Fiengo and May [1994: ch. 1] for discussion). Coreference, in turn, is simply the property of two linguistic expressions designating the same thing. But once again there is no single, linguistically privileged standard of sameness that can be applied directly to all situations. An assertion of coreference therefore needs to invoke some particular standard of sameness that is recovered from the linguistic context – a criterion of identity. I assume that pronouns themselves do not have a substantive standard of identity, because they have minimal lexical content. (This motivates my convention of giving pronouns an index that consists of only a single integer, as in (54)–(56). Since they do not correspond to equivalence relations, there is no conceptual reason to give them a second integer.) Where, then, does the necessary criterion of identity come from? The obvious answer is that it must come from the antecedent of the pronoun – the other expression that enters into the coreference relationship. It follows that the antecedent must be a noun or the projection thereof (or some functional category that also bears a referential index, like another pronoun or a full clause). This connection between anaphora and the presence of a criterion of identity is the deeper reason that I choose to express the fundamental property of having a criterion of identity by the familiar binding-theoretic notation of having a referential index.

The important role that the criterion of identity of the antecedent plays in anaphora is brought out clearly by toy castle examples of the kind discussed in section 3.2. Consider the argument in (57).

(57)   a That is a castle. Nicholas made it this morning.
        b That is a block set.
        c #That is a block set. Nicholas made it this morning.

Suppose the demonstrative that in these sentences designates the thing on the family room floor, which is a block set that Nicholas formed into a castle this morning. Then the discourse in (57a) is true. So is (57b) (putting aside metaphysical worries about exactly what the demonstrative refers to). Nevertheless, one cannot infer (57c) from (57a) and (57b); (57c) requires Nicholas to be a skilled woodworker as well as a creative child. On a simple-minded DRT-style approach that did not take criteria of identity into account, the inference in (57c) should be valid. (58) gives schematic representations for the corresponding sentences in (57), and (58c) does follow from the conjunction of (58a) and (58b). (The discourse referents are listed before the slash, and the conditions on them are listed after it.)

(58)   a x, Nicholas, y/castle(x), made-this-morning(Nick, y), y = x
         b x/block-set(x)
         c x, y, Nicholas/block-set(x) & made(Nick, y) & y = x

The problem is fixed immediately if one says that the identity statement introduced by processing the pronoun makes use of the criterion of identity of the pronoun's antecedent. Then the discourse representations of the sentences in (57) are as in (59).

(59)   a x, Nicholas, y/castle(x), made(Nick, y), same(castle)(x, y)
         b x/block-set(x)
         c x, y, Nicholas/made(Nick, y) & block-set(x) & same(block-set)(x, y)

(59c) does not follow from (59a) and (59b): we cannot infer "y is the same castle as x" from "y is the same block set as x" (or vice versa) because *castle* and *block set* have significantly different criteria of identity. This provides semantic undergirding for my syntactic claim that the antecedent of a pronoun must be a referential-index-bearing noun projection.

The contrast between nouns and the other lexical categories with respect to binding and anaphora can be seen in many environments other than derived nominals. For example, the first sentences in (60a) and (60b) are rather parallel; both contain an optional secondary predicate. The secondary predicate in (60a) contains a noun, however, whereas the corresponding predicate in (60b) contains only an adjective. As a result, *Kate* can be the antecedent of the pronoun in the second sentence of (60a), but *smooth* cannot be an antecedent in (60b).

(60)   a I threw the ball to Kate$_{\{j,k\}}$. She$_{\{j\}}$ caught it.
         b I sanded the table smooth$_{*\{j,k\}}$. #It$_{\{j\}}$caused the chair to sell quickly.

(60b) is interpretable, but only if *it* refers to the entire event denoted by the first sentence as a whole, if my sanding the table facilitates the selling of the chair in some indirect way. This suggests that the first sentence as a whole (a TP or CP) bears a referential index of some kind. But (60b) cannot have the plausible interpretation that the abstract quality of smoothness that the table comes to have as a result of my sanding also makes the chair attractive to buyers (presumably because the chair also has it). This is because the A(P) *smooth* itself does not bear a referential index. The following contrast is similar:

(61)   a Chris is sick$_{*\{j,k\}}$. It$_{\{j\}}$ also made Pat miss work.
         b Chris has a disease$_{\{j,k\}}$. It$_{\{j\}}$ also made Pat miss work.

(61a) is possible only if Chris's being sick makes Pat miss work (perhaps he was going to get a ride from Chris), not if the same sickness Chris has makes Pat too ill to go to work. (62) shows that verbs and verb phrases also cannot be antecedents for pronouns in discourse, as expected.

(62)   I made John sing$_{*\{j,k\}}$ against his will. It$_{\{j\}}$ embarrasses Bill.

It here cannot refer just to the action of singing in general, or to Bill's singing, which would be the expected meaning if it could take just the V or embedded VP of the first sentence as its antecedent. Overall, Ns and their projections constitute good antecedents for pronouns and anaphors, but As and Vs do not.

    My theory actually entails something a bit stronger than Kayne's original generalization concerning (55). Kayne suggested that an adjective cannot count as an antecedent for an NP because the two are of different categories. If I am right, one should be able to take this one step further: adjectival projections and verbal projections should not be able to be antecedents at all, even when the dependent form matches it in category. I therefore predict that there should be no such thing as "pro-adjectives" or "pro-verbs" in languages of the world that take part in anaphoric relationships with APs and VPs in the same way that pronouns enter into anaphoric relationships with NPs. Prima facie, this seems to be true: virtually every grammar has an index entry for pronouns, but very few mention pro-adjectives or pro-verbs. It is also perfectly possible to work on a language like Mohawk or Edo hard for more than five years and never encounter anything one is tempted to analyze in this way. (Edo is rich in proverbs, but that is another story.)

    There are a few possible candidates for pro-adjective or pro-verb in English, but a close look suggests that that is not exactly what they are. The element *so*, for example, can substitute for predicate adjectives in some environments:

(63)   a Chris is clever, and so is Pat.
        b Chris is brave, and Pat seems so too.
        c I consider Chris intelligent, and Mary considers Pat so.

As a result, Corver (1997) assumes that *so* is an AP pronominal. The most plausible candidate for a pro-VP in English is the empty category found in VP-deletion contexts like (64).[22]

(64)   Chris will solve the problem, and Pat will – too.

David Pesetsky (personal communication) points out to me the following paradigm, which suggests that the empty category in (64) does behave like a pronoun:

(65)   a John left when Mary did –.
        b When Mary left, John did – too.
        c ?When Mary did, John left too.
        d *John did – when Mary left.

(65a) and (65b) show that the empty category can be in either the matrix clause or the adjunct subordinate clause. (65c) shows that it is marginally possible for the empty category to precede its antecedent when it is in the subordinate clause. What is completely impossible is for an empty category VP in the main clause to precede its antecedent in the subordinate clause, as shown in (65d). This pattern of facts closely parallels the familiar behavior of pronouns, where the pronominal subject of one clause can be related to the nonpronominal subject of a second clause unless the pronominal subject comes first and is in the main clause.

(66)   a Mary explained everything when she arrived.
        b When Mary arrived, she explained everything.
        c When she arrived, Mary explained everything.
        d ?*She explained everything when Mary arrived.

The facts in (66) are explained by Condition C of the Binding Theory: a pronoun cannot c-command a nonpronominal antecedent (Reinhart [1976]; Lasnik [1989], and references cited there). (65) can be explained in the same way if one posits a null pronominal VP that cannot be anaphorically dependent on a VP

---

[22] English also has the superficially similar phenomenon of *do so*, as in *Chris solved the problem, and Pat did so too*. However, in this case *do* is the main verb *do*, co-occurring with an (anaphoric?) adverb *so*, where *so* means basically *thusly*. The *do* of *do so* acts like main verb *do* for subject–auxiliary inversion and negation, and its subject must be agentive. I assume then that the VP as a whole is not anaphoric here, although the adverb *so* might be.

that it c-commands. This suggests that VPs can participate in the same kinds of anaphoric relationships as NPs after all.

Even if I agree that *so* and the null VP are pronominal/anaphoric elements of some kind (there are also some dissimilarities that could tell against this decision), I can deny that they are pronominal APs or VPs.[23] Consider first *so*. While (64) shows some contexts in which *so* seems to be replacing an adjective, *so* is not possible in all environments where an A/AP can appear. APs can be resultative secondary predicates, but *so* cannot replace them there:

(67)   a ??John beat the iron flat and Mary beat the copper so.
       b ?*The chair is already clean, and Chris will wipe the table so too.

Adjectives can also be attributive modifiers of nouns, but *so* does not replace them in this environment either:

(68)   a *Mary is an intelligent woman, and John is a so man/so a man.
       b *I caught a big fish, and they caught a so bird.
       c *The FBI located the man responsible for the crisis, and Interpol located the woman so.

Conversely, *so* can stand for expressions that are not adjectival at all, including predicate nominals, PPs, VPs, and CPs:

(69)   a Chris is a genius, and so is Pat.
       b The unicorn is in the garden, and so is the griffin.
       c Mary will solve the problem, and so will John.
       d Kate says that she will come and Nicholas says so too.

All this implies that *so* is not a pro-adjective *per se*. The contexts where *so* can replace an AP are just those contexts in which the AP is a primary predicate, and these are the contexts in which AP is immediately dominated by PredP on my analysis (see chapter 2, chapter 4). It is thus more accurate to say that *so* is a pro-PredP than to say it is a pro-AP. This characterization can be generalized to account for (69c,d) by saying that *so* stands for a predicate of any category. It presumably belongs to some higher level functional category that contains VP and PredP but is contained in TP (see Cinque [1999] for many possible candidates). The strong prediction of my account that adjectives and their projections

---

[23] For example, the *so* in (63a) must be fronted by some kind of operator movement; this is not expected if it is merely a pronoun. The null VP in (65c) is significantly worse than the corresponding subject pronoun in (66c); this could suggest that VP deletion is regulated by linear order rather than by Binding theory. Also, I am not aware of anything like an AP- or VP-reflexive anaphor, nor of bound variable readings of *so* or the null VP. The similarities between NP anaphora and anaphora with other categories are therefore partial at best.

do not participate in anaphora is thus not falsified by *so*. The French predicate pronominal clitic *le* described by Kayne (1975) and others has essentially the same distribution as English *so*, and can be analyzed in the same way.

A similar case can be made that the empty category in VP ellipsis is not really of category VP. On the one hand, this gap cannot replace verbs/VPs in all the environments where they occur. It cannot appear under verbs that take bare VP complements, for example:

(70)   a *I made Chris laugh, and they made (Pat) – too.
        b #I heard Chris scream, and they heard (Pat) – too.

On the other hand, the same kind of gap can appear when there is no VP to replace:

(71)   a Chris is a genius, and Pat is too.
        b The unicorn is in the garden, and the griffin is too.
        c Mary is intelligent, and John is too.

(71c), for example, contains an AP, a PredP, a TP, and whatever kind of phrase is headed by *be*, but it has no VP that could be filled with a pronominal VP, strictly speaking. Again, I conclude that there is no evidence that the gap in VP-ellipsis contexts is a pronominal verb projection *per se*. If there is a pronominal element at all, it stands for some higher level predicative expression that is not category specific and includes functional structure as well as lexical. Some phrases headed by functional categories can bear referential indices, and it is not surprising that these phrases participate in anaphora. But the prediction that APs and VPs by themselves cannot holds true.

3.5   Nouns and movement

I turn next to a related topic, the fact that NPs can undergo certain movement processes that APs and VPs cannot. Kayne (1984a) also pointed out the contrast in (72), which he related to the contrast involving anaphora in (55).

(72)   a Everyone deplored China's$_{\{j,k\}}$ destruction t$_{\{j\}}$ by Russia.
        b *Everyone deplored the Chinese destruction t$_{\{j\}}$ by Russia.

A prenominal genitive NP can be interpreted as the theme argument of the derived nominal rather than as the agent argument ((72a)). This results in a passive-like structure, as has been known since the earliest work in generative grammar. When a comparable nationality adjective is used, however, this passive interpretation is impossible, as shown in (72b). It seems descriptively that an AP cannot undergo movement to become the subject of DP, whereas an NP can.

Kayne accounted for (72) using assumptions that were standard for the time. First, there must be an empty category noun phrase in the position where the theme theta-role would normally be assigned (Chomsky's [1981] Projection Principle). Second, the "traces" of movement to subject positions count as anaphors, falling under the same binding theoretic principles as reflexives like *itself*.[24] Given these assumptions, the contrast in (72) has exactly the same explanation as the contrast in (55): the NP can antecede the trace, but the AP cannot.

This analysis too can be inherited by my theory, which adds to it a deepened understanding of why adjectival projections are not possible binders. Since the prenominal AP in (72b) cannot bear a referential index, it perforce cannot be coindexed with the trace, leaving it unbound and uninterpretable. Moreover, my analysis again broadens the original generalization, predicting that A-movement of an AP or VP should be problematic even when the trace left behind is in an AP or VP position. For me, this effect depends not on a condition that the trace and its antecedent must match in relevant respects (as Kayne implied), but rather on a very basic property of APs and VPs that make them inherently unsuitable as antecedents. Examples (73)–(75) verify this prediction. The (a) sentences in each set are causative/resultative constructions in which a transitive verb is followed by both an accusative-marked object and a PP, AP, or VP. The (b) and (c) sentences show what can happen when the verb is passivized. The object NP can, of course, move to the subject position in all three cases (the (b) sentences). (73c) shows that it is possible in principle for something other than the NP – in this case, a PP – to move to the subject position, as long as certain conditions are met (for example, the NP must be indefinite). (74c) and (75c), however, show that it is impossible for an AP or a VP to move to the subject position under the same favorable circumstances.[25]

---

[24] It is not so clear that more recent theory still holds to this. In recent Minimalist work, it has been thought that this stipulation might be redundant, since the clause-boundedness of A-movement might be derived from Relativized Minimality instead, a strong condition that also holds of other kinds of movement (Rizzi 1990). But it has never been clearly shown that A-movement traces are not anaphors, and this assumption is not redundant in the arguments being reviewed here. See also Baker (1996a) for another limitation on A-movement that does not follow from Relativized Minimality and supports the idea that its traces are anaphors.

[25] The comparison sentence in (73c) suggests that PPs can bear referential indices. Anaphora also suggests this, since pro-PPs are well-attested: *there* is a pro-PP in English (*On each table still stands the trophy that Mary put there*), as are the clitics *y* 'to it' and *en* 'of it' in French (Kayne 1975). This is compatible with my theory because Ps are functional categories, not lexical ones (see appendix). There is a tension, however, with the fact that PPs cannot generally occur in argument positions the way that NPs can. See the appendix for some discussion.

(i)　　I put my book [on the table]$_{[i,k]}$. Kate put hers there$_{[i]}$ too.

(73)   a Chris put a book$_{\{i,k\}}$ on the table$_{\{n,m\}}$.
   b A book$_{\{i,k\}}$ was put t$_{\{i\}}$on the table$_{\{n,m\}}$.
   c On the table$_{\{n,m\}}$ was put a book$_{\{i,k\}}$ t$_{\{n\}}$

(74)   a Chris pounded some metal$_{\{i,k\}}$flat.
   b Some metal$_{\{i,k\}}$was pounded t$_{\{i\}}$flat.
   c *Flat was pounded some metal$_{\{i,k\}}$ t$_{(\{n\})}$.

(75)   a Chris made a child$_{\{i,k\}}$ sing.
   b A child$_{\{i,k\}}$ was made t$_{\{i\}}$ to sing.
   c *(To) sing was made a child$_{\{i,k\}}$ t$_{(\{n\})}$.

The same pattern is found with intransitive verbs of the unaccusative type: an NP or PP complement of such a verb can become its subject, but an AP or VP cannot:

(76)   a The trophy$_{\{i,k\}}$ Chris won stands t$_{\{i\}}$ on the table$_{\{n,m\}}$.
   b On the table$_{\{n,m\}}$ stands the trophy Chris won$_{\{i,k\}}$t$_{\{n\}}$.

(77)   a The woman$_{\{i,k\}}$ that was in charge became t$_{\{i\}}$ tired.
   b *Tired became the woman$_{\{i,k\}}$ that was in charge t.

(78)   a The wind$_{\{i,k\}}$ in the forest started t$_{\{i\}}$ howling.
   b *Howling started the wind$_{\{i,k\}}$ in the forest t.

This supports the theory that APs and VPs simply cannot undergo A-movement, in contrast to NPs and certain phrases with functional heads (including PPs and CPs).

For the *wh*-movement family of phenomena, the empirical situation is more complex. The traces of *wh*-movement do not count as anaphors with respect to the binding theory; as a result a *wh*-moved NP need not be contained in the same clause as its trace (Chomsky 1981; Rizzi 1982). In Minimalist thinking the traces of such movements are nothing more than copies of the moved phrase that get deleted at PF (Chomsky [1993] and much related work). There is no reason why an AP or a VP cannot undergo copying just as well as an NP can; this formal relation is not intrinsically dependent on a referential index. We thus expect that APs and VPs should be able to undergo simple instances of *wh*-movement. This is correct, particularly for APs with the +*wh* degree head *how*:

(79)   a How tall is Chris?
   b How dangerous do they consider this intersection?
   c How clean did Kate wipe the table?

    d How carefully did they open the door?
    e Jak długą napisał Paweł sztukę? (Polish [Kennedy and Merchant 2000:
      how long wrote Paweł play   104])
      How long a play did Paweł write?

AP can indeed be moved from any position where it occurs: primary predicate positions ((79a,b)), resultative secondary predicate position ((79c)), adverbial position ((79d); see section 4.5), and attributive modifier position ((79e)). ((79e) is only possible in some determiner-less languages like Polish [Kennedy and Merchant 2000]. In English a +*wh* attributive A must trigger the movement of the NP containing it, a case of pied piping, for independent syntactic reasons.) There is no similar item that can mark a VP as +*wh*, and hence subject to question movement, at least in English. VPs can, however, take part in the form of topicalization known as VP-fronting, which is in the *wh*-movement family (Rizzi 1990):

(80)   (Nicholas promised he would clean his room, and) clean his room he did.

English also has a special type of fronting known as *though*-movement. This can apply to predicative noun phrases, but it can also apply perfectly well to APs and VPs:

(81)   a Genius though he is –, Fred could not answer the question in time.   (NP)
        b Tall though she is –, Sue could not reach the jar on the top shelf.   (AP)
        c Crying though he was –, the child still held tightly to his ice cream cone. (VP)

    The *wh*-movability of nonnominal phrases can also be seen in the characteristic movements of other languages. For example, APs as well as NPs can scramble leftward in Japanese, as shown in (82) (Hironobu Hosoi, personal communication), and in Hindi (Veneeta Dayal, personal communication):

(82)   a Heya-ga   hiro-ku   nat-ta   →   ?Hiro-ku   heya-ga   nat-ta.
        Room-NOM wide-AFF become-PAST wide-AFF room-NOM become-PAST
        'The room became wide.'
        b Taroo-ga   kami-o   mikika-ku kit-ta.
        Taro-NOM hair-ACC short-AFF   cut-PAST
        → Taroo-ga   mikika-ku kami-o   kit-ta.
          Taro-NOM   short-AFF hair-ACC cut-PAST
        → Mikika-ku Taroo-ga kami-o   kit-ta.
          short-AFF   Taro-NOM hair-ACC cut-PAST
        'Taro cut his hair short.'

In a similar way, APs as well as NPs can be topicalized in German, thereby appearing before the inflected auxiliary in second position (Alexandra Zepter, personal communication).

(83)   a Gross ist John ja doch.
          tall   is John indeed
          'John is tall.'
        b Gross werden sie John schon finden.
          tall   will   they John PRT   consider
          'They will find John tall.'
        c Flach sollte er das Metall schlagen.
          Flat   should he the metal pound
          'He should pound the metal flat.'

All this is as we expect.[26]

There are, however, other constructions in the *wh*-movement family that cannot apply to APs or VPs. These include relative clauses ((84)), clefts ((85)), and so-called *tough* movement constructions ((86)).

(84)   a John will give Mary *the flower* that he promised – to her. (NP)
          Chris is not *the genius* that Pat is –.
        b *Chris is not *clever* that Pat is –. (AP)
          *I will pound the metal *flat* that the foil is –.
        c *Chris will *sing* that Pat will –. (VP)
          *I made my students *solve the problem* that Mary made her students –.

(85)   a It's *this flower* that John will give Mary –. (NP)
        b ??It's flat as a pancake that I will pound the clay –. (AP)
          ??It's smart that Chris is.
        c *It's solve this problem that I made my students –. (VP)
          *It's sing that Mary will –.

(86)   a *This brand of candy* is hard to give – away. (NP)
        b *Clean as a whistle* is hard to wipe this table –. (AP)
          (compare: It's hard to wipe this table clean as a whistle.)
          *Sharp as a tack is hard to consider John – after that blunder.

---

[26] Heavy NP shift in English has been compared to scrambling in Japanese by Saito and Fukui (1998). It can also apply to AP, as in (i). Topicalization in Modern English may or may not be the same thing as the topicalization that triggers verb-second in German. Topicalizing an AP is not terrible, but neither is it very natural, as shown in (ii).

(i)   The man became – suddenly/in a flash as nice as you can imagine.
(ii)   ?As clean as a whistle, Mary wiped the table.

The uncertainty of the judgment in (ii) may reflect some indeterminacy as to whether topicalization involves simple movement, adjoining to IP, as in Lasnik and Saito (1992), or whether it involves a base-generated topic phrase and movement of a null operator, as in Chomsky (1977). On the latter analysis, it is similar to a cleft construction, and thus is ruled out for the reasons stated below.

c *Solve this problem is hard [to make students –].   (VP)
(compare: It's hard to make students solve this problem.)

The difference between these examples and those in (79)–(83) is that these are not *simple* cases of *wh*-movement. In standard P&P analyses of the (a) examples, it is not the italicized NP itself that undergoes *wh*-movement. Rather, the NP is base-generated in its surface position, and a syntactically distinct null operator moves from the position of the gap inside the embedded clause. This movement creates a semantically open expression, capable of being applied to the italicized NP. Finally, the null operator is coindexed with the italicized NP. This is necessary to assign a value to the null operator, so that it does not violate the ban on vacuous quantification (Chomsky 1982), now seen as a special case of Full Interpretation (Chomsky 1986b). The structure of (84a), for example, is (87a).

(87)   a John gave Mary [$_{NP}$ the flower$_{\{k,n\}}$ [Op$_{\{k\}}$ that he promised t$_{\{k\}}$ to her]].
b *I will pound the metal [$_{AP}$ flat [Op$_{\{k\}}$ that the foil is t$_{\{k\}}$]].
c *Chris will [$_{VP}$ sing [Op$_{\{k\}}$that Pat will t$_{\{k\}}$]].

Consider then the possibility of creating similar structures with APs and VPs, as in (87b,c). The movement relationship between the null operator and the AP- or VP-trace can be legitimate, just as it is in cases of simple *wh*-movement and scrambling. The problem is that the empty operator in these examples cannot be coindexed with the AP or VP that the clause is adjoined to, the adjoined-to phrase not bearing an index. The operator is left unspecified, and the construction is ruled out by the ban on vacuous quantification. From the semantic point of view, connecting a relative clause to its head involves making an identity claim: (84a), for example, says that what John gave to Mary was *the same flower* as that he promised to her. Since there is a sameness claim, there must be a standard of sameness, which is provided by the head of the relative. Therefore the head must have a criterion of identity, which is equivalent to saying it must be a noun projection given (1). The same reasoning applies to the other null operator constructions. I conclude that any category can undergo simple *wh*-style copy movement, but only NPs can participate in more complex constructions that involve a null operator.[27]

[27] There is an alternative analysis of relative clauses in which what is moved is not an empty operator but the NP that ends up as the head of the relative. This head-raising analysis was originally proposed by Vergnaud (1974), and has received a great deal of attention since Kayne (1995). If one adopts the head raising analysis, however, I cannot see a principled reason for saying that relative clauses pattern with clefts and tough movement rather than with question movement and scrambling in not tolerating nonnominal categories.

One construction that requires special discussion in this regard is so-called comparative deletion. This is perhaps the best-analyzed movement-like dependency that seems to involve an AP. Evidence that *wh*-movement is involved comes from the fact that the gap can be several clauses away from its AP antecedent, but cannot be separated from it by a syntactic island (Chomsky 1977):

(88) a Chris is as *smart* as Pat is.
      b Chris is as *smart* as [$_{CP}$ they say Pat is –]
      c Chris is as *smart* as [$_{CP}$ I heard [$_{CP}$ them say Pat is –]]
      d ??Chris is as *smart* as I heard [$_{NP}$ a rumor that Pat is –]
      e ??Chris is as *smart* as Mary complained [$_{CP-arg}$ because Pat is –]

This is somewhat surprising given what we have seen so far. By rights, comparative deletion should be a null operator construction, because the AP is interpreted twice within the thematic skeleton of the clause: the sentences in (88) say that Chris is smart and that Pat is smart. In this respect, comparative deletion is like relative clause formation and unlike scrambling or topicalization. This is indeed how comparative deletion is usually analyzed (Chomsky 1977; Kennedy 1999).[28] Nevertheless, (88a) is good, in marked contrast to (84b)–(86b).

The answer to this puzzle lies, I believe, in the fact that the gap of a comparative deletion construction cannot appear in all the positions that an AP can in English. The gap corresponds to the main predicate of a tensed clause in the grammatical sentences in (88). It can also correspond to the predicate of an argumental small clause:

(89) a Chris is as *smart* as Pat seems –
      b Chris is as *smart* as I consider Pat –.

The gap cannot, however, correspond to a resultative secondary predicate ((90)), or to an attributive modifier ((91)):[29]

---

[28] Lechner (1999) argues for an AP-raising analysis of comparative deletion, similar to Kayne's (1995) head-raising analysis of relativization. If he is correct in this, then the examples in (88) are no problem for my theory. It seems strange, however, to adopt a head-raising analysis for comparative deletion but a null operator analysis for relative clauses, given that most of the same conceptual and empirical considerations apply to both.
[29] These examples improve somewhat when the two clauses are syntactically parallel ((i)), and become perfect when ellipsis applies in the comparative clause ((ii)).

   (i)   a ?John wiped the table as clean as Mary wiped the chair –.
          b ?John wrote as long a letter as Mary wrote – a play.
   (ii)   a John wiped the table as clean as Mary did –.
          b John wrote as long a letter as Mary did –.

(90)   a *The copper is as *flat* as Chris beat the iron –.
        b ?*The table is cleaner than Pat wiped the chair –.

(91)   a *Mary is as kind as John is a – man.
        b *This basket is as expensive as that is a – dish.

Comparative deletion is different in this respect from question movement, scrambling, and topicalization, all of which can apply to resultative secondary predicates as well as to other APs. The distribution of comparative deletion in English is, however, perfectly parallel to the distribution of pronominal *so* as discussed in the preceding section; both are possible in all and only those environments in which the AP is immediately dominated by Pred. This falls into place if we say that the null operator in these examples is not of category AP after all, but rather is a PredP or some higher functional category that contains it. Indeed, the operator might well be a null allomorph of *so* itself. Clausal functional projections can bear referential indices, as we saw in our earlier study of pronouns. They can thus be coindexed with the corresponding functional category of the matrix clause, making comparative deletion possible. (92) gives structures for the grammatical (88a) and the deviant (90a).[30]

(92)   a Chris be+T $[_{FP_{[i]}}$ [t Pred [as [smart]]] [OP$_{[i]}$ as [Pat be+T $[_{FP_{[i]}}$ –]]]
        b The table be+T $[_{FP_{[i]}}$ [t Pred [as [clean]]] [Op$_{[i]}$ as [Pat wiped the chair $[_{AP_{[i]}}$ –]]]

(92a) is well formed, but (92b) is bad because a PredP/FP operator binds an AP position. If instead an AP operator were used in (92b), it could not be coindexed with a matching antecedent in the matrix clause. Comparatives can thus be handled in my theory, with some positive results.

Kennedy and Merchant (2000) argue that (iib) is good because the offending trace of the AP is eliminated by ellipsis before it triggers a violation, an idea that can be extended to (iia) as well. I would like to use this insight, but need to recast it because (at least for (iia)) the problem is not so much with the trace as with the relationship of the empty operator to the AP in the main clause. This could be done by saying that the null VP of the ellipsis construction is base-generated and is interpreted by some kind of reconstruction at the conceptual-intentional interface. Then there is no source position for an operator in the sentences of (ii), and hence no operator that needs an antecedent with an index. Spelling out the details of such an account might give interesting data about the exact sequence of steps through which conditions are checked and sentences are interpreted in the LF component, but I do not pursue this here. To the extent that the sentences in (i) are better than those in the text because of the syntactic parallelism, I assume that something like ellipsis happens in them too, with the destressed material in the second clause being equivalent to deleted material.

[30] These representations are possible because *than-* and *as*-clauses can attach to PredP/FP as well as to AP/DegreeP, I assume.

Empty operator constructions in other languages should also be restricted to NPs (or the projections of functional heads) as opposed to APs and VPs. There is good evidence that this is true for West African languages. Like other languages of this region, Edo has an often-used focus construction in which a focused NP appears at the front of the sentence followed by *òré*:

(93)   a Òzó lé   èvbàré.   (simple sentence)
          Ozo cook food
          'Ozo cooked some food.'
        b Èvbàré òré Òzó lé.   (cleft of object)
          food   it-be Ozo cook
          'It's food that Ozo cooked.'

This *òré* is not an atomic focus head; rather, it consists of the neuter subject pronoun *ọ* and the nominal copula *re* (Omoruyi 1989: 280). This is confirmed by the fact that in negative clefts the nonpast negative marker í comes between the pronominal part and the copular part, giving *è-í ré* (Omoruyi 1989: 289). The structure of the Edo focus construction is thus not too different from that of the English cleft. Therefore it too is presumably a null operator construction. This predicts that APs cannot be focused in Edo, which is true:

(94)   a *Khérhé òré   ágá   yé (khérhé).
          small   it-be chair be small
          'It's small that the chair is.'
        b *Pèrhè òré   Òzó gbé èmátọ̀n (pèrhè).
          flat   it-be Ozo beat metal flat
          'It's flat that Ozo beat the metal.'

Verbs, in contrast, apparently can be focused in the West African languages. The result is known as the predicate cleft construction, introduced to the generative literature by Koopman (1984) (she calls it "the *wh*-movement type of verb movement"). Recent investigations have, however, shown that it is not really the verb that is moving, but rather a nominalization of the verb. The morphology of Edo indicates this very clearly, in that the fronted copy of the verb must bear the *u*- plus *-mwẹn* circumfix that is otherwise found in event-denoting nominals (Stewart 2001):

(95)   Ù-lé-mwẹ̀n   òré Òzó lé   èvbàré.   (predicate cleft)
        NOML-cook-NOML   it-be Ozo cook food
        'It's cooking that Ozo did to the food.'
        (compare *ù-lé-mwẹ̀n óghé èvbàré* 'the cooking of food')

Stewart (1998: ch. 3) argues for a version of Manfredi's (1993) analysis of Yoruba, which says that what is actually moved in this construction is a cognate object that originates as a sister of the verb, inside VP. The predicate cleft expresses contrastive focus on the verb, but this cannot be done simply by clefting the verb directly; rather the verb must be nominalized. This otherwise peculiar requirement makes perfect sense if the syntax of empty operator constructions forces extracted elements to be nominal, so that the operator will have a legitimate antecedent. Nominalization is also seen overtly in the predicate clefts of Yoruba and Nupe (Ahmadu Kawu, personal communication on Nupe).[31] This attests to the crosslinguistic generality of the analysis.

The last major type of movement to consider is the movement of the head of a phrase to combine with the head of a higher phrase. This is a simple movement, which is semantically vacuous (Baker 1988a; 1996b) and does not involve a null operator. Nor is there any reason to classify the trace of such a movement as an anaphor; its strict locality follows from other considerations (the Head Movement Constraint, which is a corollary of Rizzi's [1990] Relativized Minimality condition and its descendants in the Minimalist Program). This kind of movement can therefore be treated as a simple case of copy and delete, and we expect it to be equally possible for all of the lexical categories. The literature bears this out. Nouns can certainly undergo head movement, whether to determiner positions as in the Semitic languages (Ritter [1991] and others) or incorporating into verbs as in Mohawk (Baker 1988a). Verbs undergo a comparable range of head movements: they move to tense and higher functional heads in languages like Vata (Koopman 1984), French (Pollock 1989), verb second languages like German (Travis 1984), and verb initial languages like Irish, and they incorporate into higher verbs in morphological causatives and similar constructions (Baker 1988a). Adjectives are the least familiar head-movers among the lexical categories, but there is evidence that this is possible as well. Adjectives can move to degree-type functional head positions in English ((96), see Corver [1997: 124–25]), and Borer (1991) argues that they can incorporate into a verbal head to form inchoative constructions in Hebrew ((97)).

(96)　　a Chris is [$_{QP}$ proud$_i$-er [$_{AP}$ t$_i$ of our children]]
　　　　b Pat is [$_{QP}$ angry$_i$ enough [$_{AP}$ t$_i$ at the boss]]

---

[31] The nominalization is not as obvious in the morphology of some other West African languages, including those Koopman originally studied. Cleft verbs in Vata, for example, do not have the *–lI* suffix found with event nominals (Koopman 1984: 20). They do, however, have a fixed mid tone in place of the tonal tense marking found on inflected verbs. This could be interpreted as a kind of nominalizing morphology. The same forms also take genitive case subjects in a related verbal relative construction (Koopman 1984: 156), suggesting that they are nominal.

(97)   ha-simla [$_{VP}$ hilbina(=A$_i$+V) [$_{AP}$ t$_i$ kmo gir]]   (Hebrew)
        the-dress   whitened   as   chalk
        'The dress became as white as chalk.'

All lexical categories thus undergo a similar range of head movements, as predicted.

   In summary, we find that some types of movement can apply to any lexical category, whereas others are restricted to nominal projections. The restricted ones are those that involve movement to subject, and hence create a theta-chain with an anaphoric trace, and those that connect two thematically relevant positions by way of a null operator. These relationships require a referential index to tie them together. In other situations, movement is simply a matter of copying and deleting, and is not limited to one type of category.

3.6   Nouns as arguments

The idea that only noun projections have a referential index has fairly obvious utility in explaining why only noun projections can antecede anaphors, pronouns, null operators, and certain kinds of traces. The next step is to use the same reasoning to explain an even more fundamental difference between the projections of nouns and those of other lexical categories: only nouns can serve as the subject or direct object of the clause.

   The basic facts in this domain are straightforward. (98a) shows that any kind of noun can appear in the subject position, including a singular count noun (*a mistake*), a bare plural (*errors*), or an abstract mass noun (*slander*). (98b) and (98c) show that neither an adjective nor a verb can be a subject unless they are nominalized.

(98)   a A mistake/errors in judgment/slander led to John's downfall.
        b *Proud led to John's downfall. (OK: Pride led ...)
        c *Brag led to John's downfall. (OK: Bragging led ...)

Note that *led* is a causative verb that puts very few selectional restrictions on its subject; this, together with the ease of interpreting these sentences when the subject is nominalized, suggests that (98b) and (98c) are not ruled out by simple semantic selection. The ungrammaticality of the verbal subject in (98c) is not too surprising. According to the theory defended in chapter 2, verbs must have a specifier, and this property is not satisfied in (98c). Once the specifier is added, together with the functional structure that is needed to license its case, the phrase becomes a clause, and such clauses can fill argument positions (e.g. *That John boasted led to his downfall*). The impossibility of adjectival subjects is more mysterious, however, since APs (apart from a Pred) do not take specifiers. The subject in (98b) is thus a thematically complete, saturated expression. Even so, it cannot be in argument position. The same contrast is found in Edo:

(99)   Èzúrọ̀ / *zùrọ̀zùrọ̀ gbé   Òzó.
      laziness$_N$ / lazy$_A$ killed   Ozo
      'Lazy-*(ness) killed Ozo.'

The basic difference can also be illustrated by comparing nationality adjectives to names of nations, following the lead of Kayne (1984a). Although the two can look like nearly synonymous expressions of the agent argument in derived nominals ((100a)), only the NP can express the agent in a clause ((100b)).

(100)   a Italy's / the Italian invasion of Albania
      b Italy/*Italian invaded Albania.
      c The invasion of Albania   compare: *Invaded Albania.

The contrast in (100b) is related to the basic difference between clauses and nominals shown in (100c): clauses need a grammatical subject, whereas nominals do not (Chomsky 1981). (100b) with the adjective is out for the same reason as the subjectless clause in (100c), given that APs are not qualified to be syntactic subjects. In contrast, (100a) with the adjective is good for the same reason as the nominal in (100c) is: (100a) does not have a syntactic subject (only an AP), but as a nominal it does not need one.

The same contrast between nouns and the other lexical categories is found in direct object positions ((101)) and inside prepositional phrases ((102)).

(101)   a I admire a good joke / women that stand up for themselves / fine wine.
      b *I admire sincere. (OK: *sincerity*)
      c *I admire sing.   (OK: *good singing*)

(102)   a I'm looking for a unicorn/diamonds/gold.
      b *I'm looking for happy. (OK: *happiness*)
      c *I'm looking for advance. (OK: *advancement*)

Again, similar contrasts can be found in Edo. In general, adjectival roots in Edo can appear in argument position only if they are nominalized by a vowel prefix, as in (99), or if they are preceded by a determiner, as in (44). In the latter case, they are really attributive modifiers of a null noun licensed by that determiner, as argued in section 3.3. This pattern of facts is found in many languages that have a determiner system, including the Mayan language Tzutujil ((103)), Italian (Longobardi 1994), and Moroccan Arabic (Bhat 1994), to name a few.

(103)   a Nwaajo7 ya7.   (Tzutujil)   (Daley 1985: 282)
              I.want.it water
              'I want water.'
          b Nwaajo7 *(ja) kaq.
              I.want.it the   red
              'I want the red one.'

Examples like (101) and (102) show that a treatment of (98) in terms of special properties of the subject position would not be adequately general. In Minimalist work it is common to explain the surface position of subjects in English by saying that tense has "a strong D feature" that must enter into a checking relationship with a DP before Spell Out. This approach might automatically rule out (98), but does not naturally extend to (101) and (102). The correct generalization seems to be that NPs but not APs or VPs can receive thematic roles.

An easy way to derive this asymmetry between nouns and the other categories would be to follow Longobardi (1994) and say that expressions in argument positions must be DPs. We already know from section 3.3 that only an NP can be the complement of a D head, so it would follow from this that each argument must contain a noun as its ultimate semantic head. But I have already rejected Longobardi's approach, arguing (in agreement with Chierchia [1998]) that bare NPs can also occupy argument positions in many languages. If bare NPs can do this, then why cannot VPs or APs? I therefore need another angle on this question.

Even if NPs do not necessarily need to be embedded in DPs in order to be arguments, it could be that the referential index that makes them possible complements of Ds also makes them possible arguments. Why would that be? An attractive answer comes from Williams' (1989) proposal that theta-roles are inherently anaphoric, linked to the phrase that receives the thematic role in essentially the same way that an anaphor like *themselves* is linked to its antecedent. This idea takes quite literally the common notational device (with origins in Stowell [1981]) of expressing the theta-roles of a verb as an ordered list (called a theta-grid) and coindexing each theta-role in the list with a suitable NP in the neighborhood of the verb:

(104) $Chris_k$ will eat a $sandwich_n$
              $<Ag_k, Th_n>$

(If a transitive verb like eat is decomposed into three parts [v, V, and A], as in section 2.9, then the agent role is associated with v, and the theme role with V.

We can safely abstract away from this for the moment, however.) There is indeed a strong parallelism between the core properties of anaphoric dependencies and those of theta-role assignment. First, anaphors must have a syntactic antecedent; similarly, theta-roles must be related to a phrase in the syntactic structure:

(105) a *Chris$_n$ hit themselves$_k$ (An anaphor must have an antecedent.)
       b *Chris$_n$ hit<Ag$_n$, Th$_k$>   (A theta-role must have an argument.)

In the theta-theoretic domain, this is commonly known as (part of) the theta criterion. Second, the antecedent of an anaphor must c-command it; the antecedent cannot be embedded in some other constituent of the clause, for example. The same is true of theta-role assignment: NPs that are sisters of projections of the verb can receive a theta-role from the verb, but NPs that are embedded in these NPs cannot:

(106) a *[John's$_n$ mother]$_k$ criticized himself$_n$.   (Antecedent must c-command anaphor.)
       b #[Chris's$_n$ pot]$_k$ broke<Ag$_n$, Th$_k$>   (Argument must c-command V.)
          (intended meaning: 'Chris broke the pot'.)

Third, the antecedent of an anaphor must be within a local domain of the anaphor; roughly, they must be clause-mates. Similarly, a phrase can receive a theta-role from a verb only if they are clause-mates:

(107) a *John$_n$ said that Mary criticized himself$_n$.   (Antecedent must be local to anaphor.)
       b *Chris$_n$ seems that the pot$_k$ broke<Ag$_n$, Th$_k$> (Argument must be local to V.)
          (intended meaning: 'It seems that Chris broke the pot.')

Thus, there are substantive similarities between theta-role assignment and anaphora that justify using partially the same theory for both.[32]

Suppose then that theta-role assignment is a species of anaphora. I showed in section 3.4 that NPs can be antecedents for anaphors by virtue of having a referential index, but APs and VPs cannot. Therefore, it follows that NPs can also receive theta-roles, but APs and VPs cannot. An AP or VP does not have what is needed to establish the relevant kind of relation with the theta-role of the verb, as shown in (108) (these are simplified S-structures, abstracting away from neo-Larsonian predicate decomposition and the VP internal subject hypothesis).

---

[32] I do not mean to imply that Binding theory provides a complete theory of theta-role assignment. There could well be additional conditions on theta-roles that do not hold of other kinds of anaphora, enforcing an even stricter locality, for example.

(108)   a.   b.

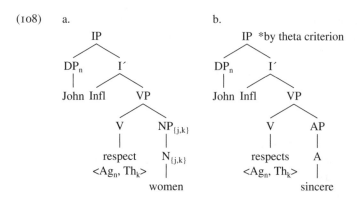

Continuing the parallelism between anaphora and theta-role assignment out-
lined in the previous paragraph, (109b) (= (100b)) is bad for the same reason
as (109a) (= (55)).

(109)   a *The Italian destruction of itselfₙ.   (Antecedent of anaphor cannot be AP.)
        b *Italian destroyed<Agₙ, Thₖ> Albaniaₖ.   (Argument cannot be AP.)

This analysis can also be seen from a semantic perspective, emphasizing
the role of the criterion of identity that underwrites the presence of referential
indices. Like anaphora, theta-role assignment makes an identity claim. To say
that in a sentence like *A man arrived* the NP *a man* is the theme of *arrive* is
essentially to say that something that is a man is the same as the something that
arrived. This is usually expressed logically as (110a), but an equivalent logical
representation would be (110b).

(110)   a $\exists x (^\cup man(x)$ and $arrive(x))$
        b $\exists x, y (^\cup man(x)$ and $arrive(y)$ and $x = y)$

The more articulated logical formula in (110b) would be forced by the following
principle, which I take to be an axiom of the grammar (I have further use for it
in chapter 4):

(111)   If X and Y are distinct lexical heads, then the variables associated with them
        in a semantic representation are distinct (unless there is explicit marking to
        the contrary).[33]

---

[33] Conjunctions like *and* might be one way of marking that the variables associated with the two
conjuncts are the same. (111) is conceptually somewhat similar to Reinhart's and Reuland's
(1993) Binding theory, which observes that two arguments of a single predicate are understood
as different unless there is explicit reflexive marking to the contrary. The two might be collapsible
into one overarching condition, but I do not pursue this here.

Given (111), one can only say *A man arrived* if there is a separate identity claim that says that the distinct variables introduced by *man* and *arrive* correspond to the same entity. But natural language does not use a universal standard of sameness; rather, a standard of sameness must be provided by some common noun. Therefore, it must be a noun projection that is involved in the thematic relationship with the theta-role bearing verb (or other head). The expression "x = y" in (110b) should really be "same(man)(x,y)" –x is the same man as y.

Block-castle examples confirm that the particular criterion of identity associated with a given noun plays an important role in constructions that involve theta-role assignment. Suppose that the demonstrative subject points to what is on the family room floor in both (112a) and (112b). One nevertheless cannot infer (112d) from (112c).

(112)   a That is a block set.
        b That is a castle.
        c Nicholas made the castle.
        d *Not*: Nicholas made the block set.

On a theory that ignores the criterion of identity, the inference should be valid, because (113d) follows trivially from (113a–c).

(113)   a x/$^\cup$block-set(x)
        b x/$^\cup$castle(x)
        c x/made(Nicholas, x) and $^\cup$castle(x)
        d x/made(Nicholas, x) and $^\cup$block-set(x)

If, however, one uses formulas like (110b) that follow principle (111) and make use of the criterion of identity, then the inference turns out to be invalid, as it should be.

(114)   a x/$^\cup$blockset(x)
        b x/$^\cup$castle(x)
        c x/$\exists$y [made(Nicholas, y) & $^\cup$castle(x) & same(castle)(x, y)]
        d x/$\exists$y [made(Nicholas, y) & $^\cup$block-set(x) & same(block-set)(x, y)]

The inference is invalid because one cannot conclude from the fact that two things count as the same castle that they count as the same block set, or vice versa. The criterion of identity of a noun therefore plays a crucial role in the knitting together of elements in a clause known as theta-role assignment. Adjectives and verbs do not have criteria of identity; for them, an expression like "same(X)(x,y)" is undefined. As and Vs therefore cannot play the same knitting-together function. In other words, they cannot receive thematic roles.

This discussion has taken it for granted that the theta-role assigning powers of a verb (or other head) are expressed in the form of a theta-grid, as in Stowell (1981). An alternative view has arisen in recent years, thanks to the work of Hale and Keyser (1993). Hale and Keyser propose to identify theta-roles with syntactic configurations in a one-to-one fashion. For example, the configuration [X [v VP]] is equivalent to X being an agent; the configuration [X [V AP]] is equivalent to X being a theme, and so on. Their proposal is motivated by two basic observations. First, natural languages seem to have roughly the same number of distinct thematic roles as they have distinguishable syntactic positions given X-bar theory and a small number of syntactic categories. Second, it seems that theta-roles are consistently assigned to particular syntactic positions (the UTAH [Baker 1988a]). Both of these properties follow immediately if theta-roles simply *are* configurations. In that case, there seems to be no need for a distinct representational device such as the theta-grid. But eliminating theta-grids as redundant would take away the foundations of my account of why only noun projections can be arguments.

The Hale and Keyser approach has attractive features, and I have integrated aspects of it into my theory. In particular, I agree that the agent corresponds strictly to the [X [v VP]] position, and the theme to the [X [V AP]] position. It may also be the case that once the heads are broken up into their component parts, no head assigns more than one theta-role. If so, there is less for a theta-grid to say than there was in Stowell's original formulation. It is not clear, however, that theta-grids are entirely redundant in this system. Even if they are, there is still a variant of my proposal that gives the intended result. Phrase structure configurations are pieces of syntax, and thematic roles are aspects of semantics and/or conceptual structure. Therefore, as I observed in chapter 2, they cannot, strictly speaking, be the same things; this would be confusing two distinct levels of representation. At most there could be an isomorphism between the two levels. This would mean that there would be correspondence rules roughly like the following:[34]

(115)   a $[X [v VP]] \leftrightarrow \exists e, x, y [VP(e) \ \& \ Agent(e, x) \ \& \ ^{\cup}X(y) \ \& \ same(X)(x, y)]$
        b $[X [V AP]] \leftrightarrow \exists s, x, y [AP(s) \ \& \ Theme(s, x) \ and \ ^{\cup}X(y) \ \& \ same(X)(x,y)]$

Here each syntactic configuration corresponds to a specific thematic predicate. Then there are no indices in the syntax; the verb and its argument are related simply by virtue of standing in a particular phrase-structural relationship. Any

---

[34] I got the idea of handling theta-roles in this way from comments by Paul Pietroski, made at a semantics workshop at Rutgers University in September 1999.

kind of category could in principle go into the X slot in these configurations as far as syntax itself is concerned. The thematic predicates in the semantic formula are inherently relational, however, so their argument positions still need to be related to those of the other expressions in the formula by way of identity conditions. X must therefore supply a standard of identity that makes the expression "same(X)(x,y)" coherent. In other words, X must be a noun projection. The same result follows, but at a different level of representation (and without assuming that theta-role assignment is anaphora). This is a specific instance of the orthodox Minimalist option of keeping referential indices out of the syntax by building their effects into the interface between the syntax and the conceptual-intentional system. I consider this a live option, but continue to use the syntactically explicit version with indices and theta-grids, because it is more perspicuous. The crucial point is that Ns differ from As and Vs with respect to theta-role assignment in the same way as they differ with respect to anaphora, regardless of whether the parallelism is best captured in the syntax proper or beyond it.

The claim that APs and VPs never receive theta-roles does not entail that they can never appear in the same syntactic positions as NPs do. APs and VPs can apparently serve as the complements of a handful of verbs in English. *Make*, for example, can take a VP instead of an NP, as shown in (116) and many examples in chapter 2:

(116)   a I made Julia *a sandwich*.
        b I made Julia *eat her sandwich*.

In a similar way, APs seem to be internal arguments of a few semantically special verbs like *seem, feel,* and *consider,* as in (117).[35]

(117)   a Chris seems intelligent.
        b Chris feels sad.
        c I consider Chris intelligent.

There are two ways that such examples can be analyzed within my system. First, what appears to be an AP or VP could really be a PredP or some larger functional phrase, the head of which happens to be phonologically null. Functional phrases of a clausal nature can bear referential indices and participate in anaphora and null operator movement, as shown in the previous two sections.

[35] See section 4.4 for an analysis of resultative secondary predicates like *Chris wiped the table clean*, in which the AP seems to have a selectional relationship to the verb and appears in roughly the same position as an argument PP or the second object of a dative construction.

It is therefore expected that they can receive a thematic role as well. This is a plausible analysis of the examples in (117), in particular.

The second possibility is that the nonnominal complement of the verb is licensed not by receiving a theta-role, but rather by entering into a relationship of complex predicate formation with the complement-taking verb. There are constructions in which even the nominal complement of a verb does not get a theta-role from the verb; these are the so-called light verb constructions found in Japanese ((118)), as well as Korean, Hindi/Urdu, and other languages.

(118)   a John-wa   murabito-ni [ookami-ga kuru-to-no   keikoku]-o shi-ta.
            John-TOP villager-DAT wolf-NOM come-COMP-GEN warn-ACC do-PAST
            'John warned the villagers that the wolf was coming.'
         b John-ga   Mary-kara [hooseki-no   ryakudatu]-o   kokoromi-ta.
            John-NOM Mary-from jewelry-GEN plunderage-ACC attempt-PAST
            'John attempted to steal jewelry from Mary.'

Saito and Hoshi (1998) and Saito (2000) analyze this construction as involving the incorporation of the noun into the light verb (possibly at LF) so that the two form a kind of complex head. The two parts of the complex head then jointly theta-mark arguments. Saito and Hoshi's premises are given in (119).

(119)   a The need for theta-role assignment can trigger head movement (at LF).
         b Both X and Y can assign a theta-role to NP in the following configuration:

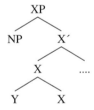

This proposal captures nicely the fact that the event-denoting noun must always be the syntactic direct object of the light verb (note the accusative case on 'warn' and 'plunderage' in (118)). The complement / direct object position is the only one from which the noun could incorporate into the light verb, given the head movement constraint. This then is a second way of having a complement that satisfies full interpretation; the complement is not present to get a theta-role from the main verb, but rather to join with the verb in assigning theta-roles.

Now it so happens that VPs and APs that seem to bear a thematic relation to a main verb are always the complements of the main verb, never its specifier or oblique argument. (120) illustrates this. The complement of a causative verb can

be either an TP/CP or a bare VP, depending on the verb ((120a,b)). The subject
of a causative verb can also be an TP/CP, as in (120c). What is impossible is
for the subject of causation to be a bare VP ((120d)).

(120)   a She would cause John to smile.   (TP/CP complement)
        b She would make John smile.   (VP complement)
        c (For the president) to smile would cause a commotion. (TP/CP subject)
        d *(The president) smile would make a commotion. (*VP subject)

This restriction on the distribution of bare VPs parallels the light verb construction in (118), strongly suggesting that they too are licensed by having their
head incorporate into the main verb, in accordance with (119). This gives a
plausible way of analyzing (116b) and (120b): *make* assigns a theme role to the
causee, and the lower verb assigns an agent role to it after LF-incorporation.
(120d) is bad because the VP subject does not have a referential index to link
it to a theta-role, neither can its head incorporate into *make* so it can assign a
theta-role.[36]

   In other languages, apparent counterexamples to the claim that APs cannot
be arguments stem from the fact that adjectives can sometimes be modifiers of
null nouns, as argued in section 3.3 above. When this happens, the adjective-
plus-null-noun combination can perfectly well appear in an argument position,
thanks to the index associated with the null noun. In English, the null noun must
be licensed by the overt determiner *the*, but other languages – especially those
without articles – are not subject to this restriction. In such a language, it can
seem that nouns and adjectives can equally well be arguments. The Australian
language Mayali is a case in point. Morphological properties make it fairly clear
that adjectives form a distinct class from nouns in Mayali: nouns in Mayali
have inherent gender, expressed by a prefix, whereas adjectives vary in gender
depending on what noun they agree with (Evans 1991). Superficially, it looks
like the object of a verb can be either a noun, as in (121a), or an adjective, as in
(121b).

---

[36] Some instances of apparent VP or AP complementation can plausibly be analyzed either as
   selection for a functional head that contains the VP/AP or as a case of complex predicate formation. For example, Stowell (1991) argues that the adjectives in examples like (117) incorporate
   into the verb to form complex predicates in English. If this is correct, then they are licensed by
   (119), in which case there is no need to posit a Pred. I will not attempt to find criteria that can
   systematically distinguish these two possibilities here.
      According to section 2.9, APs are almost always complements to a V underlyingly. This too
   is licensed by (119), given that the A incorporates into (conflates with) V to derive a lexical
   verb. Strictly speaking, the A does not assign a theta-role by itself, but it becomes a theta-role
   assigner by virtue of incorporation into Pred or V.

(121)   a Aban-yawoyh-warrkah-marne-kinje-ng   kun-kanj   (Evans 1997: 399)
           1/3pO-again-wrong-BEN-cook-PAST / PUNC   NCL-meat
           'I cooked the wrong meat for them again.'
        b Kandi-wo-Ø   man-kuyeng!   (Evans 1997: 401)
           2/1-give-IMPER NCL-long
           'You give me the long one!'

My theory predicts that there must be some covert structure in (121b): the
adjective must modify a phonologically null noun, comparable to English *one*,
which is the true head of the direct object. Confirmation that this is so comes
from incorporation. Mayali allows direct objects to be incorporated into the
verb, as shown in (122).

(122)   Abanmani-ganj-wo-ng.   (Evans 1991: 287)
        1/3dO-meat-give-PAST/PUNC
        'I gave meat to the two of them.'

If the adjective in (121b) were really an AP direct object with no hidden structure, we might expect that it too could incorporate into the verb; formally there
would be nothing to prevent this. My theory, however, predicts that this type of
adjective incorporation should be impossible. The head movement constraint
implies that one can never incorporate the attributive modifier of a noun to form
a A_k+V [$_{NP}$ t_k N] structure; such configurations are never found with an overt
noun, and the noun being phonologically null should make no difference. In
fact, Mayali does not seem to allow incorporation of "adjectival objects," in
support of my prediction.

(123)   *Kandi-kuyeng-wo-Ø!   (see Evans [1997: 404–5])
        2/1-long-give-IMPER
        'You give me the/a long one!'

The fundamental fact that NPs can be arguments but APs (and VPs) cannot is
partly disguised in simple sentences in Mayali, but the difference is revealed
by incorporation.

Other languages in which "adjectives" seem to be arguments are precisely
those that create doubt that the adjective–noun distinction is universal –
languages like Quechua, Nahuatl, and Greenlandic Eskimo. Incorporation is
a useful test for revealing that there is a noun–adjective distinction in these
languages as well, but I defer showing this until section 3.9.

3.7   Nouns must be related to argument positions

So far, my focus has been on things that noun projections can do that other categories cannot because they have criteria of identity and referential indices: they can form true plurals, they can be complements to determiners and quantifiers, they can antecede pronouns, they can undergo a full range of movements, and they can appear in argument positions. But with privileges come responsibilities. I turn now to the other side of the coin: things that a noun cannot do because of its referential index. Having a referential index makes it possible for noun projections to be related to pronominals, operators, and theta-roles by way of coindexing. I now propose to strengthen this to say that nouns and their projections *must* be coindexed with something else:

(124)   *The Noun Licensing Condition (NLC):*
         The second member of a referential index must be systematically identical to some dependent index in the structure that its bearer c-commands.

By a *dependent index* here I mean the index of an element that does not have intrinsic lexical content of its own: a theta-role, a pronominal, a trace, or a null operator. Also note that the indices associated with each projection of a noun count as a single index for purposes of the NLC. This is natural within the Bare Phrase Structure conception of things, in which the labels of larger phrases are constructed directly from the substance of their parts.

Conceptual grounding for NLC comes from the idea that noun projections bear indices because they have a criterion of identity, because they function as standards of sameness. This was my reason for conceiving of referential indices as pairs of integers, not as single integers. One of these integers – by convention, the first – is the new discourse referent contributed by each use of a nominal expression (compare Kamp and Reyle [1993]). But the second integer has a distinct role, identifying the new discourse referent with something else in the structure. It is often said that the canonical function of noun projections is to refer (Croft 1991; Bhat 1994), but the idea here is slightly different. The fundamental job of nouns is the more relational task of binding structures together and tracking sameness and difference of reference. As such, nouns must always be related to something else.

The NLC is closely related to part of Chomsky's (1981) theta criterion. The first part, that theta-roles must be assigned, I expressed by saying that theta-roles are anaphors, following Williams (1989). The NLC captures the second part, saying that argument-type categories – typically NPs – must receive a thematic role from some head or the equivalent. In my representation scheme, an NP receives a theta-role from a head X if and only if the NP is coindexed with something in the theta-grid of X and NP minimally c-commands X (i.e. they are structural sisters). This is the most obvious and important way of satisfying the NLC. As such, the NLC accounts for the badness of examples like those in (125).

(125)   a *The guests$_{\{i,k\}}$ smiled<Ag$_k$> a chicken$_{\{n,m\}}$.
         b *Some people$_{\{i,k\}}$ seem<SM$_j$> [$_{CPj}$ that the chairman$_{\{n,m\}}$ left<Th$_m$>].

The NLC is somewhat broader than the traditional theta criterion, however, in that it leaves open the possibility that there might be elements other than theta-grids which an NP can be coindexed with and thus licensed. This seems warranted. Consider, for example, the tough movement alternation in (126), as discussed by Chomsky (1981) and others.

(126)   a It is easy to fool some people.
         b Some people are easy to fool –.

Since place-holder *it* is in the subject position of the matrix clause in (126a), this particular Pred-plus-adjective combination seems to have no theta-role to assign to the Spec, PredP. Nevertheless, a meaningful NP appears in this position in (126b). This NP is not thematically related to the matrix adjective, but rather to the object position in the embedded clause by way of a *wh*-movement dependency. The usual P&P analysis is that the subject in (126b) is licensed by being coindexed with a null operator that moved from the object position into the specifier of the embedded clause, as shown in (127b).

(127)   a it is easy<SM$_k$> [$_{CPk}$ PRO$_{\{arb,i\}}$ to fool<Ag$_i$, Th$_n$> some people$_{\{m,n\}}$]
         b some people$_{\{m,n\}}$ are easy<SM$_k$> [$_{CPk}$ Op$_n$ PRO$_{\{arb,i\}}$ to fool<Ag$_i$, Th$_n$> t$_n$]

Chomsky's (1981) formulation of the theta criterion forced him to posit a powerful restructuring rule that made *easy to fool* into a kind of complex predicate that theta-marks the subject. This artifice is superfluous once we adopt the more general statement in (124): the coindexing of the matrix subject with the null operator can count as licensing the subject NP all by itself, without completely subsuming the relationship to theta-role assignment.[37]

---

[37] For a complete account of *tough*-movement, one would want to explain why this kind of operator-licensing is possible with predicates like *easy*, but not with other predicates that are thematically similar, like *likely* (*Chris is likely to catch*). But this is a quasi-independent issue that every theory must face. Part of the answer could be that the kind of infinitival tense that *likely* selects fails to license the PRO subject.

The NLC also accounts for an important difference between NPs and other categories in many languages. PPs of various kinds can often be freely adjoined to the beginning of a clause as a topic or as some kind of scene-setting expression. Adjectives in their adverb guise can also be left-adjoined to clauses (see section 4.5). NPs too can appear in this position, but they are subject to an additional condition: they must be related to a pronoun inside the clause (called dislocation) or to a gap (called topicalization). Thus, in English one finds the following pattern:

(128) a On the mountain, the trees are beautiful.   (PP)
        b Honestly, the trees are beautiful.   (AP)
        c ?*This mountain, the trees are beautiful.   (NP-no link)
        d This mountain, the trees on it are beautiful.   (NP-with pronoun)
        e This mountain, people visit – to look at the trees.   (NP-with gap)

This contrast can be replicated in many other languages, including Mohawk ((129), from Baker [1996b]) and Chichewa ((130)).

(129) a Thíkʌ o-nut-á-'ke   yó-hskats   ne okwire'-shú'a.
          that   NsO-hill-Ø-LOC NsO-be.pretty NE tree-PLUR
          'On that hill, the trees are pretty.'
        b *Thíkʌ onúta', yó-hskats   ne okwire'-shú'a.
          that   hill   NsO-be.pretty NE tree-PLUR
          '(As for) that hill, the trees are pretty.'
        c Thíkʌ onúta', í-k-ehr-e'   tsi Sak wa-há-kʌ-'.
          that   hill   Ø-1sS-think-IMPF that Sak FACT-MsS/(NsO)-see-PUNC
          'That hill, I think that Sak saw (it).'

(130) a Ku San Jose ndi-ma-sung-a   galimoto y-anga m'garaji.
          At-San Jose 1sS-HAB-keep-FV 9.car   9-my   in-garage
          'In San Jose, I keep my car in the garage.'   (Bresnan 1991)
        b *?Mkango uwu fisi   a-na-dy-a   iwo
          lion   this hyena 3sS-PAST-eat-FV it
          'This lion$_k$, the hyena ate it$_n$.'   (Bresnan and Mchombo 1987: 749)
        c Alenje   njuchi zi-na-wa-lum-a   (pro).
          2.Hunters 10.bees 10S-PAST-2O-bite-FV
          The hunters$_k$, the bees bit them$_k$.'   (Bresnan and Mchombo 1987: 745)

These contrasts are a direct consequence of the NLC: NPs as bearers of referential indices must be coindexed with some index-bearing element within the clause. This explains the ungrammaticality of the (128c), (129b), and (130b), in contrast to (128d,e), (129c), and (130c). Since PPs and APs need not bear referential indices (although the NP inside them does, coindexed with the theta-role of the P), they are not subject to this condition, so (128a,b), (129a), and

(130a) are fine. These contrasts do not follow from the theta criterion strictly speaking, but they do follow from my generalization of it. My account is very similar to Bresnan and Mchombo's (1987), where their "Extended Coherence Condition" has essentially the same relation to LFG's original Coherence Condition as the NLC has to Chomsky's theta criterion. (Bresnan and Mchombo do not explicitly discuss the NP–PP contrast, however, or how the Extended Coherence Condition applies to PP-like constituents.)

The so-called topic prominent languages of East Asia (Li and Thompson 1976) seem to work differently in this respect. In these languages, an NP can appear at the front of the clause, without any obvious relationship to anything inside the clause. (131) is a famous example from Japanese.

(131)   Nihon-wa / ga   dansei-ga   tanmei   desu.   (Kuno 1973: 67)
         Japan-TOP / NOM   male-NOM   short.lived are
         '(As for) Japan, men have a short life-span.'

The possibility of examples like (131) in East Asian languages makes the un-grammaticality of sentences like (128c), (129b), and (130b) in most other languages particularly striking. The question now is what is the nature of the parameter that makes sentences like (131) possible only in certain languages? Japanese clearly has nouns as a distinct lexical category, so I need to say that the topic phrase bears a referential index. It is implausible to say that the NLC does not hold in these languages; that would be tantamount to saying that the theta criterion is turned off for these languages, which would be a radical move with many unintended consequences. The simplest account would be simply to say that the topic marker *–wa* is the equivalent of a postposition in Japanese. On this interpretation, (131) with *–wa* would be grammatical for the same reason that (128a), (129a), and (130a) are. Most of the topic prominent languages that Li and Thompson discuss have an overt topic particle that can play this role, comparable to the complex preposition *as for* in English. This does not extend, however, to Chinese, in which the topic is a bare NP, or to those Japanese sentences in which the topic is marked only with nominative case. For these cases, I tentatively suggest that the topic NP is coindexed with the comment clause as a whole, giving the representation in (132).

(132)   nihon-ga$_{\{i,k\}}$ [$_{CP_i}$ dansei-ga$_{\{j,n\}}$ tanmei   desu<Th$_n$>].
         Japan-NOM   male-NOM   short.lived are
         'As for Japan, men have a short life-span.'

The idea that a CP can bear a referential index is not novel; we saw in previous sections that this must be so, because clauses can be the antecedents of pronouns, they can undergo movement, and they can receive thematic roles. The special property of topic prominent languages is that they allow an NP and a CP to be coindexed in this way even when there is no operator in the specifier of CP, the dependency being interpreted as an "aboutness" relationship. This account predicts that this second type of topic in Japanese *must* be an NP, because no other lexical category could be coindexed with a clause in this way. This is correct: PPs can be *wa*-marked topics in Japanese (Kuno 1973: 243–45), but they cannot be *ga*-marked topics:

(133)   *New York-(ni)-ga   gakusei-ga   itta.   (Kuno 1973: 77)
         New York-(to)-NOM   students-NOM   went
         'It's New York that the students went to.'

I also predict that the bare topics in Chinese can only be NPs. This is consistent with Li and Thompson's (1976) examples and discussion, although they do not state this explicitly. If this is on the right track, it constitutes another case in which an NP need not get a thematic role in the narrow sense, but is nevertheless licensed by a coindexing relationship.

The NLC can also be used to account for the fact that NPs cannot by themselves constitute a matrix clause, although VPs and PredPs can. A priori, one would think that this should be possible, particularly for indefinite NPs. An indefinite NP used in a sentence has the function of introducing a new discourse referent as well as saying something about the eventuality it was involved in. For example, *A dragon arrived* says that there was a dragon and that dragon arrived; this is often expressed as a formula like $\exists x\ [^{\cup}dragon(x)\ \&\ arrive(x)]$. Now suppose that one only wanted to introduce a dragon into the discussion, without (yet) saying anything about it. The contribution of the verb *arrived* to the formula is the "arrived(x)" part. Subtracting this, it seems that one ought to be able to assert that there was a dragon simply by uttering the expression *A dragon*. But this is impossible in English. Rather, the indefinite NP must be used as the complement of a verb, even though the verb is virtually meaningless:[38]

---

[38] An apparent counterexample to this generalization is discourses like: *Look! A dragon! It is about to burn the village!* Such discourses are crucially different from the ones in the text in that they must be accompanied by a gesture or other form of deixis. I conjecture that the NP in such examples is really a predicate nominal with its subject omitted; it is short for *Look! It* (the thing I'm pointing to) *is a dragon!* I do not, however, have any decisive evidence to prove this.

  An NP can also stand as a complete utterance when answering a content question. For example, one can respond to *What just flew by?* with *A dragon*. I assume that such utterances are elliptical

(134)   a *(A) dragon. It was big and fierce. It burned down the town.
        b Once there was a dragon. It was big and fierce. It burned down the town.

The same is true in other languages. (135) gives an equivalent contrast in Edo.

(135)   a *Òkpìá. Ọ̀ ghá!á kpọ́!lọ́. Ọ́ dé   ímọ́tò.
          Man   he PAST big   he bought car
          'A man. He was big. He bought a car.'
        b Òkpìá ókpá na   dòó   ghá rró!ó. Ọ̀ ghá!á kpọ́!lọ́. Ọ́...
          man   one PRT INCEP ASP be   he PAST big   he...
          'There was a certain man. He was big. He...'

In the same way, an existential verb is required in addition to an indefinite noun
to make an existential assertion in the wide range of languages in (136).

(136)   a Onʌ'ya tut-ká-yʌ.   (Mohawk)
          rock   DUP-CIS-NsS-lie
          'There is a rock there.'
        b Nge-la-y   chadi.   (Mapuche [Smeets 1989])
          be-NEG-3s salt
          'There is no salt.'
        c Guäha buteya gi hälum kähun áis.   (Chamorro)
          Exist bottle inside box   ice
          'There's a bottle in the icebox.'
        d Masa-nɪn üst-ün-de   šarap var. (Turkish [Kuno 1973: 395])
          table-GEN top-POSS-LOC wine is
          'There is wine on the table.'

I know of no language in which this is not the case. For languages like English,
one might think that nominal existential utterances are ruled out by a general
need to express tense overtly. But this would not be general enough, since many
languages do allow verbless sentences with no (overt) tense specification when
a predicate noun is predicated of a subject, as in (137).

(137)   Onʌ'ya thíkʌ.   (Mohawk)
        rock   that
        'That is a rock.'

Nevertheless, even languages that allow sentences like this do not allow bare
NPs as existential sentences. The NLC draws the relevant distinction. The NPs

forms of the full-sentence answer *A dragon flew by*, in which the NP is licensed by being
coindexed with a theta-role of the verb in the usual way. This fits with the fact that in case-rich
languages the NP answer typically bears the case marking it should have as part of the complete
sentence. I leave open how this kind of ellipsis should be handled in detail.

in (134)–(136) clearly have referential indices, since the whole point of the utterance is to introduce a new discourse referent. They are not, however, coindexed with anything in their c-command domain; therefore, they are bad. In contrast, the predicate nominal in a sentence like (137) can be coindexed with its subject (and vice versa) in a way I return to in the next section; hence the two nominal projections license each other for purposes of the NLC.

In summary, an NP's having a referential index not only gives it the possibility of being related to a theta-position, but also the necessity of being so related, either directly (the ordinary theta criterion) or indirectly by binding a pronoun, trace, or operator. Chapter 4 makes further use of the Noun Licensing Condition to explain why adjectives but not nouns can be attributive modifiers and resultative secondary predicates.

3.8   Predicate nominals and verbalization

One further domain my theory can be applied to is derivational morphology. In section 2.9, I discussed how verbs can be derived from adjectival roots. (Indeed, I claimed that all verbs are ultimately derived in this way.) In section 3.1, however, I mentioned that verbs apparently cannot be derived from nouns in the same way. Thus, in English we have *The door opened* and *The wind opened the door* corresponding to *The door is open*, but we do not have *John manned* or *The battle manned John* corresponding to *John is a man* (cf. Hale and Keyser [1993]). I return now to this curious asymmetry, showing first that it is crosslinguistically robust, and second that it can be derived from the fact that nouns have a referential index but adjectives and verbs do not.

The Australian language Nunggubuyu provides a paradigmatic illustration of this asymmetry (Heath 1984). Heath shows that adjectives generally take the same inflectional affixes as nouns, including prefixes that show gender and suffixes that show case, as in (138a). Both categories can be used predicatively, without any overt copula. The nominal gender prefix on the predicate adjective can, however, optionally be replaced with a verbal prefix that agrees with the subject of predication in person and number but not gender. The prefix on nouns cannot be replaced in this way, as shown by the contrast in (138b). A Nunggubuyu adjective can apparently become a stative verb by zero-derivation, but a noun cannot. Nunggubuyu also has two verb-creating derivational suffixes: *-ma*, which forms inchoative verbs; and *–wa,* which forms causative verbs. Heath observes that both of these morphemes attach productively to adjectives but not to nouns, as shown in (138c,d).

(138) a a-wu<u>r</u>ugu-wuy;   a-<u>r</u>unggal-wuy
           NCL-pond-DAT   NCL-big-DAT
           'to the pond'   'to the big one'
        b *wu-wurugu;   wu-runggal
           3sS-pond   3sS-big
           'it is / was a pond'   'it is / was big'
        c *wu-wurugu-ma-ny;   wu-runggal-ma-ny
           3sS-pond-INCH-TNS   3sS-big-INCH-TNS
           'it is / has become a pond' 'it is / has become big'
        d (*niwu-wurugu-wa-ny);   niwu-runggal-wa-ny
           3sS / 3sO-pond-CAUS-TNS 3sS / 3sO-big-CAUS-TNS
           'he made it into a pond' 'he made it big'

Evans (1991) describes similar facts from the related language Mayali, and
Cole (1985) presents the same paradigm in the unrelated language Imbabura
Quechua (see (13)).

    Once one becomes sensitive to this issue, one finds the same asymmetry in
many languages. Mohawk has a class of inherently adjectival roots, such as *hnir*
'hard' and *rak* 'white' (see section 4.6.3 for justification). These roots can –
indeed must–be made into verbs by one of a series of suffixes: *-u* derives stative
verbs, *-' / –ha'* derives inchoative verbs, and *-st/ –ht* derives causative verbs:

(139) a Thíkʌ yo-hnír-u.
           that   NsO-hard-STAT
           'That is hard.'
        b Wa'-o-hnir-ha-'.
           FACT-NsO-hard-INCH-PUNC
           'It became hard.'
        c Wa-ha-hnir-a-ht-e'.
           FACT-MsS-hard-Ø-CAUS-PUNC
           'He made it hard.'

Mohawk also has noun roots, which can be used predicatively either on their
own (with a null Pred) or with a lexical verb meaning 'become':

(140) a Ohkwári thíkʌ.
           bear   that
           'That is a bear.'
        b Ohkwári wa-h-átu-'
           bear   FACT-MsS-become-PUNC
           'He became a bear.'

It is, however, impossible to derive stative, inchoative, or causative verbs from
these noun roots:

(141) a *Thíkʌ yo-hkwarí-(ht)-u.
          that   NsO-bear-(NOML)-STAT
          'That is a bear.' (lit. 'That bears.')
     b *Sak wa-ho-hkwari-(ha)'-ne'
          Sak FACT-MsO-bear-INCH-PUNC
          'Sak became a bear.'
     c *Sak wa-ho-hkwari-ht-e'.
          Sak FACT-MsO-bear-CAUS-PUNC
          'It made Sak a bear.'

In Edo adjectives are frequently morphologically related to verbs. A disyllabic adjective like *pèrhè* 'flat' can be made into a verb *pèrhé* by giving it a low – high tone pattern. This verb can be stative, inchoative, or causative, depending on the tense and the number of arguments it has. But nouns do not correspond to verbs in this way. For example, the noun *e-kita* 'dog' does not correspond to any verb *kìtá that means to be, become, or cause to become a dog. The same derivational asymmetry between nouns and adjectives is thus found in Edo as well.

Other languages that bear witness to this asymmetry include Tzutujil, Mapuche, Lezgian, Finnish, and Hebrew. Daley (1985) treats inchoatives and causatives as a regular part of the derivational paradigm for adjectives in Tzutujil. Corresponding to an adjective like *saq* 'white, clear' are the verbs *saqireem* 'to become white' and *saquirsaxik* 'to make white, clear.' These affixes attach only sporadically to noun roots, however. The only example Daley cites is *ya7reem* 'to melt' related to *ya7* 'water' (1985: 122). (142) shows in a condensed way that the same is true in the other languages. In each case the verbalizing morphology that attaches to an adjective either cannot attach to a noun root, or it creates a very different meaning from what the noun would have when used predicatively.

(142) a *lif* 'clean$_A$' → *lif-* 'to become clean'   (Mapuche [Smeets 1989])
       aling 'fever$_N$' → #*aling-* 'to get a fever' (*not* 'to become a fever')
     b *hazur* 'ready$_A$' → *hazur-un* 'make ready'   (Lezgian [Haspelmath
                                         1993: 178])
       k'walax 'job$_N$' → #*k'walax-un* 'to (do) work' (*not* 'to make something
                                         be work')
     c *suuri* 'big$_A$' → *suur-nta-a* 'to make bigger' (Finnish [Klaus Laalo,
                                         personal communication])
       kirja 'book$_N$' → *kirja-nta-a 'to make into a book'
     d *lavan* 'white$_A$' → *hilbin* 'to whiten'   (Hebrew)
       'avaq 'dust$_N$' → #*'ibeq* 'to remove dust from' (not 'to make into dust')

This difference between nouns and adjectives is robust enough to show up in Stassen's (1997) study of intransitive predication in 410 languages.

Concerning languages in which adjectives alternate with verbs, Stassen writes (1997: 156–57): "In terms of frequency alone, [this] can be said to constitute a highly popular option among the world's languages. ...There are no less than 88 languages exhibiting this kind of pattern-switching, which ranks this class of languages among the largest typological groupings." He also notes that such languages are found all around the world (1997: 160), and that his count on this feature is probably a very conservative one. Concerning languages in which predicate nominals alternate with verbs, he writes (1997: 224) that this is "definitely marginal" and "restricted to small numbers of (usually closely related) languages." He identifies only about twelve such languages, including Abaza and Abkhaz (see section 2.4) and six Polynesian languages (see section 3.9 below). This confirms that we are not dealing with an accidental gap in the stock of derivational morphemes found in one or two languages. Since the same asymmetry shows up in language after language, one wants a principled explanation for it to emerge from the theory of lexical categories.

To see why this difference between nouns and adjectives exists, consider more carefully the structure of predicate nominals as compared to predicate adjectives. In chapter 2, I emphasized the similarity between the two with respect to theta-role assignment: both must combine with a Pred head in order to theta-mark a subject. But there are differences as well. If my theory is right, predicate nouns bear a referential index that predicate adjectives do not have. This follows from (1), together with the fact that the noun–adjective contrast is not neutralized in predicative environments. Predicate nominals can be singular or plural, as shown in (143a,b).[39] Singular count nouns used as predicates in English generally have to be the complement of the indefinite

---

[39] Note that the number morphology on the predicate nominal does not necessarily agree with the subject, the way predicate adjectives do in more heavily inflecting languages like Spanish. (ia) gives an example in which the subject is plural and the predicate is a morphologically singular collective; (ib) gives an example in which the subject is singular and the predicate is plural. Number morphology on the predicate is therefore determined by the predicate nominal's own criterion of identity, not by that of its subject.

(i)   They are a family; that is why they seem so comfortable together.
(ii)   That couple are both doctors, which puts stress on their relationship.

   English does occasionally use predicate nouns that refer to special human roles without an article, even though they are singular count nouns (e.g. *Who is governor of Wisconsin these days?*). This is more widespread in many European languages, including Dutch and French, where the usage extends to many profession words as long as they are not modified (*Il est professeur* 'He is professor') (Hengeveld 1992). I have no account of the special properties of these constructions, but take them to be the exception rather than the rule. (It may be significant that many of these words for roles and professions are historically deverbal forms.)

determiner *a*, unless there is a uniqueness presupposition, in which case *the* is used ((143c)). Predicate adjectives take neither plural morphology nor a determiner ((143d,e)).

(143)   a Rover is a dog.
         b Rover and Fido are dogs.
         c Rover is the smartest dog in his class at obedience school.
         d Rover is (*a) black.
         e Rover and Fido are black(*s).

The plural morpheme and the determiners require that the head they select have a criterion of identity, and hence a referential index, for reasons discussed in sections 3.2 and 3.3; therefore, the predicate nominals must retain this feature in (143). Carefully engineered discourses confirm this, showing that a predicate nominal introduces a new discourse referent, distinct from the one associated with the subject. This can best be seen when the subject and the predicate nominal have different gender or number features. A subsequent pronoun can then pick up the reference of the predicate nominal, agreeing with it in contradistinction to the subject. (144a) and (144b) give two examples; (144c), in contrast, shows that a predicate adjective does not introduce a discourse referent, as expected.[40]

(144)   a In the winter, Merlin is a wolf. It has a brown coat and sharp teeth.
            In the summer, he is a nightingale. It has wings and a beautiful song.
         b We are a committee. It meets every Friday to discuss plans for next year.
         c We are industrious. #It (industriousness) also helped John succeed.

(145) replicates these facts in Greek, a language in which gender marking is more pervasive:

---

[40] These examples may create some controversy. To me, they seem perfectly unremarkable, but one anonymous reviewer out of five and roughly 40 percent of my students do not accept them. I have also received a wide range of responses from speakers of various Slavic languages.

   Even I do not get a comparable judgment with profession names. A less-fanciful version of (144a) could be (i), but here it does not seem that the pronoun *she* can refer to the predicate nominals *professor* or *professional baseball player* as distinct from the subject Mary.

(i)   In the winter, Mary is a professor. She (the professor?) is very talented.
         In the summer, Mary is a pro baseball player. She (the player?) is not very talented.

I assume that this is because the same pronoun *she* would be used to refer to both the subject and the predicate nominal, and in this ambiguous situation the subject is a much more salient antecedent. It is conceivable, however, that profession names are different from other predicate nominals in some deeper way (compare note 39).

(145)   a Tin anixi o   Merlin   ine   zevra.   Ine   omorphi.
DET spring DET Merlin(MASC) be-3S zebra(FEM) be-3S beautiful(FEM)
'In the spring, Merlin is a zebra. She is beautiful.'
b Imaste mia epitropi.   Ine   mejali.
be-1pS DET committee(FEM / SG) be-3S big(FEM/SG)
'We are a committee. It is big.'

Together (143)–(145) show that the behavior of nouns used as predicates is not significantly different from that of nouns used as arguments with respect to these matters. There is thus converging evidence that predicate nominals bear the same referential indices as other NPs.

Since predicate nominals have a referential index, they must be coindexed with something they c-command, by the NLC. The only element that they c-command in general is the Pred head; thus, the Pred that combines with a nominal must have a theta-grid that contains a theta-role that can license its complement. Pred also creates for the predicate nominal a theta-role to be assigned to the subject out of the criterion of application implicit in the noun's entry, as discussed in chapter 2. The nominal-selecting Pred shares this second feature with the adjective-selecting Pred, but the first feature is unique to it; the adjective-selecting Pred must not have a theta-role for its complement, because the AP does not have a referential index. The difference between the two structures is shown in (146).

(146)   a Predicate nominal: b Predicate adjective:

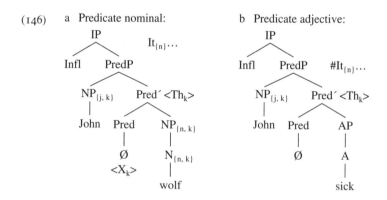

The claim that the nominal-selecting Pred has partially different lexical properties from those of the adjective-selecting Pred, which is forced upon me by my theory, fits nicely with the fact that the two Preds are phonologically distinct in some languages, such as Edo:

(147)   a Òzó *rè* òkpìá.   (nominal Pred = *rè*)
         Ozo is man
        b Ébòlù *yé* pèrhè(pèrhè).   (adjectival Pred = *yé*)
         ball   is flat(flat)

Other languages that have different Preds for predicate nominals and adjectives are Bambara, Ewe, Chinese, Hixkaryana, Mundari, Vai, and Ika (these are gleaned from Hengeveld [1992] and Wetzer [1996]). There are also languages that have a nominal Pred but not an adjectival Pred; see section 4.2. This confirms that the two Preds are, in fact, formally different entities. (The two Preds are, of course, spelled out the same in many languages [e.g. *ndi* in Chichewa, Ø in English]. This can be explained in a theory like Distributed Morphology [Halle and Marantz 1993], in which phonological forms are underspecified and inserted late in the derivation. Languages like Edo happen to have vocabulary items that are keyed to the slight difference in representation between (146a) and (146b); languages like Chichewa and English do not.)

With this background, we can now return to the asymmetry in verbalization. Why is it easy for the structure in (146b) to correspond to a verbal construction, but not for the structure in (146a)? An answer is close at hand. Verbs differ from adjectives only in that verbs license a specifier, to which they typically assign a theme (or agent) theta-role, as discussed in chapter 2. A verb is thus exactly equivalent to the combination of an adjective and an adjective-selecting Pred. In section 2.9, I interpreted this equivalence derivationally, claiming that verbs are created by moving an adjective into a Pred prior to lexical insertion. Verbs also differ from nouns along a second dimension: not only do they license a specifier, but they also do not have a referential index. Therefore, no verb could be an exact equivalent of the Pred + noun combination in (146a). A verb can replicate the theta-role assigning property of the Pred part, but not the discourse-referent-inducing property of the N part. The axiom of my theory given in (148) ensures this.

(148)   The Reference-Predication Constraint (RPC)
        No syntactic node can both theta-mark a specifier and have a referential index.

The conceptual motivation for the RPC is the truism of logic that nothing can be both a predicate and a referring expression (Geach 1962). The RPC's major empirical consequence is that Universal Grammar contains no fourth lexical category that completes the space of logical possibilities defined by the existence of nouns, verbs, and adjectives (Schachter [1985]; see the appendix for evidence that P is not a lexical category). The RPC also plays a role in constraining the derivational relationships that are our current concern, however. Verbs can be created out of adjectives by the simple, monotonic process of adding a specifier/theta-role, but adding a specifier/theta-role to a noun does not create a verb:

(149)   a A + Pred = V
         b N + Pred = * by the RPC

In derivational syntactic terms, suppose that a noun root moved into the Pred head, in an attempt to lexicalize it by conflation. Then the resulting head would have both a theta-grid and a referential index, which is an illicit representation. This explains the resistance of predicate nouns to verbalization in terms of the fundamental difference between nouns and adjectives.

The empirical prediction that emerges is actually a little more subtle. One might allow a verb to be derived from a noun by conflation or its equivalent, *as long as the noun lost its referential index.* The RPC is consistent with such a derivation. This means that the noun would lose its distinctive nominal flavor when it was transformed into a verb, becoming essentially like an adjective. This seems to be correct. Although predicate nouns resist verbalization in English and many other languages, such verbalization is not completely impossible. For example, the morpheme *–ize* in English derives verbs from adjectives productively, but it also attaches to a reasonable number of nouns, and sometimes (not always) the noun has a predicative meaning. *Crystalize* thus means roughly 'to become a crystal', and *fossilize* means roughly 'to become a fossil.' But only roughly. The verb *crystalize* does not introduce a referent to a crystal into the discourse, as shown by the contrast in (150).

(150)   a The solution became a crystal. It was two inches long ...
         b The solution crystalized. #It was two inches long ...

The counting that is made possible by a criterion of identity is also lost in such forms. There is no contrast between *crystalize* 'to turn into one crystal' and *crystalize* 'to turn into many crystals,' even though that difference is of great practical importance to materials scientists. In this respect (150b) is more closely equivalent to something like *The solution became crystalline,* where the result of the change is expressed adjectivally, than to (150a). This illustrates the possibility of a noun becoming a verb at the cost of its referential index.[41]

---

[41] This is one reason why the ban on nouns becoming verbs shows up as a tendency in Wetzer (1996) and Stassen (1997), but not as a universal. Two other sources of noise can be identified. First, languages like Abaza, in which nouns are distinct from verbs but tense and agreement morphology attaches to both (see section 2.5) get counted as languages in which nouns

A similar phenomenon can be seen in languages like Kiowa (spoken in the American Great Plains) and Mapuche (spoken in Chile). Both of these languages allow a noun to incorporate optionally into a copular verb meaning 'be.' This particular type of incorporation, however, is not meaning-preserving. The periphrastic version has the normal predicate nominal meaning, whereas the incorporated version has a pseudo-adjectival meaning: 'man-be' means 'be manlike,' and 'salt-be' means 'be salty.'

(151) a K'yạ:hị Ø-dɔ   (Kiowa [Watkins 1984: 227])
          man   3s-be
          'He's/it's a man.'
       b ... kú:tò-gɔ-àl – á-k'yạ:hị + dɔ:-mè:-dé-ẹ.
          bird-INV-too   3p-man-be-HSY-NOML-when
          'at that time when they – birds too – were manlike.'

(152) a Nge-la-y   chadi.   (Mapuche [Smeets 1989: 159–60])
          be-NEG-3S   salt
          'There is no salt.'
       b Chadi-nge-la-y
          salt-be-NEG-3S
          'It is not salty.'

These subtle but consistent contrasts follow from my analysis.

Comparing these constructions to true noun incorporation can help to clarify my distinction between incorporation and conflation, first introduced in section 2.9. Some languages allow nouns to be incorporated into verbs productively – including languages that do not allow ready verbalization of nouns, such as Mohawk, Mayali, Kiowa, and Mapuche. In some of these languages, the incorporated noun retains its referential index, and can introduce a discourse referent, as in (153) from Mohawk (Baker 1996b: sec. 7.2).

---

become / look like verbs by these authors' surfacy criteria. Second, there are languages in which the syntactic juxtaposition of a noun with a verb meaning 'be,' 'become,' or 'cause' is mistaken as a case of morphological union. The Australian language Yidin is a case in point. Bhat (1994) cites this as a language in which verbs are productively derived from nouns, based on Dixon (1977). Examples like (i) seem like excellent cases in point:

(i)   Gu<u>d</u>ugu<u>d</u>u   muray   dura:<u>d</u>inu gunduy-daga:<u>n</u>.   (Dixon 1977: 342)
      rainbow(ABS) hair(ABS) take.off   brown.snake-become
      'The rainbow shed its hair and turned into a brown snake.'

However, Dixon clearly states that the morpheme meaning 'become' is a distinct phonological word from the noun or adjective word for purposes of stress assignment and vowel deletion rules. Thus, there is reason to doubt whether this is a morphological object at all. The causative affix – *a-l* does form a single phonological word with the nonverbal root. But it is less clear that this element combines productively with nouns as well as adjectives; Dixon gives only a single example of – *a-l* attaching to a noun (the form means 'to make X into a grinding stone' [p. 342]).

(153)   Thetʌ're' wa'-ke-nakt-a-hnínu-'.   I-k-ehr-e'   Uwári
         yesterday FACT-IsS-bed-Ø-buy-PUNC Ø-IsS-think-IMPF Mary
         ʌ-ye-núhwe'-ne'.
         FUT-FsS-like-PUNC
         'I bought a bed yesterday. I think that Mary will like it.'

Why does Mohawk tolerate incorporation of an argument noun into a verb like 'buy,' referential index and all, but not incorporation of a predicate noun into a verb like 'become?' Incorporated nouns never have a predicative interpretation in Mohawk, as far as I can tell. According to my theory, nouns have a predicative interpretation if and only if they are the complements of Pred, a theta-role-creating functional head. When a referential noun incorporates into a verb, the two categories each retain their distinctive identities in the syntax. This is pure incorporation. The incorporated noun root can bear the referential index, and the verb can bear the theta-grid without violating the RPC. In contrast, when a noun or adjective incorporates into a Pred, Pred does not maintain its own independent existence; rather, the combination is recategorized as a verb (see section 2.9). This is what I mean by conflation: conflation is incorporation prior to lexical insertion, resulting in recategorization. The derived structure has only one X° node, and the RPC guarantees that it cannot have a referential index. Either this derivation is ruled out or the noun must shift its meaning, depending on the language and the particular example. The two structures (somewhat simplified) are compared in (154).

(154)   a Incorporation into V (e.g. (153))   b Conflation into Pred (e.g. (141a))

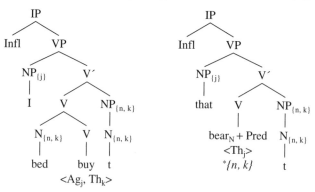

The categorial requirements of the two structures are opposite. (154a) tolerates a noun because the two heads remain syntactically distinct, and it requires a noun to be coindexed with the relevant theta-role of the verb. (154b) tolerates adjectives because the predicate does not bear a thematic relation to the Pred, and it requires an adjective – or a stripped down N – because Pred does not remain a syntactically distinct node. The particular categorial requirements of the different complex-verb forming processes of natural language thus follow from my account.[42]

The fundamental idea of this section is very simple: predicate adjectives become verbs more easily and regularly than predicate nouns do, because both adjectives and verbs lack a referential index. The nuances of this for different syntactic structures fall into place rather well, given the distinction between conflation and incorporation.

3.9 Are nouns universal?

Now that we have a precise idea of what it is to be a noun and what the grammatical consequences of being a noun are, we are well equipped to face the typological question of whether all languages have nouns as a distinct lexical category. I argue that they do. This section thus parallels section 2.10, which claimed that all languages have verbs.

Once again, one can imagine what a language without nouns could be like. Probably any human language must contain referring expressions, but these can

---

[42] An interesting case that deserves more study is Inuktitut. In this language nouns can incorporate into predicative elements like *–u* 'be' or *–nngur* 'become,' unlike in Mohawk. The syntaxes of the two kinds of incorporation are, however, significantly different. When incorporation into a lexical verb strands an adjective, that adjective is in the instrumental case and precedes the complex verb, as in (ia). In contrast, when incorporation into a copular item meaning *be* or *because* strands an adjective, the adjective must follow the complex verb and be in absolute case, as in (ib).

(i)   a   Ataatsi-nik   qamute-qar-poq. (Sadock 1985)
           one-INSTR/PL   sled-have-INDIC/3s
           'He has one sled.'
     b   Hansi nukappiaraq-u-voq   miki-soq. (Sadock 1985)
           Hans   boy-be-INDIC/3s   little-NOML/ABS
           'Hans is a little boy.'

This confirms that the two constructions have different syntactic statuses, as my analysis predicts.

My account also provides a leading idea about why this difference exists. When an N incorporates into a true verb, the verb retains its lexical status; it is the head of the derived structure. Therefore, in accordance with the head-final nature of VPs in Inuktitut, the derived word comes at the end of the clause, after complements and related material, including the stranded adjective. When an N incorporates into a Pred-type element, in contrast, Pred loses its distinct existence. The verbalized N is then dominant in the resulting word. It comes before its adjective modifier, because Ns always precede As in Greenlandic. Exactly how to work out the details of this account is far from clear, however. See Sadock (1980; 1985; 1991) for a fuller description of the facts and an analysis that captures a somewhat different intuition in terms of his Autolexical Syntax framework.

also be constructed out of functional categories that bear referential indices, such as pronouns and determiners. A nounless language would not have an exact equivalent of English's *the child*, but it might get along quite well with constructions like *the childlike one* (where *childlike* is an adjective) or *she who childs* (where *childs* is a verb). There are proposals in the literature that have roughly this character, some more radical, and others more moderate.

3.9.1   Languages that putatively have no words that are ever nouns

It is unusual to make the strongest claim of this type – that a language has no lexical items that can ever be nouns in the syntax. The one person I know of crazy enough to say exactly this is I. In Baker (2001a), I conjectured that Australian languages like Warlpiri and Jiwarli have verbs and adjectives but not nouns. I suggested that this could be the root cause of the radical kind of nonconfigurationality that those languages exhibit. I no longer believe that this is a promising line of analysis, however, and this subsection explains why.

Austin and Bresnan (1996) show that Jiwarli has the same cluster of non-configurational properties that Hale (1983) originally identified for Warlpiri: free word order ((155a)), discontinuous constituents ((155b)), and frequently dropped arguments ((155c)).[43]

(155)   a Piji-nha   mantharta-nha   wanka-rla-rninyja   ngulu-pa   martaru-lu.
          many-ACC   man-ACC   live-make-PAST   that-ERG   gum-ERG
          'That gum has cured many people.'   (OVS order, a rare basic order)
     b Karla   wantha-nma-rni   jarnpa   juma.
          fire.ACC   give-IMPER-hence   light.ACC   small.ACC
          'Give me a small fire light.'   ('fire' and 'light' separated by V)
     c Wirntupinya-nyja-rru.
          kill-PAST-now
          'They killed him.'   (V standing alone as complete clause)

These properties suggest that "nominal" expressions in Jiwarli do not sit in the normal subject and object positions of Spec, TP and Spec, VP. Jiwarli does not, however, have pronominal clitics on the verb comparable to the clitics found in most Warlpiri clauses, which Jelinek (1984) identified as the true arguments of the verb and the reason why other nominals are excluded from argument positions (see also Baker [1991; 1996b] on Mohawk). The question thus arises of what prevents nominals from occupying argument positions in Jiwarli.

---

[43] Additional information about Jiwarli, including some of the examples that follow, comes from a class I attended on the structure of Australian languages taught at Stanford University by Peter Austin in fall 1994. I thank Peter Austin for many stimulating discussions in that context.

My (2001a) suggestion was that what are called nominals in Jiwarli are really adjectives. As such, they cannot be in argument positions for the same reasons that a word like *proud* cannot be a subject in an English sentence like **Proud led to John's downfall* (see section 3.6). This proposal capitalizes on the independently known fact that Jiwarli, like many other Australian languages, makes no morphological distinction between adjectives and nouns; both bear the same range of case endings. This makes it plausible to say that they have only one of the two categories. Bhat (1994: 168–69) observes that languages in which there is neutralization of the noun–adjective distinction tend to be nonconfigurational and often tolerate discontinuous constituents. In addition to Australian languages, Bhat mentions that Latin, Sanskrit, Turkish, and Quechua are like this, and I added the North American languages Klamath and Nez Perce to the list. The overt "nominals" in Jiwarli sentences like (155a,b) were, I claimed, related to null pronouns in argument position by way of secondary predication, following Speas (1990). On this view, the structure of (155a) is the one given in (156); this structure is comparable to the structures of English sentences like *I ate it raw* and *He arrived drunk*.

(156) $[PRO_k$ Pred people(like)$]$ pro_i cured pro_k $[PRO_i$ Pred gum(like)$]$
        (lit. 'It cured them peoplelike gumlike.')

The last step in my argument was to account for the case marking on "nominals" in these languages. It so happens that both Warlpiri and Jiwarli (unlike Indo-European languages) use case markers on the verbal head of an embedded clause that agree with the case of the controller of the null subject of that clause. For example, the verb in the purposive clause in (157) bears the same ergative case marker as does the "nominal" associated with the subject position in (155a).

(157)   Kuwarti kurriya   purra-rninyja [patha-rrkarringu-*ru* jiriparri-yi].
        now   boomerang. ACC toss-PAST   pelt-intent-ERG   echidna-DAT
        'Next he threw a boomerang to hit echidna.'

This rule applies also to the structure in (156): the secondary predicate 'gum(like)' bears ergative case because its PRO subject happens to be controlled by the ergative null subject of the verb. In the same way, the accusative case on 'people(like)' in (155a) indicates that the controller of its PRO subject is the object of the verb.

This proposal had several other positive consequences for Jiwarli syntax. For example, it explained the fact that Jiwarli has no true determiners (cf. section 3.3), the fact that "nominals" cannot combine to form larger nominal phrases (cf. section 4.2), and the fact that Jiwarli does not allow incorporation of direct objects (cf. section 3.6). In these last two respects, Jiwarli contrasts minimally with the northern Australian language Mayali. Mayali does have an inflectional distinction between nouns and adjectives, and this fits with the fact that [A N] constituents are possible in Mayali, and so is noun incorporation into verbs (Evans 1991).

In spite of these intriguing successes, I now think that this is unlikely to be the correct explanation for the special characteristics of Warlpiri and Jiwarli grammar. The brief and informal discussion in Baker (2001a) left some theoretical loose ends that the current discussion of the syntax of lexical categories does not tie up. The most serious loose end is that depictive secondary predicates in English, which provide the model for the structural analysis of Jiwarli in (156), are actually quite rigidly ordered. A depictive controlled by the subject must come outside a depictive controlled by the object ((158a) versus (158b)), depictives must follow the verb ((158c)), and having two depictives related to a single argument is unnatural at best ((158d)).

(158)   a Chris ate the meat raw drunk.
        b *Chris ate the meat drunk raw.
        c *Raw Chris ate the meat drunk.
        d ??Chris only eats fish raw fresh.

The core nonconfigurational properties of free word order and discontinuous realization of arguments therefore do not follow automatically from saying that "nominals" in Jiwarli are secondary predicates. At a minimum, we would still have to say that the syntax of secondary predication is different in Jiwarli and English (Pensalfini 1997). This detracts significantly from the elegance of the proposal by multiplying differences between the two language types.

Pensalfini's (1997) analysis of another Australian language, Jingulu, casts further doubt on my (2001) proposal. Jingulu is geographically and grammatically intermediate between Northern Australian languages like Mayali and Nunggubuyu, which have a noun–adjective distinction, and Southwestern Australian languages like Jiwarli and Warlpiri, which supposedly have only adjectives. Jingulu has as clear a noun–adjective contrast as Nunggubuyu and Mayali do. It too has a gender system in which nouns have fixed gender and adjectives vary in gender to agree with nouns. Sentences with predicate nominals and sentences with predicate adjectives also display significant differences in case marking and word order in Jingulu. Now the crucial fact is that Jingulu seems to have *both* the nonconfigurationality-by-dislocation that is characteristic of Mayali and Nunggubuyu (Baker 1996b) *and* the nonconfigurationality-by-predication-and-case-marking that is characteristic of Jiwarli and Warlpiri. Argument-expressing words in Jingulu can either show up with no case marking at the edge of a clause ((159a)), as in Mayali, or they can show up as multiple words, each of which is case marked and interspersed with other constituents throughout the clause ((159b)), as in Jiwarli.

(159) a Dilkurni nginaniki, kakuwi darra-ardi.   (Pensalfini 1997: 163)
          kite   this(FEM) fish   eat-HAB
          'The white-breasted kite eats fish.'
       b Dardu-wala-rni   maja-ni-ngurru-ju wajbala-rni.   (Pensalfini 1997: 162)
          many.people-ERG get-INV-1pinO-do whitefella-ERG
          'Lots of white people took photos of us.'

The fact that dislocation is possible confirms that "nominals" in Jingulu can be nouns, bearing a referential index: it is only NPs that enter into binding chains with pronouns inside a clause (section 3.7). But the very same words also take part in Jiwarli-style nonconfigurationality-by-case-marking. This suggests that Jiwarli-style nonconfigurationality is not induced by the absence of true nouns after all. There is no decisive evidence here against the claim that Jiwarli has no nouns, but neither is there decisive evidence in its favor and it does not succeed in its goal of deriving nonconfigurational syntax from a simple difference in the stock of lexical categories plus independently known principles of syntax.

3.9.2 *Languages that putatively have no words that are always nouns*
Much more common and plausible than the claim that some languages have no words that can ever be used as nouns in the syntax is the claim that some languages have no words that can only be used as a noun. Many languages are said to have no noun–adjective contrast. What is typically meant by this is that the same roots can be used either as nouns or as adjectives, depending on needs of the situation. Huallaga Quechua (Weber 1989), Classical Nahuatl (Launey 1981), and Greenlandic Eskimo (Fortescue 1984: 102, 108, 302) are three languages for which this has been said, in addition to certain Australian languages (Bittner and Hale 1995). Authors' reasons for making this claim are fairly uniform. "Adjectival" words meaning things like 'good', 'big,' and 'plastic' can be used with noun-like inflectional affixes and functional heads to form argument expressions in all these languages:

(160)   a in cual-li   (Nahuatl [Launey 1981])
           the good-NSF
           'a beautiful or good person'
        b Hatun-ta rikaa. (cf: Rumi-ta   rikaa)   (Quechua [Weber 1989])
           big-ACC I-see   stone-ACC I-see
           'I see a/the big one.' 'I see a/the stone.'
        c Naamik, kisianni plastikki-mik pe-qar-poq.   (Greenlandic [J. Sadock,
           No   but   plastic-INSTR Ø-have-3sS   personal communication.])
           'No, but there are plastic ones.'
           (Answers the question: *Qisunnik puugutaqarpa?* 'Are there any wooden plates?')

Conversely, words meaning things like 'stone' can be used as predicates in these
languages, with adjective-like meanings:

(161)   a Ca   tetl   in metlatl.   (Nahuatl
           PRT stone the metate.   [Launey 1981])
           'The metate is (of) stone.'
        b Toqay rumi ka-yka-n. (cf. Toqay hatun ka-yka-n.)   (Quechua
           that stone be-PRES-3S That big be-PRES-3S   [Weber 1989])
           'That one is stone/a stone.' 'That one is big/a big one.'
        c Illuqarvi-u-vuq   (cf. Qursu-u-vuq.)   (Greenlandic
           town-be-INDIC/3sS   green-be-INDIC/3sS [Fortescue 1984: 70, 76])
           'It is a town.'   'It is green.'

And either type of word can combine with a noun to form an attributive modification structure:

(162)   a in   cual-li tlācatl; in   pàtli   xihuitl (Nahuatl [Launey 1981])
           the good   man   the medicine herb
           'the good man'   'the medicinal herb'
        b rumi wasi; hatun wasi   (Quechua [Weber 1989])
           stone house big   house
           'a stone house' 'a big house'
        c innu nutaaq; illirviusaq qisuk   (Greenlandic
           house new   box   wood   [Fortescue 1984: 108, 119])
           'a new house' 'a wood(en) box'

The examples in (160) seem to show that the words in question can act as nouns,
whereas the examples in (162) seem to show that they can also act as adjectives
(see section 4.2). This leads the authors to the conclusion that the adjective–
noun distinction is neutralized in these languages.

   Some languages are even said to have no noun–verb contrast, particular
words being usable in either way. Notable among these are the Salish and
Wakashan languages, based on the famous discussions of Sapir and Swadesh

(1939; 1946; Swadesh 1939), picked up by Whorf (1956) and many others (see Jacobsen [1979] for a detailed review of the early literature on this issue). Such languages have been said to have only one lexical category. Any lexical item in most of these language can be used as a predicate, with similar morphology, as shown in (163) for St'át'imcets (also known as Lillooet Salish).

(163)   a Qwatsáts-kacw.   (Dermidache and Matthewson 1995)
           leave-2sS
           'You leave/left.'
        b Smúlhats-kacw.
           woman-2sS
           'You are a woman.'
        c Xzúm-lhkacw.
           big-2sS
           'You are big.'

Any lexical item can also be used as an argument, in which case it is introduced by a determiner and comes after the predicate, as shown in (164), again from St'át'imcets.

(164)   a Qwatsáts-Ø ti   smúlhats(-Ø)-a   (Dermidache and Matthewson 1995)
           leave-3A   the woman-(3A)-the
           'The woman left.'
        b Smúlhats-Ø ti   qwatsáts-(Ø)-a
           woman-3A   the leave-(3A)-the
           'The one who left is a woman.'
        c Qwatsáts-Ø ti   xzúm-(Ø)-a.
           leave-3A   the big-(3A)-the
           'The big one left.'

The most striking illustration that all words are of the same category in these languages is the fact that two-word sentences are systematically reversible: either word can function as the subject, and either one can function as the predicate. (164a) and (164b) show one such reversal; (165) illustrates another one from the Wakashan language Nootka, which is spoken in the same general area as the Salish languages but is part of a different family.

(165)   a Mamu:k-ma   qu:?as-?i: (Nootka [Swadesh 1939])
           work-INDIC   man-the
           'The man is working.'
        b Qu:?as-ma   mamu:k-?i.
           man-INDIC   work-the
           'The working one is a man.'

Very similar issues arise in Austronesian languages, and doubts that lexical category distinctions exist have been expressed also in this family's scholarly tradition. Schachter (1985: 12), for example, shows that Swadesh's famous Nootka examples in (165) can be replicated perfectly in Tagalog. Descriptive works that do not distinguish the categories include Tchekhoff (1981), whose discussion of Tongan has influenced typological works like Hengeveld (1992), Mosel and Hovdhaugen (1992) on Samoan, and Klamer (1994: 97) on Kambera. The following data from Tukang Besi show the same root being used as an NP, as an attributive modifier, and as a verb (Donohue 1999: 81):

(166)   a te   tomba
            ART mud
            'mud'
         b te   sala   tomba
            ART road mud
            'muddy road'
         c Te   atu   no-tomba.
            ART that 3.REAL-mud
            'That's mud(dy).'

These languages, then, pose the most radical possibility of all, that there might be no distinction between nouns and any other lexical category.[44]

The examples found in grammars must, however, be interpreted with caution. Showing that there are some words that can be used either as nouns or as adjectives (or as verbs) is not enough to support the claim that there are significant typological differences among languages with respect to lexical categories. English clearly has a noun–adjective distinction; nevertheless, there are a few classes of lexical items whose category is systematically ambiguous. Designations of material, nationality, and sex can be used either as Ns or as As in English:

(167)   a The stone table stands over there.
            The stones stand over there.
         b The Italian flag waves proudly.
            The Italians sat down and began to eat.
         c The male falcon is smaller than the female.
            All males must register for the draft, regardless of age.

---

[44] In addition to Salish, Wakashan, and Austronesian, the Mundari language of India is often cited as having no distinction between nouns, verbs, and adjectives (Bhat 1994: ch. 11; Wetzer 1996; Stassen 1997). Bhat (1994) does, however, mention that not all Mundari grammarians agree on this issue. Unfortunately, I have not gained access to primary sources on this language that would allow me to make an informed judgment, so I cannot discuss it.

Given this, it is not surprising that words like 'stone', 'wood,' or 'plastic' show ambivalent behavior in Nahuatl, Quechua, or Greenlandic. Examples like those in (162) thus tell us little by themselves. Donohue (1999) is careful to point out that, while many words in Tukang Besi show the category-neutral behavior in (166) (perhaps 60 percent), there are also words like *woleke* 'rat' that behave unambiguously like nouns, words like *tode* 'flee' that behave unambiguously like verbs, and words like *to'oge* 'big' that show distinctively adjectival behavior. Mosel and Hovdhaugen (1992: 77) emphasize that in Samoan "many, perhaps the majority of, roots can be found in the function of verb phrase and noun phrase," but they concede that they have never observed *alu* 'go' as a noun or *mea* 'thing' as a verb. An important typological difference exists only if categorial ambiguity extends to an entire open class of inflectionally similar words, thereby affecting the overall grammar of the language. I argue that this is not the case in any of the languages cited above, or any others for which there is enough data to judge. Rather, all the languages have some words that cannot bear a referential index and others that must bear one, once we know where to look for relevant effects.

Our experience so far gives some fairly clear expectations as to what factors might make it hard to distinguish the lexical categories in a particular language. We expect that a noun selected by a Pred can be used as a predicate, and that a verb or an adjective that appears in construction with a pronoun or relative operator can be used as an argument. Since Preds and pronouns are functional heads, it is common for them to be phonologically null. This can be an important source of confusion when evaluating the behavior of the lexical categories. The critical task, then, is to find ways of isolating the lexical heads from their functional support systems, to see if the noun–nonnoun contrast reemerges in those environments. This is what I proceed to do.

I consider first sources of evidence that only a subset of the relevant heads can bear a referential index in these languages. Noun incorporation should be a good test to show this in languages that have it. Simple nouns that bear a referential index are in principle incorporable; they retain their index under incorporation and bind the object theta-role of the verb (see (154a)). If there are heads that cannot be used as nouns, however, they should not be incorporable. Apart from incorporation, they might sometimes look like the direct object of a verb by virtue of being in construction with a null determiner or pronoun, but these functional elements would necessarily be the heads of the phrase, blocking the non-noun from incorporating. I showed at the end of section 3.6 that this was correct for Mayali, where the noun–adjective distinction was not in doubt (see (121)–(123)). We can therefore apply the same test to Nahuatl and

Greenlandic, two other languages that permit incorporation. In both languages, words that one would expect to be nouns can incorporate, but words that one expects to be adjectives cannot. (168) gives an ordinary noun incorporation pair in Nahuatl:

(168)   a Ni-c-chīhua   in   cac-tli.
         1sS-3sO-make the shoe-NSF
         'I make the shoes.'
        b Ni-*cac*-chīhua.   (Launey 1981: 165)
         1sS-shoe-make
         'I make shoes.'

(169a) is superficially parallel to (168a), with the "adjective" *cual* 'good' being used as a noun. *Cual* cannot, however, be incorporated to form (169b).[45]

(169)   a Ni-c-chīhua   in cual-li.
         1sS-3sO-make   the good-NSF
         'I make the good one.'
        b *Ni-*cual*-chīhua.   (Kenneth Hale, personal communication;
         1sS-good-make   no examples of this form in Launey [1981])
         'I make good ones.'

(170a) shows ordinary noun incorporation in Greenlandic, and (170b) shows that similar incorporation of an "adjective" is impossible. ((170b) contrasts with the grammatical (160c), in which 'plastic' is not incorporated.)

(170)   a Qisun-nik   puuguta-qar-pa?
         wood-INSTR/PL   plate-have-INTEROG/3S
         'Are there any wooden plates?'
        b ??Naamik, kisianni plastikke-qar-poq.
         No   but   plastic-have-3sS
         'No, but there is a plastic one.'

---

[45] The adjectival root *cual* can be incorporated into the verb in Nahuatl, but the verb consistently retains an object pronominal prefix, unlike in (168b). Incorporated *cual* is interpreted not as the direct object of the verb, but as a predicate of the object of the verb. Some examples are:

(i)   a *te*-cual-itta   (Andrews 1975: 433)
        3O/INDEF-good-see
        'to enjoy seeing someone, to like the appearance of someone'
        (lit. 'to see someone as good'), but *not* 'to see a good one'
       b te-cual-ihtoa   (Kenneth Hale, personal communication)
        3O/INDEF-good-speak
        'to praise someone, speak well of someone'

These facts fit well with my theory. Modifier incorporation is generally possible in Nahuatl, and there is no reason for this not to apply to *cual*. The crucial point is that since *cual* has no referential index it cannot by itself be the antecedent for the verb's object theta-role. That is why a distinct object prefix like *te*- is needed in these examples, unlike in (168b).

These examples prove that, for all their noun-like inflection, roots like 'good' and 'plastic' cannot have a referential index. They are thus adjectives, contrasting with other roots, which are nouns.

Further evidence for a distinct class of nouns comes from the distribution of determiners in some languages. In section 3.3, I discussed the fact that adjectives can modify a null noun only if that noun is governed by a definite determiner in English, Italian, and Edo (*I worship *(the) rich*). This syntactic restriction is not universal, but it is common in languages that have determiners at all. We might therefore expect adjectives and verbs that are masquerading as nouns to require such a determiner, whereas true nouns will not necessarily require one. This is clearly case for the Wakashan language Makah, as discussed by Jacobsen (1979). As in Salish and Nootka, any word in Makah can function as an argument when followed by a determiner such as *-ºiq* ((171a,b)). Yet Jacobsen (1979: 121) writes: "Probably the clearest defining characteristic of nouns as opposed to verbs is that they may directly occur as subjects (and other nominal arguments), whereas verbs may so occur only by being nominalized with the article *-ºiq*." Thus, examples like (171c) are possible in Makah, but not examples like (171d).

(171)   a Ła:pxu: huktu:b-iq.   (Jacobsen 1979: 122)
            fly-INDIC-3S bird-DET
            'The bird is flying.'
        b Da:s?its   t'iq'ʷas-iq.   (Jacobsen 1979: 123)
            see-PASS-INDIC-1sS sit-on.ground-DET
            'The one sitting on the ground sees me.'
        c ?u:šaba:c'a:l   wa:q'it   (Jacobsen 1979: 121)
            talk-now-INDIC-3S frog
            'The frogs are croaking.'
        d *Da:s?its   t'iq'ʷas.   (Jacobsen 1979: 123)
            see-PASS-INDIC-1sS sit-on.ground
            'One sitting on the ground sees me.'

This shows that *wa:q'it* 'frog' has a referential index and so is a noun intrinsically in Makah, whereas *t'iq'ʷas* 'sit on the ground' does not and is not.

The Austronesian languages seem to be similar to Wakashan in this regard. Klamer (1994: 100) says that verbs in Kambera may be used as arguments *with a definite determiner*. The requirement of having a determiner does not apply to words that are intrinsically nouns; they can appear as bare NP arguments when understood as indefinites.

(172)   a Na   ma-kaloru-nya   na   manganga...   (Klamer 1994: 100)
            ART REL-arrange-3sD ART steal
            'One who is engaged in theft' (lit. 'the [one] who arranges the steal')

   b Mbàda manahu-da-ka   uhu.   (Klamer 1994: 70)
     already cook-3pG-PERF rice
     'They have already cooked (some) rice.'

Argument phrases headed by true Ns can also appear with or without determiners in Samoan. (Whether a determiner is present affects word order and case marking because all and only determined NPs move out of the verb phrase to check case prior to verb phrase fronting, according to Massam's [2001] analysis of "noun incorporation" in related Niuean.)[46]

(173)   a Na   fa'atau e   le   tama le   pua'a. (Det + Obj; VSO order)
           PAST sell   ERG ART boy ART pig
           'The boy sold the pig.'
         b Fia   faatau puaa oe?   (Bare Obj NP; VOS order)
           want sell   pig you
           'Do you want to sell pigs?' (Mosel and Hovdhaugen 1992: 738)

Verbs can generally be preceded by the singular specific determiner *le*, in which case they seem nondistinct from nouns and can appear in argument positions:

(174)   'o   le   alu o   le   pasi i Apia
          PRT ART go POSS ART bus to Apia
          'the go(ing) of the bus to Apia'

There are, however, no examples in the grammars of an expression like (174) appearing without a determiner as the direct object of the verb, parallel to (173b). If it is confirmed that such constructions are ungrammatical, then I conclude that there is a noun–verb contrast even in Samoan and Tongan, although it is concealed in part by the presence of determiners (and null relative operators).

---

[46] The more traditional Austronesianist view is that the bare noun that immediately follows the verb in (173b) has undergone noun incorporation. Which of these views is ultimately correct is not crucial for my argument; the crucial point is that verbal roots cannot appear in this context.
     The noun–verb distinction is more obvious in Tukang Besi because it has special morphology on verbs that shows when a *wh*-extraction has taken place, similar to Tagalog. Subject extraction morphology appears when an intransitive verb is used as an argument, but not when a noun is so used, proving that there is a distinction (see also Klamer [1994] on Kambera):

(i)   a te   woleke
           ART rat
           'the rat'
         b te   t-*um*-ode   (Donohue 1999: 79)
           ART REL-flee
           'the fleeing one'

The Oceanic languages do not have these morphological reflexes of relativization, so the difference between (ia) and (ib) is less noticeable in them.

But whenever there is no determiner, as in the special "incorporation" construction in (173a), the expected contrast between nouns and verbs emerges more clearly.

This form of argument applies also to Quechua, except that the licensing function of the definite determiner is played by the accusative case marker *–ta*. I assume that Quechua *–ta* heads the functional category Kase, as in Lamontagne and Travis (1987) and Bittner and Hale (1996). In his review of Weber (1989), Adelaar (1994) points out that although both adjectives and nouns can serve as objects of the verb when marked by *–ta* (see (160b)), this does not generalize to subjects. A "noun" can be the subject of the intransitive verb in (175a), but an "adjective" cannot be. In order to express the equivalent of (175b), one must use a headless relative clause construction, in which the "adjective" functions as a predicate, not as an argumental expression ((172c); examples from David Weber, personal communication).

(175) a Runa čaya-mu-ša.
          Man arrive-CIS-PAST /3sS
          'The man arrived.'
       b *Hatun čaya-mu-ša.
          big   arrive-CIS-PAST /3sS
          'The big one arrived.'
       c Hatun ka-q   čaya-mu-ša.
          big   be-NOML arrive-CIS-PAST /3sS
          'The one that is big arrived.'

This suggests that words like *hatun* 'big' cannot be nouns inherently in Quechua either; rather they can be modifiers of an empty noun head that must be governed by a case marker like *–ta* (or perhaps by the verb itself). David Weber has changed his (1989) view in response to Adelaar's point, now distinguishing "adjectival nouns" from ordinary nouns.[47]

Arguments from determinerless expressions cannot be applied to the Salish languages in exactly the same way, because all argument phrases must contain an overt determiner in these languages. The Salish equivalent of (171c) is thus just as ungrammatical as the Salish equivalent of (171d). Conceivably this could be taken as evidence in favor of Jelinek's and Demers' (1994) view that all lexical items are inherently predicates (i.e. verbs) in Salish. A more conservative possibility, however, is that the parameter that requires determiners to be used with all common noun arguments in Italian and French (see section 3.3)

---

[47] Weber is, however, still sympathetic to the view that the distinction between As and Ns in Quechua is purely a semantic one. See chapter 5 for discussion relevant to this class of ideas.

also holds in Salish. Determiners do, however, reveal the noun–nonnoun contrast in Salishan languages in a different way. Recall that only a subset of the determiners licenses null noun heads in languages like English: *the* does, but *a*, *that*, and *this* do not (*I admire the /*a / ?*that rich*). This parallels Davis' (1999) observation that, whereas all categories can appear as arguments together with the determiner *ti – a* in St'át'imcets, only true nouns can follow a demonstrative plus the non-referential determiner *ku*:

(176) a Áts'x-en=lhkan   ti7   ku=sqaycw.
          see-DIR=1sS   DEM DET=man
          'I saw that man'
       b *Áts'x-en=lhkan ti7   ku=qwatsáts / tayt.
          see-DIR=1sS   DEM DET= leave / hungry
          'I saw that one that left / that hungry one.'

This contrast can be understood in the same way as the English one: nonnouns like 'leave' and 'hungry' can only count as arguments by virtue of forming a construction with a null noun, and this null noun is licensed by *ti – a*, but not by the determiner *ku*. Determiners thus provide a sensitive test for revealing the noun–adjective distinction in languages that have them.

   If only some of the words in a given language have a referential index intrinsically, we might expect the difference to show up also in the way that those words participate in movement relationships (see section 3.5). This prediction is confirmed in St'át'imcets, where some lexical heads can function as the head of a relative clause but others cannot, as discussed by Dermidache and Matthewson (1995) and Matthewson and Davis (1995). (177) illustrates one kind of relative clause construction, in which the discontinuous determiner *ti – a* sandwiches a clausal expression, and the whole phrase is followed by the understood head of the relative. (177a) and (177b) show that this relative construction is well-formed when the head is intrinsically nominal, but (177c,d) show that it is ungrammatical when the final head is a word corresponding to a verb or adjective in English.

(177) a Ats'x-en-Ø-lhkan   [[ti qwatsáts-Ø-a] sqaycw]
          saw-TRAN-3A-1sE   the leave-3sA-the man
          'I saw the man who left.'
       b Ats'x-en-Ø-lhkan   [[ti xzúm-Ø-a] spzúza7]
          saw-TRAN-3A-1sE   the big-3sA-the bird
          'I saw the big bird.'
       c *Ats'x-en-Ø-lhkan   [[ti sqáycw-Ø-a] qwatsáts].
          saw-TRAN-3A-1sE   the man-3A-the leave
          'I saw the leaving one who is a man.'

d *Ats'x-en-Ø-lhkan　　[[ti xzúm-Ø-a] tseqwtsíqw].
　saw-TRAN-3A-1sE　　the big-3A-the red
　'I saw the red one who is big.'

The exact structure of these relative constructions is an interesting topic in itself (Dermidache and Matthewson 1995; Matthewson and Davis 1995), but the details are not particularly crucial for my purposes. Whatever other structure they may have, these relative clauses contain a gap, which is bound by an empty operator (assuming Salish is like Mohawk in this respect). Words like *sqaycw* 'man' and *spzúza7* 'bird' have a referential index that allows them to control this empty operator, but words like *qwatsáts* 'leave' and *tseqwtsíqw* 'red' do not. This is further evidence that not all words belong to the same category in Salish.[48]

So far, I have concentrated on evidence that only a proper subset of the lexical items in the languages under consideration *can* have a referential index. There is also evidence that many of these items *must* have a referential index. Consider, for instance, the possibility of attributive modification. In English, adjectives but not nouns can be attributive modifiers of a noun (*a smart woman* versus **a genius woman*). Anticipating the discussion in section 4.2, this is because the referential index of a noun in attributive position cannot be coindexed with anything in its c-command domain, violating the noun licensing condition. If no (nonverbal) word was intrinsically nominal in a particular language, we would expect that any word could be used as an attributive modifier. This is not, however, the case. A noun in Greenlandic, for example, can be followed by a second "nominal," which is understood as an attributive modifier of the first, as seen in (162c) and (178). But not just any "nominal" can be the second member of this construction (Jerrold Sadock, personal communication). The second nominal must come from a short and familiar list: it must refer to a material (wood, stone, plastic . . .), a gender (male, female), a nationality/place of origin (French, Greenlandic . . .), or it must be an "adjectival noun" (new, old, green, . . .). As a result, attributive constructions in Greenlandic are not reversible, as shown by the ungrammatical examples in (178).

(178)　a ilinniartitsisoq franskeq;　but　??franskeq ilinniartitsisoq
　　　teacher　　　Frenchman　　　　Frenchman teacher
　　　'a French teacher'　　　　　　　'a teacher Frenchman'

---

[48] Matthewson and Davis (1995) also discuss a second kind of relative clause in Salish, which has two instances of the determiner *ti – a*, the first sandwiching the understood head and the second sandwiching the predicate. In this construction too only a subset of the lexical items – the true nouns – can be used in the head position.

b puugutaq qisuk;   but   ??qisuk puugutaq
plate   wood   wood   plate
'a wooden plate'   'a plate(like) piece of wood'

Both versions should be possible in principle if any nonverb can be used as either an adjective or a noun in Greenlandic. If, however, words like 'teacher' and 'plate' are unambiguously nouns (unlike 'wood' and 'French') then the asymmetry is explained, since they cannot be attributive modifiers. In a similar way, "noun" plus "adjective" is possible as a complex NP in Kambera, but not "adjective" plus "noun" (*Pàu rara* ['mango red/ripe'] 'a ripe mango', but **rara pàu* ['ripe mango'] Klamer 1994:104, 114), showing that the word classes are distinct in that language too.[49] For St'át'imcets, Dermidache and Matthewson (1995) show that only a limited class of "adjectives" can be pre-nominal modifiers to a predicate nominal; most words that translate as nouns (or verbs) cannot. (179a) is a grammatical example, in which the predicate consists of an adjective and a noun in that order; (179b,c) show that similar combinations in which the first word is a verb or noun rather than an adjective are impossible.[50]

(179)   a Kwikws spzúza7 i   sáq'w-a.   (OK: A+N)
           small   bird   PL/DET fly-DET
           'The ones who flew were small birds.'
        b *Saq'w spzúza7 ti   ats'x-en-Ø-án-a   (* V+N)
           fly   bird   PL/DET see-TRAN-3sA-1sE-DET
           'The ones I saw were fly(ing) birds.'
        c *plísmen naplít ti   ats'x-en-Ø-án-a   (*N+N)
           policeman priest PL/DET see-TRAN-3sA-1sE-DET
           'The one I saw was a policeman (and) priest.'

Davis (1999) refines this generalization slightly, pointing out that some words can appear as either the first member of a complex predicate or as the last member, including gender words like 'woman/female' and nationality words like 'Indian.' But this is no surprise: these are precisely the kinds of words that

---

[49] In contrast, either order of words is said to be possible in a Huallaga Quechua NP (Weber 1989). I assume this is because the word order of attributive constructions is freer in Quechua than in Greenlandic or Kambera. In other words, 'stone house' and 'house stone' are both possible because the adjectival modifier 'stone' can adjoin to the inherently nominal head 'house' on either the right or the left, not because 'house' is a possible attributive modifier of 'stone.'

[50] The asymmetry does not show up in nominals used as arguments for independent reasons. As already mentioned, nouns used as arguments need to be embedded in determiner phrases and the determiners in question can license verbs or predicate nominals as a kind of relative clause.

Dermidache and Matthewson (1995) also show that a sequence of two adjectives cannot form a complex predicate in Salish; the last word of the complex predicate must be a noun. This recapitulates exactly the English contrast between *John is a big (strong) man* and **John is big strong*. See section 4.2 for an analysis.

are ambiguously nouns or adjectives crosslinguistically. The important point is that some words apparently must have a referential index, and other words can never have one; these are the unambiguous nouns and the unambiguous adjectives of Salish. A similar range of complex predicates is found in Straits Salish (Jelinek and Demers 1994: 708, ex. (28)) and in Wakashan languages (Jacobsen 1979; Wojdak 2001).

Attributive constructions also reveal a noun–adjective distinction in Austronesian languages. For example, in Tukang Besi words like *to'oge* 'big' and *woleke* 'rat' can both be used with an article to form an argumental expression ((180a)), potentially causing one to doubt that there is a difference in category. But *to'oge* can modify a true noun directly, as shown in (180b), whereas *woleke* cannot; a genitive particle is required between the two nouns ((180c)).

(180)   a te   to'oge; te   woleke   (Donohue 1999: 78, 80)
          ART big   ART rat
          'the big one; the rat'
    b te   woleke to'oge   (Donohue 1999: 77)
          ART rat   big
          'the big rat'
    c te   iku *(nu) woleke   (Donohue 1999: 80)
          ART tail GEN   rat
          'the rat('s) tail'

The ungrammaticality of (180c) without the genitive marker shows that words like *woleke* 'rat' must bear a referential index; this cannot be freely suppressed to give it the distribution of an adjective as well as that of a noun.[51]

A second test of whether some words must have a referential index in these languages comes from verbalizing morphology. Section 3.8 showed that in languages with a noun–adjective distinction, it is normal for predicate adjectives to correspond to stative, inchoative, and causative verbs, but not for predicate nouns to do so. The reason is that the referential index of the noun cannot coexist with the theta-marked subject added by verbalizing morphology, by the Reference-Predication Constraint. If referential indices were only optionally associated with noun-like words in a particular language, then this asymmetry should disappear; all roots should be equally eligible for productive

---

[51] Attributive constructions also point toward there being a noun–adjective distinction in Samoan, although the evidence is more subtle. Nouns that modify other nouns do not require a genitive marker in Samoan. But Mosel and Hovdhaugen (1992) point out an asymmetry in linear order: when a noun is modified by both a "noun" and an "adjective," the order must be head noun-modifying noun-adjective, not head noun-adjective-modifying noun. I interpret this as showing that nouns can only combine with other noun projections by way of nonsyntactic root compounding, whereas adjectives can combine with nouns by syntactic merge.

and semantically transparent verbalization. But this is not what we find in any of the languages with relevant derivational morphology. Launey (1981: 275) discusses two Nahuatl affixes – inchoative *ya* and causative *–lia* – which he describes as attaching only to "adjectives." His examples have glosses like 'become white,' 'become sour,' 'become green/fresh,' 'become yellow,' 'make something white,' 'make sad,' and 'become big':

(181)   a Iztā-ya   in tepē-tl
            white-INCH the mountain-NSF
            'The mountain became white.'
         b O-quim-iztā-li   in cepayahui-tl in tē-tepe'.
            PAST-3pO-white-CAUS the snow-NSF   the PL-mountain
            'The snow has made the mountains white.'

These affixes apparently cannot attach to roots with clearly nominal meanings– the same asymmetry we find in languages like English.[52] Salish also has an inchoative derivation, produced by adding a glottal stop infix or a *–p* suffix to a root. This derivation too can apply to "adjectives," but not to nouns, as shown in (182) (van Eijk and Hess 1986; Davis 1999).[53]

(182)   a *za7Xw* 'to melt', from *zaXw* 'melted'   (adjectives)
            la7kw 'get loose' from *lakw* 'loose, untied'
            tsa-7-k 'get cool' from *tsek.tsák* 'cool'
            qwa-7-ez' 'go blue', from *qwez.qwáz* 'blue'

---

[52] Andrews (1975) describes another Nahuatl morpheme, *-ti*, as being a verbalizing suffix that can be added productively to nouns to create inchoative verbs meaning 'to become (like) X.' He implies that this is a relatively common process in Nahuatl, citing examples like *tlāc-ti* 'to become a person, to be born' and *teō-pix-cā-ti* 'to become a priest.' Launey's (1981: 274) discussion of the same affix, however, gives a different impression. He lists 'become' as only the fourth gloss of this affix when it attaches to nouns; other glosses that he puts first are 'to do,' 'to be for the moment,' and 'to behave like a.' A typical example of his is *ni-tequi-ti* 'I work' (from *tequi-tl* 'job, task'), which means 'I do work,' not 'I became a job.' I assume that Launey's discussion is the more accurate and complete one.

[53] Davis (1999) mentions briefly that there is another inchoative affix in Salish that attaches exclusively to nouns, the so-called "developmental" affix *–wil'c*:

(i)   a *sama7-wíl'c*   'become a white person'
       b *sk'uk'mi7t-wíl'c* 'become a child'

While this further supports the point that there are category differences in Salish, it does call into question my generalization that nouns cannot productively form inchoative verbs. The striking difference between this affix and the one in the text is that the developmental affix is phonologically heavier, constituting a full syllable. Perhaps this shows that it is lexically a verb rather than a Pred, and it combines with the noun by true incorporation rather than conflation. In that case, the N root and the V morpheme count as two separate nodes in the syntax, and the noun root can continue to bear its referential index (cf. also note 41 on Yidin).

The verbalization of predicate nouns is perfectly productive in Greenlandic; see note 42 for data and a tentative suggestion toward an analysis.

    b **qá-7-y'ecw* 'become a man', from *s-qaycw* 'man'   (nouns)
     *k'u-7-k'wm'it 'become a child' from *s-k'úk'wm'it* 'child'

There may not be a clear difference in the productivity of verbalizing "adjectives" and "nouns" in the Austronesian languages, both apparently being very common. But there is a predictable difference in the meaning of the verbalized form. Verbs that correspond to inherently adjectival roots in Tukang Besi have very simple and regular meanings, in which the state denoted by the root is predicated of the subject. The verbal form of *to'oge* 'big' means (unremarkably) 'to be big,' for example (Donohue 1999: 77). In contrast, the verbal form of a nounish word like *ha'o* 'hammer' means not 'to be a hammer,' but 'to use a hammer.' In the same way, the verbal form of *ba'e* 'fruit' means 'to bear fruit,' and the verbal form of *hoti* 'food' means not 'to be food' but 'to give food or clothing to the poor' (Donohue 1999: 81–82). This reconfirms that the two classes of roots have different grammatical properties, the one being free to take on a specifier directly, the others doing so only as the result of more complex and indirect lexical manipulations that remove or satisfy their referential index.

This difference is detectable even in Huallaga Quechua, the discussion in Weber (1989) notwithstanding. Weber cited the two examples in (183) as evidence that there is no morphological difference between "nouns" like 'stone' and "adjectives" like 'big' in Quechua:

(183)   rumi-ya-n;   hatun-ya-n.
        stone-INCH-3S   big-INCH-3S
        'It becomes stone'   'It becomes big'

But 'stone' is a material-denoting word, which one expects to be ambiguous between noun and adjective. To clarify the situation, David Weber (personal communication) performed a computer search on a large text (the Bible) to pull out examples that contained the morpheme –ča, an affix that creates transitive verbs. This affix is commonly glossed as 'cause to be,' but this gloss turned out not to be very accurate. In four cases, it attached to a root that English eyes see as an adjective. In these cases, it does consistently mean 'cause to be'; (184a) is typical.

(184)   a lanu-ča:-
        thin.round-VBZR
        'to make something thin' (e.g. yarn, when spinning)
    b wamra-ča:-
        child-VBZR
        'to adopt someone' (not: 'to make someone a child')

c pampa-ča:-
   ground-V B Z R
   'to bury something' (not: 'to make something be ground')
d kači-ča:-
   salt-V B Z R
   'to salt (meat), to put salt on' (not: 'to cause to be salt')

Weber also found approximately fifteen cases in which *–ča*: attached to a proto-typical noun root. In none of these examples does *–ča*: have a simple causative meaning, as shown by the representative examples in (184b,c,d). These have the same kinds of argument-like readings that nouns zero-derived into verbs have in English: (184c) is like Hale's and Keyser's (1993) location verbs (*to corral the horses*) and (184d) is like Hale's and Keyser's locatum verbs (*to salt the meat*). Quechua derivational patterns are thus sensitive to the same difference in categories as Nahuatl and Salish derivations are, once one digs beneath the surface.

Summarizing all this material, I have shown that there is evidence that some words in each language considered may not have a referential index, and there is evidence that some words in each language must have a referential index. For each language considered, there are at least two converging lines of evidence for this. Often there are also a few roots for which a referential index is optional, but that is true even in languages like English. Therefore, nouns seem to exist as a universally distinct lexical category after all. Furthermore, the grammatical consequences of being a noun are quite stable over this wide range of languages. These consequences can be masked in some situations by the presence of functional categories – Preds that make nouns look more verbal, and pronouns / determiners that make adjectives and verbs look more nominal. In languages in which both Pred and pronouns are systematically null, it is easy to get the impression that there is no difference in the lexical categories. For Salish, some Wakashan languages, and some Austronesian languages, this impression is magnified by two other quirks of the grammar: the fact that determiners happen to be required even with nouns, and the fact that tense and subject agreement are clitics rather than true affixes. The obligatoriness of determiners means that verbs and adjectives seem to be just as good arguments as nouns, since the crucial contrast in (171) does not show up as such. The clitic nature of tense and agreement means that they attach just as well to predicate nominals as to verbs, the extra Pred projection that usually blocks the attachment of T-related affixation to nouns having no effect on clitics attached in the PF component. This magnifies the impression that nouns are just as good predicates as verbs.

None of these properties – null Preds, null pronouns, obligatory determiners, and tense particles that are PF clitics – is remarkable in itself, but appearing all together in the same languages they largely conceal the otherwise obvious differences in categories. Nevertheless, for each language, a clearly recognizable class of nouns emerges once we know where to look, guided by the fundamental definition of nouns given in (1).

4 Adjectives as neither nouns nor verbs

4.1 The essence of having no essence

In chapter 2, I considered what distinguishes verbs from nouns and adjectives. The difference, I claimed, was that only verbs take a specifier, a syntactic position that is normally assigned a theme or agent theta-role. This is a sharpened version of the widespread intuition that verbs are the prototypical predicates of natural language (see, for example, Croft [1991] and Bhat [1994]). In chapter 3, I turned to nouns, asking what distinguishes them from adjectives and verbs. The answer was that nouns alone have criteria of identity, which allows them to bear referential indices. This is a sharpened and generalized version of the common intuition that nouns are uniquely suited to the task of referring. Now it is time to look more closely at adjectives, not as a foil for the other categories, but in their own right. What distinctive property do adjectives have that underlies their various morphological and syntactic characteristics?

The strongest and most interesting answer to this question would be to say that there is nothing special about adjectives. They are already distinguished from verbs by not licensing a specifier, and from nouns by not having a referential index. Ideally, this should be enough to completely characterize their behavior. Such a theory would preserve an important aspect of the Chomskian insight that one needs only two binary features to distinguish three or four categories ($+/-$N and $+/-$V from Chomsky [1970], or $+/-$Subj and $+/-$Obj from Jackendoff [1977]). Any additional features would be logically superfluous and would raise questions about why there are not more categories than there are. My particular theory contains an axiom that stipulates that there cannot be the equivalent of a $+$N, $+$V category, the Reference-Predication Constraint of chapter 3. One can, however, have a category that is $-$N, $-$V, and in this chapter I argue that is what adjectives are; one needs no new features and no new principles to account adequately for their basic properties across languages. This sharply distinguishes my approach from the descriptive and functionalist traditions, which often see adjectives as being by definition the prototypical modifiers of natural language (Croft 1991; Bhat 1994). My view is also distinguished from formal semantic attempts to characterize adjectives as being inherently gradable predicates (e.g. Larson and Segal [1995: 130–32], see also Kamp [1975] and Croft [1991]). Adjectives can be used as modifiers in many languages, and they can be compared, but I argue that these are derived properties of adjectives, not basic defining ones.

To defend this view, I consider three syntactic environments in which only an adjective can appear. First, adjectives can be direct attributive modifiers of nouns, but nouns and verbs cannot be (section 4.2):

(1)   a *a smart woman
        b *a genius woman
        c *a shine coin

Second, adjectives can be the complements of degree heads like *so, as, too*, and *how* in English, but neither nominal nor verbal projections can be (section 4.3):

(2)   a Mary is too smart for her own good.
        b *Mary is too a genius/a too genius for her own good.
        c *If you polish it, the coin will too shine in the dark to miss.

Third, adjectives can be resultative secondary predicates, unlike nouns and verbs (section 4.4):

(3)   a They beat the metal flat.
        b *They beat the metal a sword.
        c *They polished the coin shine.

These, then, are contexts in which adjectives do not form a natural class with either nouns or verbs.

How can these environments select for adjectives, if adjectives have no distinctive properties to select for? The logic of my theory permits only one answer to this question: these must be structures in which the theta-role as-signing property of verbs and the index-bearing property of nouns causes them (independently) to run afoul of general conditions. When that is the case, ad-jectives emerge as the only category that can be used, not because of any posi-tive feature that the adjective has, but by default, because nothing disqualifies them. I develop this type of theory in the next three sections. Section 4.5 then considers the relationship between adjectives and adverbs, claiming that they are essentially the same category. Finally, section 4.6 looks at the question of whether all languages have one and only one category of adjective. I argue that the answer is "yes," in spite of the conventional wisdom that this category is the most prone to crosslinguistic variation (Dixon 1982; Schachter 1985; Bhat 1994).

4.2   Attributive modification

4.2.1   Framing the issues

The most obvious distinctive characteristic of adjectives is that they modify nouns directly, in the so-called attributive construction. Nouns and verbs can not do this. (4) gives more examples illustrating this in English:

(4)   a a rich man; a shiny coin
       b *a wealth man; a genius man   (OK: a man of wealth, a boy-genius)
       c *a shine coin; a hunger man   (OK: a coin that shines, a shining coin)

The same generalization holds in Edo ((5)), in Tukang Besi ((6) [Donohue 1999]), and in a great many other languages.

(5)   a òkpìá zùròzùrò.   (Edo)
          man   lazy/foolish$_A$
          'the/a lazy man'
       b *òkpìá zùró   (OK: òkpìá nè ó zú!ró)
          man   be.foolish$_V$ man that he be.foolish(REL)
          'the laze man'   'the/a man that is foolish'
       c *òkpìá òzùrò   (OK: òkpìá óghé òzùrò; ekẹn-òkhókhò)
          man   laziness   man   of   laziness egg-chicken
          'the/a laziness man'   'chicken egg'

(6)   a te   woleke to'oge   (Tukang Besi)
          ART rat   big
          'the big rat'
       b *te   woleke tode   (OK: te   woleke t-*um*-ode)
          ART rat   flee   ART rat   REL-flee
          'the flee rat'   'the fleeing rat'
       c *te   iku woleke   (OK: te   iku *nu* woleke)
          ART tail rat   ART tail of rat
          'the rat('s) tail'   'the tail of the rat'

This is, indeed, the most common way for descriptive grammars to recognize a distinct class of adjectives: see, for example, Smeets (1989) on Mapuche, Heath (1984) on Nunggubuyu,[1] Feldman (1986) on Awtuw, Renck (1975) on Yagaria, Dixon (1977) on Yidin, Daley (1985) on Tzutujil, among others.

---

[1] In Nunggubuyu there is the interesting wrinkle that the attributive adjective–noun combination shows up as a morphological compound. Thus, Heath says that N–A compounds like *ani-dunggu-runggal* (NCL-word-big) 'big words' are found in the language, but N–N compounds are rare.

Nouns and verbs can, of course, modify nouns in less direct ways, if they are embedded in the right additional functional structure. For example, verbs can be the main predicate of a relative clause that modifies the head noun in all three languages. Nouns can become modifiers when they are embedded in a prepositional phrase headed by *of* in English, *ọghé* (which often reduces to just a floating high tone) in Edo, or *nu* in Tukang Besi. Nouns can also modify other nouns within a compound, where compounds can often be distinguished from syntactic modification on morphological and phonological grounds (e.g. the special stress pattern of many English compounds). Finally, nouns and verbs can modify nouns if they are transformed into adjectives by derivational morphology, as in *a wealthy man* or *a shiny coin*.[2] This range of options is available to adjectives as well: they can modify a head noun by being embedded in a relative clause (*a man who is rich*), by forming a compound (*a blackbird*), or by being derived into another adjective (*a reddish flower*). But adjectives also have an option that is unique to them: that of being merged directly with the head noun, with no obvious functional structure mediating the relationship.[3] (5a) shows that even the Pred head (spelled out overtly as *yé* in Edo) is not present in the attributive construction. This then gives us a descriptive characterization of the attributive construction: it consists of a(n almost) bare head in tight syntactic construction with a noun or noun projection. And the only heads that can, in point of fact, be in such a configuration are adjectives.

I already mentioned in section 4.1 that some functionalist authors like Croft (1991), Hengeveld (1992), and Bhat (1994) take the ability to modify nouns to be the defining – or at least the characteristic, prototypical – property of adjectives. In this, they follow traditional grammar. When medieval grammarians such as Peter Helias and Thomas of Erfurt first began to distinguish "adjectival nouns" from "substantive nouns," it was precisely because their new emphasis on syntax led them to realize that the one word class is essentially syntactically

---

[2] Participial forms of the verb can also modify nouns, as in *a shining light*. Two analyses of these are compatible with my theory: the participle suffix could be (among other things) a derivational affix that forms adjectives (Borer 1990), or the participle could be a kind of reduced relative clause (Kayne 1995). I leave a detailed study of participles to future research.

[3] There are languages such as Tagalog (Norvin Richards, personal communication) and Tzutujil (Daley 1985) in which a linking morpheme appears between an attributive adjective and a modified noun:

(i)   k'ay-i   nequun   (Tzutujil)
        bitter-LK thing
        'a bitter thing' (compare *k'ay* 'it is bitter')

One might think this is a functional head involved in modification somehow. In Tzutujil, however, the presence of this linker is phonologically conditioned: it appears after one syllable adjectives but not after longer ones. It could thus be purely a PF phenomenon. None of the languages I know well has a linker, so I take it to be of marginal significance and ignore it here.

independent whereas the other occurs essentially in construction with another noun (Robins 1989: 95).[4] Bhat (1994: ch. 12) legitimately criticizes generative grammar for being preoccupied with predicate adjectives, in which the adjectives are partially "verbalized" (for me, by the presence of a Pred) while neglecting the attributive construction that is more characteristic of adjectives. Pursuing this intuition would presumably lead one to identify some special positive property of adjectives that underlies their ability to be attributive modifiers.

Nevertheless, I believe that it is wrong to make the ability to modify nouns the defining or characteristic property of the category adjective. It is well known that English has adjectives that cannot be used as attributive modifiers, but only as predicates, as shown in (7a) and (7b). Other adjectives can be used attributively or predicatively, but only with a substantial change of meaning (Bolinger 1967; Siegel 1980).

(7)   a The dog is asleep.
          *The asleep dog.
        b Mary is ready.
          #The ready woman.
        c John is responsible (e.g. for losing the report).
          ≠The responsible man.

Such purely predicative adjectives are not uncommon across languages. The Athapaskan language Slave is an extreme case, in which all adjectives are restricted to predicate position, as complement to the copular verb; adjectives are never used as attributive modifiers in direct construction with a noun (Rice 1989: ch. 21).

(8)   a Yenene (be-ghǫ) sho   hįlį   (Rice 1989: 389–90)
          woman 3-of   proud/happy 3-is
          'The woman is happy/proud (of him/her).'
        b *yenene sho   (Keren Rice, personal communication)
          woman   proud/happy
          'a proud/happy woman'

In order to use a word like *sho* as a restrictive modifier of the noun, one must use a relative clause – the Slave equivalent of 'a woman that is proud' – which contains a copula and a complementizer as well as the adjective. One can very well say that the adjectives in (7) and (8) are not prototypical adjectives,

---

[4] In antiquity, the parts of speech were distinguished primarily on the basis of inflection, and adjectives happen to take the same range of number, gender, and case forms as nouns in Greek, Latin, and Sanskrit. For this reason, the distinction between nouns and adjectives was usually not noticed before the Middle Ages.

and (at least for (7)) that the properties they denote are not canonical ones. Nevertheless, they are adjectives.

It is not even clear that the attributive use of adjectives is the most common one statistically. In Croft's (1991) study of how adjectives are used in texts, attributive modification was the most common use, but the predicative use was far from rare: fully 33 percent of the tokens were predicate adjectives. Croft acknowledges that this is only weak support for his view that modification is the defining function of adjectives. Other counts put the percentage of predicative adjectives even higher: Thompson (1988: 174) and Hengeveld (1992: 59) found that 68 percent of adjectives were used predicatively, and only 32 percent were used attributively. Some functions of adjectives are doubtless more common than others, but no one use constitutes such an overwhelming majority that it is certain to hold the key to the category as a whole. This suggests that it is wrong to build a theory of adjectives around the property of noun modification. It would be better to do it the other way around, and derive the possibility of noun modification (for most adjectives) from a more general theory of what adjectives are.

4.2.2 *Explaining the basic restrictions*

On my conception, adjectives are simply lexical heads that are not nouns or verbs. Within my system, that adjectives alone can be attributive modifiers can be derived directly from this. The range of structures to consider is shown in (9), where a word of each category is merged directly with a noun projection to create a larger noun projection that functions as the argument of a verb. (I use a bare nominal without a DP projection for simplicity, but nothing significant changes if a determiner projection is added above the NP projection.)

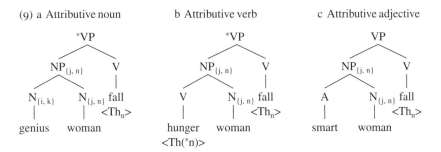

(9) a Attributive noun   b Attributive verb   c Attributive adjective

The target structure in (9c) looks a bit odd to those whose eyes have been blinded by X-bar theory. It violates the X-bar theoretic tenets that every head

must correspond to a maximal projection, and that every constituent of a phrase
other than its head must be a maximal projection. These axioms of X-bar theory
have led most previous researchers to say that the structure of attributive modification is either [DP D [NP AP [NP N]]] (the standard view) or [DP D [AP A
[NP N]]] (Abney [1987] and a few others after him). Both of these structures
square with X-bar theory by positing a maximal projection that the adjective
heads. Chomsky (1994; 1995), however, points out that these conditions are
merely conventions of the theory, with little true substance. He suggests that
one should not make a principled theoretical distinction between minimal, intermediate, and maximal projections, and that any two phrase-structural objects
should be allowed to "merge" to form a new phrase, as long as no independent
condition is violated. This less constrained "Bare Phrase Structure" perspective
is very much to be welcomed when it comes to the study of attributive modification, because there is plenty of straightforward evidence that (9c) is essentially
correct. On the one hand, the attributive adjective cannot take a complement
(*the proud of Mary parent*), nor can it be preceded by a degree element (*the
too/so proud parent*). If the structure is really [DP D [NP AP [NP N]]], as the
orthodox theory would have it, then it is completely mysterious why the AP
can contain little more than a bare A, and not the other usual ingredients of an
AP.[5] On the other hand, it is very clear that the A + NP constituent has the
external distribution of an NP, not that of an AP. It can be the complement of
a determiner but not a degree head, for example (*the proud parent, *too proud
parent*), and it can be the argument of ordinary NP-selecting verbs but not of
AP-selecting verbs like *seem* (*I respect proud parents, *John and Mary seem
proud parents*). These facts are problematic for Abney's [DP D [AP AP [NP N]]]
structure. There are thus compelling reasons to take (9c) to be the correct structure for attributive modification, and its existence gives empirical justification
for the move from X-bar theory to Bare Phrase Structure. My theoretical task,
then, is to take up the Bare Phrase Structure challenge of saying why the combination in (9c) is possible, but the combinations in (9a) and (9b) – which can
be formed just as easily by an unconstrained operation of merge – run afoul of
general principles.

---

[5] Whereas it is true that attributive adjectives cannot take complements, and cannot appear with a
fully fledged degree system, they can be a little more than just a head: the attributive adjective
can be modified by an adverb (*an extremely tall man*) or by *very* (*a very tall man*). Apparently it
is possible for one head to adjoin to another to make a new head within an attributive modifier,
but that is all. I discuss the adjunction of adverbs to adjectives in section 4.5 below. *Very* has
properties that distinguish it from all other words in English, but I tentatively assume that it is a
specialized adverb that falls under essentially the same analysis. Why A can merge with NP but
AP cannot is unclear and the basic facts seem to vary from language to language; see note 12.

Consider first (9a), in which a noun is merged with another noun (projection). Both nouns bear a referential index, by definition. Moreover, the two indices must be distinct, given that neither noun is inherently anaphoric. Elements with little or no intrinsic lexical content, such as pronouns, null operators, NP-traces, and theta-roles, have dependent indices. A noun projection that c-commands any of these items can bind it, so that they share an index, which helps to license the noun in accordance with the Noun Licensing Condition of chapter 3. The indices of lexically specified nouns, however, are not dependent in this way. As a result, one noun phrase cannot bind another one that it c-commands (Condition C of Chomsky's [1981] Binding theory), giving the contrast between (10a) and (10b) (Lasnik 1989: ch. 9).

(10)   a *Mary$_{\{i,n\}}$ thinks the genius$_{\{k,i\}}$ will win big on the quiz show.
        b Mary$_{\{i,n\}}$ thinks that she$_{\{i\}}$ will win big on the quiz show.
        c Mary's$_{\{i,n\}}$ mother thinks the genius$_{\{k,i\}}$ will win big on the quiz show.

(10a) is bad even though it is perfectly possible for the same person to be both Mary and a genius; indeed, the two phrases can refer to the same person as long as neither one c-commands the other, as in (10c). Because one lexical noun cannot bind another, lexical nouns cannot license each other for purposes of the NLC, as shown in (11).

(11)   a That woman$_{\{j,n\}}$ will win<Ag$_n$> big on the quiz show.
        b That woman$_{\{j,n\}}$, she$_{\{n\}}$ will win big on the quiz show.
        c That woman$_{\{j,n\}}$, Op$_{\{n\}}$they are sure to pick t$_{\{n\}}$ to be on the quiz show.
        d *That woman$_{\{j,n\}}$, the genius$_{\{k,n\}}$ will win big on the quiz show.

These considerations also imply that *genius* cannot be licensed by being coin-dexed with *woman* in (9a). Therefore, both nouns must be coindexed with something else in the c-command domain of their maximal projection, in order to pass the NLC. One of the nouns can fulfill this requirement by being chosen as the head of the phrase at the time of its construction. Whichever noun is chosen as the head of the newly formed category provides the label of the cat-egory as a whole (Chomsky 1995: sec. 4.3), and the referential index is part of this label, I assume. Indeed, since being a noun reduces to having a referential index in my system, it is natural to say that the referential index *is* the label N. The index of the head is therefore visible to the outside world and can be li-censed, for example by being coindexed with the theta-role of the nearby verb *fall* in (9a). The elementary operation merge is, however, unable to combine two indices into a new index.[6] The index of the noun that is not chosen as the head is thus trapped inside the noun phrase; it is unable to enter into a binding relationship with anything else in the structure, because it does not c-command anything but the head noun.[7] It therefore violates the NLC. This explains the ungrammaticality of the attributive noun construction in (9a).

There are, of course, other syntactic resources that can achieve approximately the intended effect. A noun can modify another noun if it is first theta-marked by a preposition, as in expressions like *a man of sorrows*. Such constructions are particularly common in African languages, including Edo and Chichewa. A noun can also be transformed into an adjective by derivational morphology, after which it can be used attributively. But a pure attributive noun construction is impossible. The minimally different representations are compared in (12).

(12)   a *a $[_{N\{i,j\}}$ power$]$ $[_{N\{k,l\}}$ man$]$
        b a $[_{N\{i,j\}}$ man$]$ $[$of$<$Th$_1>$ $[_{N\{k,l\}}$ power$]]$
        c a $[_A$ powerful$]$ $[_{N\{i,j\}}$ man$]$

Consider next the possibility of an "attributive verb" configuration, in which a verb is merged with a noun to form a noun projection, as in (9b). The characteristic property of verbs is that they have a specifier, to which they generally assign an agent or theme theta-role. If this theta-role is not properly assigned, the structure is ruled out by the theta criterion. What could the verb assign its theta-role to in (9b)? Theta role assignment is a very local relationship: a verb can only discharge its theta-role to a maximal projection that is a structural sister of the verb or its projection. The verb does not, however, project a phrase in (9b), by hypothesis. Therefore, the only expression that the verb *hunger* could conceivably assign its theta-role to is the head noun *woman*. But this element is not a

---

[6] In this respect, pure merge contrasts with a conjunction head like *and*, which can combine the indices of the two conjuncts into a new, plural index which is the sum of the two constituent indices. Thus, a tentative representation for *the woman and the genius* would be:

(i) $[_{NP\{m=i+k,\ n=j+l\}}$ The woman$_{\{i,j\}}$ and the genius$_{\{k,l\}}]$ fell $<$Th$_n>$

[7] The attributive noun certainly could never get a theta-role. It is conceivable that it could c-command a pronoun, however, if the NP it modified contained a complement. The attributive noun probably does c-command the pronominal possessor of the complement in (i), for example.

(i)   *The $[$genius$_{\{i,j\}}$ $[$sister$_{\{k,l\}}$ of his$_{\{j\}}$ best friend$_{\{m,n\}}]]$

But even if *genius* could technically be licensed by binding *his* as a kind of resumptive pronoun in (i), it could not thereby be interpreted as a modifier of *sister*. Thus, even this odd structure is ruled out by the theory.

maximal projection according to the Bare Phrase Structure principles of Chomsky (1995), since it provides the label for the phrase as a whole, and non-maximal projections cannot be theta-marked. The noun phrase *hunger woman* as a whole is a maximal projection, but *hunger* cannot theta-mark this phrase because it is contained in it. There is no phrase that is both a maximal projection and the sister of a projection of *hunger*; *hunger* thus cannot assign its theta-role, and the structure is ruled out.

Things would come out differently if merge took the verb to be the head of the projection in question, rather than the noun. Then the noun *woman* would count as both a maximal projection and a sister of the verb, and theta-marking could take place. But the resulting structure would be a VP, not an NP at all. As such, it could not bear a referential index, and could not serve as the argument of another verb, such as *fall*. It follows, then, that verbs cannot be attributive modifiers either.[8] They can be modifiers of nouns if they are part of a more complex structure, such as a relative clause, in which there is an additional noun phrase that the verb can assign its theta-role to (see (13b)). Alternatively, verbs can become modifiers of nouns by losing their theta-role in the process of being transformed into an adjective (see (13c)). But a pure attributive verb construction is as impossible as an attributive noun construction ((13a)).

(13) a *a $[_{N\{k,l\}}$ $[_V$ shine<Th$_{??}$>] $[_{N\{k,l\}}$ coin]]
      b a $[_{N\{k,l\}}$ coin] $[Op_l$ that $[t_l$ shines<Th$_l$>]]
      c a $[_{N\{i,j\}}$ $[_A$ shiny] $[_{N\{i,j\}}$ coin]]

Let us turn then to the possibility of merging an adjective with a noun or noun projection, as in (9c). The adjective does not have a referential index that needs to be equated with something else in the structure, so it is not in danger of violating the NLC. Nor does it have a theta-role that it must assign, so it is not in danger of violating the theta criterion. This structure thus violates none of the basic principles, and it is grammatical (subject to the lexical semantic properties of the heads involved). This completes the explanation of why only adjectives are suited to being attributive modifiers. Adjectives have no special property that equips them to be attributive modifiers, but neither do they have

---

[8] This reasoning can be extended to verbs like *seem* and *appear*, which do not theta-mark their specifier position, but do have a subject-matter theta-role to assign to a complement. Weather verbs like *rain* are the only ones that might not have any theta-role to assign at all (but see Rizzi [1986a] on quasi-argumental theta-roles). But even they are subject to a related requirement: they must have an expletive *it* subject. There is no such subject in *a rain day*, and this can be used to explain why this combination is bad, as compared to *a rainy day*.

a special property that conflicts with this role. They are thus used as attributive modifiers more or less by default.[9]

4.2.3   *Further consequences of the analysis*

Certain further properties about attributive modification follow directly from this analysis. The structure in (9c) can, for example, be iterated. Another adjective could be merged with the nominal projection formed by merging the first adjective with the noun. This second adjective is also not in danger of violating the NLC or the theta criterion. I thus explain the fact that a noun phrase can in principle be made up of one noun together with any number of adjectives. This freedom is realized in English and, to a more limited extent, in Edo.

(14)   a a big dog
       b a big black dog
       c a big black hungry dog
       d an angry big black hungry dog
       e ágá   khérhé pèrhè   (Edo)
          chair small   flat
          'a little flat chair'

This full freedom is, of course, restricted by the lexical meanings of the adjectives (which combinations make sense), as well as by language particular factors.[10] But the attested possibilities are the ones the theory expects.

My theory also correctly predicts that the result of merging an adjective with a noun must always be a noun phrase, never an adjective phrase. Under Bare Phrase Structure assumptions, such facts do not go without saying. Merge can apply freely to combine any two categories, and can in principle pick the label of either category to be the label of the phrase as a whole. This freedom is, however, restricted by other principles in practice. What, then, would it mean

---

[9] My theory implies that there is no connection of theta-role assignment between an attributive adjective and the head noun. Some researchers have seen a thematic relation here, given that *a smart woman* entails that the woman in question is smart. The entailment does not, however, go through in full generality (Bolinger 1967) (see the discussion of *responsible* below (27) for an example). Also Cinque (1990) shows that some predicate adjectives take external arguments (e.g. *long, dangerous*) and others take internal arguments (e.g. *unlikely, clear*). This difference is neutralized when the adjectives are used attributively: *an unlikely event* and *a clear proposal* have the same syntactic structure as *a long story* and *a dangerous proposal*. If theta-role assignment were involved, this would be a problematic violation of the UTAH. But if theta-role assignment is not at issue, this problem does not arise. See below for some preliminary remarks on the semantic relationship between the attributive adjective and the head noun.

[10] There are languages that allow only one adjective to combine attributively with a noun, including Yimas (Foley 1991) and Nunggubuyu (Heath 1984). The restriction may be prosodic or phonological in nature rather than syntactic, since the two words become a single phonological unit, at least in Nunggubuyu.

to say that the merger of an adjective and a noun was an adjective? It would mean that the newly formed phrase had no referential index; otherwise the phrase is nominal, by definition. But the noun part does have a referential index. The referential index of the noun must then be trapped inside the phrase as a whole, and cannot enter into a binding relationship with some dependent element that it c-commands, a violation of the NLC. An AP consisting of an A and an N is thus ruled out for essentially the same reason that an NP consisting of two Ns is. The correctness of this for English is illustrated in (15).

(15) a Mary is *(an) intelligent professor.
         (compare: Mary is (*an) intelligent; Mary is *(a) professor.)
      b *Mary seems intelligent professor.
         *Mary seems professor intelligent.
         (compare: Mary seems intelligent; ??Mary seems a professor.)
      c *I pounded the metal [flat bar]
      d *I built a [big dog] house (intended meaning: 'a house for a big dog')

(15a) shows that the merger of an adjective and a singular count noun in predicate position must be introduced by the indefinite determiner; in this respect, the phrase as a whole necessarily behaves like a singular count noun, not like an adjective. Verbs like *seem* select an AP predicate but not an NP predicate for most speakers of American English. (15b) shows that, for such speakers, *seem* also cannot select the combination of an A and an N, because it must be nominal. (15c) shows that an A+N cannot be used as a resultative secondary predicate (see section 4.4), and (15d) shows that an A+N cannot be used as an attributive modifier. This truth can also be seen in a different way in Edo. When an adjective and a noun are merged together in Edo and the result is used as a predicate, it must be the complement of *rè*, the Pred that selects for a nominal phrase, not *yé*, the Pred that selects an adjective phrase (see section 3.8 on this distinction).

(16) a Òzó yé   zùròzùrò̩.
         Ozo Pred$_A$ lazy/foolish
         'Ozo is foolish.'
      b Òzó rè   òkpìá.
         Ozo Pred$_N$ man
         'Ozo is a man.'
      c Òzó rè   / *yé   òkpìá zùròzùrò̩.
         Ozo Pred$_N$ / *Pred$_A$ man   lazy/foolish
         'Ozo is a lazy/foolish man.'

The structure of the ungrammatical version of (16c) is given in (17); note that the nonhead 'man' of the AP is not properly coindexed with anything.

(17)

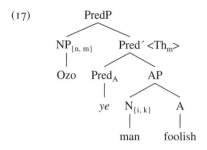

Attributive modification structures contrast minimally with modificational compounding in many of these respects. Both constructions express a kind of restrictive modification. But whereas the nonhead in an attributive construction must be an adjective, the nonhead in a compound can perfectly well be a noun, as shown in (18).

(18) a the grèen hóuse.   (attributive adjective)
      b the gréenhòuse (place for growing plants)   (A–N compound)
      c *the dòg hóuse   (*attributive noun)
      d the dóghòuse   (N–N compound)

My theory explains the contrast between (18a) and (18c), but this contrast disappears in comparable compounds, as shown by (18b) and (18d). Modificational N–N compounds are also found in Edo (e.g. *ekọnkhọ́khọ̀*, 'chicken egg,' from *ekẹn* 'egg' and *ọ̀khọ́khọ̀* 'chicken') and many other languages. The combination of a noun plus an adjective can also be an adjective, if the combining is done by compounding, rather than by syntactic merge:

(19) a Chris seems *girl-crazy*.   (N+A = A compounds)
      b You took my *pea-green* sweater.

The crucial point is that an attributive construction is a *syntactic* combination of heads. Both parts of the attributive relation are thus fully specified syntactic objects and are subject to syntactic principles like the NLC. Modificational compounding between N roots and A roots in English, in contrast, happens in the morphological component, apart from the syntax. Thus, referential indices are not assigned to the parts of the compounds in (18) and (19), but only to the word as a whole if it is a noun. There is thus no violation of the NLC in these examples. This means, of course, that in order to evaluate the predictions of the theory one must be able to distinguish compounds from attributive constructions in a noncircular way. In some languages this can be difficult to do in practice. In many cases, however, there will be evidence from morphophonological considerations such as stress assignment (like the Compound Stress Rule in English), from internal sandhi processes, or from inflectional morphology that distinguish the two. In such cases, the predictions of the theory should show up clearly. (I return to the implications of this contrast for the overall structure of the grammar in chapter 5.)

One fact that does not follow from my theory so far but should is the fact that it is not usually possible for two As to combine to form an AP, as shown by the striking contrast in (20).

(20)   a John is a big strong man.
         b *John is big strong.

The same contrast is found in Edo ((21)), in St'át'imcets Salish ((22)), in the New Guinean language Awtuw (Feldman 1986: 127), and in others.

(21)   a ágá   khéré pèrhè.   (Edo)
           chair small flat
           'a small flat chair'
         b *Né!né ágá   yé   khéré pèrhè.
           the   chair PRED small flat
           'The chair is small flat.'

(22)   a Kwikws spzúza7 i   sáq'w-a. (St'át'imcets)
           small   bird   DET/PL fly-DET (Dermidache and Matthewson 1995)
           'The ones who flew were small birds.'
         b *Kwikws tseqwtsíqw i   ats'x-en-Ø-án-a.
           small   red   DET/PL see-TRAN-3sA-1sE-DET
           'The ones I saw were small red.'

(The contrast in (22) further illustrates the point, argued in section 3.9, that Salish distinguishes the same three categories as English; a complex noun phrase is possible in this language if and only if the first word is an adjective and the second is a noun.) It seems that there must be a noun in one of these constructions to hold the adjectives together. According to Bare Phrase Structure theory, however, the merger of an adjective and an adjective could in principle form a larger adjectival projection. Only one of the two adjectives would count as the head of the newly created phrase, but since the nonhead is an adjective, it is not in danger of violating the theta criterion or the NLC. The first adjective has no referential index that must be licensed by coindexing, and it has no theta-role that it must assign. Therefore, simple A+A combinations should be possible as far as my syntactic principles are concerned.

This is, I believe, a job for the semantic side of the analysis. It is not the referential index of the noun *per se* that is required for an attributive construction to cohere, but its criterion of identity. To see this, consider in crude terms the semantics of attributive modification. The usual semantic formulas do not work directly off the shelf, because they assume that As and Ns are one-place predicates, of type $<e,t>$. In contrast, I assume they are saturated expressions, of type $<e>$, using the technology of Chierchia (1985). Chierchia and Turner (1988: 287) give a first-pass semantics for the attributive construction using the "join" operator, as follows:

(23) $[_N \text{ A N}]' = A' \cap N'$

The join operator is defined in such a way that the predicate corresponding to $A' \cap N'$ (written as $^\cup(A' \cap N')$) is the conjunction of the predicate that corresponds to A and the predicate that corresponds to N, in the usual way:

(24) $\lambda x \, ^\cup(A' \cap N')(x) = \lambda x \, [^\cup A'(x) \, \& \, ^\cup N'(x)]$

A sentence like *That is a red book* thus entails *That is red* and *That is a book*, just as in the usual account in which *red* and *book* are predicates.[11]

Chierchia and Turner's schema as is could interpret an $[_A \text{ A}_1 \text{ A}_2]$ construction just as well as $[_N \text{ A N }]$. The interpretation would be $A_1' \cap A_2'$, the predicate version of which is $\lambda x \, [^\cup A_1'(x) \, \& \, ^\cup A_2'(x)]$, a coherent and well-defined expression. A slight adaptation of this semantics can, however, bring out why a criterion of identity is crucial. In my discussion of the semantic side of theta-role assignment in section 3.6, I invoked the following condition:

(25)   The variables introduced by each lexical item are distinct.

The schema in (24) does not obey this dictum; rather the A and N correspond to predicates of the same variable. If (25) is valid, then the variables corresponding to the two parts of an attributive construction need to be equated by an additional condition, which has the form of an identity statement. Thus, in place of (24), I propose to define the join operator as follows:

(26) $\lambda x \, ^\cup(X' \wedge Y')(x) = \lambda x \, \exists y \, [^\cup X'(y) \, \& \, ^\cup Y'(x) \, \& \, \text{same}(Y)(x, y)]$

---

[11] This is, of course, only the simplest case, in which the adjective and noun are understood intersectively. In many cases the A+N is interpreted subsectively (a *good violinist* is a violinist, but not necessarily good in any general sense), or even nonintersectively (an *alleged communist* is not necessarily a communist). I assume that the refinements that are needed to generalize to these cases are orthogonal to my point about the role the criterion of identity of a noun plays in making attributive constructions interpretable.

According to (26), X is a red book if and only if there is something that is
red and that thing is the same book as X. This is a reasonable rendering of an
A+N combination. (26) can also be applied recursively to give a meaning for
an [A+[A+N]] combination, in the obvious way. (26) is undefined, however,
for an A+A combination. The expression "same(Y)(x,y)," in particular, is undefined when Y is an adjective, because adjectives do not have a criterion of
identity. This explains why there is no attributive A+A construction. In informal
terms, an attributive construction involves a statement of sameness (a red book
means that *the same thing* is both red and a book), and a noun is needed to supply
the standard of sameness that makes this possible. An attributive construction
must thus modify a noun for much the same semantic reason that theta-role
assignment must be to a noun. In both cases, a noun is necessary to bind the
structure together in the face of (25). I consider the contrasts in (20)–(22) to be
one of the most striking demonstrations that the criterion of identity associated
with nouns is linguistically significant. (Of course, there may be other ways for
two As to become a coherent semantic unit; I suggest other ways in sections 4.4
and 4.5 below.) This completes my account of what lexical items can participate
in this kind of direct merge.[12]

4.2.4   On adjectives that are always or never used attributively

My analysis is designed to capture the fact that the same lexical items can
normally be used both as attributive modifiers and as predicates under a Pred
head. For example, the same word *tall* appears in both *the tall woman* and

---

[12] One notable fact about attributive constructions in English that does not follow from my analysis
is the fact that the adjective cannot take a complement (*the angry woman* versus **the angry at
social injustice woman*). Given my Bare Phrase Structure-style approach, there should be no
inherent difference between the features and properties of a simple A head and those of a larger
phrase that gets its label from the A head. Thus, the expressions *angry* and *angry at social
injustice* should be equivalent with respect to the principles I have discussed.

The standard assumption in the literature has been that **the angry at social injustice woman*
is ruled out by some kind of "Head Final Filter," which stipulates that the head of the AP must
be linearly adjacent to the N it modifies (Emonds 1976; Williams 1982; Giorgi and Longobardi
1991: 95–100). Such a filter would work within my theory too, although it is not very satisfying.
More crosslinguistic work needs to be done to see if the restriction is particular to English or
not. Bhat (1994) claims that the same contrast is found in head-final Kannada, but it is not found
in head-initial Greek (Natalia Kariaeva, personal communication).

Where the restriction holds, it might be a sign that a restructuring process applies, reanalyzing
the adjective and noun as a single complex head. There are a number of syntactic similarities
between A+N constructions and the V+V restructuring studied by Rizzi (1982) and others. For
example, the NP cannot be moved away, stranding the A, just as VP cannot move, stranding
the restructuring verb. Also, the distinction between unergative and unaccusative adjectives is
neutralized in attributive constructions (see note 9), just as the difference between unergative and
unaccusative first verbs is destroyed by restructuring. The fact that attributive adjectives cannot
take a complement fits into this pattern, since restructuring verbs also cannot take complements
distinct from those of the verbs they restructure with.

The woman is tall. There is, however, a line of semantically oriented research, initiated by Siegel (1980), that is built on the opposite intuition. Siegel points out that some adjectives in English can only be used predicatively, and others can only be used attributively (see also Bolinger [1967]):

(27)   a The main idea escaped Chris.
        b *This idea is main. (compare: This idea is the main one.)

(28)   a The woman is ready now.
        b ?*The ready woman waited impatiently for her husband.

Other adjectives can be used in both environments, but only with a significant shift in meaning; for example, saying *That person is responsible* (e.g. for the fiasco) does not allow us to refer to her or him as *the responsible person*. Other languages seem to show a derivational difference between attributive adjectives and predicative adjectives. Russian, for example, has "short form" adjectives that are used only predicatively and "long form" adjectives that are used attributively:

(29)   a Dom   novyj/   nov.   (Pereltsvaig 2000)
          house new(long)/new(short)
          'The house is new.'
        b Novyj/   *nov   dom   stoit   na gore.
          new(long)/new(short) house stands on hill
          'The new house stands on a hill.'

   Siegel's point can be extended to other typological facts. Some languages use adjectives only in attributive environments. The West African languages of Vata and Gbadi are like this, according to Koopman (1984: 64–66):

(30)   a kO! *Kad*-Ò   'a big man, old man'   (attributive As [Vata])
          kUà *kad*-Uà   'old men, big men'
          slí *kád*-à   'a big house'
        b *Wa (lÈ)   *kad*-Uà.   (no predicate As)
          they PRED old

(*lÈ* is a copular particle that is used with predicate nominals in Vata.) Tamil (Wetzer 1996), Hua (Schachter 1985: 16), and the Yagaria language of New Guinea (Hengeveld 1992) are other languages of this type. In Yagaria, for example, the effect of a predicate adjective is achievable only by combining the adjective with (if nothing else) the nominal element *na* 'matter, thing' (Renck 1975):

(31)   a haga' dote'na   (attributive adjective)
          tasty food
          'tasty food'

b Ma'i ege-mo   haga-*(na)-(e')
  this banana-CON tasty-thing-PRED
  'This banana is tasty.' (lit.... 'is a tasty thing')

Other languages use adjectives predicately but not attributively. I have already mentioned Slave as being such a language; the examples are repeated in (32).

(32)   a Yenene (be-ghǫ) sho   hįlį   (Rice 1989: 389–90)
         woman 3-of   proud/happy 3-is
         'The woman is happy/proud (of him/her).'
       b *yenene sho   (Keren Rice, personal communication)
         woman proud/happy
         'a proud/happy woman'

The Ika language of Columbia is another such: most adjectives cannot modify a noun directly, but must combine first with a copular verb like *kawa* 'seem' (Frank 1990). The modification structure that results is a kind of internally headed relative clause, as is normal in the language:

(33) (i)   Aná?nuga [awʌn? *(kawa)] guákʌ-ža
           animal   big   seem   kill-MED
           'It kills big animals.'

In the light of such facts, Siegel (1980) argues that there is not one lexical category, corresponding to the traditional adjective. Rather, there are two fundamentally different categories: attributive adjectives and predicative adjectives. Within Siegel's Categorial Grammar assumptions, the two are assigned to very different types. Attributive adjectives combine with a common noun to form a new common noun phrase; for Siegel, they are of category <CN/CN>. Predicative adjectives, in contrast, are of the same type as ordinary intransitive verbs; they are <e/t> (they take an entity – the subject – and produce something that has a truth value – a clause). In principle, these have no more in common than any other two categories. Siegel could analyze Slave as a language that has only the <e/t> adjectives and Vata as a language that has only the <CN/CN> adjectives. Russian has both categories, with a rule of derivational morphology that maps one type of adjective into the other. English is like Russian, except that there is no morphology associated with the lexical rule that maps most <e/t> adjectives into <CN/CN> adjectives (or vice versa). English and similar languages can thus easily give the impression that there is a unified class of adjective, but this is an illusion, according to Siegel.

While it is true that not every adjective can be used both predicatively and attributively, I believe that the English situation is the rule and Siegel's cases are the exception, not vice versa. There are several reasons for this. First, the large majority of adjectives can be used both predicatively and attributively in a majority of languages that have surface adjectives in the first place. It is true not just in English, but also in the Romance languages, Celtic languages, Semitic languages, Kwa languages, Bantu languages, Australian languages, some New Guinean languages, Mapuche, Abaza, and many others. Second, we saw in chapter 2 that predicate adjectives are not of category <e/t> at all; this view wrongly blurs the distinction between adjectives and verbs and fails to account for the differences between them that are revealed by unaccusativity diagnostics and other morphosyntactic tests. If predicate adjectives are not of category <e/t>, it is not so clear that they differ from attributive adjectives in category after all, making it more tempting to relate the two. Finally, the difference between the two kinds of adjectives in Russian looks more like an inflectional difference concerning adjectival agreement than a derivational one. Attributive adjectives must agree with the noun head in all features in Russian, including case, whereas case agreement is not required for predicate adjectives (perhaps because their subject is generally in the unmarked, nominative case).[13] This, then, is not such compelling morphological evidence that two distinct lexical categories are involved.

What, then, can be said about those adjectives that can only be used in one way? I believe that the answer is different for English-like languages in which the majority of adjectives can be used either way, and for Vata- or Slave-like

---

[13] This statement might bring it to the reader's mind that I have said nothing about adjectival agreement. Nor do I intend to say much about this. One thing is certain: on my theory agreement in gender and number between an adjective and a noun cannot be an instance of specifier-head agreement. The subject of the predicate adjective is never in the specifier of the adjective in my view, nor are the head noun and its attributive adjective in a specifier-head configuration. This is not a serious theoretical problem, however, Minimalism already having retreated from the claim that all agreement is spec-head agreement.

The basic facts about adjectival agreement seem to be quite language-particular, which is my excuse for not studying them in detail. Some languages never show agreement between an adjective and a noun (English, Edo); some languages always show agreement between an adjective and some nearby noun (Spanish, Chichewa); a few languages show more agreement in attributive constructions than in predicative ones (Russian, German). I tentatively assume that a statement like (i) holds in languages that have agreement morphology on adjectives:

(i)   An adjective assumes the phi-features (e.g. gender, number, case) of the closest nominal that c-commands it.

Some apparent counterexamples to (i) are easily solved by positing null noun phrases (e.g. PRO) in control structures. Some languages might make the stronger requirement that the noun projection and the agreeing adjective must c-command each other; such languages will have agreement in attributive constructions but not in predicative ones. This view predicts that no language will have agreement on predicative adjectives but not on attributive ones – unless the agreement is really the agreement in person as well as number that is associated with tense, appearing on the adjective as a result of cliticization (as in Abaza; see section 2.5).

languages in which all adjectives have a limited distribution. For English-type languages, the effect seems to be semantic. The adjectives that can only be used predicatively all denote very transitory properties, which typically hold for a short time: *ready*, *present*, *handy*, *asleep*, *awake*, and so on. This is a robust generalization, noted by Bolinger (1967) and others. Enç (1986) points out that attributive adjectives do not have a time parameter different from the noun they are associated with. For example, *Abraham Lincoln was a good president* can only mean that he was good at the same time as he was a president; it cannot mean that he was good up to age 10 and a president as an adult. Now nouns typically correspond to properties held for some extended period of time. This leads to a near contradiction when the noun is modified by a highly transitory adjective, as in *?*Abraham Lincoln was an asleep president*. The property denoted by *asleep* could not be true of Lincoln over the same period of time that the property *president* was, or even for a meaningful subperiod of that time. The same observation accounts for the shift in meaning that some adjectives show depending on how they are used. *That employee is responsible* can have a very transitory meaning, in which he is responsible right now for some specific duty. In contrast, *the responsible employee* does not have this meaning; it means that being responsible is characteristic of the person's whole tenure as an employee.

This semantically based account predicts that roughly the same words should be predicate adjectives in other languages, and this seems to be true. Kilega, for example, is a Bantu language that has a few words that can only be used predicatively, never attributively (Kinyalolo, personal communication). They stand out in the language on formal grounds because they do not have the noun class prefixes that most other lexical items have. They also refer to very transitory conditions, as predicted:

(33) (ii)   a Muntu   úmozi á-li   lugali.   (Kilega)
            1.person 1.one 3sS-be lying
            'The person is lying down.'
         b *[Muntu lugali] a-ku-tend-a.
            1.person lying   2sS-PROG-talk-FV
            'The lying-down person is talking.'

To develop this suggestion fully would require a complete discussion of how time denoting expressions are used in natural languages, which I cannot engage in here. But I assume that these details can be filled in, so that the inability of an adjective like *asleep* to be used attributively does not undermine my overall theory of categories.

The adjectives that can be used attributively but not predicatively in English (*main, principal, mere, former. . .*) also seem to be a semantically coherent class, but it is harder to put one's finger on just how to characterize it. This impression is confirmed by the fact that semantically similar adjectives show the same behavior in unrelated languages like Edo:

(34)   a ọ̀tá   kpàtàkì
          speech main
          'the main idea'
        b *Ọ̀tá   nà   yé kpàtàkì.
          speech that be main
          'That idea is main.'

The striking fact about these adjectives is that they do not seem to mean very much by themselves. It is known that the meaning of an adjective is often filled out by the meaning of the noun that it modifies: a good pianist is good in a very different way from a good carpenter, and a good villain has quite different traits from a good hero. In the same way, the meaning of *main* or *mere* is interpreted relative to its head, and this fills out its meaning. I suggest then that *main* and *mere* are so semantically underspecified that they cannot be used on their own to characterize a well-defined state. This is why *This idea is main* is defective, but *This is the main idea* is not. Again, more work needs to be done to fill out this account – in particular one would have to face the semantics of nonintersective adjectival modifiers – but this should be enough to show how a unified syntax of adjectives can be maintained.

Languages like Vata and Slave call for a more syntactic approach. In these languages, all adjectives have a limited distribution, regardless of their lexical meanings. For Vata, it is easy to see why this might be. Adjectival predication does not come for free in my theory; rather the adjective must appear as the complement of a Pred head, which creates the theta-role for the subject. Vata, then, can be analyzed as a language that happens not to have the relevant Pred, as an accidental lexical gap. This "parameter" is stated in (35).[14]

(35)   Some languages do not have $Pred_{Adj}$ (Vata, Tamil, Hua, Yagaria, etc.).

Conversely, we can capture the fact that adjectives can only be used as primary predicates in Slave with the parameter in (36).

---

[14] In contrast, all languages apparently have an NP-selecting Pred, given that all languages permit predicate nominals of some kind (Hengeveld 1992). The difference can be explained functionally. Some languages have few adjectives and a paraphrase for predicate adjectives is always available; one can replace 'That house is old' with 'That house is an old one,' for example. Therefore it is rather easy to get by without a $Pred_A$. But all languages have many nouns, and there is no trivial paraphrase for a predicate nominal, so doing without $Pred_N$ is harder.

(36)   In some languages, A must be in the minimal domain of a Pred (Slave, Ika, Japanese, etc.).

There is nothing particularly insightful about this proposal, but it does the job in a straightforward way. (35) is a rather normal-looking parameter of variation, since we expect languages to differ to some extent in their inventories of functional categories; it is not markedly different then from the familiar fact that English has articles and Japanese does not. (36) is somewhat more peculiar, in that it cannot be tied to the presence or absence of one particular vocabulary item. In the best case scenario, it would be deducible from more basic properties of the languages in question.[15] But even if this does not prove to be possible, (36) seems preferable to Siegel's wholesale fragmentation of the category adjective into subcategories – especially since one still needs to explain the systematic patterns that we see in adjective usage across languages. One would still want to ask *why* Slave has <e/t> adjectives but not <CN/CN> adjectives, for example. (36) at its worst is no more shallow than the alternative in this respect. The essential claim of (36) is that adjectives fail to be used attributively in Slave not because of any defect in their own nature, but because of some property of the language as a whole. ((36) is important in section 4.6.3; it plays a role in explaining why some languages seem not to distinguish between adjectives and verbs.)

Overall, then, we have seen that adjectives are particularly suited to being used as attributive modifiers because they are free of the burden of having a theta-role to assign or a referential index to be licensed. As a result, they can show up buried inside a noun phrase without the need to enter into linguistic relationships with anything outside that noun phrase. Being an attributive modifier is not part of the definition of being an adjective, but it does follow naturally from the definition. The general expectation, then, is that any adjective can be used attributively as well as in other contexts to be discussed. Lexical and grammatical factors sometimes intervene, so that the full range of possibilities is not realized in particular cases; for example, *asleep* gives a deviant meaning when used attributively in English, and *kadU* does not get the support it needs to be used predicatively in Vata. But these local complications should not detract from our unified understanding of what it is to be an adjective.

---

[15] For example, it could be relevant that attributive adjectives so often agree with the noun that they modify in number, gender, and case in languages that inflect for these things (see note 13). Suppose that this agreement is actually necessary to the existence of an attributive construction, for some reason. Then if adjectives could not bear agreement (not even covert agreement) in a particular language, they would be barred from attributive constructions in that language. They could only show up in predicative environments, where the "glue" of agreement is not so necessary. Perhaps this is the case for Slave. Indeed the fact that predicate adjectives are completely uninflected is somewhat striking, given that Slave is otherwise a language rich in agreement inflections.

4.3   Adjectives and degree heads

Another distinctive property of adjectives is that they are selected by a certain class of functional heads, known as degree heads. In English, this class includes the particles *how*, *too*, *so*, and *as*.[16] These functional heads appear with adjectives, but not with nouns or verbs:

(37)   a   Mary is *too* intelligent (to make such a mistake).   (degree plus adjective)
               ...*as* intelligent as Einstein
               ...*so* intelligent that she solved the problem immediately.
             How intelligent is Mary?
         b   *Mary is *too* (a) genius (to make such a mistake).   (degree plus noun)
               *...*as* (a) genius as Einstein
               *...*so* (a) genius (that she solved the problem immediately).
             How (a) genius is Mary?
         c   *Mary too hungers (to think straight).   (degree plus verb)
             *Mary as hungers as John.
             ?Mary so hungers that she could eat a horse.
             *How hunger does Mary?

These degree words were analyzed as AP specifiers by Jackendoff (1977), but since Abney (1987) the standard P&P view has been to treat them as functional heads that take an AP complement. Among other things, this explains why they cannot be extracted, stranding the associated AP. The AP must be carried along with a +*wh* degree, as expected if the degree element is a head and the AP its complement:

(38)   a   *How is Chris [– tall]?
         b   [How tall] is Chris – ?

See Corver (1997) for other arguments that these elements are functional heads in English and Dutch, a result I assume without further discussion. The crucial question for me is why do such heads select only adjectives? The simple answer that these elements are lexically specified as selecting a +N,+V complement is

---

[16] There are semantically similar elements that are not category-specific in this way, such as *more*, *less*, and *enough*. Like the true degree heads, these specify the grade argument of an adjective (*more intelligent, less intelligent, intelligent enough*), but they also combine with other heads, including mass nouns (*more water, less water, enough water*). Another difference is that *more*, *less*, and *enough* can combine directly with the predicate pronoun *so* (*Mary is intelligent, and Sue is more so*), whereas the degrees require a dummy *much* in this environment (*Mary is intelligent, in fact, she is too *(much) so*) (Corver 1997). These differences show that *more*, *less*, and *enough* are not degree heads. I follow Doetjes, Neeleman, and van de Koot (1998) in taking these elements to be adjuncts, not projecting heads. Since they can adjoin to any lexical category, they are not so interesting for my topic, and I put them aside here. There is an important warning here for crosslinguistic comparison, however, because there is no guarantee that items with similar meanings will have similar syntactic categories in this domain.

not available to me, because my goal is to eliminate these as primitive features. I seek instead a principled account in which no head could do what degree heads do if their complement had an agent or theme theta-role or a referential index.

Just as some researchers take modification to be the defining property of adjectives, others take "gradability" to be the defining property. A predicate is gradable if it corresponds to an ordered set of predicates. Degree words are one way of fixing the meaning of the predicate, by specifying the extent to which the quality in question holds of the subject. If all and only adjectives were semantically gradable in this sense, then it would follow that only adjectives can combine meaningfully with degree words. This is a fairly common view in the formal semantics literature (see, for example, Larson and Segal [1995]); it also plays a role in characterizing the difference between adjectives and other categories in some functionalist discussions, including Croft (1991) and Bhat (1994).

It seems dubious that this could really be the essential, defining property of adjectives, however. First, gradability does not extend to the class of As as a whole. Some adjectives express absolute, ungradable properties, and thus cannot appear with degree heads:

(39)   a *Seven is as prime as two is.
         b #Mary is too pregnant to go on the trip.
         c *How three-legged is that stool?

Nevertheless, *prime, pregnant*, and *three-legged* are still clearly adjectives. Second, there is reason to think that some nouns and verbs are gradable, corresponding to properties that can hold to different degrees. There are different levels of being a genius, for example, just as there are different levels of being smart, and one can hunger to different degrees, just as one can be hungry to different degrees. The degree parameter can even be expressed linguistically for nouns and verbs, although not with one of the degree heads:

(40)   a Chris likes scuba-diving *a lot.*
           Chris likes scuba-diving *as much as Pat does.*
         b Chris is a *great* genius.
           Chis is *as much* (of) a genius *as Einstein was.*
         c Chris is *extremely* smart.
           Chris is smart *as much as she is kind.*

The degree of the predicate can be fixed by an adverb ((40a)) or an adjective ((40b)); it can even be fixed by a degree word like *as*, so long as the degree word takes a dummy A *much* as its complement prior to merging with the VP or NP/DP. There is nothing special about the fact that degrees can be specified in this way; the degree of an adjective can also be expressed by an adjoined adverb, as shown in (40c). Adjectives are special only in that they have another way of fixing this lexical semantic parameter, provided by the dedicated degree heads.[17] The correct generalization is not that all and only adjectives are gradable, but rather that only adjectives can have their grade specified by a functional head that projects its own phrase.

Why this is so can be explained using my theory of categories together with the widespread assumption about the status of "grades" in the grammar, given in (41) (see Corver [1997: 131–32], Larson and Segal [1995], and others).

(41)   "Gradable" expressions have an extra position in their theta-grids for the specification of the degree to which the property holds.

This means that expressions like *is hungry*, *hunger*, and *is a genius* are not simple one-place predicates that holds of an entity; they are actually two-place relations that hold of an entity-degree pair. *Chris is too hungry* is true if the person Chris is hungry to a degree x that exceeds the contextually given standard. The role of a degree head or comparable adverb is to saturate this extra position in the theta-grid of the lexical head by establishing a relationship of theta-role binding (see Higginbotham [1985]).[18] If a degree head takes a complement that does not have a grade position in its theta-grid, the structure is ruled out as an instance of vacuous quantification. This explains the ungrammaticality of examples like those in (39). The structure of a simple example in which a degree word takes an AP complement is given in (42), where theta-binding is represented by a link between the theta-role binder and the bound role.

(42)

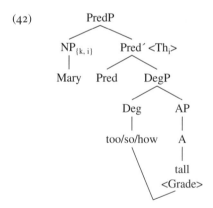

---

[17] See also Doetjes, Neeleman, and van de Koot (1998) for related discussion, showing that grade specification by degree heads and by adverbial modification are semantically equivalent.

[18] In this I follow Corver (1997), who (following Higginbotham [1985]) distinguishes theta-role binding as a mode of theta-discharge that is partially distinct from ordinary theta-role assignment. I leave open whether the two relations can ultimately be reduced to one or not. (If so, then the degree head must be coindexed with the grade theta-role, given the logic of section 3.6. This is

Gradable verbs are more complex than adjectives, in that they typically have (at least) two positions in their theta-grid: the grade position and the theme (or agent) role that the verb assigns to its specifier. We must therefore consider how these two theta-roles relate to each other with respect to the configurational mapping into syntactic structure. Such matters are usually thought to be regulated by a thematic hierarchy (Larson 1988), but in the research tradition that I reviewed and extended in section 2.9, the thematic hierarchy effects are derived from more basic facts about how words are decomposed in the syntax. In that section, I claimed that verbs are always derived syntactically by (in part) the conflation of an adjectival part into a BE operator equivalent to Pred. The theme argument of the verb originates in the specifier of BE/Pred, by definition. UTAH-type considerations suggest that the grade role of a gradable verb should (like the verb's goal or subject-matter arguments) be associated with the adjectival part. What, then, are the prospects for having a verb with a distinct degree head? The answer is: not good. The semantically natural place for this degree head to appear is above the adjectival component of the verb, but below the Pred component, just as in (42). But then the degree head blocks the movement of the A into Pred by the Head Movement Constraint. The context for verb insertion thus cannot be created from this structure. The alternative would be to generate the degree head higher, with the whole PredP/VP as its complement, as shown in (43a).

(43) a   b

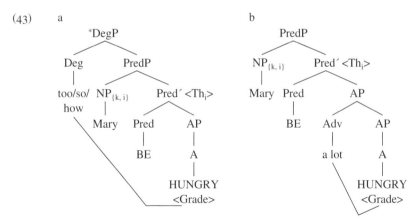

Here there is no problem in conflating HUNGRY with BE to derive the verb *hunger*, but there is a problem with the theta-binding of the grade role by the

how Corver [1997] does choose to represent the theta-binding relationship, but he does not have my theory-laden idea of the nature of indices in mind.)

degree head. The degree is no longer in a local syntactic configuration with the bearer of the role that it is supposed to theta-bind; thus it runs afoul of the basic condition stated in (44) (Higginbotham 1985: 565).

(44)   A head X can theta-bind a role in the theta-grid of Y only if Y is in the minimal domain of X.

The HMC and (44) thus conspire in such a way that it is impossible for a degree head to appear with a gradable verb.

Why, then, is it possible for the grade role of a verb to be discharged by an adverbial constituent, as shown back in (40a)? The minimal difference is that when an adverb is merged with the AP component of the verb, the A is the head of resulting category, rather than the degree-expressing adverb, as shown in (43b). This makes all the difference. The degree adverb is in the necessary local configuration to bind the grade role, but it does not intervene between the A head and Pred in the way that triggers an HMC violation. The A can then conflate into Pred, deriving a sentence like *Mary hungers a lot*. Verbs can combine with degree-specifying elements, then, but only if they are adverbs, not functional heads that project their own phrases. In contrast, conflation does not apply to surface adjectives, so nothing is violated if the degree-expressing item is counted as the head of the phrase, as in (42).[19]

This analysis makes the additional prediction that the degree-like adverbs must be argument-like elements that are generated relatively low in the structure – the kind of adverb for which Larson's (1988) analysis of adverbs as innermost arguments seems appropriate. This prediction is borne out by the data in (45). With eventive verbs, the degree-like adverb *a lot* has a frequency meaning, making it a near synonym of *often*, as shown in (45a). But *a lot* is clearly different from *often* in that it has to appear inside VP, to the right of the verb's objects. *A lot* cannot be adjoined to tense, as many other adverbs can, including *often* ((45b)). This low positioning of *a lot* correlates with the fact that *a lot* (unlike *often*) can receive a degree-like interpretation when it occurs with a gradable verb ((45c)).

---

[19] The core idea of this analysis can be maintained even if one does not accept the idea that verbal predicates are decomposed in the syntax. What is then required is that one stipulate that theme ranks higher on the thematic hierarchy than grade does (as seems natural). If a verb like *hunger*, which assigns a theme theta-role, is generated as the complement of a degree head, then the grade role is discharged after the theme role, violating the thematic hierarchy. If *hunger* is merged with the degree head prior to being merged with an NP specifier, then the thematic hierarchy is respected but the verb does not assign the theme role within its maximal projection, a violation of the theta criterion. The tension can be resolved by using a grade-binder that does not project its own phrase – i.e. one that is syntactically an adverb rather than a functional head.

(45)   a Mary eats spinach often/a lot.
        b Mary often/*a lot didn't eat her spinach.
        c Mary likes Chris a lot/*often.

This confirms the prediction: only low-attaching (AP-internal), argument-like adverbs can merge with the structure soon enough to discharge the grade role, while still not blocking conflation.

Consider next the possibility of embedding a noun projection under a degree head. Nouns are not derived by conflation the way that verbs are, so this is not an issue. But nouns do have a referential index that must be coindexed with some dependent element in its c-command domain (the NLC). Suppose, then, that a noun projection is merged with a degree word, and the degree word is chosen to provide the label for the new projection, creating the structure in (46).

(46)

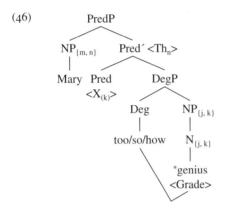

Since the label of the node in question comes from Deg, and not from N(P), it does not include the referential index of the noun. This index is thus trapped inside DegP, and does not c-command anything that could license it.[20]

---

[20] Degrees differ minimally in this respect from determiners, which do pass on the index associated with their nominal complement. The reason determiners can do this is presumably related to the fact that determiners require a complement that has a referential index (section 3.3). Determiners may also bear a referential index themselves; certainly pronouns do, and I assume that they constitute a subclass of the determiners. We can tie these two observations together technically by saying that determiners bear an index that matches the index of their complement, if they have one. (This matching shows up morphologically in languages like Spanish, where the determiner agrees with its complement in gender and number features.) This entails that the complement must have an index, and since this index is also on the determiner, it is automatically passed up to the DP projection as a whole and is accessible to the rest of the structure.

The theta-role associated with the Pred, in particular, is too far away to license this NP. Therefore, the structure violates the NLC.

Once again, things come out differently if the noun is chosen as the label of the category formed by merging the noun projection and the element that saturates its grade role. Then the referential index does percolate up, and it does bind (say) the theta-role of the Pred. In this case, the grade-discharging element is syntactically an adjunct, not a functional head. This is a legitimate structure for a phrase like *a great genius*, although not for **too (a) genius*.

Crosslinguistic comparison unfortunately does not add much perspective on this particular topic. In part, this is because degree expressions have not been studied much in non-Indo-European languages. It may also be that degree heads are not very common in languages of the world, just as articles are not. Edo, Chichewa, and Mohawk, for instance, do not have degree heads in the English sense, even though Edo and Chichewa clearly have adjectives. These languages exclusively use adverbs similar to *a lot* to express degrees (*sʌha* 'more,' *eso* 'much, very,' *sotsi* 'too much' in Mohawk; *kàkàbó* 'much, very' in Edo). Japanese does have a degree-like word, *totemo* 'very' that appears only with adjectives, according to Ohkado (1991). The Muskogean language Creek has special comparative forms that only appear with adjectives (Sakaguchi 1987), which are otherwise rather difficult to distinguish from verbs (see section 4.6.3 for discussion of this in Choctaw, a related language). Degree heads that are specific to adjectives are also found in the Mayan language Tzutujil (Daley 1985), and in Bangla, Tagalog, Fijian, and Turkish (Bhat 1994: 27). Such elements may be of some use in confirming that these languages have adjectives as a distinct lexical category. But none of these examples illustrates any possibilities that are not realized in English.

There is a deep similarity between my explanation of why only adjectives can be attributive modifiers and my explanation of why only adjectives can be complements of a phrase-projecting degree word. In both constructions, the lexical head is embedded in some phrase that prevents it from entering into local syntactic relationships with other linguistic elements – a noun phrase in the case of attributive modification, and a degree phrase in the case studied in this section. Nouns and verbs are required to enter into local syntactic relationships, by the theta criterion and the NLC. But adjectives are not so required, because they have neither a theme/agent theta-role nor a referential index. In this respect, I have arrived at a unified explanation of what otherwise seem like two very different properties of adjectives, properties that are hard to connect to each other by any one positive quality that one might associate with adjectives.

4.4 Resultative secondary predication

A third way adjectives are distinguished syntactically from both nouns and verbs is in their ability to be resultative secondary predicates. These are phrases that combine with an eventive verb and help to characterize the final state of the theme argument of the verb. In English, such resultative predicates can be APs (or PPs), but not VPs or NPs:[21]

(47)   a I beat the metal flat.   (AP)
       b *I beat the metal break/broke/breaking.   (VP)
       c *I beat the metal (a) sword.   (NP)

Relatively little is known about resultative predicates crosslinguistically, except that the construction is not all that common. Even a language like French, which has a robust category of adjectives and is similar to English in its overall structure does not generally permit resultative adjectives (Legendre, 1997, no. 567; see below). But in other languages that do allow resultative secondary predication, the same category specificity seen in English shows up. The examples in (48) illustrate this construction for Edo and Japanese.[22]

(48)   a Òzó kòkó Àdésuwa mòsèmòsè.   (Edo)
          Ozo raised Adesuwa beautiful$_A$.
          'Ozo raised Adesuwa so that she was beautiful.'
       b John-wa pankizi-o   usu-ku   nobasi-ta. (Japanese [Washio 1997: 9])
          John-TOP dough-ACC thin-AFF roll-PAST
          'John rolled the dough thin.'

This, then, is a third testing ground for my theory of adjectives: can it explain why only adjectives appear in this syntactic environment without positing a positive quality for adjectives?

4.4.1   The basic analysis

In developing an analysis of resultative secondary predicates, it is useful to contrast them with depictive secondary predicates. These two constructions look very similar at first glance: both can consist of an AP attached to the clause

---

[21] The "resultative noun phrase" in (47c) becomes grammatical if it is embedded in a PP, giving *I beat the metal into a sword*. This emphasizes that there is something reasonable that this example could mean, if it were grammatical. On how PPs fit into the big picture, see the appendix.

[22] Edo also allows a kind of resultative VP as well as resultative APs. This verbal resultative is one particular type of serial verb construction among the several kinds found in the language (Stewart 1998). I return to these serial verb constructions at the end of this section.

Washio (1997) says that Japanese resultative constructions are found with nouns and adjectives, although not with verbs. "Resultative nouns" are marked with the dative particle *–ni*, which I take to be a postposition, equivalent to *to* in English (see note 21).

to supplement the meaning of the verbal main predicate, the AP expressing a property of the underlying object of the clause. (49a) and (49b), for example, are parallel as surface strings.

(49)   a The file sanded the wood smooth.   (resultative)
         b I ate the meat raw.   (depictive)
         c I left Chris angry.   (depictive)

There are, however, instructive differences between the two constructions. From a semantic perspective, the AP in a resultative construction expresses a property that the theme acquires as a result of the event characterized by the main verb; the AP in depictive constructions expresses what the object is already like at the time of the event. Correlated with this is a family of syntactic differences that point to the conclusion that resultative APs are more tightly integrated into the verb phrase than depictives are. First, resultatives must come before instrumental PPs, whereas depictives felicitously follow them:

(50)   a I wiped the table (clean) with a damp cloth (*clean).
         b I ate the meat (?raw) with a fork (raw).

Second, when both occur in the same clause the resultative must come before the depictive:

(51)   a I washed the car clean cold.   (Rothstein 1983)
         b *I washed the car cold clean.

Third, resultative secondary predicates cannot follow a double object construction, possibly suggesting that the AP competes with one of the objects for a unique structural position. Depictive predicates, in contrast, are perfectly compatible with double object constructions:[23]

(52)   a *I broke Chris a coconut open.
         b I gave Chris the meat raw.   (Williams 1980)

Fourth, a resultative predicate can only be associated with the underlying direct object of the verb, whereas depictives can be predicated of either the subject or the object (Simpson 1983; Levin and Rappaport-Hovav 1995). Thus, (49c) is ambiguous as to who was angry at the time of leaving, whereas in (49a) it must be the wood that becomes smooth, not the file.

---

[23] (52a) improves if the adjective is placed between the two objects, in the same position as a prepositional particle would appear (Kayne 1984b; Dikken 1995), giving *I broke Chris open a coconut*. Whatever this means for the theory of double object constructions and the relationship between resultative APs and verb-particle constructions (which I leave open), this certainly confirms that resultative APs appear in a different syntactic position than depictive APs.

Depictive constructions also differ from resultative constructions in another way, which is particularly relevant to this study: depictives need not be APs. NPs and participial VPs can function as depictive predicates as well, as shown in (53) (contrast with (47)).

(53)   a I left Chris cursing her bad fortune.
         b The army sent Chris home a hero.

These differences between depictives and resultatives are presumably not independent of each other, but form a cluster of interrelated effects attributable to one basic cause. One can thus seek an explanation for why resultatives (but not depictives) have to be APs in terms of the distinctive syntactic position that APs appear in when they get a resultative interpretation.

An explanation of this nature can be developed in terms of the lexical decomposition of verbs presented in section 2.9. There I argue that ordinary transitive verbs are decomposed into (at least) three elements: they have a representation like [x CAUSE [y BE [ADJECTIVE]]], where x stands for the agent and y for the theme. The lexical verb is the result of conflating CAUSE+BE+ADJECTIVE into a single X^0 by successive head movement. For example, *wipe* is CAUSE TO BE WIPED$_A$, *gbe* 'beat' in Edo is CAUSE TO BE BEATEN$_A$, and so on. I suggest that resultative constructions arise when a second adjective is adjoined to the adjectival component of the verb in the pre-conflation representation. The adjectival component of the verb then moves out of the complex AP to combine with BE and CAUSE, as shown in (54).

(54)

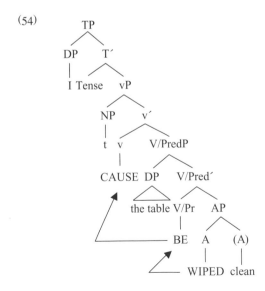

This separating of the abstract adjectival head WIPED from the lexicalized adjective *clean* by head movement is syntactically the same as the way that verb roots are moved away from particles in English and from separable prefixes in German.[24]

The structure in (54) explains the basic properties of the resultative construction quite nicely. The A+A combination at the bottom of the structure is syntactically well formed, as discussed in section 4.2.3. (See below for discussion of why it is not semantically deviant, as most other A+A combinations are.) It is interpreted roughly as two adjectival elements working together to describe more precisely the resulting state of the event. This gives natural expression to Levin's and Rappaport-Hovav's (1995) observation that the resultative adjective must be a further specification of the result already inherent in the verb; Washio (1997) gives elegant examples demonstrating that such a condition holds (even more strongly) in Japanese. The construction thus has a semi-productive, semi-lexicalized flavor, whereby adjectives cannot be freely combined with plausible verbs. (54) also answers a question raised by Bittner (1999): the question of where the sense of causation comes from in resultative constructions. If I wipe the table clean, then I cause the table to become clean by wiping it. But *clean* by itself does not have a causative or inchoative element of meaning, and there is no sign of a causative connective that links the adjective to the verb in these structures. In (54), the causative element comes from the lexical decomposition of the verb *wipe*. The formation of a resultative construction is nothing more than the putting of a (second) adjective inside the domain of this operator, so that I not only cause the table to be wiped, but I also cause it to be clean.

Within my framework one should expand Bittner's question, asking not only where the causative force of these examples comes from, but where their predicative power comes from. I established in chapter 2 that an adjective cannot be predicated of an NP unless it is the complement of a Pred head. Resultative secondary predicate constructions look like exceptions to this: the AP attributes a

---

[24] My account has both similarities and differences with the one found in Hoekstra (1992) and Rapoport (1993). The similarity is that we all take the adjective to characterize the resulting state in the abstract representation of an accomplishment predicate. The difference is that Hoekstra and Rapoport say that the A *adds* a resulting state to a verb that otherwise does not have one, whereas my view is that the A *supplements* the resulting state inherent in the verb meaning. I thus predict that AP resultative constructions are not so tightly limited to atelic process verbs as Hoekstra and Rapoport claim. For example, *John broke the coconut open* is a perfectly good resultative construction, even though *break* clearly includes a result in its lexical meaning and does not express an atelic process (see Levin and Rappaport-Hovav [1995] for more discussion). Throughout this discussion I put aside resultatives with unergative verbs such as *John drank the kettle dry*. These are typologically much more restricted than resultatives with transitive verbs, being possible in English, but not in Edo or Japanese (Washio 1997).

property to the structural object, but no Pred is present. This can be seen clearly in Edo, where Pred is realized overtly as *yé*. Although *yé* must be present whenever an adjective is used as a primary predicate, it is absent when the adjective is used as a secondary predicate. One thus finds minimal contrasts like the one in (55).

(55)   a Òzó gbé èmátòn (*yé) pèrhè.   (secondary predicate;
           Ozo beat metal   (be)   flat   'metal' is object of 'beat')
           'Ozo pounded the metal flat.'
    b Úyì yá   èmátòn *(yé) pèrhè.   (primary predicate;
           Uyi made metal   be   flat   'metal' is a small clause subject)
           'Uyi made the metal to be flat.'

The structure in (54) explains this too. The resultative AP is in fact embedded under a Pred, but this is disguised on the surface because the Pred does not show up as an independent formative; rather, it is merged together into the verb root by the conflation process. The basic semantic properties of the resultative construction are thus readily explained in terms of (54).[25]

The structure in (54) also accounts for Simpson's (1983) Direct Object Restriction. *Clean* must be predicated of the object of *wipe* because it forms a unit with the adjectival part of *wipe*, and this is predicated of the object of *wipe* by the axioms of the system. The participant in the event that becomes clean as a result of the event is necessarily the same participant as the one that becomes wiped, because *clean* and WIPED form a constituent.

Finally, (54) accounts for the fact that resultative predicates are more deeply embedded in the verb phrase than depictives are. It is precisely because the adjective *clean* is adjoined at the deepest level of the structure that it is in the domain of BE/Pred and CAUSE/v, making it a resultative. Adverbial elements, including instrumental PPs and depictive predicates are right-adjoined to the verb phrase; thus, they necessarily follow a resultative AP in English. This

---

[25] This line of reasoning also predicts that depictive AP predicates, which are not embedded under BE but rather adjoined to VP, should require *yé* in Edo. In fact, depictive secondary predication seems to be impossible in Edo, with or without *yé*. I have not investigated why this is so. Possible support for the prediction comes from Japanese: the so-called "nominal adjectives" are followed by *de*, which Nishiyama (1999) analyzes as a realization of Pred, when they are used as depictives but not when they are used as resultatives. As resultatives, they are followed by *ni*, which is not otherwise an element with predicative force.

(i)   a John-ga   sakana-o nama-*de*   tabe-ta.   (depictive)
         John-NOM fish-ACC raw-PRED eat-PAST   (Nishiyama 1999: 188)
        'John ate the fish raw.'
    b Kanozyo-wa teeburu-o kirei-*ni*   hui-ta.   (resultative)
         she-TOP   table-ACC clean-DAT wipe-PAST   (Washio 1997: 16)
        'She wiped the table clean.'

accounts for the word order effects in (50) and (51). Without going into the structure of Double Object Constructions in detail, it is plausible to think that the goal object of a double object construction originates as a complement of the A part of a verbal complex. If so, then it is not surprising that there would be interference between having a goal complement inside the AP and having a resultative AP. In contrast, no interference is expected between a goal object and a depictive AP adjoined to the VP as a whole (see (52)). The basic syntactic and semantic properties of resultative secondary predicates thus follow in a unified way from the structure in (54).

Now that we know what the structure of resultative constructions is, we can face the issue of the categorial restrictions on that construction. The key question takes the following form: why can an adjective be adjoined to the adjectival part of a decomposed verb, whereas a noun or a verb cannot be? My answer has the same structure as before: only adjectives are permitted, because a verb in this position would be unable to assign its theta-role, and the referential index of a noun in this position would not be licensed.

First, imagine that a verbal projection like *sparkle* were merged into this position instead of an adjective like *clean* to give **I wiped the table sparkle*. Unlike the adjective, the verb has a theme role. This theme role needs to be assigned to an NP that is a sister of a projection of the verb. There is, however, no such NP in (54). The closest NP available is the direct object in the specifier of PredP/VP, but this is too far away to receive the verb *sparkle*'s theta-role. Structures with a bare resultative verb thus violate the theta criterion. *Sparkle* can be the predicate of a kind of resultative construction, as in *Chris wiped the table until it sparkled*, but here the resultative phrase is crucially a full clause, containing its own, independently licensed subject pronoun that *sparkle* can theta-mark.

Next suppose that a nominal projection like *a sword* were merged into the resultative position of the clause *I beat the metal*, rather than an adjective like *flat*. This nominal projection would bear a referential index, by definition. There are two subcases to consider: either the index associated with *a sword* is inherited by the phrase [BEATEN *a sword*], or it is not inherited. If it is not inherited, then the index is trapped inside this complex AP, unable to bind another index in the outside world, in violation of the NLC. If, on the other hand, the referential index of *a sword* is inherited by [BEATEN *a sword*], then the BE/Pred head could potentially theta-mark it, as in ordinary predicate nominal constructions (section 3.8). But [BEATEN *a sword*] would then count as a noun phrase, with *sword* as its head. BEATEN could not move out of such a noun phrase to combine with BE/Pred and CAUSE/v, since only the head of a phrase can move out of the phrase into a higher head position (the HMC). In this case, the transitive verb *beat* fails to be assembled out of its component parts, and the structure crashes. Therefore no licit structure can be built out of (54) with a noun projection in place of the adjective in the smallest phrase. Noun phrases can be used in a kind of resultative construction, but only if there is a preposition that theta-marks them, as in *I beat the metal into a sword* or *I bored the students to death*.

Merging an adjective into the resultative position avoids both these problems. Since an adjective does not have a theme theta-role or a referential index, it is not in danger of violating either the theta criterion or the NLC. It has no positive nature to get it into trouble, so it can occur in this rather particular syntactic environment where other categories cannot.

It is not crucial to this analysis that the resultative expression be only an adjective; any larger phrase will do as well, as long as it has neither an undischarged theta-role nor a referential index. One can therefore have resultative APs that contain a complement, as in (56a), or resultative degree phrases, as in (56b).

(56)   a Chris drained the pot *empty of water.*
        b Pat wiped the table *as clean as a whistle.*

The presence of this extra structure does not affect the reasoning, in accordance with the Bare Phrase Structure view that there is no principled difference between projections of different sizes that bear the same label.

This analysis of resultative constructions contains one important gap that needs some patching: I need to say something about why the merger of two As makes a good AP in resultative constructions, but not in many other cases. (57) illustrates this difference with some minimal pairs: the syntactic merger of two ordinary adjectives is not good ((57b)), but the merger of an adjectival passive with a simple adjective that expresses its result is better ((57a), cf. Levin and Rappaport-Hovav [1995: 43–46]). (It is also possible for two simple adjectives to form a lexical compound, as shown in (57c).)

(57)   a This door remains opened wide/wiped clean.
        b ??The door remains open wide/bright clean.
        c The door remains wide-open/squeaky-clean.

I showed in section 4.2.3 that nothing in the syntax *per se* rules out the merger of an A with an A; I claimed that examples like (57b) are defective only at the semantic level. In the semantics, a noun is needed to provide a criterion of identity that links the variables associated with the individual lexical items together (thus *a bright clean door* is fine). Something else apparently accomplishes this semantic linking in resultative constructions. Verbs derived from adjectives and their adjectival passives differ minimally from simple adjectives in that they imply an event. I propose that this implicit event variable is what provides the semantic connection that is needed to hold the A+A construction together in resultatives. Without going into all the gory details, the intuition is as follows. In an example like *The table is bright clean*, each adjective introduces a distinct variable in the semantics and there is no noun to support saying that the two variables refer to the same thing. A substructure like [CAUSE [x BE [WIPED+clean]]] says a bit more. In this case, the two adjectives denote states that must be proper subparts of the single event introduced by the CAUSE operator; in particular, they must be terminating parts of the event (Pietroski 1998). The event of causing can only have a single theme, by thematic uniqueness (Carlson 1984), and this theme must be the element that is in any state that results from the event, by the definition of theme. Since both adjectives characterize a resulting state, the variables of the predicates they correspond to must perforce refer to the same thing. In resultative constructions, the fact that the two adjectives apply to the same variable is imposed from above, as it were, by the mereology of events, whereas in normal attributive constructions it is imposed from below, because both adjectives are modifiers of the same noun. Formalizing this idea would be a nontrivial endeavor, requiring among other things that one become precise about the semantics of the CAUSE element. I will not attempt this here. For now, I am content merely to suggest that there could be principled reasons why the A+A constituent found in resultatives is semantically well formed, even though most other A+A constituents are not.

4.4.2   *Crosslinguistic variations*

Turning to other languages, one finds two variations on the English pattern, one fairly boring, and the other more interesting theoretically. The boring variation, which I already alluded to above, is that many languages that have adjectives still do not allow those adjectives to form resultative secondary predicates. Such languages may have resultatives, but only with PPs, not with adjectives. French is one language of this type (Legendre 1997: 46–47) (see (58)); others include Hindi, Hebrew, and Chichewa.

(58)   Pierre a   peint   les murs en blanc/ *blancs.
        Pierre has painted the walls in white/ *white.

This may be related to the fact, discussed in the previous paragraph, that A+A combinations are usually bad and require special interpretative considerations to rescue them. If these special considerations do not apply in other languages, then even adjectival resultatives will be ruled out by general principles. Snyder (2001), for example, relates the existence of resultative constructions across languages to the existence of productive N+N compounding in the language, showing that children master the two constructions at the same time. This connection is not implausible in my theory, given that resultative constructions involve forming a kind of adjective+adjective "compound" in the syntax. This could be why resultative adjectives are possible in languages like English, Edo, and Japanese, which have productive compounding of various kinds, and not in compound-poor languages like French and Chichewa.

The more interesting variation is found in Edo, as well as other West African languages (e.g. Nupe, Yoruba) and South East Asian languages (e.g. Vietnamese). In these languages, a transitive verb can combine with a stative verb to form a kind of resultative construction. The verbal resultative can be nearly synonymous with the adjectival resultative, as shown in (59).

(59)   a Òzó kòkó Àdésuwa mòsèmòsè.   (Edo)
          Ozo raised Adesuwa beautiful$_A$
          'Ozo raised Adesuwa beautiful.'
       b Òzó kòkó Àdésuwa mòsé.
          Ozo raised Adesuwa be.beautiful$_V$
          'Ozo raised Adesuwa to be beautiful.'
       c *Òzó kòkó Àdésuwa ìmòsè.
          Ozo raised Adesuwa beauty$_N$
          'Ozo raised Adesuwa (to have) beauty.'

((59c) shows that nouns are ungrammatical as secondary predicates in Edo, as in English; there is no crosslinguistic variation on this point, as far as I know.) Examples in which the second verb is not stative and does not correspond to an adjective are also possible:

(60)   Òzó suá Úyì dé.
         Ozo push Uyi fall
         'Ozo pushed Uyi down.'

These resultatives constitute one coherent subclass of the so-called serial verb construction (SVC). Stewart (2001) shows in detail that this type of SVC acts like more familiar resultative constructions in many ways. For example, the second verb makes the construction into a telic accomplishment, and it is in complementary distribution with other delimiting expressions, such as resultative APs, second objects, or prepositional phrases. (60) illustrates the incompatibility of a resultative verb phrase with a double object construction; it is perfectly parallel with the bad example (52a) in English except for the category of the resultative.

(61)   Úyì sùá Òzó èwé (*dé).
        Uyi push Ozo goat fall
        'Uyi pushed the goat (down) on Ozo.'

The resultative verb also must come before locatives and other VP-adverbials, showing that it is deeply embedded in the verb phrase (compare (62) with (50a) in English):

(62)   *Òzó kòkó Àdésuwa ègìégìé mòsé.
        Ozo   raised Adesuwa quickly be.beautiful$_V$
        'Ozo raised Adesuwa quickly to be beautiful.'
        (OK is: Òzó kòkó Àdésuwa mòsé ègìégìé.)

The structure of these resultative SVCs thus seems to be essentially the same as that of AP resultatives in English (and Edo), despite the difference in the category of the resultative head.

Building on Baker and Stewart (1999), Saito (2000) analyzes these resultative SVCs by saying that the second verb undergoes head movement at LF to adjoin to the first verb. From this position, it can assign its theta-role to the NP in the specifier of the first verb's projection. The LF structure of (60) would then be something like (63).

(63)   [$_{vP}$ Ozo$_{\{i,j\}}$ v<Ag$_j$> [$_{vP}$ Uyi$_{\{k,l\}}$ fall<Th$_l$>+push<Th$_l$> [$_{vP}$ <*fall*>]]]

This sort of head movement for the purpose of theta-role assignment is also found in a variety of other constructions, including light verb constructions and restructuring constructions (see Saito and Hoshi [1998] and Saito [2000]; section 3.6 above gives a brief review). The head movement takes place overtly in other languages, creating resultative V–V compounds on the surface in languages like Igbo and Mandarin Chinese.

Of course, once I open up this new theoretical option to account for resultative verb phrases in Edo, I have to consider why English and other languages do not also take advantage of this option. Why cannot verb incorporation happen at LF in English, to give a sentence like *John pushed the goat fall*? Baker and Stewart (1999) explain this in terms of properties of the tense–verb relationship (see Déchaine [1993] for a very similar idea). A rough typological generalization that has been noticed by many linguists is that true SVCs exist only in languages with little or no verbal inflection; tense is either unmarked in these languages, or it is indicated by morphologically independent particles. Thus West African languages, Caribbean Creoles, and South East Asian languages are all known for the poverty of their verb inflection as well as for having SVCs.[26] This correlation suggests that the parameter that makes SVCs possible has something to do with the relationship between tense and the verb. The details of Edo confirm this. Unlike the nearby serializing languages Nupe and Yoruba, Edo has one tense marker that is realized as a segmental suffix on the verb: the past perfective affix. It is significant that this one tense is incompatible with the resultative serial verb construction:[27]

(64)   *Àkhé ọ̀-ré Òzó suá-rè   dé(-rè).
        pot   it-be Ozo push-PAST/PERF fall(-PAST/PERF)
        'It's the pot that Ozo has pushed down.'

(64) is bad regardless of whether or not the tense suffix shows up on the second verb as well as on the first. In contrast, resultative AP constructions are possible in the past perfective, showing that there is no semantic incompatibility between this tense and complex achievement predicates.

(65)   Àdèsúwà ọ̀-ré Úyì kòkó-rò   mòsèmòsè.
        Adesuwa it-be Uyi raise-PAST/PERF beautiful$_A$
        'It's Adesuwa that Uyi raised beautiful.'

Thus in the one subarea of Edo in which verbs are like Indo-European verbs in bearing tense inflections, we find the same limited range of resultative constructions that Indo-European languages allow. This is language-internal evidence that the tense–verb relationship is crucial to whether resultative VPs can be generated or not.

This range of data can be explained by appealing to principles like the following:[28]

(66)   a The two verbs of a serial verb construction must match morphologically.
        b Each tense node has a unique morphological realization in the clause.

---

[26] Within the Kwa languages of Nigeria, Igbo is unusual in that every verb bears an inflectional suffix. Igbo is also special in that it does not have SVCs on the surface, but rather V–V compounds (Déchaine 1993). This is further evidence that the two properties are related.

[27] If the verb has a direct object, it must be clefted in this particular tense; see Baker and Stewart (1998) for discussion.

[28] These principles are independently motivated in that they apply also to what Stewart (2001) dubs the "Consequential Serial Verb Construction," which otherwise has quite different syntactic properties from resultatives. (The consequential VP is more like a depictive secondary predicate, Stewart claims.) (66a) does not, however, apply to all constructions that involve verb-movement for purposes of theta-role assignment in the Saito–Hoshi theory. Restructuring constructions, for example, sometimes have verbs with matching inflection, but more often the moved verb is some kind of nonfinite form. As a result, restructuring is much more common crosslinguistically than resultative serialization. Why this difference exists is unclear to me.

(64) without the tense affix on the second verb violates (66a); (64) with the tense affix on the second verb violates (66b). In contrast, if tense is not realized morphologically – either because there is no expression at all, or because it is an independent particle – then an SVC like (59b) or (60) is possible in languages like Edo. In Indo-European languages, almost every verb is inflected; as a result, resultative serial verb constructions are not allowed. (I must, of course, assume that there are Ø present tense affixes in English which are subject to (66) in order to explain the fact that *They always push pots fall* is no better than **They pushed the pot fall/fell*. This assumption is independently motivated by the fact that *do*-support takes place in present tense in English, giving sentences like *They do-Ø not push the pot* [Halle and Marantz 1993].)

This completes my explanation of why there are no resultative verb constructions in English, but there are in some languages with different morphosyntactic properties. The more accurate generalization, then, is that adjectives are the easiest lexical category to use as a resultative predicate, verbs can be used as resultatives given certain parameter settings involving tense, and nouns can never be used as resultatives.

4.5   Adjectives and adverbs

So far I have considered three syntactic environments in which one finds adjectives and their projections but not nouns or verbs: attributive modification configurations, complements of degree heads, and resultative secondary predication. In each case, once the exact structural configuration was determined, I was able to explain the categorial restriction without inventing any new principles that refer to properties of APs *per se*. The facts in question follow from the theoretical devices already proposed in earlier chapters – the theta criterion and the NLC. Adjectives thus appear in these positions by default. Within this theory, one does not have to find any particular characteristic that these three environments have in common in order to explain why adjectives appear in all of them. Adjectives are simply the "elsewhere case" in the world of lexical categories; they appear wherever no more specialized category will do. This is an attractive feature of the analysis, because it is not at all clear what these three environments share.

The potential danger with this kind of theory is that it could run wild, allowing adjectives in all kinds of other, unexpected positions. For example, my analysis of the attributive construction is based on the idea that adjectives (and only adjectives) can freely be merged with noun projections without changing the basic character of the projection because they do not have to worry about assigning a thematic role or binding an index. But if this is so, then why can not adjectives also merge with VPs? Or with TPs? Or with APs?

The most interesting answer to these questions is to say that adjectives *can* merge with all these categories – except that in these environments we normally call them adverbs. Adjectives do appear in construction with VPs, TPs, and APs in English, as long as they are followed by –*ly*:

(67) a Chris will quickly/carefully/casually solve the problem.   (VP)
      b Probably/luckily/hopefully, Chris will win the race.   (TP)
      c Chris is extremely/mildly/thoroughly sick.   (AP)

This –*ly* is usually thought of as a category-changing derivational affix that creates adverbs out of adjectives. There are, however, reasons to doubt this. First, -*ly* is otherwise used in English as a derivational affix that creates adjectives, as in *worldly*, *manly*, and *daily*. Second, there are many syntactic affinities between adverbs and adjectives that can be used to justify taking them to be members of a single syntactic category, as argued by Emonds (1976) and others. For example, adverbs appear with the same degree heads as adjectives:

(68) a Chris entered the house as quietly as a mouse.
      b   . . . so quietly that no one noticed.
      c   . . . too quietly to be heard.
      d How quietly did Chris enter the house?
        (also: more/less quietly than a mouse, quietly enough to not disturb us)

Third, adverbs are like attributive adjectives in English in that (with a handful of exceptions) they cannot take complements when they appear before the modified head (Jackendoff 1977):

(69) a John is a proud (*of his daughter) man.
      b John proudly (*of his daughter) showed everyone his photo album.

Fourth, it is well known that adverbs in verbal or adjectival projections correspond closely to adjectives in semantically parallel derived nominal projections:

(70) a Italy *brutally* invaded Albania.
        Chris is *extremely* shy.
      b Italy's *brutal* invasion of Albania
        Chris's *extreme* shyness

Fifth, issues of adjective ordering and placement with respect to the head noun are highly similar to issues of adverb ordering and placement with respect to the verb, as can be seen by comparing Cinque (1994) on NP syntax with Cinque

(1999) on clausal syntax. All these facts fall into place if adverbs in *–ly* really are adjectives. Similar arguments apply to the Romance languages, in which many adverbs are adjectives followed by *–mente*.

There is also support for the idea of reducing the category of adverb to the category of adjective in non-Indo-European languages. What I have been calling adjectives in Edo can also be interpreted as manner adverbs when they appear in VP-final position. Comparing (71) with (59a) shows that some words in Edo can have either a manner adverb interpretation or a resulting state interpretation with no morphological change.

(71)   Òzó kpèé èmà mòsèmòsè.
        Ozo play drum beautiful
        'Ozo played the drum beautifully.'

Adjectives can also be used as adverbs in Mapuche (Smeets 1989: 91) and Kilega (Kinyalolo, personal communication).

(72)   Pichi dungu-n.   Compare: pichi wentru   (Mapuche)
        small speak-1sS   small man
        'I spoke briefly.'   'a small man'

(73)   Kasíbá á-ku-ímb-ag-a   bu-soga. Cf. kasíbá   mu-soga (Kilega)
        1.singer 3sS-PROG-sing-HAB-FV   14-nice   1.singer 1-nice
        'The singer sings beautifully.'   'a beautiful singer'

Even Mohawk gives a kind of negative support for there being a close relationship between adjectives and adverbs. We have seen that Mohawk has no free adjectival roots, but only stative verbs. Mohawk also does not have an open class of adverbs. Rather, adverbial notions – when expressible at all – also have the morphology and perhaps the syntax of stative verbs:[29]

(74)   Yó-hsnor-e′   ro-[a]teyahr-ú-tye′   ne owirá'a.
        NsS-be.quick-STAT MsO-grow-STAT-PROG NE baby
        'The baby is growing quickly.' (lit. 'It is quick that the baby is growing.')

That adverbs belong to the same category as adjectives is indirectly confirmed by the fact that a language without the latter does not have the former either.

---

[29] Mohawk, like many other languages, has a variety of closed class particles that can appear at various points in the clause. Some of these might be considered adverbs, just as English has some adverbial particles that are not related to adjectives, such as *now* and *soon*. These are probably functional categories of some kind, and hence outside my primary domain of inquiry. The traditional label "adverb" almost certainly does not pick out a natural class of elements with respect to the syntax.

To complete this account, it would be nice to say something about the "adverbial" affix *–ly* and equivalents like *–mente* in the Romance languages. Why is it that these elements must appear with adjectives used as modifiers *unless* the modified element is a noun? (75) further illustrates this robust generalization.

(75) a Honestly, I think we should quit. (TP versus NP)
     Chris's honest opinion
    b Chris quickly ate lunch.   (VP versus NP)
     Chris had a quick lunch.
    c Chris is greatly upset with you. (AP versus NP)
     Chris is a great cook.
    d Chris is hopelessly in love.   (PP versus NP)
     Chris is a hopeless romantic.

This difference between lexical categories is the kind of thing my theory aspires to explain.

The only thing that is special about nouns, in my view, is that they have criteria of identity, represented syntactically as referential indices. So the explanation must be in these terms. Why might having a criterion of identity make them easier to modify? I gave an answer for this within a narrower context in section 4.2.3, when I analyzed the fact that A+N phrases are easily made, but A+A phrases are not. My answer made use of a principle regulating the syntax-semantics interface repeated in (76).

(76) The variables associated with distinct lexical items are distinct.

The consequence of this is that the direct merger of two lexical items can only receive the conjunctive interpretation typical of modification if there is an extra statement that equates the distinct variables that (76) requires. If a noun is involved in the merger, its criterion of identity makes such an equation possible; otherwise it is not. The semantic value of a (predicativized) modification structure is repeated in (77).

(77) Pred $[X\ Y] = \lambda y\ \exists x\ [{}^{\cup}X'(x)\ \&\ {}^{\cup}Y'(y)\ \&\ \text{same}(Y)(x, y)]$

The expression "same$(Y)(x, y)$" is well defined if and only if Y is a noun. This proposal already covers the question of why [$_{NP}$ great cook] is well formed but [$_{AP}$ great upset] is not. It also extends naturally to account for the ill-formedness of [$_{VP}$ quick eat]. A sentence like *Chris quickly ate* is often given the semantic value in (78), in which *quick* and *ate* are both predicates of the same variable ranging over events and no semantic significance is attached to *-ly* (Davidson 1967; Parsons 1990).

(78)   ∃e [eating(e) & Agent(e, Chris) & [∪]quick(e)]

This logical representation violates (76): *quick* and *eat* are distinct lexical items but correspond to predicates of the same variable. (76) can then be used as the cornerstone of an explanation for the badness of **quick eat*. In general, it explains why only nouns can be modified directly.

What contribution, then, does *–ly* make, so that nonnominal phrases can be modified? Following Déchaine and Tremblay (1996), I suggest that *–ly* is itself a noun, and thus has its own criterion of identity. Déchaine and Tremblay give several arguments in favor of this. First, they remind us that adverbs in *–ly* are semantically equivalent to PPs in which the adjective modifies a noun: *carefully* is synonymous with *in a careful manner*, for example. Second, both *–ly* and Romance *–ment(e)* are nouns historically: *-ly* comes from Old English *lijk* 'body' and *–ment(e)* comes transparently from Latin *mente*, the ablative form of 'mind.' Third, some signs of attributive modificational syntax still survive. For example, *-ment(e)* attaches specifically to the feminine form of adjectives, as shown in (79) from French:

(79)   a lente-ment,   *lent-ment   'slowly'
          b grande-ment,   *grand-ment   'greatly'
          c maladroite-ment, *maladroit-ment 'clumsily'

This is surprising if *–ment* is a category-changing derivational affix, since such affixes typically attach to an uninflected stem or to the unmarked form of the base word, which in French is the masculine. It makes perfect sense, however, if *–ment* is a noun and the adjective is its attributive modifier: *-ment* is itself feminine, and the adjective agrees with it in gender, as attributive adjectives always do. (This argument does not, of course, apply to Modern English, because it does not have gender as an inflectional category.) In Spanish (although not in English or French) two adjectives can be coordinated in combination with a single *–mente*:

(80)   a [inteligente y   profunda] -mente
             intelligent and profound -ly
             'intelligently and profoundly'
          b [directa o   indirecta] -mente
             direct   or indirect   -ly
             'directly or indirectly'

Finally, Jackendoff's (1977) observation that adverbs generally cannot take complements is relevant to this point too. Adverbs are unlike predicative adjectives in this respect:

(81)   a John showed everyone his photo album proudly (*of his daughter).
            (compare: You often meet men proud of their daughters.)
         b Chris gazed over the water fondly (*of the view).
            (compare: People fond *(of the view) should request an ocean side room.)
         c John is behaving responsibly (*for this project).
            (compare: The person responsible for this project should report
            immediately.)

This difference is explained if the adjectival root is really an attributive modifier
of –*ly*, since attributive modifiers generally do not take complements. *Proudly
of his daughter* is then ruled out for exactly the same reason as *a proud man of
his daughter*. There is thus converging evidence that –*ly* and –*mente* are not
grammatically innocuous, quasi-inflectional suffixes, but rather nominal heads
meaning 'manner' that enter into attributive modification constructions.[30]

Since –*ly* is nominal, it has a criterion of identity. This criterion of identity
can then provide the glue that binds together modificational structures whenever
the modified element is not already nominal. The details can be filled in for an
example like *Chris ate quickly* as follows. Let us suppose that many verbs have
an optional "manner" theta-role, in addition to their usual theta-roles of agent,
theme, and the like.[31] Since the head of *quickly* is the noun –*ly*, it can bind
this theta-role. The criterion of identity of –*ly* can then be invoked to say that
the manner in which the eating was done and the manner referred to by –*ly*
are the same manner. (This is how theta-role assignment usually works out
semantically; see section 3.6.) At the same time, *quick* is an attributive modifier
of –*ly*. The criterion of identity of –*ly* is used again to say that the thing that
is quick and the thing that –*ly* refers to are the same manner. (This is how
attributive modification usually works semantically; see section 4.2.) The verb
phrase in (82a) thus expresses the logical formula in (82b) (I ignore the agent
argument for simplicity).

---

[30] There are syntactic differences as well. Perhaps the most important one is that –*ly* adverbs can
left-adjoin to verb phrases, whereas more explicitly phrasal modifiers cannot, as shown in (i).

(i)   a Mary opened the jar carefully/in a careful manner.
        b Mary carefully/??in a careful manner opened the jar.

This difference may be phonological in nature, with elements that are left-adjoined in a right-
branching language needing to be a single prosodic word (the so-called head-final filter). If so,
the fact that –*ly* cliticizes onto its adjectival modifier at PF makes all the difference.

[31] The alternative would be to say that –*ly* adverbs are governed by a covert preposition that assigns
them a theta-role and makes them adjoinable to a verb phrase, parallel to the *in* of *in a careful
manner*. Dechaine and Tremblay take this tack, pointing out that –*mente* in Romance comes
from an oblique (ablative) form of the Latin word for 'mind.' I take the position in the text for
expository purposes: it gives me one fewer null head to argue for and it allows me to give a
precise semantics without taking a stand on the semantic value of prepositions. But I would be
inclined to adopt the null P idea in a fuller exposition, as I do for other bare NP adverbs (see the
appendix).

(82)   a [$_{VP}$ eat<Ag, manner$_j$> quickly$_{\{i, j\}}$]
        b ∃e,x,y,z [eating(e) & manner(e, x) & $^\cup$manner(y) & same(manner)(x, y) &
            $^\cup$quick(z) & same(manner)(y, z)]

Notice that there are two conditions of the form "same(manner)(i, j)" here: one
is introduced by the interpretation of the theta-role assignment to *–ly* by *eat*,
and the other is introduced by the interpretation of the attributive modification
of *–ly* by *quick*. This is no different from how the ordinary verb phrase [$_{VP}$ eat
a big sandwich] is interpreted, except that the lexical content of the head noun
-ly is different (more abstract) and the particular theta-role it receives is different
(manner as opposed to theme). The logical formula in (82b) is little more than an
expanded version of the traditional one in (78). It has the same desirable quality
that *Chris ate quickly* implies that *Chris ate* by simple conjunction reduction
(Davidson 1967; Parsons 1990). Unlike (78), however, (82b) is consistent with
the fundamental principle in (76). The three lexical heads *eat*, *quick*, and *ly*
are predicates of different variables (x, y, and z), which are tied together into a
coherent interpretation by *–ly*'s criterion of identity.

The same techniques work for cases of "adverbs" modifying adjectives, with
the minor difference that adjectives do not have a manner theta-role but do have
a grade theta-role, as discussed in section 4.3. The *–ly* form thus expresses the
degree to which the adjectival head holds, rather than the manner. The logical
formula expressed is as in (83b).[32]

(83)   a Chris$_{\{k,l\}}$ is [t$_l$ Pred<Th$_l$> [extreme-ly$_{\{i,j\}}$ tall<Grade$_j$>]]
        b ∃ x, y, z [$^\cup$tall(Chris, x) & $^\cup$degree(y) & same(degree)(x, y) &
            $^\cup$extreme(z) & same(degree)(y, z)]

(83b) says that Chris is tall to a certain degree, and that degree is the same as a
degree that is extreme. Again, the criterion of identity of *–ly* holds the formula
together. This explains why *–ly* is required whenever the modified constituent
does not have a criterion of identity of its own.

Since (76) is a universal principle, I expect nominal elements to be found in
adverbial modification structures in other languages as well. Not all languages
wear this on their sleeve; there is no sign of something like *–ly* in (72) from
Mapuche, for instance. Some Edo examples, however, do support the prediction.
Adjectives and verbs in Edo always begin with a consonant, whereas nouns
invariably begin with a vowel. Most VP-final adverbs also begin with a vowel:

---

[32] Notice that I give *–ly* the meaning 'degree' here, and the meaning 'manner' in (82b). This seems
to be an instance of semi-accidental homophony. We might, then, expect to find languages in
which the form of an adjective that modifies an action verb is different from the form of an
adjective that modifies a gradable adjective. I do not know whether this is true.

(84)   a Òzó kòkó ọ̀gọ́ è-gìẹ̀gìẹ̀.
          Ozo gather bottle quickly
          'Ozo gathered the bottles quickly.'
        b Òzó gíẹ́!gíẹ́ kó!kó ọ̀gọ́
          Ozo quick   gather bottle
          'Ozo was quick in gathering the bottles.'

The VP-adjoined manner adverb *è-gìẹ̀gìẹ̀* in (84a) is morphologically related
to the inflected form *gíẹ́!gíẹ́* in (84b) (possibly an auxiliary verb), but it has the
noun-like vowel prefix *è-*. I take this prefix to be a noun, the Edo equivalent of
English *–ly*. (Note that attributive adjectives follow the head noun in Edo, so it
is not surprising that *è-* comes before the associated adjective, the reverse of the
order seen in English.) Similarly, Bhat (1994: 75) writes that some adjectives
can be used as adverbs in Kannada, "but they need to take the affix *age* for this
purpose":

(85)   A: kabbiṉavannu kemp-age   ka:yisa-be:ku.
            that iron-ACC   red-ADV   heat-must
            'That iron must be heated red(ly).'
            (compare: *kempu baṭṭe* 'red cloth')

Here *–age* follows the adjective root, in the position where one would expect
a modified noun in head-final Kannada. Adjectives used adverbially in Kilega
begin with a special noun class prefix *bu-*, which does not agree with any other
noun phrase in the sentence (see (73)). It is reasonable to say that this is a
nominal element in its own right, the Kilega version of *-ly*. As a final example,
adverbial expressions in Tagalog are regularly formed by combining adjectives
with the fixed element *nang* (Schachter 1985: 22). Thus, the prediction that a
nominal element is needed when adjectives modify categories other than nouns
garners some crosslinguistic support. Examples like (72) in Mapuche may have
a phonologically null noun head as well.

  If further research into adverbs across languages confirms that many semantically rich adverbs really belong to the same lexical class as adjectives, this
will be a double success for my theory. First, I will have been right not to posit a
positive character for the category adjective, thereby putting relatively few explicit constraints on the syntactic structures they can appear in. Taken together,
adjectives/adverbs do show up in a wide range of syntactic environments, including as modifiers of categories of all types. Second, I will have succeeded in
subsuming part of the problematic and ill-understood category of adverbs into a
better understood category that has a well-defined place within my disciplined
theory of the lexical category distinctions.

4.6   Are adjectives universal?

Finally, now that we have an idea of what it is to be an adjective and what the grammatical consequences of being an adjective are, we can consider whether all languages have essentially the same category of adjectives or not.

Ever since Dixon (1982), adjectives have been widely held to be the most varied and least universal of the lexical categories, the locus of significant crosslinguistic differences (see also Schachter [1985], Hengeveld [1992], Bhat [1994]). Functionalist linguists in particular often see a continuum of possible lexical semantic meanings, with nouns at one end of the continuum and verbs at the other. Particular languages then divide this continuum into distinct lexical categories at a semi-arbitrary number of places. English happens to divide the space into three categories: nouns, verbs, and adjectives, as shown in (86a). One might, however, perfectly well expect some languages to divide the same continuum into four or more parts. This would result in languages with two distinct categories in the intermediate range where English has only one class of adjectives ((86b)). (Wetzer [1996] envisions an extreme case of splitting, in which a language could have as many as six lexical categories, ranging from true verbs, to adjectival verbs, to verby adjectives, to nouny adjectives, to adjectival nouns, to true nouns.) Alternatively, some languages could divide the continuum into only two parts. This would produce languages that have only a noun-verb distinction, with words that correspond to adjectives in English being grouped either with the nouns or with the verbs ((86c,d)).[33]

(86)   Transitory situations   Permanent situations
   a X—(verbs)—X————(Adjs)————X—(nouns)—X   (English)
   b X—(verbs)—X–(A_1s)—X–(A_2s)————X–(nouns)——X   (Japanese?)
   c X—(verbs)—X————————————(nouns)————X   (Chichewa?
                                                            Quechua?)
   d X————(verbs)————————————X—(nouns)—X   (Mohawk?)

Languages of all these types (and more) have been thought to exist.

The typological expectations that emerge out of formal accounts that use arbitrary distinctive features on the model of Chomsky (1970) are not so different.

---

[33] The single category partition could also fall in the middle of the region that constitutes adjectives in English. This would give a language in which some words with "adjectival" meanings have the grammar of nouns and other words with "adjectival" meanings have the grammar of verbs. Greenlandic Eskimo is a plausible language of this type (Fortescue 1984). The possibilities discussed in the text are thus idealizations, but sufficient to investigate the basic question.

   One can also imagine languages that do not divide the putative lexical–semantic continuum at all, and thus have only one undifferentiated lexical category. This is a traditional view of Salish, Wakashan, and Austronesian languages, which I argued against in section 3.9.

These features are modeled after the use of features like $+/-$continuant and $+/-$voiced in phonology. In the phonological domain, some languages clearly use more distinctive features than others, causing the sizes of phonemic inventories to vary considerably. For example, Edo has twenty-four vowels (a core seven vowel system, plus distinctive nasality and tone) whereas other languages have as few as three. The sizes of consonant inventories also varies widely. Parallel to this, if the lexical categories are *complexes* of features, then one expects category inventories to show the same kind of variation. The English category system seems to be built around two distinctive features, which define three or four lexical categories, depending on whether or not prepositions are included. Another language could in principle add a third distinctive feature, giving it as many as eight lexical categories if none of the combinations violates syntactic principles. Other languages might use only one distinctive feature; they would have only two categories, noun and verb. The lexical items that are adjectives in English would fall together with nouns if the language in question employed only the $+/-$N distinction, and they would fall together with verbs if the language employed only the $+/-$V distinction. Therefore, in the usual formalist picture, languages could have a greater or lesser number of lexical categories, and different patterns of category neutralization are possible, just as in the usual functionalist picture.

Contrary to these traditions, I argue that all languages for which adequate information is available have one and only one syntactic category of adjectives. (In this I agree with Croft [1991]; Croft does not discuss any detailed evidence for his view, however.) My theory says that each category is defined not by a region in a continuum or by a complex of features, but by the presence or absence of a single, privative feature. Given this, there is no other way for the ingredients to be combined without a major change to the system. One cannot have some category that falls between the adjective and the verb: this would be a head that takes half a specifier – which is absurd. Nor could one have some category that bears 66 percent of a referential index, and hence falls between the noun and the adjective. My view, then, leads to the strong expectation that all languages should have essentially the same three-way category system, certainly no more, and probably no less. In this section, I show that this expectation squares with the facts. First, I consider a claim from the literature that Japanese has four lexical categories, including two in the adjective family. Next, I assess whether there are languages in which "adjectives" are all nouns. Finally, I turn to the question of whether there are languages in which "adjectives" are all verbs. (Recall that in section 3.9, I already argued against one commonly claimed two-category system: a system that has verbs and "substantives," the latter being usable as either nouns or adjectives.)

4.6.1   Are there languages with two kinds of adjectives?

Probably the best-known case for a language having four distinct lexical categories is Japanese, as analyzed by Miyagawa (1987) (see also Murasugi [1990]). Miyagawa's claim has already been argued against by Ohkado (1991) and Nishiyama (1999), and I will do little more than repeat their arguments, showing how they are validated by my more comprehensive theory of categories. While this is not my most creative work, it is a worthwhile case study because it provides a pattern for how claims that a particular language has an additional lexical category can be evaluated within my theory.

Miyagawa shows that Japanese has two different classes of words, both of which translate naturally into English as adjectives. The difference between the two can be observed both when the words in question are used attributively and when they are used as predicates. The attributive facts are shown in (87).

(87)   a utskushi-i   onna   versus   kirei-na   Hanako
          beautiful-PRES woman   beautiful-?? Hanako
          'a beautiful woman' (A)   'beautiful Hanako' (AN)
        b hashi-ru   onna   versus   sensei-no (*na)   Hanako.
          run-PRES woman   teacher-GEN   Hanako
          'a woman who will run' (V)   'Hanako, who is a teacher' (N)

Both kinds of words can come immediately before a noun that they modify, but they take different suffixes when they do so: one group of adjectives takes the present tense ending *–i*, whereas the other takes the suffix *–na*. The present tense ending is similar but not identical to the present tense suffix used on verbs in relative clauses;[34] the *–na* suffix is similar but not identical to the genitive suffix *–no* used on nouns ((87b)). The predicative facts are shown in (88).

(88)   a Hanako-wa   utsukushi-i   versus   Hanako-wa   kirei-da
          Hanako-TOP beautiful-PRES   Hanako-TOP beautiful-COP
          'Hanako is beautiful.'(A)   Hanako is beautiful. (AN)
        b Hanako-wa   hashi-ru   versus   Hanako-ga   sensei-da
          Hanako-TOP run-PRES   Hanako-NOM teacher-COP
          'Hanako is running.' (V)   'Hanako is a teacher.' (N)

[34] The fact that noun-modifying adjectives in Japanese must bear tense inflections suggests that there is no true attributive construction in Japanese, but these are predicate adjectives in a relative clause construction. This also fits with the fact, noted by Sproat and Shih (1991: 582), that Japanese adjectives do not show the same ordering restrictions that adjectives in many other languages do. If this is correct, then I would say that Japanese is like Slave in requiring adjectives to be in the minimal domain of a Pred (see section 4.2.4). The Japanese adjective apparently does not incorporate into Pred, however, because it retains its identity as an adjective, as shown below (in contrast to the languages discussed in section 4.6.3).

Again, both types of adjectives can be used in this way, but the morphology is different. *Utsukushi* takes a simple tense ending –*i* (as in (87a)), distinct from but parallel to the tense ending –*ru* that attaches to verbs. *Kirei*, in contrast, must be followed by the copular morpheme –*da*, which is identical to the morpheme that is found when nouns are used predicatively ((88b)). In this respect, *kirei* is more like a noun than *utsukushi* is, although (87) shows it is not identical to a noun. For these reasons (and a few others), Miyagawa concludes that words like *kirei* are neither true adjectives nor true nouns, but some other category that falls between the two in terms of its properties. He therefore calls them "nominal adjectives." He makes room for the new category within the familiar +/−V, +/−N system by allowing one of the features to be left unspecified (cf. Stowell [1981]). More specifically, he gives nominal adjectives the same feature complex as adjectives in English, whereas words like *utsukushi* are +V but unspecified for the N feature. This gives him the following system of lexical categories for Japanese:

(89)   a Noun = +N, −V
         b Adjectival Noun = +N, +V
         c Adjective = +V
         d Verb = +V, −N

Miyagawa can then state the desired morphosyntactic generalizations in terms of these features. For example, words that are +N need the copula –*da* when used predicatively. This applies to *kirei* 'beautiful' and *sensei* 'teacher', but not to *utsukushi* 'beautiful' or *hashi* 'run.'

Part of the reason it was relatively easy and attractive for Miyagawa to make this proposal is because the features +/−N, +/−V had almost no theoretical content. One could thus tinker with the features to achieve a desired morphological effect without any obviously embarrassing consequences. The freedom that comes from having theoretical entities that do not have theoretical consequences is not the kind of freedom that one ultimately wants, however. My approach therefore seeks to either deepen such proposals or to foreclose on them by giving the features more content. In this particular case, it is clear that I must foreclose, rather than deepen. On my theory, the features "N" and "V" are privative. Either a word has a referential index (the feature N) or it does not; there is no meaningful third option. In the same way, a word either has a specifier (the feature V), or it does not, with no third option. By taking this approach, I both give the features some meaning and constrain sharply the set of possible categories one can have. If there are two features that can take three values each (+, −, and 0), then there could in principle be nine distinct kinds of lexical categories – which seems like too many. Two privative features create only three or four categories, which is closer to the truth. But on this approach Miyagawa's analysis becomes impossible.

That this is a good result is shown by Ohkado (1991). Ohkado argues that *utsukushi* and *kirei* are really in the same lexical category – adjective – and that the differences between the two are purely morphological in nature (see also Nishiyama [1999]). In addition to rebutting Miyagawa's evidence, he gives some positive data in favor of his claim, which are particularly meaningful in this context. Ohkado shows that adjectives and nominal adjectives can both be used as resultative secondary predicates (see also Washio [1997]):

(90)   a Taroo-ga   kami-o   mizika-ku   kit-ta.
         Taro-NOM   hair-ACC   short-AFF   cut-PAST
         'Taro cut the hair short.' (*mizika* is an A)
       b Taroo-ga   kami-o   kire-ni   kit-ta.
         Taro-NOM   hair-ACC   beautiful-AFF   cut-PAST.
         'Taro cut the hair beautiful.' (*kire* is an AN)

This is significant because we saw that, among the lexical categories, only adjectives can take part in such a construction for principled reasons (section 4.4). *Kire* is not intermediate between a noun and an adjective in this respect; it is exactly like an adjective. Ohkado also shows that only adjectives and adjectival nouns can appear with degree-like expressions such as *totemo* 'very':

(91)   a Hanako-ga   totemo kirei-da.   (AN)
         Hanako-NOM   very   pretty-COP
         'Hanako is very pretty.'
       b Hanako-ga   totemo utsukusi-i.   (A)
         Hanako-NOM   very   beautiful-PRES.
         'Hanako is very beautiful.'
       c *Hanako-ga   totemo sensei-da.   (N)
         Hanako-NOM   very   teacher-COP
         'Hanako is very (much a) teacher.'
       d *Hanako-ga   totemo okasi-o   tabe-ru.   (V)
         Hanako-NOM   very   sweets-ACC   eat-PRES
         'Hanako very (much) eats sweets.'

This also holds true for comparatives and superlatives in Japanese. This fits well with section 4.3's explanation of why adjectives but not verbs can co-occur with degree heads.[35] Third, Ohkado points out that both As and ANs can be used as manner adverbs (see also Murasugi [1990: 70] and Nishiyama [1999]):

[35] *Totemo* 'very' does not, however, appear where a degree head should: it comes before the adjective, not after it as would be expected in a strict head-final language like Japanese.

(92)   a *ryuuchoo-ni* 'fluently'   (AN)
        b *utukusi-ku* 'beautifully'   (A)

This too shows that both must be adjectives, given section 4.5's conclusion that adverbs are the same category as adjectives. Finally, I can add to Ohkado's evidence the observation that As and ANs take part in the same causative and inchoative alternations in Japanese. (93a) gives an example of an A that becomes an inchoative verb by suffixing *–mar* and a causative verb by suffixing *–mer*; (93b) shows that ANs can undergo exactly the same derivations.

(93)   a tsuyo-i;   tsuyo-mar-u;   tsuyo-mer-u   (A)
          'be strong'   'become strong'   'strengthen'
        b shizuka-da;   shizu-mar-u;   shizu-mer-u   (AN)
          'be quiet'   'become quiet'   'cause to become quiet, calm'

Such derivations are usually possible with adjectives but not with nouns (section 3.8), and indeed true nouns in Japanese do not take part in this pattern: one has *sensei-da* 'be a teacher' but not **sensei-mar-u* 'become a teacher' or **sensei-mer-u* 'make someone a teacher.' ANs thus behave systematically like As and not like Ns in all the ways that matter most, according to my theory.

One might consider going in a different direction with this data. One might accept that ANs in Japanese are just normal adjectives, but say that there is something special about the As. One could say that words like *utukushi* are "adjectival verbs," halfway between true adjectives and verbs, and get a four-category system in that way. This is more accurately what Miyagawa's feature system in (89) (as opposed to his terminology) expresses. There is a grain of truth in this in that "verbal adjectives" cannot be used attributively without a tense marker in a relative clause-like construction in Japanese, as seen in (87a) (see note 34). The data, however, also speak against this approach. The ability to act as a secondary predicate, as an adverb, or to appear with a degree word distinguishes adjectives from verbs just as much as from nouns. One can create causatives from verbs as well as adjectives in Japanese, but this requires a different morpheme (*-sase*, rather than *-mer*). In the light of section 2.6, this suggests that the basic thematic properties of the roots are different. Finally, "adjectival verbs" behave like unergative predicates rather than like unaccusative predicates according to Miyagawa's (1989) floated quantifier test, as expected of true adjectives (and so do "adjectival nouns"; see section 2.8.4 for discussion):

I tentatively suggest that *totemo* is actually in the specifier of a head final but phonologically null degree head. This would be consistent with both the word order and the categorical restrictions seen in (91).

(94)   a Kyaku-ga   ryokan-ni (2-ri) tui-ta.   (V)
          guests-NOM inn-to   2-CL   arrive-PAST
          'Two guests arrived at the inn.'
        b Kodomo-ga   eeyoo-busoku-de (*san-nin) yowa-kat-ta.   (A)
          children-NOM malnutrition-from three-CL weak-PRED-PAST
          'Three children were weak from malnutrition.'

This suggests that the subject originates in a higher position, to the left of
the PP, in (94b) as contrasted with (94a). In all these respects, words like
utsukushi behave exactly like adjectives should, not halfway between a verb
and an adjective.

Overall, words like *utsukushi* and words like *kirei* behave alike in ways that
are uniquely characteristic of adjectives crosslinguistically and that distinguish
them from the other categories in Japanese. I conclude that both are adjectives,
and there is no good evidence for the existence of a fourth lexical category in
Japanese.

What, then, should we make of the evidence for two categories that motivated
Miyagawa's original proposal? My answer is "not much." Most of the differences turn out to be morphological in nature. It is perfectly familiar that not all
roots that share a category take exactly the same morphological endings. Nouns
in Latin, for example, come in different declension classes that cause them to
appear with different inflectional ends, even though their syntax is the same. I
claim that Japanese is similar: there are simply two different declension classes
of adjectives that are identical syntactically and semantically. The potential for
confusion comes from the fact that, for historical reasons, some of the endings
that go with one class of adjectives happen to look like endings found with
nouns (copular *–da*, dative/resultative/adverbial *–ni*), although others do not
(attributive *–na* versus genitive *–no*).[36] This kind of difference in declension
class does not justify expanding the list of lexical categories. Nishiyama (1999)
works out in some detail what the relevant morphological rules look like within
the framework of Distributed Morphology, presupposing a syntactic analysis
close to (but not identical to) mine.

I have lingered somewhat on Miyagawa's proposal, partly because it is one
of the few well-documented cases of a language claimed to have more lexical categories than English, and partly because it illustrates certain themes of

---

[36] The "adjectival nouns" were borrowed into Japanese from Chinese at a time when Japanese had
relatively few native adjectives (Murasugi 1990). As is often the case, the borrowed words could
not readily take the characteristic inflectional morphemes of the native words. Thus, noun-like
affixes were pressed into service – perhaps because these were really encliticized heads.

general interest. In particular, it shows clearly the pitfalls of taking inflectional morphology at face value when trying to identify categories. One must look at the overall weight of evidence, including evidence from relatively obscure sources like resultative predicates and inchoative formations. My theory has particular value in cases like this in which the evidence seems mixed, because it can guide decisions about which evidence is likely to be more reliable. For example, it predicts that evidence from resultative secondary predicates (if they exist) will usually be more enlightening than evidence from the more obvious source of simple matrix predication. In matrix predications, the existence of an often-null functional head like Pred, whose presence can be revealed only by subtle diagnostics, can confuse the issue. Pred is not involved in resultative secondary predication, however, so the essential properties of adjectives come across more clearly in this context. This gives a model for how other proposals that there are additional categories in particular languages can be investigated – and a precedent for how the inquiry is likely to turn out.

4.6.2 *Are there languages that have nouns instead of adjectives?*
Next let us turn from languages that putatively have more lexical categories than the Indo-European languages to languages that putatively have fewer. Recall that there are at least two distinct ways that a language could have nouns and verbs but not adjectives: words with adjectival meanings like 'big' or 'good' or 'white' could be included in the category of nouns, or they could be included in the category of verbs.[37] In this subsection, I dispense with the possibility that there are languages that always use nouns in the place of adjectives, saving the harder case of languages that seem to use verbs in the place of adjectives for the next subsection.

There are three distinct ways that a language could fail to distinguish adjectives from nouns. First, a language could have no nouns but only adjectives. In the terms of my theory, this would be a language in which no lexical item is ever associated with a criterion of identity or a referential index. Second, a language could have a large class of words that can be used as either nouns or adjectives – words that optionally bear a referential index. Third, a language could have nouns but not adjectives; in my terms, this would be a language in which all nonverbal lexical categories must bear a referential index. Such

---

[37] A third possibility is that some "adjectives" could be nouns while others are verbs, as mentioned in note 33. I put this aside to simplify the discussion. The subset of "adjectives" that appear to be nouns in such a language can be evaluated using exactly the same considerations as apply to a language in which all the "adjectives" appear to be nouns.

a language could have words for qualities, but these would be abstract nouns rather than adjectives; the language would have words like 'wealth,' but not 'rich,' words like 'intelligence,' but not 'intelligent.' The first two logical possibilities were considered and rejected in section 3.9, in the course of discussing whether the category noun is universal. It now remains to consider the third possibility.

It is not hard to imagine what a language that used nouns in the place of adjectives would look like: it would look a lot like Chichewa. (The data in this section are from Sam Mchombo [personal communication]). Many other African languages seem roughly similar to Chichewa in the relevant respects.) The syntax of nouns would be essentially the same as in English, but there would be none of the distinctively adjectival constructions discussed in this chapter. There would, for example, be no direct attributive modification of a noun by another word. Instead, an abstract noun could be connected to a head noun by way of a prepositional element, as in examples like *a man of wealth* in English. The Chichewa equivalent of this construction is indeed common and productive:

(95)   m-kango *(w-a)   nzeru
        3-lion   3-ASSOC 10.intelligence
        'a lion of intelligence, a smart lion'

Second, there would be no dedicated degree words that act as functional heads. Rather, degrees would have to be indicated with nonprojecting adverbs that can combine with any VP or PredP. This is the case in Chichewa:

(96)   a Mi-kango ndi   y-a   mphamvu *ku-posa njovu*.
          4-lions   PRED 4-ASSOC strength INF-pass 10-elephants
          'Lions are stronger than elephants.' (lit., 'Lions are of strength to pass elephants.')
        b Mi-kango i-ma-imb-a   *ku-posa njovu*.
          4-lions   4S-HAB-sing-FV INF-pass 10-elephants
          'Lions sing more than elephants.'

Third, the language would not have resultative secondary predicate constructions comparable to *I beat the metal flat*. This is also the case in Chichewa:

(97)   *Ndi mkango u-mene   a-lenje   a-na-meny-a   (w-a)   u-kali
         PRED 3-lion 3-which 2-hunters 2S-PAST-hit-FV   3-ASSOC   fierce(ness)
         'It is the lion that the hunters beat fierce/(to) fierceness.'

Finally, such a language should have no productive morphology for transforming nonverbal roots into stative, inchoative, or causative verbs, because nouns typically resist this kind of derivation (section 3.8). Causative and inchoative propositions would have to be expressed periphrastically, by a predicate nominal together with a syntactically distinct verb meaning 'become' or 'cause to become.' This is indeed the only option in Chichewa:

(98) a M-kango ndi   m-lenje / w-a   u-kali.
         3-lion   PRED 1-hunter   3-ASSOC 3-fierce
         'The lion is a hunter/fierce.'
      b M-kango u-na-khal-a   mfumu / w-a   u-kali.
         3-lion   3S-PAST-become-FV chief   3-ASSOC 3-fierce
         'The lion became a chief/fierce.'
      c Mbidzi   zi-na-khal-its-a   m-kango mnkhungu / w-a   u-kali.
         10.zebras 10S-PAST-become-CAUS-FV 3-lion   robber   3-ASSOC 3-fierce
         'The zebras made the lion (become) a robber/fierce.'

This, then, is what a language that had only nouns but not adjectives would look like.

Although Chichewa is a powerful aid to imagining what a language without adjectives would be like, it is clearly not such a language. It has approximately six words that behave like true adjectives, including *kali* 'sharp, fierce,' *kulu* 'big,' *tali* 'long,' *fupi* 'short,' *ng'ono* 'small,' and *wisi* 'raw, unripe, immature.' Bresnan and Mchombo (1995) take care to establish that these are adjectives and not nouns in Chichewa. The most obvious difference is that words like *kulu* 'big' do not have a fixed gender prefix; rather, its prefix varies to match the gender of the noun it modifies or is predicated of:

(99)   m-kango w-a   *u*-kulu;   mbidzi z-a   *zi*-kulu
         3-lion   3-ASSOC 3-big   10.zebra 10-ASSOC 10-big
         'the big lion'   'the big zebra'

The adjectives contrast in this respect with abstract nouns like *nzeru* 'intelligence,' the prefix of which is always class 10 regardless of the class of the modified head (see (95)). This variability of gender is characteristic of adjectives as opposed to nouns in gender-rich languages with a noun/adjective distinction, including the Indo-European languages, Hausa, Australian languages, and certain New Guinean languages. I have taken this to be a sign that adjectives are not associated with their own criterion of identity, which fixes the referent within the folk classificatory system associated with the language. These adjectives can be used either as attributive modifiers of nouns, as in (99) or as primary predicates, as long as they are complements of the Pred *ndi*, as in (100).

(100)   M-kango ndi   w-a   u-kulu.
        3-lion PRED   3-ASSOC   3-big
        'The lion is a big.'

These adjectives cannot function directly as the arguments of verbs; rather they must be nominalized by the prefix *u*- (Bresnan and Mchombo 1995) in such environments:

(101)   a *Kulu ??-ma-ndi-sanalats-a.
           big   ??S-HAB-1sO-make.happy-FV
           'Big pleases me.'
        b U-kulu u-ma-ndi-sanalats-a.
           14-big 14S-HAB-1sO-make.happy
           'Bigness pleases me.'

This is what we expect if these words do not bear a referential index in and of themselves.[38] Many other African languages are similar in that they have an identifiable class of adjectives, but it has a very small membership. Kilega also fits this description (Kinyalolo, personal communication), as do Igbo (8 As [Dixon 1982]), Ngamambo (5 As [Siegel 1980]), and Hausa (about 25 As [Newman 2000: 32]).

This leaves us in a somewhat awkward situation when trying to assess whether universal grammar permits a natural language not to have a noun–adjective distinction. On the one hand, Chichewa makes it easy to imagine that there could be such a language. Chichewa would itself become such a language if it happened to lose its eight adjectives, either by fixing their gender prefixes so that they acted like abstract nouns such as *nzeru* 'intelligence' or by having the words drop out of the language altogether. On the other hand, Chichewa is not an adjectiveless language, nor have I found one that is either from Africa or some other part of the world.[39] This result is similar to what we already saw in sections 2.10 and 3.9: languages that lack a certain lexical category are

---

[38] It is also marginally possible to have *m-kulu* as the subject of (101). This would mean 'the big one,' understood as anaphoric to some class 1 noun in the discourse. This is an instance of the familiar situation in which an adjective modifies a phonologically null noun, agreeing with it in gender and number (see section 3.3).

[39] It could also be that this discussion seriously underestimates the importance of the category adjective in Chichewa and similar languages. In the text, I assume that the "associative" element *a*, which introduces abstract nouns in many "adjective-like" environments, is a preposition comparable to *of* in English. But this may not be accurate. *A* differs from uncontroversial prepositions in Chichewa in at least two ways: it itself bears number and gender agreement with an associated noun projection (see (95), (96), (99), (100)), and when used predicatively it is preceded by the nonverbal copula *ndi* rather than the verbal copula *li* ((100)). These are both properties that one expects of adjectival projections, but not of PPs (see the appendix on a PP predication's need for a full verb). This raises the possibility that *a* is really an adjectival head that takes a noun or adjective as its complement and projects an AP. If so, then there are many more adjectival projections in Chichewa and related languages than has been thought.

theoretically conceivable, but they either do not exist or at least are extremely rare. I return to why this might be in chapter 5.

4.6.3   *Are there languages with verbs instead of adjectives?*

The last possibility of crosslinguistic variation in lexical category systems to consider is languages that seem to use verbs in place of adjectives. The literature expresses relatively little doubt that such languages exist. Mohawk, for example, seems to show exactly the properties my theory predicts such a language should have. Mohawk words that correspond to English adjectives do not need a copular particle and they inflect like verbs, bearing the same agreement morphemes and those tense/aspect morphemes that are semantically appropriate to them:

(102)   Ra-kowan-ʌ'-hne'   ne   Sak.
         MsS-big-STAT-PAST   NE   Sak
         'Sak used to be big.'

The syntax of these words is like that of unaccusative verbs such as 'fall' or 'arrive.' Mohawk thus allows noun incorporation into "adjectival verbs" as well as into other unaccusatives:

(103)   a Ka-wis-a-hútsi   thíkʌ.
            NsS-glass-Ø-black that
            'That glass is black.'
         b T-a'-ka-wís-ʌ'-ne'   thíkʌ.
            CIS-FACT-NsS-glass-fall-PUNC   that
            'That glass fell.'

(See Baker [1996b] for other unaccusativity diagnostics that treat 'fall' and 'black' the same in Mohawk.) The same causative morpheme that attaches to ordinary eventive verbs also attaches to "adjectives," suggesting that they have similar powers of theta-role assignment:

(104)   a Wa-shakó-ye-ht-e'.
            FACT-MsS/FsO-wake.up-CAUS-PUNC
            'He woke her up.'
         b Wa'-e-rák-ʌ-st-e'
            FACT-FsS-white-STAT-CAUS-PUNC
            'She made it white.'

The same benefactive applicative suffix also attaches to both verbs and "adjectives."

   A language with verbs instead of adjectives should not have the distinctive constructions that require an adjective. This is also true of Mohawk, for the most part. For example, degree specification is done by adverbs of intensity

and frequency, not by special phrase-projecting heads with purely degree interpretations:

(105)   a Éso / sótsi kowán-ʌ.
           much / too NsS.big-STAT
           'It is very big / too big.'
         b Sak sótsi éso   ra-hnekír-ha'
           Sak too   much MsS-drink-HAB
           'Sak drinks too much.'

Resultative secondary predicates are also impossible in Mohawk, as expected
given that verbs are inflected (so serial verb constructions are impossible). An
English sentence like *Mary pounded the dough flat* can only be translated into
Mohawk using the causative form of the "adjective" 'flat' with the process-
denoting main verb 'pound' left unexpressed (or in another clause):

(106)   Wári oshérha wa'-t-ye-takwʌtʌ-st-e'
         Mary dough   FACT-DUP-FsS-be.flat-CAUS-PUNC
         'Mary flattened the dough.'

Finally, there seems to be no special attributive modification of nouns distinct
from the possibility of forming a relative clause that is open to all verbs. The
modificational structure using 'white' in (107a) has the same word order as the
one using the verb 'buy' in (107b), and the two content words are inflected for
the same aspect and similar agreement.[40]

(107)   a Tyer [ka-rák-ʌ   atyá'tawi] wa-ha-hnínu-'
           Tyer NsS-white-STAT   shirt   FACT-MsS-buy-PUNC
           'Tyer bought a white shirt.'
         b Sak wa-hó-[a]ti-'   ne [wak-hnínu-Ø   áthere'].
           Sak FACT-MsS-lose-PUNC   NE   IsO-buy-STAT basket
           'Sak lost the basket I bought.'

Mohawk thus seems to be as clear a case of a language that has verbs rather
than adjectives as one could hope to find.

    Languages that fit this profile seem to be rather common, particularly in North
America, East Asia, and the Pacific; see Wetzer (1996) and Stassen (1997) for
extensive lists. Even some of the languages that I discussed previously as possible instances of noun–adjective neutralization fit partially under this heading as
well. Nahuatl, Greenlandic, and Chichewa all have some words that correspond
semantically to adjectives in English and act like nouns, but they have others

---

[40] More common than (107a) is a structure in which the noun is incorporated into the modifying
    head. This is possible with both "adjectives" and true verbs, but with some subtle differences
    that I return to below.

that act like verbs. For this segment of their vocabulary, these languages behave very much the same way that Mohawk does. Edo also has fewer adjectives than English does, and correspondingly more stative intransitive verbs. This, then, is the least controversial and best attested of all the possible cases of variation in lexical categories.

There is, however, reason to take a closer look even at this case. Many languages that seem to have no adjective–verb distinction still allow a subclass of verbs to modify nouns in a special way. This subclass of verbs always looks suspiciously like adjectives, and I will argue that that is what they are. To see how this can happen, I begin by considering the Muskogean language Choctaw, as described by Nicklas (1972) and Broadwell (1990).

Choctaw is like Mohawk in that "adjectives" are freely used as predicates, with no copula and with the usual tense and agreement prefixes, as shown in (108). This is Broadwell's primary reason for saying that they are really verbs (1990: 112).

(108)   a Issobah-pat   chito-h.   (no copula, tense)
           horse-DEM/NOM big-PRES
           'This horse is big.'
        b *Sa*-litiiha-*tok*.   (agreement, tense)
           1sII-dirty-PAST
           'I was dirty.'

Moreover, these are probably unaccusative verbs. Davies (1986: ch. 2) argues for this based in part on the fact that these verbs take class II agreement prefixes, which are the same as the agreements that normal transitive verbs show with their objects; compare (108b) with (109).[41]

(109)   Is-*sa*-hottopali-tok   (contrast: Chi-bashi-*li*-tok)
        2sS-1sO-hurt-PAST   2sO-cut-1sS-PAST
        'You hurt *me*.'   '*I* cut you.'

Davies (1986: 22) also shows that the sole arguments of predicates like 'dirty' do not necessarily act as subjects for switch reference marking in Choctaw, patterning in this respect too with canonical unaccusative verbs like *kobafa* 'break.' Nicklas (1972) adds the information that the same productive causative morpheme *–chi* that attaches to verbs also attaches to "adjectives": just as *ishkochi* 'to make drink' is derived from *ishko* 'to drink', so *hommachi* 'to make red' is derived from *homma* 'to be red'. Following the reasoning of

---

[41] Davies' claim that verb agreement reveals underlying grammatical functions is, however, controversial among Muskogeanists; see Munro and Gordon (1982) for another view.

section 2.6, it appears that these stative predicates in Choctaw already select a theme argument, and do not require a different causative morpheme to add that argument. This means that these words are verbs, it seems.

There is, however, a complication concerning the restrictive modification of nouns that is observable in Nicklas (1972) and discussed explicitly by Broadwell (1990). If Choctaw truly does not have adjectives, then there should be no special attributive construction that only "adjectival verbs" can enter into; they should have to form relative clause constructions on a par with all other verbs in the language. But this is not entirely borne out. (110) shows a standard relative clause construction, containing the intransitive eventive verb *illi* 'die.'

(110)   [Alla-ma   ofi-it   im-illi-kaash-ma]   ii-hoppi-tok (Gordon 1987)
         child-DEM   dog-NOM   3III-die-past-DEM/ACC   1pII-bury-PAST
         'We buried that child's dead dog.'

Notice that Choctaw has internally headed relative clauses: the bracketed clause in (110) has the same internal structure as any normal sentence. In particular, there is no gap, and the understood head of the relative clause *ofi* 'dog' bears nominative case, showing that it is the subject of the relative clause, not the accusative case one might expect given that 'dog' is the understood theme of the matrix event of burying. The accusative case marker *–ma* attaches instead to the relative clause as a whole, ending up as a suffix on the embedded verb. We need not go into the exact analysis of such internally headed relative clauses here. The point is that if "adjectives" are really just stative verbs, then they should form relative clauses that look exactly like (110). This is not correct, as shown in (111). The gross word order is indeed the same, with the understood head noun, followed by the predicate, followed by a demonstrative element that bears the case of the argument as a whole (this time the nominative *–mat*). The difference is that in (111) the internal head cannot take its own nominative case marking, whereas in (110) it must.

(111)   Hattak-(*at)   chaaha-mat   chahta   kiiyoh. (Broadwell 1990)
         man-(NOM)   tall-DEM/NOM   Choctaw   not
         'That tall man is not Choctaw.'

Broadwell (1990) analyzes (111) as a special kind of reduced relative clause, built on a type of small clause constituent that does not have a tense node. It is striking, however, that it closely recapitulates the properties of attributive modification: it is a special construction that involves the merger of a bare noun with a bare "adjective" in the absence of any distinctively clausal material. "Adjectives" enter into this construction, but eventive verbs do not. (111) thus raises the possibility that Choctaw has adjectives after all.

There is a way to account for these seemingly contradictory facts. Suppose that Choctaw roots like *litiiha* 'dirty' and *chaaha* 'tall' are inherently adjectives, not verbs. We already know from section 4.2.4 that adjectives in some languages are required to be embedded under a Pred head; Slave and Ika are clear examples. This parameter of variation is repeated in (112).

(112)   In some languages, A(P) must be in the minimal domain of a Pred.

Suppose that this is true in Choctaw too, but Choctaw adds a wrinkle: its Pred is phonologically null and requires its adjectival complement to incorporate into it whenever possible. Section 2.9 established that the result of incorporating an adjective into a Pred prior to lexical insertion is a verb. Thus, all I am saying so far is that Choctaw has adjectives underlyingly, when syntactic structure is first constructed, but because of its particular combination of lexical properties those adjectives usually get transformed into verbs. This is only slightly different from saying that Choctaw has verbs rather than adjectives from the start. In particular, it is consistent with the observations that stative predicates end up being inflected for tense and number, that they act like unaccusative predicates, and that they can incorporate into causative verbs like *–chi*. There is, however, one difference: my more-abstract theory opens up the possibility that an adjective could combine with a noun to form a distinctive attributive construction *before* it is embedded under Pred. On this view, the structure of the relative clause in (111) is approximately (113) (note that Choctaw is a head-final language).[42]

(113)

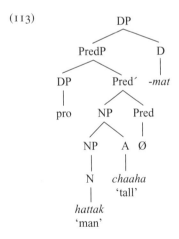

---

[42] I leave open both the exact structure of the internally headed relative clause (e.g. whether there is a null operator or not) and the question of whether additional functional categories such as tense come between PredP and DP. These details are orthogonal to the main point at hand.

This structure satisfies (112), because the adjective is adjoined to the NP that is the complement of the Pred. As such, it is technically not dominated by NP, given the definition of domination in terms of segments in Chomsky (1986a: 7, 9). It is dominated by PredP, however; it is thus in the minimal domain of PredP, just as if it were the true complement of Pred.[43] In this structure, the noun 'man' is not the subject of the relative clause at all; rather, it is the head of an attributively modified nominal that constitutes the predicate of the relative clause. This explains why it is not marked nominative in (111): predicate nominals are not marked for case in Choctaw, as shown also in the simpler example in (114).

(114)   Hattak-mat   alíkchi.   (Nicklas 1972)
         man-DEM/NOM doctor
         'That man is a doctor.'

The real head of the relative clause is a phonologically null subject pronoun – a configuration that is independently known to be possible in Choctaw. On my analysis, then, the most literal gloss of (111) is not 'The man who is tall is not a Choctaw,' but rather 'The one who is a tall man is not a Choctaw.' The two are truth-conditionally equivalent.

True verbs like 'die,' in contrast, cannot enter into the structure in (113), because there is no attributive verb construction, for the reasons discussed in section 4.2.2. Even if verbs like 'die' are decomposed into an adjectival part and a verbal part, as proposed in section 2.9, the adjectival part must be able to incorporate into the verbal part for lexical insertion to take place. This head movement is not possible in (113), since the adjective is not the head of the complement of Pred. Therefore, a lexical verb can only modify a noun by forming a full relative clause, with the head NP case-marked internal to that clause, as in (110). The fact that intransitive stative predicates generally act like verbs in Choctaw can thus be reconciled with the fact that there is a distinctive attributive construction involving what look like adjectives by making crucial use of (112) and the syntax of conflation. I conclude that Choctaw does have a verb–adjective distinction after all, but it is neutralized on the surface in most contexts.[44]

---

[43] On this interpretation of (112), one might expect adjectives to be able to attributively modify nouns even in Slave, as long as the noun is used predicatively. This is probably not possible, given Rice's (1989) silence on the matter. Perhaps the fact that As incorporate into Pred in Choctaw (and Mohawk) makes a difference in how this condition applies.

[44] Nicklas (1972: 185) also mentions that Choctaw has special degree-like constructions that can co-occur only with a subclass of verbs – roughly the adjectival ones. An example is:

This analysis may also hold for many other languages that seem to have verbs rather than adjectives. Mojave (a Yuman language), for instance, is strikingly similar to Choctaw in these respects. Mojave "adjectives" look for the most part just like intransitive verbs. For example, the word *havasu:* 'blue' appears as a predicate without an overt copula in (115), and it bears a typical Mojave tense/aspect suffix *–pč*.

(115)   Hatčoq-č havasu:-pč   (Munro 1976)
         dog-NOM   blue-TNS
         'The dog is blue.'

As in Choctaw, relative clauses are internally headed in Mojave. When the understood head of the relative clause is the subject of that clause, a special prefix *kw-* attaches to the verb. (116a) shows what this looks like with a normal transitive verb, and (116b) illustrates the same construction with an "adjectival" verb.

(116)   a [hatčoq poš k^w-taver]   ?-iyu:-pč   (Munro 1976)
           Dog   cat REL-chase 1sS-see-TNS
           'I saw the dog that chased the cat.'
         b [hatčoq k^w-əvasu:-n^y] m-iyu: ?
           Dog   REL-blue-DEM   2-see Q
           'Have you ever seen a blue dog?'

Uninflected stative intransitive predicates also have another way of modifying nouns, however, which is open to them but not to canonical verbs. Munro (1976: 45) writes: "[(117)] illustrates a standard construction in which an uninflected (deverbal) "adjective" (*iraw*) immediately follows the noun it qualifies (*?ahat*)." The subject relativizing prefix *kw-* is not present here, and the "adjective" is not inflected for tense or aspect.

(117)   [?ahat iraw] mat ičo:-k   (Munro 1976: 45)
         horse fast self make-TNS
         'He changed himself into a fast horse.'

(i)   Chaahah chóyyoomih.
         tall   quite
         'He is really tall.'

This *choyyoomih* apparently does not appear with true verbs, like *balilih* 'run.' Also note that *choyyoomih* comes at the end of the clause, after the verb, consistent with the claim that it is a functional head (rather than an adverb) in head-final Choctaw. It is very possible that additional evidence in favor of saying that there are adjectives in Muskogean languages can be gleaned from this material. I do not pursue the matter here, however, because the constructions are not described in detail. (I would want to know what the past tense of (i) is, for example.)

Elsewhere, (p. 187) Munro suggests that this "adjective" construction might be thought of as a type of reduced relative. But just as in Choctaw, this so-called relative clause duplicates precisely the distinctive properties of attributive modification: it consists of only a noun and something that looks like an adjective merged into a tight constituent that contains no distinctively clausal elements. This suggests that Mojave also has adjectives that normally must combine with a Pred to form a verb, but that can create an attributive construction when the circumstances are right. I do not attempt to derive the particular morphosyntactic properties of this Mojave construction, however, which are not as straightforward as Choctaw. (See Hengeveld [1992: 47–48], who also appeals to sentences like (117) as a reason to resist reducing adjectives to verbs in Mojave.)

Very much the same situation can be discerned in Austronesian languages. Donohue (1999) shows that in predicative environments, "adjectives" in Tukang Besi seem indistinguishable from verbs, as is typical for languages in this family:

(118) a No-to'oge   na   woleke iso.   (A [p. 79])
          3/REAL-big NOM rat   yon
          'That rat is big.'
       b No-tode=mo   na   woleke.   (V [p. 77])
          3/REAL-flee-PERF NOM rat
          'The rat's bolted.'

A difference appears, however, when the two types of words are used to modify nouns: true verbs require a morpheme that shows that relative extraction has taken place, whereas adjectives do not:

(119) a te   woleke to'oge   (A [p. 77])
          ART rat   big
          'the big rat'
       b te   woleke t-*um*-ode   (V [p. 79])
          ART rat   REL-flee
          'the fleeing rat'

Donohue's own informal analysis of this is that Tukang Besi has a class of distinctively adjectival roots, but they are bound elements that must be incorporated into some other category on the surface (1999: 82–89). In (118a), the adjectival root is combined with a null verb; in (119a) it forms a kind of compound with a noun. These suggestions fit very well into my theory: in my terms, (118a) is a case of A conflating into a null Pred to yield a V, and (119a) is a normal case of attributive modification forming a complex N projection. (I do not treat this as asyntactic compounding, however, because N roots apparently cannot modify nouns in the same way; see sections 4.2 and 5.1.)

The same story seems to hold straightforwardly in other Austronesian languages such as Kambera (Klamer 1994), and it can be extended to Oceanic languages like Samoan and Tongan as well. The distinction between attributive modification and relativization is less obvious in Samoan, simply because the verbal affixes like –*um*- that are concomitants of relative extraction in the western branches of the Austronesian family are not found in this eastern branch (Mosel and Hovdhaugen 1992). Thus, no morphological difference between the Samoan equivalents of (119a) and (119b) is expected, and none is observed. There is a hint that the basic syntactic difference is present, however, in Mosel and Hovdhaugen's observation that "adjectival" modifiers come closer to the head noun than (other) relative clauses do. This word order difference follows from the fact that only adjectives can merge directly with nouns; verbs must form relative clauses, which adjoin to the NP/DP as a whole.

Once one becomes alert to this theoretical possibility, one can recognize a little bit of evidence that distinctively adjectival roots exist even in Mohawk, although the evidence is more subtle than in the other languages and requires some work to uncover. (120) shows another simple example of a clause the predicate of which is a stative "adjectival" verb.

(120)   Ra-kowán-ʌ   ne   ra-ksá'-a.
        MsS-big-STAT   NE   MsS-child-NSF
        'The boy is big.'

The predicate here consists of three morphemes: the root *(k)owan*, the subject agreement *ra*-, and the stative aspect suffix –ʌ. The stative aspect can be used with verbs of all kinds in Mohawk, but "adjectival" roots are special in that (apart from certain instances of derivational morphology), they must always be followed by a stative morpheme. They cannot appear by themselves, and they cannot take any other aspect morpheme:

(121)   *Ra-kowan-(ha')   ne   ra-ksa'-a.
        MsS-big-(HAB)   NE   MsS-child-NSF
        'The boy is (always) big.'

The crucial question is whether roots like *kowan* are by themselves adjectival or verbal.

Either view is plausible a priori. On the one hand, we could say that *kowan* is inherently adjectival, meaning that it has no theme theta-role of its own to assign. The theme theta-role would be created by the stative morpheme –ʌ which functions as a Pred. Then (120) is grammatical, but (121) violates the theta criterion, there being no-theta role to assign to the subject *raksa'a* 'boy.' The fact that *kowan* is always followed by –ʌ and cannot appear in resultative constructions, degree constructions, or simple attributive constructions can be attributed to parameter (112)'s holding also in Mohawk. On the other hand, *kowan* could be inherently verbal, and hence capable of assigning a theta-role to the subject itself. On this view, the difference between (120) and (121) is a semantic one: it supposedly follows from the type of eventuality that *kowan* describes that it can appear in stative aspect but not in any other aspect.

The way to choose between these two hypotheses is to look carefully to see if anything special happens when the intransitive stative root appears in tight construction with a modified noun. The answer seems to be yes. The relevant "tight construction" in Mohawk is not the periphrastic one shown back in (107a) but the more common incorporation structure shown in (122), in which the noun root and the "adjective" root form a single morphological word.

(122)   Ka-nuhs-owán-ʌ.   (Deering and Delisle 1976: 109)
         NsS-house-big-STAT
         'The house is big, it's a big house, the big house.'

So far this is not distinctive, since many uncontroversial verbs also allow noun incorporation. It is suggestive, however, that examples like (122) are frequently translated into English as attributive adjective plus noun combinations, as 'It is a big house,' rather than as 'The house is big.' This seems to be the translation of choice in Deering and Delisle (1976), for example. The expression in (122) is also used frequently as a noun phrase, glossed as 'the big house.'

The plot thickens when one considers examples parallel to (122) in which the noun is animate. In this case, Mohawk speakers have a choice: the complex verb can bear true agreement with the understood gender of the incorporated noun ((123b)), or it can bear default neuter agreement *ka-*, in which case the gender of the incorporated noun is not specified ((123a)).

(123)   a ka-ksa-ht-owán-ʌ
            NsS-child-NOML-big-STAT
            'a big child'
         b ra-ksa-ht-owán-ʌ
            MsS-child-NOML-big-STAT
            'a big boy'

The agreeing version in (123b) seems, if anything, to be the more normal of the two. In this respect, "adjectival" verbs differ from eventive verbs, for which the pleonastic agreement is normal, as Baker (1996b: 315–19) shows in detail:

(124) a T-a'-ka-wír-ʌ'-ne'.
           CIS-FACT-NsS-baby-fall-PUNC
           'The baby fell.'
       b *T-a'-e-wír-ʌ'-ne'.
           CIS-FACT-FsS-baby-fall-PUNC
           'The baby girl fell.'

There also seems to be a semantic distinction between agreeing forms like (123b) and nonagreeing forms like (123a). For many examples, the glosses 'That boy is big' and 'That is a big boy' seem equally felicitous, but there are some for which the translation in which the noun is part of the predicate rather than the subject is clearly more appropriate. These are cases in which there is a so-called nonintersective relationship between the "adjective" and the noun, the "adjective" being interpreted relative to the meaning of the noun. Siegel (1980) shows that nonintersective interpretations are associated with attributive modification, not with predicative uses of an adjective. For example, *beautiful* in (125a) easily gets a special reading in which it does not assert ordinary physical beauty, but rather a special kind of beauty that is relevant only to being a dancer – the beauty of dancing well. In contrast, when used as a simple predicative adjective ((125b)), the salient reading of the adjective is the one of ordinary physical beauty.

(125) a She is a beautiful dancer.
       b That dancer is beautiful.

Noun plus "adjective" combinations in Mohawk get similar nonintersective readings only when the noun is incorporated and the combination shows full gender agreement. Some examples are:

(126) a Yako-skar-a-kstʌ′ha.
           FsO-friend.of.opposite.sex-Ø-elderly
           'She is too elderly to be a girlfriend.' (not 'The girlfriend is elderly.')
       b ra-[a]tʌro-hser-íyo
           MsS-friend-NOML-good
           'He is a good friend.' (not the same as 'The friend is good'; he may
           be faithful, loyal, and supportive, but a corrupter of youth.)
       c te-y-atʌro-hser-áks-ʌ
           DUP-MdS-friend-NOML-bad-STAT
           'They are bad friends to each other.' (not the same as 'The friends are bad';
           they may be morally good, but unable to get along.)

Putting these facts together, I conclude that there is a distinctive attributive construction in Mohawk, which only adjectival roots can enter into. The characteristics of this construction are (i) showing full gender agreement on the complex word, (ii) requiring noun incorporation, and (iii) allowing non-intersective readings of the adjectival element.

The root *–iyo* 'good' is of special interest in this connection. This root has two properties that distinguish it from other verbs in Mohawk, including typical "adjectives" like *(k)owan*. First, incorporation is strictly obligatory with this root (Postal 1979). Second, if the incorporated root is animate, gender agreement is not only possible but required, as shown in (127).

(127)   a *Ra-iyo   ne   ra-ksa-'a.
            MsS-be.good   NE   MsS-child-NSF
            'The boy is good.'
        b #ka-ksa-ht-iyo[45]
            NsS-child-NOML-be.good
            'the good child'
        c Ra-ksa-ht-iyo
            NsS-child-NOML-be.good
            'the good boy; He is a good boy.'

These peculiarities can be explained if *–iyo* is not only adjectival, but the kind of adjective that can only be used in attributive constructions, like *main* in English (see section 4.2.4). Connected with this is the fact that *–iyo* seems to have only nonintersective readings. This means there is no uniform sense of goodness in Mohawk, but goodness must always be evaluated relative to some common noun. For example, one can compare (126b) with *r-uhkwe-ht-iyo* 'MsS-person-NOML-good,' which has the sense 'He is a good-looking (attractive) man,' and with *ra-yo'tʌ-hser-iyo* 'MsS-work-NOML-good,' which means 'he is a good (hard) worker.' In each case, the type of goodness varies with the associated noun. This semantic property would then explain why *–iyo* must be used attributively in Mohawk. I conclude that roots like *iyo* 'good' *(k)owan* 'big,' *aks* 'bad,' *rak* 'white,' *'ts* 'dirty,' *hnin* 'hard,' and so on are fundamentally adjectival in Mohawk.

Given this assumption, the morphosyntactic details of the two constructions in (123) can be analyzed as follows. The difference boils down to whether the adjectival root merges with Pred first and then the noun, or with the noun first and then Pred. Suppose that the adjectival root combines with Pred first. Then no nonintersective reading is possible (so *–iyo* is impossible). The adjective root

---

[45] This example is marginally possible as 'the good pushy female child,' in which *ka-* is interpreted as a feminine zoic agreement, not a default neuter agreement.

immediately incorporates into Pred, creating an unaccusative verb. That unaccusative verb takes a nominal specifier, to which it assigns a theme role. Finally,
this nominal argument can move to adjoin to the derived verb, by the normal process of noun incorporation in Mohawk. Since the incorporated noun discharges
the only thematic role of the verbal complex, there is no other argument, and
tense takes default neuter agreement, as is normal for noun incorporation into
verbs (see (124)). The result is the structure in (128a), which is no different
from any other structure with noun incorporation into an intransitive verb.

(128)   a   b

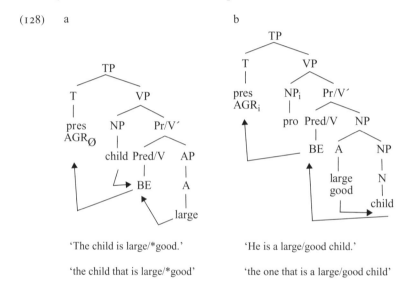

'The child is large/*good.'   'He is a large/good child.'

'the child that is large/*good'   'the one that is a large/good child'

Suppose, on the other hand, that the adjectival root combines with the noun
first, as in (128b). This is an instance of attributive modification, which supports a nonintersective interpretation of the adjective relative to the noun (so –*iyo*
'good' is possible here). This N+A combination is then merged with a Pred
head, satisfying the need for the A root to be in the minimal domain of Pred, just
as in Choctaw. Unlike Choctaw, however, incorporation takes place within the
attributive construction itself, making a single word out of the noun–adjective
combination. (This is compatible with the Head Movement Constraint, given
that the A and the N are both contained in all the same maximal projections.)
This combined head then incorporates as a whole into Pred. This explains why
incorporation is required in attributive constructions in Mohawk (see (127a)): if
the A head does not incorporate with the N, it is unable to reach Pred, as it must.
The result of this incorporation is again an intransitive verb, which combines

with tense in the usual way. The derived verb also assigns a theme theta-role
to its specifier position. This time, however, the incorporated noun is not the
recipient of Pred's theta-role, but rather part of the complement of Pred. Thus
the thematic role must be assigned to something else – such as a *pro*, licensed
by the agreement on tense. This explains why the distinctive attributive
construction has full gender agreement in Mohawk, unlike other incorporation structures. The agreement is not with the incorporated noun after all, but
with a null argument that the incorporated noun is predicated of. This second
construction is identical to the structure I proposed for Choctaw, except that
incorporation takes place in Mohawk. As in Choctaw, the structure in (128b)
can be made into a nominal by taking the *pro* subject to be the head of an
internally headed relative clause. The result means literally 'the one who is a
big child,' which is equivalent to 'the big child.'

To complete this account, I must explain why the attributive construction
in (128b) is not possible with all verbs, given that all verbs decompose into
an adjective part plus a verbal part on my analysis. The answer comes from
cyclic lexical insertion. An adjectival root like *(k)owan* 'big' lexicalizes only
A, whereas a verbal root like *hri'* 'shatter' lexicalizes an A+Pred unit. There
is no A+Pred constituent in (128b); rather, the derived head crucially has the
structure [[N+A]+Pred]. Therefore, an adjectival root can be inserted, but a
verbal root cannot.

This analysis makes one additional prediction. The agreeing attributive construction has an open subject position, filled only by *pro*. One would expect that
this *pro* could be replaced by an ordinary referential noun phrase. In contrast,
the subject position in the nonagreeing verbal construction is occupied by the
trace of the incorporated noun. Therefore, no other nominal should be possible
here (apart from the very limited possibilities for a free nominal to double an
incorporated one, discussed in Baker [1996b]). This prediction is verified by
(129).

(129)   a *Ka-ksa-ht-owan-Λ   ne   Sak.
           NsS-child-NOML-big-STAT   NE   Sak
           'Sak the child is big.'
         b Ra-ksa-ht-owan-Λ   ne   Sak.
           MsS-child-NOML-big-STAT   NE   Sak
           'Sak is a big child.'

The grammaticality of (129b) confirms that there is something special about
incorporation into "adjectives," and that the incorporated element is not really

the subject, but rather part of a predicate nominal. Thus even Mohawk has adjectives of a sort.

Overall, I have looked in varying degrees of detail at four languages that seem at first to have verbs but not adjectives. Upon closer examination, the "verbs" that correspond to adjectives in all of these languages have subtle grammatical properties that distinguish them from true verbs. In each case, the roots of such verbs can enter into a special attributive construction with a noun instead of or prior to "verbalization." From this, I conclude that all of these languages have adjectives. Each language also has roots that cannot enter into the distinctive attributive constructions; these are the true verbs. These languages thus have a verb–adjective distinction after all, despite the fact that adjectives always become verbs in simple structures. Once again, I have not found genuine examples of a type of category neutralization that seemed at first glance to be plausible and even common. This does not, of course, guarantee that every single language in the world has a distinct class of adjectives. But even careful large-scale typological studies of predication such as Wetzer (1996) have observed that many languages that do not distinguish predicate adjectives from verbs do have special constructions of attributive modification that only some roots can participate in. In addition to some of the languages discussed above, he mentions Tigak, Chinese, Sudanese, Chemehuevi, and Guarani in this regard.[46] I am therefore prepared to conclude that the adjective–verb distinction will turn out to be a universal at the appropriate level of morphology and syntax. Combined with the results of sections 2.10, 3.9, and 4.6.2, I arrive at the conclusion that all natural languages have essentially the same three-category system, which distinguishes nouns, verbs, and adjectives. Exactly what this claim means, and why it should be true, is the topic of the concluding chapter.

---

[46] See also Koopman (1984: 64–65) on the West African language Vata. She observes that while many "adjectival" notions are expressed as stative verbs on the surface in Vata, these verbs contain roots that have special derivational possibilities that show them to be inherently adjectives. She concludes that a class of adjectives exists in Vata "at the lexical level," but they can only be inserted into the syntax if they are verbalized by either *mall* or a null equivalent. This is equivalent to my proposal, where *mall* is a Pred head that the adjectival roots must be in the minimal domain of and into which they must incorporate.

5 *Lexical categories and the nature of the grammar*

In the core chapters of this book, I have defended particular claims about what it is to be a noun, a verb, or an adjective. I have also argued that all natural languages have essentially the same three-way distinction among lexical categories. Grammatical systems that do not have one of these categories are perfectly imaginable. Such systems could achieve approximately the same expressive power as a three-category language by using periphrastic constructions built around the functional category that corresponds most closely to the absent lexical category. But such languages seem not to exist. In this final chapter, I step back from the details of particular languages and particular lexical categories to reflect briefly on what these results might show about the basic design of the human language capacity.

Some large-scale questions that are still to be faced are these. What exactly bears a category? Is it fundamentally roots that are categorized as nouns, verbs, and adjectives, or is it stems, or inflected words, or the minimal leaves of a syntactic tree, or the maximal X^0s, or even larger phrases? For which of these linguistic units is category inherent, and for which is it derivative or even undefined? A logically similar and partially related set of questions concerns whether the category distinctions are fundamentally syntactic, semantic, or morphological in nature. One intriguing (and maddening) aspect of this topic is that whether something is a noun, verb, or adjective seems to have relevance in all three of these domains. Yet presumably the category distinctions inhere fundamentally in one domain and then project into the others; otherwise it would be a kind of coincidence that parallel categorial distinctions exist in each domain. Which domain, then, is the most fundamental one in this respect? Can the apparently crossmodular nature of the lexical category distinctions be used to gain any new insight into the relationships of syntax, semantics, morphology, and the lexicon within the architecture of human language? Finally, what is one to make of the somewhat surprising fact that the lexical category distinctions are not conceptually necessary but do as a matter of fact seem to be universal to human language? What does this imply about the nature of Universal Grammar, how detailed and specific to language it is, and how it is related to other aspects of cognition? I do not aspire to give definitive answers to these very broad questions in what follows, but do attempt to tease out the implications of the material I have considered for them as best I can. Doing this should help prepare for a future inquiry that combines evidence from lexical categories with evidence from other domains into a truly comprehensive picture of these matters.

5.1 What has a category?

The least abstract of these questions is the one of what linguistic unit fundamentally bears a category. Some of my analyses have quite specific implications for this question, and data can be brought to bear on it fairly directly. We can begin here and then use what we learn as a wedge into the even bigger questions.

Probably the most traditional and widespread view about category distinctions is that they are essentially morphological in nature. Particularly in well-inflected languages, it is a salient fact that some roots take one class of inflections whereas other roots take a different class of inflections. Some roots take case and number endings, for example, whereas other roots can be inflected for tense and mood. The fully inflected words then feed into the syntax, and their syntactic possibilities are determined in large part by the ways they have been inflected. Words inflected for nominative case, for example, can be used as subjects, whereas words inflected for tense can be used as predicates. This is one of the oldest views about categories, the one that was held by most ancient Greek and Roman grammarians, and it has played into the way that European languages have been taught ever since (Robins 1989). It is also a dominant view in many structuralist-influenced and descriptive grammars, which are generally morphocentric, especially if the language being described is a synthetic or agglutinative one. Those generative approaches that subscribe to strong versions of the lexicalist hypothesis also fall into this broad class of theories. For this wide range of linguists, category is first and foremost a property of roots and stems. From there it projects into the syntax by determining how a word can be inflected and hence what its syntactic possibilities are.

Essentially the opposite view has recently been adopted by Marantz (1997) and the other Distributed Morphologists, and by Borer (2000). For these theorists, categorial identity is determined by the syntactic environment of the category. Inflections often originate in different syntactic nodes from roots, as shown by English *do*-support, by differences in syntactic position that correlate with how a word is inflected in languages like French, Welsh, and Edo, by incorporation phenomena, and so on. Given this, it can strictly speaking be

meaningless to ask what the category of an inflected word is; the different components of the inflected word come from different nodes in a syntactic structure,
each of which has its own category. It is true that typically only one of these
components is a lexical category, and hence a semantic head in the sense of
Abney (1987). It is thus natural to see this as the central ingredient of the expression as a whole, giving rise to the common intuition that an inflected verb (say)
is itself a verb. But these inflected words strictly speaking may have a different
syntactic status, or even no syntactic status at all, given that an inflected word
need not constitute a coherent subpart of a syntactic representation.

For Marantz and Borer, this nonlexicalist, syntax-oriented conception has
further developed into the view that roots project syntactic phrases that have
no intrinsic category. The category of the phrase as a whole is then determined by that of the functional category that it is the complement of. A "root
phrase" that is the complement of a determiner is/becomes an NP; a root phrase
that is the complement of an Aspect head (or v) is a VP, and so on. This
is clearly a syntactocentric approach; indeed, Marantz claims that the internal structure of words is "syntax all the way down" (Halle and Marantz 1994).
To some extent, this approach takes the old Sapir and Swadesh (1946) view
that there is a single kind of lexical category prior to inflection in Wakashan
and Salish languages and applies it to all languages. Marantz's and Borer's
approaches also foreground the phenomenon of zero derivation – the fact that
many words one usually thinks of as being members of one category can also be
used as members of another category in a suitable context, especially in English.
For example, we think of *dog* as being a noun, and indeed it is in sentences like
The pesky dog followed us home. But the same root can also be used as a verb
with a partially related sense, as in *This problem has dogged us for a long time.*
Conversely, we normally think of *run* as a verb, having in mind examples like
Mary runs every morning, but it can also be used as a noun, as in *Mary goes
for a run every morning.* Such ambivalence of category is fairly widespread,
and can be exploited in creative ways by speakers in response to a particular
communicative situation.[1] On this view, then, it is syntactic phrases as a whole
that bear a category. Phrase structure also determines how complex words are
created and inflected by way of processes like incorporation and morphological

---

[1] I strongly suspect that the freedom of roots to switch categories is much freer in English (and
languages like Tongan, Mandarin, and Hebrew) than it is in languages like Mohawk, Edo,
Chichewa, and Australian languages. This could raise questions about the suitability of the
Marantz/Borer theory of category-neutral lexical heads. At least the implications of such a
"parameter" of variation for this view have not been considered. I do not, however, attempt
to document the difference here.

merger. Roots are inserted into functional contexts wherever they make sense, and our judgments about the categories of roots are derived from that.

Vaguely similar to this Distributed Morphology (DM) view are some functionalist theories, in which category differences are fundamentally pragmatic in nature (Hopper and Thompson [1984]; see also Croft [1991]). For these authors, the categorization of a given word follows from the role it plays in the more general context. This is like DM in that categorization is seen as a top-down phenomenon, enforced by the larger units that contain a given word, in contrast to the bottom-up perspective of lexicalist approaches. Hopper and Thompson also tentatively suggest, like Marantz and Borer, that particular roots are not intrinsically associated with particular categories.

The view that emerges from my inquiry is similar but not identical to the DM view. My approach is also syntax-oriented, as opposed to lexically or morphologically based. This is most obvious for verbs, which are defined as lexical categories that have a specifier. "Specifier" is a patently syntactic notion, defined in terms of the theory of phrase structure, and it has no intrinsic relevance to other linguistic domains. The syntactic property of having a specifier is naturally related to the morphological property of bearing tense inflection and to the semantic property of assigning an agent or theme theta-role, but it is not in perfect correspondence to them. A word that has a syntactic specifier but no tense marking or theta-role is still a verb, as *seem* is in a sentence like *Julia made it seem that she was tired*. The referential index of a noun is also a syntactic element, as shown by the fact that it is subject to the Noun Licensing Condition, a syntactic condition that crucially refers to relationships of c-command that are defined in terms of phrase structure. The referential index typically corresponds to reference in the semantic domain, but not in any straightforward way, as shown by Chomskian examples like *the average man* and *the flaw in the argument*. These NPs behave like perfectly normal noun phrases in the syntax – and hence bear a referential index – but they do not correspond to "things" in the real world in any mind-independent notion of "thing" (Chomsky 1981: 324). Nor is there any particular morphological marking that nouns must have that corresponds to this index; nouns must have determiners in some languages, for example, but not in others. Finally, since adjectives are defined as lexical elements that have neither a referential index nor a specifier, and these are syntactic notions, it follows that adjectives are syntactic entities too. In this respect, my approach is similar to the DM vision. And like DM, I want to derive a substantial amount of morphology – most inflection as well as the classic cases of "incorporation" and some derivation – from the syntax (Baker 1988a; 1996b; Cinque 1999).

However, I differ from Marantz (1997) and Borer (2000) on what the syntactic determinants of the category of a lexical item are. For me, the category of an expression is not a function of the functional category that takes that expression as a complement. Rather, it is determined by the local configuration of the expression, whether it has a specifier, or bears an index, or neither. This view has at least two significant advantages over the original DM view. First, my view predicts that category-specific behavior can arise even when there is no sign of any functional superstructure dominating the lexical head. Perhaps the clearest case in point is incorporation structures, where the presence of a functional head between the incorporating head and the host head would block movement by the Head Movement Constraint and the Proper Head Movement Generalization. The DM view seems to predict that category-specificity would disappear in this case, that one would have incorporation of bare roots that are undifferentiated for category. It is true that it is normally roots (or perhaps stems) that incorporate, as opposed to inflected words. However, it is not true that those roots show neutralization of category. On the contrary, I showed in sections 2.6, 3.6, and 3.9 that category-specificity is usually *enhanced* in these contexts. For instance, Mayali, Nahuatl, and Greenlandic all allow what look like APs to function as direct objects in simple sentences, and they all allow incorporation of direct object nouns. They do not, however, allow the incorporation of "adjectival" roots (see (3) below). In a similar way, free-standing causative verbs like *make* in English can take AP and NP small clause complements as well as VPs, but affixal counterparts in languages like Quechua, Chichewa, and Japanese allow only an intrinsically verbal root to be incorporated. Thus, exactly where there is less functional structure, we find more categorial distinctiveness. This is expected on my account, where category is determined for lexical nodes themselves, and functional elements are as likely to confuse the matter as to reveal it, because they can introduce their own referential indices or specifiers into the structure. My theory is also compatible with Chierchia's (1998) proposal that bare NPs as well as DPs can stand as argument expressions in many languages – although bare APs and VPs cannot. The difference shows up rather clearly in languages like Quechua, in which both nouns and adjectives can function as direct objects when followed by the determiner/case marker –*ta*, but only nouns can function as subjects, where there is no case marker. In the same way, my proposal allows there to be such a thing as a bare VP complement to a verb in (say) restructuring constructions. Such a complement is still distinct from an AP or NP complement, which I take to be warranted by the facts. Overall, I see no evidence that the categorial nature of a lexical element comes from independently motivated functional elements, and some evidence against it in those environments where the two proposals can be separated.[2]

The second major advantage of my approach is that the co-occurrence restrictions between lexical categories and functional categories can potentially be explained in terms of the inherent nature of each. Much work on functional categories since Abney (1987) has taken it as axiomatic that Ds take NP complements, Ts take VP complements, and Degrees take AP complements. For many, it is a straightforward fact about syntactic selection that functional heads can only select one kind of complement. An alternative view is that of Grimshaw (1991), who builds the restrictions into her theory by giving functional categories the same categorial features as the corresponding lexical categories and stipulating that these features must match throughout an "extended projection." The Marantz/Borer approach tries to capitalize on the inherent redundancy in these systems by saying that only the functional heads have category intrinsically, and the category of their lexical complements is

---

[2] In more recent work, Marantz's (2000) view has evolved in a way that that bears on this discussion. Marantz (1997) and Borer (2000) assume that lexical category distinctions are induced by familiar, independently motivated functional categories like determiner and aspect. In contrast, Marantz (2000) assumes that an NP is defined as the complement of an "n" node, where n is a novel category type, parallel to the v of Chomsky (1995: ch. 4). In the same way, an AP is the complement of a novel "a" node. Depending on how this is developed, the differences between Marantz's view and mine could largely collapse. The incorporation facts, for example, can be accounted for if the incorporation of a root into an n and then on into a verb is compatible with the PHMG, n (in contrast to D) not being "functional" in the relevant sense. In the same way, Chierchia-like results could be achieved by saying that in some languages nP must be embedded in DP and in other languages it need not be. One might also be able to give a principled explanation for why D selects nP but not aP or vP in terms of the inherent properties of the parts. My work can thus be harmonized with this version of Marantz's by saying that I have given the theory of the grammar of n, a, and v, rather than N, A, and V. More generally, I see no fundamental conflict between what I am saying and the fundamental tenets of DM, and it can be offered as a friendly amendment to that general approach.

The crucial question for choosing between these proposals, then, is whether there is enough evidence for decomposing all nouns and adjectives into two categories, "n/a" and "root," which head separate syntactic projections. So far, I see no evidence that these two projections have separate existences in which they interact in a differential way with other syntactic phenomena. There is also the obvious fact that the vast majority of languages have many noun stems that are not obviously bimorphemic, consisting of a root and some category-specific ending, making Marantz's view quite abstract. Third, if one accepts the distinction between n and a versus roots, one probably has to explain why root phrases can only be generated as the complements of n, a, or v, and thus always receive a categorization; it is not obvious why this should be so. (Within my theory, for example, an uncategorized root phrase could potentially appear in the same range of positions as APs, given that neither has intrinsic lexical properties; see below.) Marantz's fundamental reason for positing a syntactic distinction between n/a and "root" seems to be that the n/a node provides a home for derivational morphemes like *–ous* and *–ity*, preserving the idea that syntax is the only "generative engine" that can combine elements. It is less important to me than to him that all morphology be syntax, so I explore a somewhat more conservative version in what follows. It should be borne in mind, however, that the difference here is a very narrow one.

derivative, predictable from that of the functional head. In contrast, by attributing an inherent nature to the lexical categories (as well as to the functional ones), my theory makes it possible in principle to derive the familiar co-occurrence relationships as theorems, rather than stipulating them as axioms. I have even taken steps toward fulfilling this promise: section 3.3 explains why quantifiers and determiners select only noun complements (following the lead of Geach [1962] and Gupta [1980]), and section 4.3 explains why degree heads can select only APs. The idea that tense can select only a verbal projection is the shakiest of these co-occurrence relations crosslinguistically, since predicate adjectival and nominal clauses can also be tensed in some languages, including Abaza and Turkish. Nevertheless, section 2.5 makes a proposal about why tense affixes attach most easily to verbs in most languages. In this way, one can work toward a deeper and more explanatory theory of the possible relationships between lexical and functional categories by giving the lexical categories inherent content. (Note that these co-occurrence patterns show up most clearly in the syntax of some languages and in the inflectional morphology of others, depending on whether markers of definiteness, degree, and tense happen to be independent particles or bound affixes in the language in question. Like DM, my syntactically oriented theory explains the two kinds of co-occurrence in a unified way. The syntax of particles and inflections is generally the same, except that inflections combine with the lexical category either by head movement or by morphological merger in PF. The equivalence of particles and inflections is harder to capture in a morphocentric, lexicalist approach to categories.)

As a consequence of these primary differences, there is little room in my theory for DM's "root phrases" – phrases that are projected from a root before it is associated with a particular lexical category. On my view, every X^0 that participates in the syntax necessarily has a syntactic category. To a large extent, this view is forced upon me as a theory-internal consequence of my treatment of the adjective as a kind of default category, a category with no positive defining essence. This has the large advantage of creating a very stable and restrictive typology of lexical categories, with little room for crosslinguistic variation in the number or nature of the categories. It also makes the system more explanatory, because it accounts for the morphosyntactic behavior of three categories with only two features and the principles associated with them. It would, however, be very tricky to incorporate root phrases in Marantz's sense into this kind of theory. A root phrase would be a constituent that has not yet been assigned a categorial nature contextually, whereas an AP would be a category that has been assigned a null/default categorial nature. This is a very slender difference, particularly from the static perspective of a final syntactic representation. Perhaps it could be maintained dynamically, if expressions have no category when they first enter merge, but get a category as they go along – for example, they become a verb if they are merged with a specifier, or if an item with lexical content is incorporated into a Pred head that has a specifier. (I say that something like this does indeed take place below.) But once a syntactic structure has been assembled, there could be no distinction between a RootP and an AP within my terms. And I know of no compelling reason why one would want such a distinction. To the extent that the different lexical categories take different types of complements (or complements that are marked differently) those differences show up immediately when the lexical head is first merged with another expression. There is no reason to say that these head-complement structures are readjusted later, after the category of the root phrase is established by its broader context.

These considerations, then, point to a theory in which category is a primary property of all X°s, the leaf-nodes of a syntactic representation, rather than of XPs (as in DM) or of morphological entities such as roots or stems (as in lexicalist theories). An instructive way of illustrating this point is to compare root compounding in English to both attributive modification and incorporation. The first member of a root compound in English is not very fussy as to its category. It can easily be a noun or an adjective, and even verb roots and bound roots that are never used as independent elements in the syntax are possible. It is also possible for two adjectives to combine to make an adjective, or for a noun and an adjective to form an adjective.

(1)   a doghouse, strawberry, suspension bridge, breezeway   (N+N)
        b greenhouse, blueberry, high school, fairway   (A+N)
        c drawbridge, runway   (V+N)
        d cranberry, huckleberry   (X+N)
        e red-hot, icy-cold, bitter-sweet   (A+A)
        f pea-green, steel-cold, sky-high   (N+A)

In contrast, the attributive construction is highly category-specific. Only an adjective can modify a noun in this way, not a noun or a verb, or a category-less root. Thus, *blackbird* contrasts with *black bird* and *greenhouse* contrasts with *green house*; the latter examples have simpler, more compositional meanings. But there are no expressions such as *dog house*, *draw bridge*, or *cran berry* (with no compound stress) that correspond in the same way to *doghouse*, *drawbridge*, and *cranberry*. Nor can a noun modify an adjective, or an adjective modify another adjective without the mediation of an affix like *–ly*:

(2)   a *dog house, *straw berry, *breeze way   *N—N
       b green house, blue berry, fair way   A—N
       c *draw bridge, *run way   *V—N
       d *cran berry, *huckle berry   *X—N
       e Chris is *tall strong; The table is *big black. *A—A

Incorporation constructions in languages like Mayali and Nahuatl are also very sensitive to category; nouns can incorporate but adjectives (and verbs) cannot, even when the latter can plausibly be understood as expressing the theme argument of the host verb in context.[3] This was originally shown in section 3.6, and is repeated here as (3).

(3)   a Aban-yawoyh-warrkah-marne-kinje-ng   kun-kanj. (Mayali)
         1sS/3pO-again-wrong-BEN-cook-PAST/PUNC IV-meat
         'I cooked the wrong meat for them again.'
       b Kandi-wo-Ø   man-kuyeng!
         2S/1sO-give-IMPER   III-long
         'You give me the long one!'
       c Abanmani-ganj-wo-ng.
         1sS/3dO-meat-give-PAST/PUNC
         'I gave meat to the two of them.'
       d *Kandi-kuyeng-wo-Ø!
         2S/1sO-long-give-IMPER
         'You give me the/a long one!'

It is also generally bad to incorporate into any category except a verb; noun-to-noun incorporation seems to be universally impossible, for example. The attributive construction is very much like root compounding in its communicative function (both are forms of restrictive modification) and incorporation is very much like root compounding in its formal properties (both combine two uninflected roots into a new inflectable stem). Given these comparisons, it might seem puzzling that both attributive constructions and incorporation constructions display strong category specificity, but root compounding does not. Why should this be?

   Within my theory, the answer to this puzzle is that syntax draws the line. There is a cluster of reasons for saying that incorporation in languages like Mayali is a syntactic process (Baker 1988a; 1996b), none of which apply to root compounding. First, the incorporated noun in languages like Mayali can be referentially active, corresponding to a discourse referent (Evans [1997: 405];

---

[3] Of course, there are other heads, with different lexical properties, into which a verb root can incorporate, but not a noun root. The point is that there are no heads into which any root can incorporate, regardless of its inherent lexical category.

see also [Mithun 1984; Baker 1988a; 1996b]), whereas this is not true of the first member of a root compound (*#The new doghouse seems to disturb it (the dog).*) Second, an incorporated noun can be modified by something not contained inside the complex verb in Mayali, but the noun head in a root compound cannot be; *#the black doghouse* does not refer to the white house of a black dog. Third, the distribution of incorporation can be derived from syntactic principles, with the incorporated noun counting as the theme argument of the incorporating verb. There is no comparable syntactic/thematic relationship between the parts of a root compound: the *dog* in *doghouse*, for example, is not the theme of *house*, nor does it bear any other identifiable thematic role.

The reasons for saying that attributive modification is a syntactic construction also do not apply to root compounding, for the most part. First, both the modifying adjective and the modified noun can combine with other syntactic material before they merge with each other (see (4a,b)). This is not possible with root compounding (**a very greenhouse*) unless the pre-combined elements themselves constitute a root compound.

(4)   a a [very tall] man
        b a nice [picture of Venice]
        c la   loro   aggressione$_i$ [$_{NP}$ brutale [$_{NP}$ t$_i$ all'Albania]] (Cinque 1994: 88–89)
          the their attack   brutal   to-Albania
          'their brutal attack of Albania'

Second, the head noun in an attributive construction can undergo head movement to higher positions such as D in a variety of languages, including Romance and Semitic languages, leaving the modifier behind (see (4c) from Italian). In contrast, head movement never separates the two parts of a root compound. Third, the attributive construction is subject to the general convention of assigning stress to phrases in a language like English. Phrasal stress is typically assigned to the last word in the phrase, as it is in the good examples in (2b), whereas compounds in English often have main stress on the first element of the compound (see Halle and Vergnaud [1987: sec. 7.9], among others). Similarly, the rules of internal sandhi such as vowel hiatus apply to A–N compounds in Kannada, but not to attributive modification structures.[4]

---

[4] Marantz (1997) argues persuasively against Lexical Morphology's strict interpretation of these facts, which was that phonological domains of a certain kind *always* correlate with syntactic word boundaries. But this does not take away from the fact that phonological domains *sometimes* correlate with word boundaries, and when they do they can provide evidence for structural distinctions. I do not infer that root compounds must be lexical from this phonological data alone, only that they are different from attributive modification.

(5)   a bellulli 'garlic', literally 'white onion' (Bhat 1994: 117–18)
        b bili ulli 'white onion, onion that is white'

Finally, in richly inflected languages like Greek, the attributive adjective bears
its own inflectional affix, distinct from that of the noun, although related to it
by the rule of concord in gender, case and number. In contrast, the first member
of a compound has (at most) a dummy inflection *–o*:

(6)   a o   kal-*os*   fil-*os*   (attributive modification)
            the good-MASC/SG friend-MASC/SG
            'the good friend'
        b kal-*o*-kardh-os   (root compounding)
            good-(NEUT?)-heart-MASC/SG
            'a good-hearted person'

   Pulling these pieces together, we see that the two constructions for which
there is good reason to say that the parts are combined syntactically are both
very restricted as to what categories of words can take part in the construction.
In contrast, the construction for which there is no independent reason to say
that syntax is involved is precisely the one for which the category of the parts
does not much matter. These correlations make perfect sense if it is the X°s
of a syntactic tree that intrinsically bear category specifications. Then category
will be crucial to all syntactic combinations, but not to those that are purely
lexical/morphological in nature. It is also noteworthy that an attributive modifier and an incorporated head are both very small pieces of syntax, typically
consisting of only a single X°. Neither can have a functional head above it:
the so/that/too tall man is a bad attributive construction in English and *meat-
the-give* is a bad noun incorporation in incorporating languages. Therefore, it
is not plausible to say that category specificity is enforced from above by a
selecting functional head in these cases. Attributive adjectives in English and
incorporated noun roots in Mohawk cannot even have complements. As such,
they are at most X°-level expressions. Therefore, even the smallest chunks of
syntax have lexical categories, although the roots of morphology need not.
I agree with the spirit of the following quotation from Bhat (1994: 112):

> We can, in fact, regard compounding and [certain] other processes of word-
> formation as involving the demotion of lexical items belonging to different
> categories to a level which is *lower* than that of categorial items; lexical items
> not only get decategorized, but also fail to get recategorized (i.e. fail to take
> on characteristics of any other category) when used in a compound.

In my view, however, it is not exactly the level of the two elements that are
combined that provides the crucial distinction in terms of category, but the nature

of the component of grammar that combines them. The roots of a compound do not get decategorized by compounding; it is just that they have not been categorized automatically by entering into a syntactic merge operation.

Another of my analyses that has direct implications for these matters is the derivational relationship between As and Vs that I proposed in section 2.9. There I observed that the arguments of an A are a proper subset of those of a V and that As are often transformed into Vs by morphological derivation or category conversion. From these facts, plus a desire to preserve the UTAH, I concluded that all verbs are derived from As by conflation. I defined conflation as incorporation that applies prior to lexical insertion. If this is correct, then no language has Vs as primitive elements of syntactic structure; all Vs are the result of a nontrivial syntactic derivation. At the same time, some languages have no free adjectives on the surface; factors conspire in such a way that all adjectives become verbs by the surface. As a result, adjectives exist only as a kind of bound root in Mohawk, Tukang Besi, Vata, and other languages. These patterns cannot be well expressed if one associates syntactic category primarily with some designated morphological unit. On the one hand, if we say that independent, fully inflected words bear category designations, then we miss the distinctively adjectival elements (bound roots) that are present in some languages. On the other hand, if we say that the syntactic elements that are the inputs to merge have category, then we miss the verbs in all languages. The middle way here is to say that it is the X^0 nodes that are the targets of lexical insertion that have category. One has an adjective when lexical insertion applies prior to or in the absence of incorporation into Pred, and one has a verb when lexical insertion applies after incorporation into Pred. This makes sense if it is X^0s that are the locus of categorial identity, not phrases or morphological units.

5.2   Categories and the architecture of the grammar

With this clarification in hand, we can go on to consider the implications of this view of categories for the overall architecture of the human language faculty. I begin with the relationships between syntax, morphology, and the lexicon, because this topic has already been set up by the preceding discussion. I then move on to the relationship of these three components to semantics.

5.2.1   *Syntax, morphology, and the lexicon*
In order to find considerations that bear on the relationship of syntax to morphology and the lexicon, we can consider more carefully what kinds of

morphological entities can be inserted into a given syntactic node in the schemas discussed in the previous section. What kinds of morphological entities can, for example, be inserted for the complex X^0 derived by incorporating an A into Pred in the syntax?

A little reflection shows that virtually any kind of morphological unit can be inserted into such a node. By hypothesis a morphologically simple verb root can be inserted into such a position; this results in stative unaccusative verbs such as *hunger* and *shine*, and perhaps also in eventive ones, like *fall* and *die*.[5] Not surprisingly, a deadjectival derived verb stem can also be inserted into this position – a stem such as *legalize, enlarge, redden, intensify*, or *open*. In this case, the morphological derivation of the stem happens to match the syntactic derivation of the node it is inserted into. This is presumably more or less a coincidence, however, the result of two independent derivations happening to reach the same point by similar paths. The alternative would be to say that in this case the adjective root *legal* is inserted into the A node, the verbal affix *–ize* is inserted into the Pred node, and the two combine by incorporation proper, rather than by conflation. I doubt that this is correct for these cases, however, because then the Pred would still count as a functional category, even after the incorporation. In that case, it would not act like an unaccusative verb that can license traces in its specifier, when in fact it does (sections 2.8 and 2.9).

The element inserted into the V node can even have an internal morphological structure that goes counter to its syntactic derivation. This is the case with denominal inchoative or causative verbs like *fossilize, crystalize, symbolize, classify, originate* and *knight*. Section 3.8 showed that these formations are not particularly productive, and they do not correspond exactly to comparable periphrastic constructions like *become a crystal* or *become a symbol*. The differences come from the fact that no referential index can be associated with the noun root in this case. The morphological structure thus cannot be derived by head movement in the syntax in these cases, because if *fossil* by itself counted as an X^0 node it would, by hypothesis, have to have a referential index. Rather, a verbal stem morphologically derived from a noun root happens to be inserted into a V node that (according to my theory) is derived syntactically from an adjectival element. Given that the morphological derivation and the syntactic

---

[5] Alternatively, inchoative unaccusative verbs might be inserted after V conflates with a non-theta-assigning v node with a meaning like BECOME. This would be geometrically the same syntactic position that transitive verb roots are inserted into. Tense and other inflections will be inserted into the T node and other similar functional categories as the verb moves into them – at least in languages with overt verb movement, such as French. I leave open just how verb inflection arises in languages without syntactic verb movement; morphological merger in the sense of Marantz (1988) and Bobaljik (1994) is a likely possibility; see also Baker (2002).

derivation can take independent paths in this way, there is no reason not to treat the deadjectival derivations in the same manner. What is inserted into the verb node can even be a stem derived from a category-less bound root (*magnify*, *colonize*) or a root compound (*pan-fry, hand-wash*). In short, almost any kind of morphological structure can be inserted into this syntactic position.

Consider now a syntactic structure in which the A element does not conflate into Pred to create a V node, but is itself a target for lexical insertion, resulting in a predicate adjective construction. What kinds of morphological objects can be inserted into this position? Certainly morphologically simple adjective roots can be, such as *red, big, good*, and *new*. So presumably can adjectival stems that are derived from verb roots, such as *shiny, restrictive, defiant*, or *forgetful*. For these relatively idiosyncratic and unproductive instances of morphology it does not seem very plausible to say that there is a complete VP node embedded under the adjectival affixes *–y, -ive, -ant*, or *–ful*, the head of which subsequently incorporates. Such a VP must by definition include a specifier, on my view, which would be stranded by the V incorporation. Yet there is no possibility of seeing this specifier overtly in any of these cases (for example: *These rules are [$_{AP}$ restrict-ive [$_{VP}$ (of) what you can wear to school t]]*). An adjectival stem that is derived from a noun can also be inserted into a syntactically simple A position. Thus, we can say that something is *foggy, childish, natural, reptilian, legendary, peaceful*, or *metallic*, even though there is little chance of deriving an A node by conflating a true noun into some functional category within my system. Adjectival X° can also be filled with stems derived from category-less bound roots (*uncanny, native, curious*), and by root compounding (*red-hot, snow-white, overripe*). Putting these cases together, I conclude that there is not always a simple relationship between the size of a morphological unit and the complexity of the syntactic node it corresponds to. A morphologically simple expression can be inserted into a syntactically complex V node, and a morphologically complex expression can be inserted into a syntactically simple A node. The units of one level do not correspond directly to the units of another level, but are partially independent of each other within the narrow domain of category-changing derivational morphology. This result is not unprecedented. It agrees with what I found in my studies of incorporation back in Baker (1988a; 1988c): a lexicalized applicative verb in Chichewa was not necessarily derived by P incorporation in the syntax, whereas a morphologically simple verb like *give* in English might contain an incorporated P in the syntax. Borer (1988; 1991) has been led to a similar conclusion by various aspects of Hebrew morphology. There are thus several testimonies to the partial independence of morphology and syntax.

Similar considerations apply to noun positions. Noun nodes cannot be related to nodes of other lexical categories by conflation, because of their association with a referential index. Thus, an N node will almost always be syntactically simple. Nevertheless, noun stems with various morphological structures can be inserted into an N node, including simple roots (*dog, house,* etc.), deverbal stems (*steerage, defendant, rebellion*), deadjectival stems (*modernist, honesty*), stems derived from a bound root (*courage, nation*), and compounds of various kinds (*doghouse, greenhouse,* etc.). It is even possible to insert a noun stem derived from a noun root into such a position: *brotherhood, orphanage, librarian, prisoner, robbery, despotism.* Here too a syntactically simple position does not necessarily correspond to a morphologically simple unit.

This partial independence of morphology and syntax probably includes even some aspects of inflectional morphology. In richly inflected languages, what is inserted into an A head is not an adjectival stem, but rather an adjectival word, inflected for gender, number, and case. This holds for both predicative and attributive positions, as shown in (7) from Spanish.

(7)   a Las camisas son roj-a-s/   *roj.
        the shirts   are red-FEM-PL/ red
      b las camisas roj-a-s/   *roj
        the shirts   red-FEM-PL/ red

The adjective phrase could conceivably be dominated by functional heads such as gender and number in these cases. I have, however, found no positive evidence in favor of such additional structure; it would only complicate my syntactic analyses to have to explain why this structure and no other must be present in these cases. (Note that degree elements, which are clearer instances of functional heads, are not possible in attributive positions (*a so tall person*).) In the absence of compelling evidence to the contrary, I prefer to say that "theme vowels" like *a* and semantically vacuous agreeing elements like *s* are absent in the syntax and are added in the PF/morphological component, in agreement with Halle and Marantz (1993: 135–36). For my purposes, this is equivalent to saying that an inflected word is inserted into the A node in these cases.

N nodes in Mohawk are also ordinarily filled not by noun stems, but by nouns that are inflected with a prefix and a suffix that have no known syntactic significance, as shown in (8a).[6]

---

[6] In Baker (1996b), I did attach syntactic significance to the nominal prefixes in Mohawk. I claimed that they were agreement prefixes, registering the syntactic subject of the noun. The noun-initial prefixes are indeed cognate with the neuter subject prefixes found on verbs. But this view is not so plausible in the context of the current theory. Nouns do not have an "R" theta-role to assign to a

(8) a Wa'-k-hnínu-'   thíkʌ ka-nákt-a'/   *nakt.
       FACT-IsS-buy-PUNC that   NsS-bed-NSF/ bed
       'I bought a bed.'
     b Wa'-ke-nakt-a-hnínu-'   thíkʌ. (*wa'-ke-ka-nakt-a'-hnínu')
       FACT-IsS-bed-Ø-buy-PUNC that   FACT-IsS-NsS-bed-NSF-buy
       'I bought that bed.'

The situation is different, however, when noun incorporation takes place, as
in (8b). In this case, an uninflected noun root must be inserted into the N
position and then move to adjoin to the verb node. This verb node also must
have been filled by an uninflected verb root, because the incorporated noun root
shows up adjacent to the verb root. Verb inflection gets added only after noun
incorporation, presumably as a result of moving the verb into higher functional
heads. In English, by contrast, there is evidence that the verb does not move
higher in the syntax (Pollock 1989). Perhaps then an inflected root is inserted
into the V node in English, just as inflected adjectives are inserted into A nodes
in Spanish and inflected nouns are inserted into N nodes in Mohawk. If all
this is correct, then a morphological constituent of any type can in principle
be inserted into a syntactic X° node, whether root, affixed stem, compound, or
inflected word.

This is not to say that all of these choices are possible in each particular
syntactic structure. On the contrary, it is ungrammatical to insert a root in
Mohawk if there is no noun incorporation, or to insert an inflected noun if there is
noun incorporation. Morphological well-formedness conditions filter out wrong
choices of lexical insertion. For example, if a bare root is inserted into the noun
position in (8a), then an improper (and phonologically ill-formed) Mohawk
word is present in the final representation. Conversely, if an inflected word is
inserted into the noun position in (8b) and then incorporated, the resulting word

subject apart from the presence of a Pred; therefore within my current assumptions no agreement
prefix corresponding to R is needed to satisfy the Polysynthesis Parameter. Indeed, some other
polysynthetic languages do not have any (overt) agreement affix on nouns. It was also something
of an embarrassment for my earlier view that the noun prefix usually does not vary with the
gender of the intended referent of the noun. For example, the bear in Lounsbury's (1953) folktale
is male, and it invariably triggers masculine agreement on verbs. Nevertheless, the noun prefix
is neuter o-, just as in the citation form of the noun, and cannot be masculine *la-/lo-*

(i)   Wa-ha-ilu-'   ne'n o-hkwali (*lo-hkwali)...
      FACT-*MsS*-say-PUNC the   NsO-bear MsO-bear
      'The bear said . . .'

This shows that "agreement" on nouns does not have the same syntactically productive status as
agreement on verbs, but is lexically fixed for most nouns. I conclude that these affixes are added
apart from the syntax purely to satisfy the morphological properties of Mohawk, the same way
that inflection is added to adjectives in Spanish.

violates the widespread ban against having inflectional morphology internal to a compound (a house for several dogs is not a *dogshouse*). In this way, surfacy morphological conditions exert a restraining influence on the freedom that is characteristic of the morphology–syntax interface, even though morphology and syntax are in a sense independent of each other. (See Baker [1988c] for earlier discussion of essentially the same notions.)

This suggests that Halle and Marantz (1994) go a bit too far in saying that the internal morphological structure of words is "syntax all the way down." I certainly agree that much of surface morphological patterning is derivable from syntactic structure via incorporation and similar processes, particularly in polysynthetic and agglutinating languages. This accounts for the widespread parallels between morphological and syntactic structure that have often been discussed in terms of the Mirror Principle (in addition to Baker [1988a; 1996b: sec. 1.6], see Cinque [1999], Julien [2000], and others). But once the syntactically predictable morphology has been stripped away, there remains a residue of morphology that seems to have nothing to do with syntax. This residue includes a rather wide range of not-very-productive and semantically idiosyncratic derivational morphology, as well as root compounding and those language-particular aspects of inflection that revolve around grammatical gender, concord, and purely formal matters of inflection such as the Indo-European theme vowels and the Mohawk noun suffixes. There is perhaps a generative morphology of quite modest power after all, distinct from syntax, that deals with the internal structure of these linguistic objects.[7] I have no reason to be dogmatic on this point; if good reasons come to light for saying that the adjective *foggy* is formed in the syntax, so much the better. For the time being, however, complicating the syntax with derivations of this kind seems likely to do more harm than good.

There are two ways to apply DM's "syntax all the way down" dictum to a word like *foggy*: either it is base-generated in the manner of Sproat's (1985) and Lieber's (1993) approach to derivational morphology ((9a)), or it is derived from

---

[7] I can see two possible ways of implementing this "nonsyntactic morphology" technically. One is a kind of limited lexicalist approach, in which the morphological objects in question are constructed before lexical insertion, independently of the syntax. The second is a kind of interpretative approach in which only roots undergo lexical insertion but these are then enriched with inflectional and derivational endings by rules in PF. The second is clearly what Halle and Marantz (1993) have in mind, but I am not sure I see a difference from the point of view of the syntax and its interface with morphology. Both views include a kind of generative morphology distinct from syntax proper; the difference is a narrow one of how exactly two derivations, each with their own internal logic are ordered with respect to each other. Elsewhere condition phenomena may decide in favor of the interpretative version for inflection, but not for root compounding or some derivation.

a structure like (9b) by incorporation. (Whether *fog* is an N in these structures or an uncategorized root is not crucial.)

(9)   a $[_A x \ fog_N \ -y_A]$
         b $[_{AP} \ fog_i\text{-}y \ [_{NP} \ t_i]]$

Neither approach is particularly attractive. Internal to my framework one would have to cook up a thematic role for *–y* to assign to the noun in construction with it, so that the NLC is satisfied. There is no obvious theta-role within the usual typology to use. On all accounts, (9a) would have the additional awkwardness that it violates word order generalizations of English, which require a head to come before its complement (see Di Sciullo and Williams [1987: 23–25] and Anderson [1992: sec. 2.1], who use this as an argument that morphology is distinct from syntax). As for (9b), it requires a complementation structure that is not otherwise well attested: As in English do not take NP complements (*proud *(of) Mary*). Nor is there any evidence from stranding arguments in favor of an incorporation analysis of these constructions, as shown in (10).

(10)   a Mary is childish.
            (She acts like a (spoiled) child.)
          b *Mary is $[_{AP} \ child_i\text{-}ish \ [_{NP} \ that \ t_i]]$
            (She acts like that child.)
          c *Mary is $[_{AP} \ child_i\text{-}ish \ [_{NP} \ t_i \ of \ Chris]]$.
            (She acts like a child of Chris's.)

Thus, pending new empirical or conceptual breakthroughs, it seems best to spare syntax the job of accounting for some of this morphology.

It would, of course, be nice to have some reliable tests for distinguishing morphological structure that is derived in the syntax from morphological structure that is not. There is no a priori guarantee that there will be any such tests that are crosslinguistically valid and easy to apply, but one can always hope. I take stranding arguments, where available, to be particularly good evidence in favor of a syntactic derivation involving head movement.

One might even be able to use category specificity itself as a probe into this issue. This tactic is suggested by the comparison between root compounding and attributive modification discussed in the previous section. Root compounding is a nonsyntactic process, and it is not particularly sensitive to the categories of the roots involved. Attributive modification is a syntactic process, and it is very sensitive to the categories of the words involved; one member of the construction must be a noun and all the others must be adjectives. This could serve as a model for addressing the syntax–morphology question in general. The inherent natures of the three lexical categories are different enough that it is rare that one can replace another in a given syntactic environment. If a noun can appear in position X, then typically an adjective or verb cannot, and vice versa. Some contexts look like they tolerate more than one lexical category, but further examination usually reveals that there is a phonetically null functional head with one category but not the other. If this is typical of syntax, then it should also hold of those aspects of morphology that are derived from the syntax. In contrast, morphological roots and stems need not be assignable to any particular lexical category, as shown by the phenomenon of bound roots like the *cran* in *cranberry* and the *nat* in *nation*, *natal*, *native*, and *innate*. Therefore, we might expect that purely morphological processes would be relatively insensitive to category, lexical category not being a crucial notion outside of the syntax. Category-sensitivity, then, would be a way of distinguishing the syntactic from the purely morphological.

This criterion gives promising results in several particular cases. For example, the Chichewa causative affix *–its* is known to be highly category-specific: it attaches only to verbs, not to nouns or adjectives, as shown in (11).

(11)   a Mwana a-ku-d-ets-a   zovala.
          child   3sS-PRES-be.dirty$_V$-CAUS-FV   clothes.
          'The child is making the clothes be dirty.' (Alsina and Mchombo 1991)
        b *Mbidzi   zi-na-kali-its-a   m-kango.
          10.zebras 10S-PAST-fierce$_A$-CAUS-FV   3-lion
          'The zebras made the lion fierce.' (Bresnan and Mchombo 1995: 242, n. 58)
        c *Mbidzi   zi-na-mfumu-(i)ts-a   m-kango.
          10.zebras 10S-PAST-chief$_N$-CAUS-FV   3-lion
          'The zebras made the lion a chief.' (Bresnan and Mchombo 1995: 242, n. 58)
        d Nungu   i-na-phik-its-a   kadzidzi maungu.
          9.porcupine 9S-PAST-cook-CAUS-FV   1a.owl   6.pumpkins
          'The porcupine made the owl cook the pumpkins.' (Alsina 1992: 518)

–Its is also the type of causative affix that is well analyzed as a trigger of verb incorporation in the syntax, à la Baker (1988a). It is productive and semantically transparent, and (more importantly) it creates complex multiple-object constructions of a kind not found with simple verbs (see (11d)). It also interacts in a complex way with clearly syntactic processes like *wh*-movement (Baker 1988a: 215–24).

This Chichewa affix can be contrasted with the causative affix -*ar* in Lezgian. Like -*its*, -*ar* attaches to verb stems, as shown in (12a), but it can also affix to noun or adjective stems (Haspelmath 1993: 163–65). (The affix –*un* in these examples is an infinitive-like ending, producing a citation form of the verb.)

(12) a *agáq'-ar-un* 'to bring, deliver'   from *agáq'-un* 'arrive, reach'
         qhit'q'ín-ar-un 'make burst, crack' from *qhit'q'ín-un* 'burst, crack'
         ksu-r-un 'put to bed'   from *ksu-n* 'fall asleep'
         q'eží-r-un 'wet, soak'   from *q'eží-n* 'become wet'
      b *ačux-ar-un* 'open'   from *ačux* 'open, clear' (Adj)
         behem-ar-un 'complete'   from *behem* 'sufficient' (Adj)
      c *ajib-ar-un* 'make ashamed'   from *ajib* 'shame' (N)

–*Ar* can also attach to a bound root, and there are examples in which it attaches to a root that is already transitive and does not change the meaning or argument structure of the verb (e.g. *at'um-ar-an* 'prop, lean' from *at'um-un* 'prop, lean'). Therefore, the category-sensitivity criterion predicts Lezgian –*ar* to be a nonsyntactic affix. This correlates with the fact that it is far from fully productive even on verb stems, and there is no special syntax associated with causative verbs that calls for an incorporation derivation. –*Ar* does not causativize transitive verbs to create multiple object constructions, for example, nor does it attach to unergative verbs like 'talk' to create a clause with two agents. It attaches primarily to unaccusative verb roots, and the result is a perfectly ordinary transitive clause, with an agent subject and a theme object. There is no sign of a syntactic difference between morphologically derived causative verbs and simple transitive verbs in Haspelmath's discussion. Thus, in the domain of causative affixes, category-specificity seems to correlate with positive evidence of syntactic derivation, as expected.

This category-specificity test can also be applied to English, with plausible looking results. Fabb (1988) presents a convenient list of forty-three not-too-uncommon derivational affixes, together with their category selection and creation properties. Of these, almost half exists in doublets, where what is arguably the same affix can attach to roots of more than one category:

(13) a -*age* Attaches to V (*steerage*) or N (*orphanage*); makes an N.
      b -*er*   Attaches to V (*killer*) or N (*prisoner*); makes an N.
      c -*ful* Attaches to N (*peaceful*) or V (*forgetful*); makes an A.
      d -*ify* Attaches to N (*classify*) or A (*intensify*); makes a V.
      e -*ism* Attaches to A (*modernism*) or N (*despotism*); makes an N.
      f -*ist* Attaches to A (*formalist*) or N (*Methodist*); makes an N.
      g -*ize* Attaches to A (*specialize*) or N (*symbolize*); makes a V.
      h -*y*   Attaches to N (*foggy*) or V (*shiny*); makes an A.
      i -*y*   Attaches to A (*honesty*), V (*assembly*), or N (*democracy*); makes an N.

The expectation, then, would be that these are purely morphological creatures. And that is probably true; no evidence has been put forward that any of these is derived by incorporation in the syntax.[8]

Working from the other direction, Fu, Roeper, and Borer (2001) present two arguments that deverbal process nominals like *arrival* and *destruction* can be created by the incorporation of a verb into a noun in the syntax. Such nominals can (marginally) be followed by a manner adverb ((14a)), and they can provide the antecedent for the predicate anaphor *do so*, which otherwise needs a VP antecedent. They conclude that there is a VP present in the syntactic structure of these examples, proposing a structure like (14c) (simplified for expository purposes).

(14)   a (?)Kim's removal of the evidence deliberately impeded the investigation.
        b Sam's destruction of his documents this morning was preceded by Bill's doing so.
        c [$_{DP}$ Kim$_i$'s [$_{NP}$ remove$_k$+al [$_{vP}$ t$_i$ t$_k$ (of) the evidence deliberately]]]

I find it significant that the various affixes associated with this kind of nominalization – *-(at)ion*, *-al*, *-ure*, *-ment*, *-ence*, and *-ing* – are all categorially restricted, attaching only to verb roots (and bound roots). None of them has a doublet that attaches to another category (*-al* has a homophone that makes As from Ns, but it is quite different). There are abstract nominalizers for adjectives too, of course, namely *–ity* and *–ness*, but these never go on verb stems. The productivity and semantic transparency of *–ity/–ness*, together with their category-specificity, makes them candidates for a syntactic derivation as well. Indeed, Fu, Roeper, and Borer's *so*-anaphora argument for incorporation in process nominals can be replicated for *–ity* and *–ness*:

(15)   a John's happiness was caused by Mary's being so.
        (contrast: *John's joy was caused by Mary's being so.)
        b (?)Chris's insanity and Pat's being so too cannot be a coincidence.
        (contrast: *Chris's disease and Pat's being so too cannot be ...)

(To get this judgment, it is crucial that the nominalized phrase have its fact-denoting reading, not its degree-denoting reading; *John's happiness* can mean either 'the fact that John is happy' or 'the extent to which John is happy', but only the first interpretation supports *so*-anaphora.) Both *–ness* and *–ation*

---

[8] One possible exception to this is the *–er* that attaches to verbs, which is very productive, has a robust meaning, and participates in synthetic compounding. See below for some discussion.

Borer (1991) argues explicitly that an incorporation account is not appropriate for verbs derived with *–ize*, based on the fact that stranded adjectival modifiers do not appear with such verbs. Thus, *#The senator popularized the income tax more than the sales tax* does not mean 'The senator made the income tax more popular than the sales tax.'

are probably triggers of syntactic incorporation, then, but they select crucially different complements, one a VP and the other an AP. This is typical of syntax, where the lexical categories are not generally intersubstitutable.

Synthetic compounds like *deer hunting* or *tree removal*, which are related to process nominalizations, might, by extension, also be accounted for in the syntax via incorporation (Roeper 1988). Unlike root compounds, these are category sensitive in that that first member of the compound must be a noun. They are also highly productive and semantically regular, and the head has a theta-role that can be coindexed with the nonhead, allowing it to be a noun in the syntax. This probably applies also to synthetic compounds built from agentive nominals, like *deer hunter*, which have similar properties. (See also below for some evidence that the *–er* that attaches to verbs is a syntactic affix, rather than a purely morphological one.)

Another English affix that has sometimes been claimed to involve a syntactic derivation is (some instances of) *–able*. This affix has the productivity and semantic regularity one would expect of a syntactic derivation. Kayne (1984a: 140–41) suggests that these have a syntactic derivation that includes an NP-trace, similar to the passive. As evidence for this, he mentions that an agentive *by*-phrase can appear with an *-able* adjective ((16a)), that preposition stranding is possible ((16b)), and that even a retained second object is conceivable ((16c)). (It is never possible for a bare NP to follow a simple adjective in English.)

(16) a This book is readable by a 10-year old.
      b The existence of stranded prepositions is not accountable for under
         Schwartz's assumptions.   (attributed to John Ross)
      c ?Prisoners are sendable linguistics books under certain conditions.
         (contrast: *Linguistics books are sendable prisoners.)

A plausible construal of these facts within a contemporary framework is to say that *–able* is generated as an adjectival head that takes a passive verb phrase as its complement. The head of this verb phrase then incorporates into A. The *by*-phrase is licensed inside VP, just as it is in ordinary passives, and the same constraints on NP movement apply:

(17)   This book$_i$ is [$_{AP}$ read$_k$-able [$_{VP}$ t$_i$ t$_k$ by a 10-year old]].

This fits nicely with the fact that *–able* is also categorially restricted, attaching to verb stems but not to nouns or adjectives.[9]

---

[9] I ignore a small handful of exceptional forms like *marriageable* and *companionable*, which do not show evidence of syntactic structure (*This girl is marriageable only by a boy with a good job*).

There might also be a semantic test for syntactic versus nonsyntactic morphology. Morphemes are traditionally said to have a constant meaning as well as a constant sound. There are, however, fairly clear cases of morphemes for which this is not the case. An example that has afflicted my beginning morphology students for years is the following, from Tzeltal.

(18)   a *bet* 'debt'   *bet-an* 'to loan'
        b *ʔip* 'strength'   *ʔip-an* 'to nourish'
        c *ʔinam* 'wife'   *ʔinam-an* 'to take a wife'
        d *ʔabat* 'servant'   *ʔabat-an* 'to serve'
        e *k'op* 'speech'   *k'op-an* 'to speak with'

There is clearly a morpheme *–an* that derives verbs from nouns, but its meaning is not so clear. A reasonable try might be to gloss it as 'give,' because to nourish someone is (sort of) to give them strength, to speak with someone is to give them speech, and to loan something to someone is to cause them to have a debt. The notion of giving here becomes rather vague and metaphorical, however. Moreover, this schema does not work at all for *ʔinaman*, which does not mean to give someone a wife, but rather to take a wife for oneself. Also *ʔabatan* does not mean to give someone a servant (parallel to *ʔipan*), or to take a servant (parallel to *ʔinaman*), but rather to give someone service, i.e. to serve them. The temptation then (which morphology students frequently indulge) is to say that X+*an* means 'some action that is plausibly related to Xs.' Such examples are not rare. A plausible conjecture is that morphemes that are like *–an* in this regard are not syntactically derived. If *bet* and *-an* were separate heads in the syntax, combined by incorporation, one would expect each to have its own meaning. The meaning of the whole derived word should be compositionally derived from the meanings of the parts in the usual way (apart, perhaps, from a limited number of idioms). If, however, *–an* is a purely morphological affix, intended to increase the stock of basic words in the language, then it makes sense that the primary consideration for the meaning of words that contain it is not "how can its meaning be calculated from its parts?" but rather "what notion, vaguely related to 'debt' do I need a word for?"

    The last conjecture that I will offer about the boundary between syntactic and nonsyntactic derivation concerns the possibility of recursion. It is the splendor of syntax to be recursive, thereby making an infinite number of expressions possible. For those aspects of morphology that are derived by syntactic incorporation, one expects this recursive nature to be shown up as well, as long as the incorporation-triggering structures can be embedded under another. This expectation is fulfilled, at least in some cases, as shown in Baker (1988a: ch. 7).

Some languages allow the causative of a causative, for example ((19a)), and Kinyarwanda allows the applicative of an applicative (Alexandre Kimenyi, personal communication). Causative and desiderative-like affixes can also be stacked on top of each other in various combinations in Quechua ((19b)) and Eskimoan languages ((19c)).

(19)   a ?Asilikali a-na-vin-its-its-a   atsikana kwa akaidi. (Chichewa)
           Soldiers   3sS-PAST-dance-CAUS-CAUS-FV girls   to   prisoners
           'The soldiers made the prisoners make the girls dance.'
       b Mikhu-naya-chi-wa-n   (Quechua)
           eat-want-CAUS-1sO-3S
           'It makes me feel like eating.'
       c Utit-ti-tau-kqu-vauk.   (Labrador Inuttut)
           return-CAUS-PASS-want-3sS/3sO
           'He wants it to be returned (made to come back).'

If I am right about the nature of nonsyntactic morphology, however, we might expect not to find this kind of recursion. To see why, consider the prospects for a word like *honestyful*. In purely algebraic terms, this should be possible: *-y* makes *honest* into a noun, and then *–ful* should be able to make it back into an adjective. Nor is there anything contradictory about its meaning, which should be something like "full of the quality of being honest." But the example is impossible. A plausible reason why comes from the previous discussion. Suppose the derivation exists primarily to create stems that can be inserted into positions with a new category, without directly specifying their meaning. Then it will be silly and superfluous to iterate such affixes. From this perspective *honestyful* should mean something like 'some property that is plausibly related to some quality that is plausibly related to being honest.' The obvious property that satisfies this description is the property of being honest itself – for which there is already a word. Therefore, there is little or no motive for these recursive derivations. By the same token, we would expect examples like *originalize* or *originalify* to be bad, in which a noun becomes a verb by way of becoming an adjective within the nonsyntactic morphology. If a nonsyntactic adjective-forming affix like *–al* has little or no meaning beyond what is naturally associated with the category adjective, there is no reason to have it unless it determines the final category. The conversion from noun to verb may as well be direct, as in *originate*.

These expectations fit well with Fabb's (1988) discovery that most derivational affixes in English attach only to roots, not to previously affixed forms.[10]

---

[10] Anderson (1992: 281) criticizes Fabb on this point, producing some counterexamples. But many of Anderson's counterexamples contain affixes that were not on Fabb's list (*truthful*, with perhaps

Roughly two-thirds of his affixes (28 of 43) have this behavior. Here is his list:

(20)   a -age (steerage, orphanage)
        b -al (betrayal)
        c –an (librarian, reptilian)
        d –ant (defendant, defiant)
        e –ance (annoyance)
        f –ate (originate)
        g –ful (peaceful, forgetful)
        h –hood (manhood)
        i –ify (classify, purify)
        j –ish (childish)
        k –ism (modernism, despotism)
        l –ist (Methodist, formalist)
        m –ive (restrictive)
        n –ize (symbolize, specialize)
        o –ly (deadly, ghostly)
        p –ment (containment)
        q –ory (advisory)
        r –y (hearty, shiny)
        s –y (assembly, robbery)

Another 6 affixes attach to only one other affix each, forming a special bundle (examples: *-ist+ic, -ion+ary, -ent+y = -ency*). This restriction was the single most important factor in determining which affix combinations are possible in English, according to Fabb's investigation. The notion that only one nonsyntactic derivational affix can attach to a root thus looks like an important one, and my view explains why this might be the case.

Finally, there are some encouraging signs of convergence between my tentative criteria for syntactic versus nonsyntactic derivation. The reader has probably noticed that the list of categorically unspecific affixes in (13) is very much like the list of nonrecursive affixes in (20); indeed, it is a subset. For every affix doublet on Fabb's list, at least one member of the doublet is constrained to attach only to a bare root, and usually both members are. (There are two exceptions to the stronger claim: *-er*, which attaches to verbs of any structure but only to bare noun roots, and *–ize* which attaches to bare noun roots and to

---

the suffix *–th*; *favoritism*, with perhaps the suffix *-ite*), affixes that do not create intermediate words (*northerly*, where there is no **norther*), or have other kinds of irregularities. Fabb's generalization may have to be qualified in some respects, but I assume there is something to it as a hint about how one type of morphology works.

adjectival stems that contain *–ive, -ic, -al*, or *–an*. I assume that there are two homophonous *–er* affixes.) These are also affixes with no robust meaning, for which no evidence of an incorporation derivation has been given. Conversely, the only affixes in Fabb's sample that can attach to stems of any morphological structure are *–er, -able*, and *–ness*, to which I add nominalizing *–ing*.[11] These affixes can create recursive cycles, such as *foolishness* (N to A to N), *purifiable* (A to V to A), *originator* (N to V to N), and *crystalizing* (N to V to N). Two other affixes that probably fit here are *–ion* and *–ity*; these can attach to a stem of any internal structure, so long as it is latinate in origin. As a result, they too can create cycles (*crystalization, originality*). These are precisely those affixes for which evidences of a syntactic derivation have been given in the literature. They are also affixes with relatively robust meanings, and affixes that can only attach to roots of one particular category (with very minor exceptions, noted above). This thus seems to be a promising set of criteria to use in exploring the question of which derivations are syntactic and which are not.

The overall picture that this points to is the following. Morphological distinctions like root, stem, compound, and word are essentially independent of the syntax. One implication of this is that the leaves of a syntactic tree do not correspond to any designated type of morphological entity. What is inserted into an X^0 slot can be a root, a derived stem, or an inflected word, depending on several factors: whether or not incorporation takes place, what kind of syntactically inert inflections the language has (e.g. theme vowels, gender affixes, some concord markers), and what roots are available in the language's basic stock. Wrong choices are filtered out by the morphology internal to PF whenever an ill-formed morphological object results (e.g. words with no inflection, words with internal inflection, unattached affixes, etc.). Conversely, morphologically complex words do not always correspond to any particular type of syntactic entity; they can correspond to a single X^0 node, to a node that has one X^0 adjoined to another, or to distinct X^0 nodes that are combined by incorporation or merger. Linguists – and children – can distinguish syntactically derived words from nonsyntactically derived words by a cluster of criteria, although these may not be adequate to determine the status of every single element unambiguously. One of these criteria is category-specificity, whether a given type of word formation is tightly restricted to one syntactic category or can apply to roots of various categories. This particular criterion is underwritten by the observation

---

[11] Fabb presumably avoided the nominalizer *-ing* because it is homophonous with the present participle suffix *–ing*. One of these *–ing*'s is presumably derivational and the other inflectional, but it is not always so clear which is which.

that lexical categories are primarily syntactic in nature, and syntactic constructions cannot be oblivious to category distinctions. In contrast, these distinctions
exist in the morphology only in a parasitic way and can be ignored until the
morphology interfaces with the syntax, in the phenomenon known as lexical
insertion.

5.2.2   Syntax and semantics

My brief discussion of the semantic value of different kinds of derivational
morphology helps to raise the more general question of the relationship of syntax
to semantics in this domain. The idea that there is a semantic basis for the lexical
category distinctions has an ancient lineage and continues to be prominent into
the present. The Ancient Greeks observed that nouns are words that "signify a
concrete or abstract entity," whereas verbs are words that "signify an activity or
process performed or undergone" (Robins 1989: 39). Schoolchildren are taught
similar definitions to this day. These notional characterizations of the lexical
categories also come up often in the professional literature, as can be seen in
Croft (1991), Bhat (1994), Anderson (1997), and others. My view, in contrast,
is syntax-centered, defining verbs in terms of having a specifier, nouns in terms
of c-commanding something with a shared index, and adjectives as having
neither a specifier nor an index. There are, however, natural correspondences
between these syntactic properties and the corresponding semantic properties,
the significance of which needs to be considered.

The notional characterizations of the lexical categories have an undeniable
appeal, especially for the obvious core cases. There are also more technical
interrelationships between syntactic and semantic notions that arise within my
approach. For example, there is a close connection between the syntactic property of bearing a referential index and the lexical–semantic property of having
a criterion of identity, and this in turn seems related to applying to a "thing"
as opposed to a property or an event. It is not surprising that physical objects
with clear and consistent perceptual boundaries that stay together over time (the
canonical things) should be easily identifiable, good for reference tracking, and
prone to being expressed as nouns. Not every noun token denotes such a thing
by a long shot – but there is a strong connection.

There is also a natural relationship between the syntactic property of having
a specifier and the lexical semantic property of being associated with a theme
theta-role, and this in turn is related to applying to an event. Events are inherently
relational in the sense that there cannot be an event without there being some
participant in the event that undergoes some kind of change. Events are thus
appropriately individuated in terms of their participants (Strawson 1959: ch. 1).

As such, events correspond naturally to the inherently relational category of verbs, which never stand on their own without a specifier and a complement. Not every verb token designates an event or assigns a theme role – the verb *seem* does neither, for example – but most verbs do both.

Finally, adjectives have neither a specifier nor a referential index in the syntax, they have neither a criterion of identity nor a theme theta-role, and in the semantics they denote properties that do not fit so comfortably into our conceptions of things or events. The overarching question is what are we to make of these correspondences, which seem nonaccidental but also nonessential? Which of these properties are primary and which are secondary? Which are causes and which are effects? What status do they have in linguistic theory?

To start with, I am happy to stick to the position that the syntactic characterizations of the lexical categories are primary, and the relationships between these and the traditional notional characterizations are natural but not axiomatic. The reasons for holding this view should by now be fairly familiar, and have been pointed out by others (although not always endorsed by them).

First, it is well known that there are crosslinguistic mismatches between meaning and category. Two words can express the same notion, in so far as one can tell, but belong to different syntactic categories. For example, the overall category systems of Chichewa, Edo, and English seem to be very much alike; the same three categories exist in all three languages, and they have similar syntactic distributions. Nevertheless, *big* is an adjective in English and the corresponding Edo word *kpòló* can only be a verb. *Intelligent* is also an adjective in English, but it corresponds to the Chichewa noun *nzeru* 'intelligence'. Noun–verb mismatches of this kind are less well known, but they exist. One case in point is cognition words, which are often verbs in English (*know*, *want*) but are nominals in Warlpiri (*pina* 'knowledge[able],' *ngampurrpa* 'desire[ous]'; see Bittner and Hale [1995: 83], Simpson [1991: 123]). A case that goes the other way comes from comparing the lexicons of English and Mohawk. English has a set of morphologically simple words that refer to garments that one wears on a particular part of the body: *shirt*, *hat*, *gloves*, *pants*, etc. Mohawk does not have basic nouns like this. Rather, Mohawk has a set of verbs with meanings like 'to cover the body,' 'to cover the hands,' 'to cover the head,' notions that can only be expressed by phrases in English. The Mohawk words for 'shirt,' 'coat,' 'hat,' and 'glove' are the nominalizations of these verbs. The basic syntactic category of a morphologically simple word thus cannot always be predicted from a language-independent characterization of what that word means.

A similar lesson can be learned by looking at clusters of related words within a single language. English, for example, has a noun *hunger*, a verb *hunger*, and

an adjective *hungry*. Each of them can be used to express essentially the same
state of affairs:

(21)   a Chris is hungry.
        b Chris hungers.
        c Chris has hunger; Chris is experiencing hunger.

(21a) is a perfectly ordinary sentence. (21b) is a bit archaic – there has been a
shift in the history of English away from using intransitive stative verbs and toward using adjectives – but it is certainly grammatical. (21c) is somewhat stilted
in English, but possible; it is also the normal way to express the proposition in
question in Spanish (*Diego tiene hambre*). Overall, there is no clear difference
in what is expressed that can be used to ground the differences in the category of
the central word. What meaning does *–y* add to *hunger* that goes along with the
conversion of the category into an adjective? A notional definition of the categories seems committed to the idea that *hungry* and *hunger* express different
notions, and *–y* adds something to create the one meaning from the other. The
syntactically oriented view is not committed to this. I do not need to assign any
determinate meaning to *–y* in (21a); it could be that *hungry* is just a positionally
defined allomorph of the basic vocabulary item *hunger*, suitable for insertion
into a syntactic slot that is adjectival. This seems like an advantage for the
syntactic theory.

   Perhaps the most fundamental concern with a notionally based characterization of the lexical categories is that it may not be well defined. At first glance, the
assertion that words denoting things are nouns seems meaningful and plausible.
But what exactly is a *thing*? When one stops to think about it, this becomes a
very troubling question. We know that medium-sized, solid objects, the parts of
which are contiguous and stay together in a constant relationship over time are
things. Such entities seem to play a special role in infant cognition, as shown
by Elizabeth Spelke and her colleagues. But there are many denotata of nouns
that are not things in this sense or any obvious extension of it. Here are some
examples:

(22)   a photon, electron, quark
        b idea, theory, hypothesis
        c lightning bolt, fire, flash
        d battle, war, truce
        e liberty, justice, beauty
        f joke, word, game
        g firm (in the business sense), country

It is clear that one is not going to get a coherent definition of "thing" that includes
all of these as special cases out of folk physics or any scientific refinement of it.

This raises the suspicion that what we really mean by *thing* is "whatever can be referred to by a noun." To the extent that this is true, it is circular to define noun as "a word that refers to a (person, place, or) thing." The same point can be made with respect to verbs and adjectives. The usual notional view of verbs is that they denote events. But it is no clearer what an event is in objective terms than what a thing is. What kind of events are existing, staying, remaining, persisting, or enduring, for example? Not the kind that can be captured on a video camera and traced out frame by frame. Nor do I have any clear sense of what a property or quality is as distinct from the other denotata that I can separate from the knowledge that they are the kinds of things that adjectives express.

One simple, language-independent way of trying to ground the event/thing/ property distinction that functionalist linguists often appeal to is in terms of time. Givón (1984: ch. 3) suggests that verbs typically express states of affairs that change rapidly, lasting only for a short period of time, whereas nouns express states of affairs that are stable, enduring for a relatively long period of time. Adjectives express states of affairs that endure an intermediate amount of time. Croft (1991), Hengeveld (1992), Bhat (1994), Wetzer (1996), and Stassen (1997) all invoke Givón's notion of time stability in one way or another in developing their theories of categories. This notion of events, things, and properties has the potential of being well defined apart from language, thereby avoiding the charge of circularity. It can also leave vague the exact cut-off point as to how long a state of affairs must last to be expressed as an adjective rather than as a verb, or as a noun rather than as an adjective. This provides a possible account of why some particular notions are expressed by an adjective in one language but not in another. The problem is that it does not fit the facts very well. For example, when someone from the Judeo-Christian tradition uses the verb *exist* to assert that God exists from eternity past to eternity future, what she asserts is as long-lasting a state of affairs as one can imagine. In contrast, the state of affairs denoted by the noun *lightning bolt* never lasts longer than an instant. In the domain of adjectives, we can say of someone's death that it was instantaneous, or we can say of the human soul that it is eternal. These cases may not be "prototypical," but neither are they particularly exceptional. The same notions are often denoted by the same categories in other languages, and closely related notions are often systematically expressed with the same category. Thus, the simple time-based characterization of event versus thing versus property will not go very far. Nor is it clear what more enriched but still language-independent characterization can be put in its place. Therefore, it is not clear that a notional view of the category distinctions as being rooted in lexical semantics can be spelled out in a noncircular way. I am inclined to agree with the medieval grammarians (Robins 1989: 88–90), with Sapir (1921: 117–19), and with Langacker (1987): the lexical category distinctions correspond not so much to ontological distinctions in the kinds of things that are out there in the world, but rather to the different perspectives we can take on those things, the different ways our linguistic capacities give us of describing them. This points away from a notional approach to the categories, and toward a syntactic one.

A more technical version of this issue concerns how the lexical semantics of a particular vocabulary item constrains the process of lexical insertion into a syntactic tree. The traditional generative view is that vocabulary items are tagged with labels as being of one or the other lexical category, just as they are in ordinary dictionaries. The label on the inserted item must then match the character of the syntactic node it is being inserted into. The alternative to this would be to say that lexical entries do not have explicit tags. Lexical insertion would then be free, but whenever an incoherent or crazy interpretation results the sentence is deemed ungrammatical (or unacceptable, or unusable). As far as the syntax and morphology proper are concerned, then, one might just as well generate *The bark will dog* as *The dog will bark*; it just so happens that the second version means something reasonable and the first does not. This second view would be a technical way of spelling out the idea that the lexical category distinctions are primarily semantic in nature, contrary to what I have been assuming.

For some cases, this version of a semantic-centered approach might work out quite well. Indeed, I have used this form of reasoning from time to time to rule structures out, particularly in the case of nouns. For example, I argued in chapter 3 that the X in a frame like "A X will bark" must correspond to something that has a criterion of identity, because the construction is supposed to mean $\exists \ x, y \ [\ |x| = 1 \ \& \ bark(y) \ \& \ same(X)(x,y)]$. This formula is only coherent if same(X) is well defined, which is true if and only if X is a common noun. Similar considerations might derive the fact that Y in a frame like "The dog will Y" must be a verb. The expression *the dog* is nominal, so it has a referential index that must be linked to something else in the clause. Perhaps the only possibility would be a theta-role associated with Y, which might imply that Y is a verb. There would be nontrivial details to work out here, because nouns and adjectives can have theta-roles too. How feasible this is depends on just how one works into the theory the idea that agent and theme roles in particular can only be assigned to subject positions (see chapter 2). But at least we can say that the semantically oriented view has potential here.[12]

---

[12] While it is relatively easy to see how a particular semantic character is required for one given word once all the other words in its syntactic environment have been fixed, this is not enough to

The idea that semantics filters out the errors of a very free syntax is less plausible in other cases, however. It is not so hard to see how the positive semantic properties associated with a noun or a verb might be required in order to create a valid interpretation for some syntactic arrangements. The harder task is to see why the positive semantic properties associated with a noun or a verb get in the way of creating a valid interpretation for a configuration that in fact requires an adjective. One such configuration is the attributive modification construction, where we find the following range of facts, discussed in chapter 4.

(23) a *A fog day is no fun.   (OK only if *fog day* is a novel compound, like *snow day*.)
      b A foggy day is no fun.
      c *A shine coin is more valuable.
      d A shiny coin is more valuable.

The criterion of identity for *fog* is not needed in (23a), but why does it do any harm to the interpretation? Why cannot the relevant aspect of its lexical semantics simply be ignored when it is not needed to construct a good meaning? Similarly, there is no need for the theme theta-role of *shine* in (23c), but why cannot it just be automatically suppressed? If lexical insertion is left totally free, subject only to the condition that some coherent interpretation be constructable, these examples should be possible with essentially the same meaning as their counterparts in (23b,d). One would have to add some additional constraint that said that all of the important lexical semantic features of a given word need to be used in the course of constructing an interpretation. But this seems like a strange, difficult, and potentially dangerous condition to impose. The approach in which the category differences are primarily a matter of syntax seems more plausible, particularly given my view of adjectives.

Also if language users are so free to adjust words to their contexts in the semantics, it seems odd that natural languages would contain derivational morphemes like –*y*, the primary function of which seem to be to mark a change of category rather than to add an element of meaning. These considerations point again to a syntax-centered approach to lexical categories, rather than a semantic one. I assume, then, that some vocabulary items are explicitly tagged

---

prove that lexical insertion can be left to operate freely. There may be problems that come from the possibility of making several "wrong" choices of lexical insertion simultaneously, where the mistakes cancel out in such a way that a crazy structure would wrongly be allowed. For example, it might be harder to rule out a structure like *The bark will dog*, with two degrees of craziness, than to rule out *The bark will run* or *The pet will dog*. The verb *bark* cannot receive a theta-role, for example, but neither does the noun *dog* assign one. It would take a great deal of care to show that no such crazy sentences slipped through in a semantically based theory. Since I do not adopt such a view anyway, I will not explore this issue fully.

as being insertable into particular kinds of positions – *fog* into one that has a referential index, *shine* into one that has a specifier, *foggy* and *shiny* into one that has neither. The primary role of nonsyntactic derivational morphemes like –*y* is precisely to change the tag on a particular item.

All this being said, there is still a very basic syntax–semantics correlation to account for. The categorization of morphologically simple words in a particular language, while not fully determined by notional considerations, is certainly not random either. The words meaning 'rock,' 'dog,' 'child,' and 'tree' are nouns in every language, and the words meaning 'buy,' 'hit,' 'walk,' and 'fall' are almost always verbs. Dixon (1982) showed long ago that even in languages with very few adjectives 'good' and 'bad,' 'big' and 'little,' 'old' and 'new,' 'black' and 'white' are adjectives. The fact that each category has a stable core of members is part of what has inspired functionalist linguists and others to take a semantic/notional line. The problematic examples that I listed above for notional approaches usually do not bother the functionalists much, because they take properties like "referring to an event" or "referring to a thing" not as *definitions* of the categories verb and noun, but as characterizations of the prototypical verb or the prototypical noun. Languages can also have nonprototypical verbs and nouns; these are expected to share some of the lexical semantic properties of the prototypes but not others. And there seems to be something right about this.

Newmeyer (1998: ch. 4) discusses the functionalist claim that lexical catego-ries have a semantic/pragmatic prototype structure in some detail, and I would like to take up his basic point into my own theory. Newmeyer argues that there is no evidence that any notion of prototype plays a direct role in explaining gram-matical phenomena. There is thus no reason to say that prototypes for the lexical categories are represented as such in the minds of mature speaker–hearers of a language. My results agree with Newmeyer's in this respect; throughout we have seen that the lexical category of a word has sharp and discrete implications for its grammatical behavior, and these implications are generally the same for nonprototypical members of the category as they are for prototypical ones. *Exist* has the same morphosyntactic properties as *fall*, for example, and *theory* has the same properties as *rock*. Where the prototypical notional characterizations may play a role, Newmeyer suggests (1998: 179–80), is in language acquisi-tion. Grimshaw (1981) makes the influential proposal that language acquisition is guided by a notion of *canonical structural realization* (CSR), that for each lexical category there are certain core semantic notions that match it (see also Macnamara [1982]; Pinker [1984]). Some plausible canonical structural real-izations relevant to the lexical categories are:

(24)   a solid physical object → noun
        b dynamic physical event → verb
        c value, color, age, or physical dimension → adjective

These mappings crucially go from concepts to lexical categories, not the other way around. They are held to be part of the language acquisition device in a narrow sense; they provide a way for children to break into the system of grammar, but they have no status in the final grammar. In Macnamara's (1982: 134) metaphor, "The child climbs to grammar on a semantic ladder and then kicks the ladder away." The crucial advantage of this perspective is that the categories on the left side of the CSRs in (24) need not partition the space of things in the world. There need not be any CSR at all for an electron or a lightning bolt, for a joke or existence or jealousy. It will be enough for language acquisition to proceed if there are a few clear cases of physical objects within the child's perceptual and linguistic experience that correspond to nouns, a few actions that correspond to verbs, and a few properties that correspond to adjectives. Children will then use this "semantic bootstrapping" as a way of identifying their first nouns, verbs, and adjectives. Once they have a grasp of the linguistic properties of these elements, they can use these properties to learn other words, which may not fall directly in the domain of any CSR. This gives essentially the same end result as the functionalist notion of prototype, in which the core members of each lexical category are consistent across languages but there is variation at the periphery, without including prototypes explicitly in linguistic knowledge. That statistical, imperfect, notional characterizations of the lexical categories should play a role in language acquisition (as opposed to grammar) should come as no great surprise, since language acquisition is a messy, statistically driven, heuristic process even for the generative linguist. It is an issue of linguistic performance *par excellence*, not an issue of linguistic competence.

This way of looking at things makes the substantive prediction that the earliest words children learn should be among the words whose category membership is most consistent across languages. This question has not been investigated explicitly to my knowledge, but seems likely to be true. Ingram (1989) and Clark (1993) provide examples and analyses of the first 50–100 words to emerge in child language, when there is little or no evidence that the child is actively using syntactic knowledge. First, it is striking that there seems to be virtually no difference in the kinds of words that appear first in the productions of children learning different first languages (Clark 1993). Roughly 65 percent of these are words for concrete objects; these include proper names for people and pets, terms for animals (*dog, kitty, bird*), foods (*milk, cookie*), body parts (*eye, nose*), and various kinds of household artifacts (*sock, car, ball, cup, doll,* etc.) Another 20 percent of the vocabulary are words for dynamic actions – words like *do, make, get, go, put, give, eat, look, kiss, see,* and *sit.*[13] Finally, about 6 percent of the vocabulary concerns properties, including dimension words like *big* and physical properties like *hot, dirty, cold,* and *wet,* plus a few others such as (of course) *mine!* (The last 9 percent of the vocabulary are "social words" (interjections?) like *hi, bye-bye,* and *peekaboo.*) These are indeed the kinds of words for which there is relatively little crosslinguistic variation in category: 'dog,' 'nose,' 'milk,' and 'cup' are nouns in every language I know; 'give,' 'make,' and 'eat' are consistently verbs; and 'big' is an adjective if anything is (Dixon 1982). I also find it significant that property words/adjectives are the smallest class of words found in the earliest child language, and they are the class that varies the most in size crosslinguistically. All this, then, is perfectly compatible with maintaining syntax-oriented definitions of the lexical categories. The notional characterizations, to the extent that they are valid, are very partial and play a role in language acquisition but not in the steady state of mature grammatical knowledge.

5.3   Why are the lexical categories universal?

These remarks about language acquisition and how it applies to lexical categories might finally help to explain our remaining mystery of why all languages have at least a few nouns, verbs, and adjectives, even though there is no logical necessity that this be so. There have been long-standing controversies about whether language acquisition guides conceptual development, or whether it is the other way around. Empiricist philosophers like Quine and linguistic relativists like Whorf and Sapir thought language guided conceptual development, that children learned (say) the somewhat opaque distinctions "individuated object" versus "substance" versus "property" by attending to the grammatical distinctions among count nouns, mass nouns, and adjectives. Before the

---

[13] There is another intriguing aspect of early verb use, mentioned by Clark (1993), which my theory of categories might shed light on. Clark points out that children use a very small number of verbs – particularly *do* and *make* – over and over again to express all kinds of events. Virtually any action can be expressed by the child as "X do it." The use of a small number of verbs with very general meaning plus an object is reminiscent of the phenomenon of light verbs in adult language such as *do a dance* (for *dance*) or *take a bath* (for *bathe*). It is tempting to see this as support for my claim that verbs are the result of conflating an adjectival element with a very small number of functional operators like Pred/BE, v/CAUSE, Aspect/BECOME, and the like. Perhaps children begin by simply lexicalizing this closed class of verbal operators and then go on gradually to learn a fuller class of verbs as they acquire conflation.

significance of the different quantifiers in English or the use of the word *same* dawns on them, they have no difference in their concepts of water, red, and Mama. Thus, Quine (1960: 92) writes:

> His first learning of the three words is uniformly a matter of learning how much of what goes on about him counts as the mother, or as red, or as water. It is not for the child to say in the first case 'Hello, Mama again,' in the second case 'Hello, another red thing,' and in the third case, 'Hello, more water.' They are all on a par: 'Hello, more Mama, more red, more water.'

(See Carey [1994] for a helpful review of Quine's position.) On this view, one would expect there to be languages that never get around to distinguishing 'red' from 'water' or 'Mama,' perhaps because their quantifier system is less articulated than that of English. The result would be a different kind of category system, one with no noun–adjective distinction, as well as a different kind of mental life.

Rationalist theorists, in contrast, think of the conceptual categories of physical object, dynamic event, and physical property as being innate within the human mind. As such, they could be available to play a role in guiding language acquisition from the beginning. Although the discussions continue and there are still interesting cases to consider, research on infant cognition over the last two decades gives striking support for this rationalist perspective. Infant attention experiments by Elizabeth Spelke, Susan Carey, and others, for example, have shown that 9–12-month-old children distinguish canonical countable objects from substances from properties and show different reasoning patterns appropriate to these different conceptual categories. These differential responses also seem to be universal, which is not surprising given that young children presumably have exposure to physical objects, substances, properties, and events the world over (although not necessarily the same ones). Carey and Xu (1999: 324–25) write:

> This series of studies provides preliminary evidence that 12-month-old infants represent the distinction between kinds and properties, and that their successes in the above series of studies are indeed based on their early sortals for kinds of objects . . . We tentatively conclude, then, that Quine's speculations have been shown to be false. At the very outset of language acquisition, children represent the distinction between properties and sortals, well before they have even begun to master the syntactic reflection of these distinctions in any natural language.

(For Carey and Xu, a sortal is precisely a concept that has a Geachian criterion of identity.)

Suppose, then, that the conceptual apparatus to distinguish properties from individuated physical objects from actions is already present in children's minds at the point that lexical and syntactic acquisition is beginning. Then knowledge about the left-hand side of the Canonical Structural Realizations in (24) is in place early enough for them to guide the very first steps of this acquisition. On the first step of language acquisition, children cannot by hypothesis know anything about the language that can override their tendency to assume that objects are designated by nouns, actions by verbs, and properties by adjectives. They then jump to the conclusion that there are a few nouns, verbs, and adjectives in the language they are learning. Moreover, if grammatical learning is largely monotonic, they will never revise this hypothesis. Once they start to realize that nouns in their language are introduced by certain fixed gender prefixes, as they are in Chichewa, this will cause them to realize that all the new words for "properties" they are learning are nouns, not adjectives, contrary to what they might otherwise have guessed. But the first six words that they learned in this semantic domain are stuck as being adjectives because there was no grammatical knowledge to tell them otherwise. In this way, we can understand the fact that languages vary significantly in which particular notions are expressed by which lexical category, even though each language seems to have at least a few core elements in each lexical category. This follows from the fact that innate conceptual knowledge happens to precede and prepare for grammatical knowledge, rather than the other way around.

A mathematical analogy might help to bring this point home. The axioms of Euclidean geometry are of two kinds: there are existence axioms ("there are at least three points") and behavioral axioms ("two lines meet in a point"). Universal Grammar surely contains behavioral axioms, such as "a noun must be coindexed with a node that it c-commands," and perhaps parameters relevant to them. Universal Grammar need not, however, include existence axioms like "there are at least three nouns." Rather, the existence statements can be derived as consequences of the nature of prelinguistic cognition and its – possibly quite small – role in jumpstarting language acquisition. If Universal Grammar does not explicitly say anything about the existence of the lexical categories, it *a fortiori* cannot state parameters that determine variation in the existence of these categories. It thus follows that languages can differ somewhat as to which words belong to which categories, but there can be no overall parameterization of languages in terms of which lexical categories they have. This is just what we observe.

The lexical categories are probably different from functional categories in this respect. The functional categories do not seem to be universal; English has members of the categories determiner and degree, for example, whereas Japanese and Mohawk do not. But determiner and degree are categories that are not the Canonical Structural Realizations of any clear-cut conceptual category. Nor are determiners and degrees among the first words a child learns, prior to acquiring any knowledge of the overall grammar of the language being learned. The cognitive/acquisition-based reasons for saying that nouns, verbs, and adjectives are universal thus do not apply to functional categories such as determiners. And this is a good thing, given that these categories do not seem to be universal.

5.4   Final remarks

Like many things passed down from the ancient world, the parts of speech have become the locus of many myths and traditions. There is a myth that there is no simple definition of the lexical categories, but they are fuzzy prototype notions that shade into one another in a continuous fashion. There is a myth that there is no simple definition of the lexical categories, but they are complexes of distinctive features that cross-classify words in interesting and substantive ways. There are myths that lexical categories can be characterized notionally, and myths that they can be characterized morphologically. There are myths that they cannot be characterized in any crosslinguistically valid way at all. There are myths that some languages have lexical categories not found in any Indo-European languages, and counterbalancing myths that some languages do without part of speech distinctions that seem foundational in the Indo-European languages. There are myths that languages can make the same lexical category distinctions but deploy those lexical categories differently in the grammar. And perhaps most serious of all, there is a generative tradition of more or less ignoring the lexical categories, taking it for granted that the topic is too easy, or too hard, or not that important. It is never easy in such a situation to sort out the literally true from the myths that have some basis in fact from the completely false.

In my own investigations into these matters, as reported in this book, I have been led to a distinctive package of ideas. Some of these I dimly expected to be true, some I sort of hoped might be, and many of them were great surprises to me – even disappointments at first. The key elements of this package are as follows. First, crisp and simple definitions of the lexical categories do exist. Second, categories are defined by (at most) one feature each, not by complexes of features, and their various grammatical behaviors can be deduced from their one essential feature in an explanatory way. Third, the definitions of the categories are primarily syntactic in nature, although they project into the morphology and semantics in various ways because of the interconnections between these components. Fourth, all natural human languages have the same three lexical categories, and these have recognizably the same core grammatical behavior. Languages differ to some extent in how many members each category has, and in some details about how they are packaged, depending on which conflations of elements happen to be favored or disfavored. But these differences seem remarkably minor compared to the shared common core. Thus, if I am on the right track, this has been a bad day for radical linguistic relativity and the search for exotic parameters and a very good day for Universal Grammar.

Appendix
Adpositions as functional
categories

Throughout this book, I have assumed that adpositions (prepositions and post-positions) are not lexical categories, but rather functional categories. As such, they have more in common with determiners, pronouns, Pred, and complementizers than they do with nouns, verbs, and adjectives. It is therefore a good thing that my theory of lexical categories has no natural place for them. While this view of adpositions is far from unprecedented, it runs contrary to the more standard generative treatment, championed by Jackendoff (1977: 31–33), in which adpositions constitute a fourth lexical category, filling out the logical space of possibilities defined by the two binary-valued features $+/-$N and $+/-$V. In this appendix, I briefly outline some arguments in favor of classifying adpositions with the functional categories, focusing on evidence from incorporation patterns. I also claim that adpositions create a projection that has neither a referential index nor a theta-role. As a result, PPs do not make good arguments or good predicates, but make excellent modifiers. P can thus be thought of as an adjective-like functional category, much as determiner/pronoun is a noun-like functional category and Pred is a verb-like functional category. The properties I have discussed throughout this book as defining the lexical categories can thus be seen also to provide a partial typology of the functional categories.

A.1   Evidence that adpositions are functional

There has always been some uneasiness about including adpositions as a lexical category. The popularity of treating them as such has perhaps been caused more by the theoretical attraction of having all combinations of the features $+/-$N and $+/-$V be attested than by compelling empirical considerations. Within my more substantive theory of what it means to be $+$N or $-$N and $+$V or $-$V much of this attraction disappears. The two features do not define four categories in my system, because of the Reference Predication Constraint, the axiom of the system that says that no syntactic node can be both +N (have a referential index) and +V (have a specifier). This frees us – and forces us – to attend to the evidence that P is really a functional category.

There are historical precedents to this claim. Chomsky (1970), for example, did not include P in the original X-bar system; it was only added later by Jackendoff. Croft (1991: 144–46) also denies that P is a major lexical category from a functionalist perspective. Grimshaw (1991) takes P to be a functional head in the extended projection of nouns, playing a role in nominal projections similar to that played by complementizers in verbal extended projections. Emonds (1985: ch. 7) also argues that prepositions and complementizers are the same category, which is presumably functional. Adpositions are by all accounts closely related to case markers, and hence to the functional category K proposed by Lamontagne and Travis (1987) and Bittner and Hale (1996). Since K and C are clear instances of functional categories, the close affinities that P has to K and C suggest that P is functional too.

There is also the obvious fact that P is a closed class: languages do not have many adpositions and are reluctant to acquire more. English is rumored to have on the order of fifty prepositions, as compared to its thousands of verbs, nouns, and adjectives. Moreover, the fifty-odd prepositions of English and related languages like Dutch may be close to a world record. Many other languages have significantly fewer clear instances of adpositions, sometimes around ten, and often less than five. Mohawk, for example, has no more than four simple adpositions (*-(a)ke* 'at,' *-oku* 'under,' *-(a)ku* 'in', and *-akta* 'near'), which show up as locative suffixes on nouns as a result of incorporation (Baker 1996b: ch. 9). Chichewa has either two prepositions (*ndi* 'with,' *ku/kwa* 'at, to') or five, depending on whether one counts the three locative gender prefixes as prepositions or not (Sam Mchombo, personal communication; cf. Bresnan [1991]). Edo has three clear cases of prepositions (*yè* 'in(to),' *nè* 'to, for,' *vbè* 'at, general location'), plus perhaps a few others that have recently evolved from serial verbs (e.g. *la* 'into' from the verb 'enter'; *gbe* 'against' from the verb 'hit'). Some languages indeed have only one preposition, such as Wari (Everett and Kern 1997: sec. 2.1.5). In many languages, then, adpositions are just as much of a closed class as uncontroversially functional elements like tenses, complementizers, or determiners.[1]

---

[1] Languages with few Ps often create complex locative expressions by using a location-denoting relational noun as the complement of a P with a very general meaning. (i) is a typical example of such a construction in Edo.

More striking even than the raw numbers is the fact that adpositions do not take part in derivational morphology, as either inputs to or outputs of word formation rules. English illustrates this clearly. It has a rather complete system of derivation, with any lexical category being derivable from any other (although with differences in productivity and semantic transparency). But there are no derivational processes that involve Ps. This is summarized in (1).

(1)   Derivational processes in English:

Source/result	Noun	Verb	Adjective	Preposition
Noun	-hood, -ship	-ize, en-, de-	-ish, -ful, -ly	–
Verb	-ing, -ment, -er	re-, un-, out-	-able, -ive, -ed	–
Adjective	-ness, -ity	-ize, -en, -ify	un-, in-, -ish	–
Preposition	–	–	–	–

This also holds for other languages. Adpositions stand out as being different from the lexical categories in this respect. They are, however, like functional categories: there are also no morphemes for deriving nouns from tenses, determiners, or degrees, or for deriving any of these from verbs.

Perhaps the richest and most compelling evidence that adpositions count as functional categories comes from the study of incorporation patterns across languages. The lexical–functional distinction is known to play an important role in the theory of head movement. In particular, the generalization in (2) holds true over a wide range of constructions and in a wide range of languages (compare (Li [1990]).[2]

(i)   Èsósà vió   èbé yè úwé   ékpétìn.
        Esosa put(pl) book to inside box
        'Esosa put the books in the box (lit. to the inside of the box).'

This happens even to some extent in English (e.g. *I put the letter on top of the book*). This suggests that English might have a relatively large number of prepositions on the surface because it permits relational nouns to conflate into an abstract P head prior to lexical insertion. This proposal would capture nicely the fact that preposition seems to be a hybrid category in English, neither clearly functional nor clearly lexical. It might also explain the fact that phrases headed by a semantically rich P can sometimes be used as NPs, as in (ii) (Neeleman 1997). These expressions would arise when the relational N component of *under* fails to conflate with P.

(ii)   a Under the elm is a nice place for a picnic.
        b I prefer under the maple.

[2] This statement is a bit different from the PHMG I stated in chapter 2. There I followed Li's (1990) discussion rather closely in saying that it is bad to move from a lexical category to a functional category and then back to a lexical category. But in fact it is evidently the second step of such a derivation that is ruled out, not the first step, as the evidence reviewed below shows. The version in (2) is thus both more accurate and more general.

(2)   The Proper Head Movement Generalization (PHMG)
           It is impossible to move from a functional category into a lexical category.

For example, nouns can incorporate into verbs in a variety of languages, but always as bare roots; they never carry morphemes that mark definiteness, number, or case – morphemes that they might have picked up by moving through functional categories on their way to the verb. Similarly, verbs can incorporate into other verbs, but in almost all instances they do so without bringing along any tense marking, agreement, or complementizing morphology. I already used this principle in the body of this book to detect whether a null determiner or Pred dominates adjectives used as nouns or verbs (see sections 2.6 and 3.6). Determiners also do not incorporate into transitive verbs when no noun has incorporated into the determiner, nor do complementizers incorporate overtly into a matrix verb, with or without the lower verb. Exactly why this type of movement is forbidden is not fully understood, but it is empirically well established.[3] For current purposes we can take it to be a primitive of the theory and use it to test whether Ps count as functional heads or lexical heads.

First imagine that a P is the intermediate head in a series of three heads, where the highest and lowest heads are clearly lexical. If the P is also a lexical category, then movement of the lowest head through P and into the highest head should in principle be possible. In contrast, if P is really a functional category, then this sequence of head movements will be ruled out universally by the PHMG. Candidate structures that instantiate this possibility are common, arising whenever a PP contains an NP complement and is generated in VP. Nevertheless, incorporation seems to be consistently impossible under these circumstances. Nouns in Mohawk, for example, do incorporate into P, thereby forming a single complex word with the various locative morphemes, as shown in (3) (Baker 1988a; 1996b).

(3)   Ka-nakt-óku   y-a-há-yʌ-'.
           NsS-bed-under TRANS-FACT-MsS-put.down-PUNC
           'He put it down under the bed.'

---

[3] An idea that I consider promising is that the PHMG might follow from a theory in which functional structure and lexical structure begin as two different levels of representation that get fused together relatively late in the derivation (see Lebeaux [1988]; his theory has its roots in the psycholinguistic theories of Merrill Garrett). Lexical-to-lexical movement would take place at the level where only lexical heads are present, and functional-to-functional movement would take place at the level where only functional heads are present. Mixed cases of movement would be ones that take place as a part of the procedure that unifies the two structures. Patterns of speech errors show that this unification procedure is asymmetric: the lexical items get inserted into the syntactic frames defined by the functional items, not vice versa. From this asymmetry it should follow that lexical items can have the appearance of moving to functional heads, but not the other way around. (I thank David Lebeaux for discussion of these issues.)

Nouns also frequently incorporate into verbs in Mohawk. But the combination of a noun plus a locative element never incorporates into a verb, as shown in (4).

(4)   *Wa-ha-nakt-oku-(tsher-a)-yʌ-'.   (Baker 1996b: 430)
       FACT-3sS-bed-under-(NOML-Ø)-lay-PUNC
       'He laid it down under the bed.'

There is nothing obviously wrong with the phonotactics or the superficial morphological structure of (4) that can explain its ungrammaticality. In Baker (1996b: 430), I claimed that examples like these were ruled out by a kind of morphological filter, which stipulated that P–V compounding happens not to be allowed in Mohawk, just as V–V compounding is not normally allowed in English, although it is in many other languages (Selkirk 1982). A simpler and more general explanation comes by saying that P is a functional category. It then blocks incorporation of the noun into the verb, just as uncontroversially functional heads like determiner do. More generally, instances of locative or obliquely marked nouns incorporating into verbs are conspicuously absent from the literature on noun incorporation.

   The one case I know of in which a noun-plus-adposition seems to incorporate into a verb is sentences like (5) from Greenlandic, but this turns out to be the exception that proves the rule.

(5)   Palasi-p   illu-a-nu-kar-poq.   (Sadock 1980: 315)
       Priest-ERG house-3sP-to-go-3sS
       'He went to the priest's house.'

In Baker (1988a: 485–86 n. 25), I used this example to illustrate my prediction of the time that this type of incorporation should be possible. This kind of incorporation differs, however, from more normal noun incorporation in Greenlandic in two important ways. First, the incorporated noun in (5) bears not only the adpositional affix *–nu* 'to,' but also the inflectional possessive agreement marker *–a-*, which should originate in D or some similar functional head. This possessive agreement never appears on other incorporated nouns in Greenlandic, as expected given the PHMG. Second, when the complement of an oblique-incorporating verb like *–kar* is modified, it is the modifier that is morphologically united with the verb, not the head:

(6)   Illu-mut angisuu-mut-kar-poq.   (Sadock 1985: 423)
       house-to big-to-go-3sS/INDIC
       'He went to the big house.'

This is an apparent violation of the Head Movement Constraint, and contrasts with other cases of noun incorporation in Greenlandic, in which the head incorporates into the verb stranding the modifier, as expected. Taken together, these facts suggest that verbs like –*kar* do not trigger incorporation in the sense of syntactic head movement at all. Rather, they are more like clitics – morphophonologically bound elements that attach to the immediately preceding word in the PF component. On this view, the PHMG is not relevant to (5) at all. The Greenlandic facts are thus perfectly consistent with and partially explained by the claim that P is a functional head.

One can also consider structures in which P is the highest in a series of three heads, where the lowest head is lexical and the middle head is known to be functional. Here the predictions of the two hypotheses are reversed. If P counts as a lexical head, the incorporation of all three heads should be ruled out by the PHMG. If P is functional, however, the incorporation is expected to be possible, just as it is possible for a verb to move through a functional category like tense on its way to C in German and many other languages. Once again, candidate structures are easy to find: they arise whenever the nominal complement of P includes some functional superstructure. We can check whether nouns inflected for notions like number and definiteness form a morphological unit with an adpositional element. In fact, such cases are abundantly attested. For example, in Mohawk the agreement prefix that represents the possessor of the noun is preserved when one incorporates into a P:

(7)   a rao-'neróhkw-a-ku
          MsP-box-Ø-in
          'in his box'
       b *rao-'nerohkw-Λ''-Λ.
          MsP-box-fall-STAT
          'His box has fallen.'

In contrast, the possessive prefix is never maintained when a noun incorporates into a verb, as shown in (7b). In a similar way, (8) shows that prepositional prefixes in Chichewa can attach outside of the prefixes that express number and gender, which arguably reside in a number head.

(8)   pa-[mu-dzi]   (Bresnan and Mchombo 1995).
       in-[3.NCL-village]
       'in the village'

Number suffixes also appear on nouns that are incorporated into adpositions in Southern Tiwa ((9a)), even though these suffixes cannot appear on nouns that are incorporated into verbs ((9b)).

(9)   a seuan-*ide*-'ay.   (Allen, Gardiner, and Frantz 1984)
          man-S G -to
          'to the man'
        b Ti-seuan-(*ide*)-mū-ban
          1sS/A-man-S G -see-P A S T
          'I saw the man.'

The Greenlandic example in (5) is another case in point. This type of data confirms that adpositions are functional categories, in marked contrast to verbs.

If P is a functional head, one would expect functional categories like D to target it, even if there were no N projection inside DP. This also seems to be the case. Pronouns are often analyzed as Ds that do not take an NP complement, and they often incorporate into the P that governs them; (10) gives examples from Abaza (Caucasian) and Slave (Athapaskan).

(10)   a wə-qa-z   (Abaza [O'Herin 1995: 277])
          2sE-head-for
          'for you'
        b se-gha   (Slave [Rice 1989: 299])
          1sO-for
          'for me'

In contrast, the incorporation of true pronouns into verbs is often said to be impossible in the noun incorporation literature (see, for example, Allen, Gardiner, and Frantz [1984]). Some languages do, of course, have clitic pronouns that are homophonous with determiners and that seem to attach to verbs; the Romance languages are a prominent example. But in these languages there is evidence that the cliticization (if it is a case of head movement at all) targets not the lexical verb, but rather T or some other functional head in the clause (Kayne 1989; Kayne 1991). We thus have D-to-T incorporation, rather than D-to-V incorporation, which would be forbidden:

(11)   a Jean les+a   mangé.   (French)
          Jean them-has eaten
        b *Jean a   les+mangé.
          Jean   has them-eaten

We can also consider the possibility of incorporating Ps all by themselves. Does P incorporation target the lexical category V or a functional category such as T or aspect? In Baker (1988a: ch. 5), I claimed that P-to-V incorporation was reasonably common, using this as the analysis of the applicative constructions found in Bantu languages and many others. A canonical example is (12) from Chichewa.

(12)   Ndi-na-phik-ir-a   ana   nsima.
        1sS-PAST-cook-APPL-FV children corn.mush
        'I cooked nsima for the children.'

Subsequent research has, however, shown that this is not correct. The incorporation in (12) does seem to involve lexical categories because the applied affix appears next to the verb root and no functional/inflectional morphemes can appear between them. But there is little evidence that the applied affix is actually an adposition (see, for example, Sadock's [1990] criticism of Baker [1988a] on this point). Another plausible source for these benefactive applicative constructions is a structure in which a triadic verb similar to 'give' takes a VP as its complement, as in (13) from Japanese.

(13)   John-ga   Mary-ni   hon-o   kat-te   age-ta.
        John-NOM Mary-DAT book-ACC buy-AFF give-PAST
        'John gave Mary the favor of buying a book.'

Examples like (12) can be derived from underlying structures like that of (13) by ordinary verb-to-verb incorporation. In Baker (1996b: sec. 9.3), I argued that this is the correct derivation for languages in which the applied affix is a suffix that attaches close to the verb root. I also detected a distinct class of applicatives, in which the applied affix is a prefix. Such prefixes have slightly different case-theoretic properties from suffixal applicatives, and the prefix is sometimes recognizably the same as a free-standing postposition in the language (see, for example, Craig and Hale [1988]). For this class of applicatives, I maintained an adposition incorporation analysis. The significant point for current purposes is that prefixal applicatives do not always appear adjacent to the verb stem. On the contrary, it is common for them to be separated from the verb root by tense markers, agreement markers, or other inflectional morphology. (14) gives examples of this from Abaza and Slave, in which the incorporated adposition is transparently related to free-standing adpositions and has a pronoun incorporated into it. The adposition comes outside of subject agreement and (in Slave) the tense/mood affix.

(14)   a Y-[*l-zə*]-s-ž^w-d.   (Abaza [O'Herin 1995: 271])
           3sO-[*FsE*-BEN]-1sS-drink-DYN
           'I drank it for her.'
        b Sǫ́ba   [*ne*-**ghá**]-wo-h-lee   (Slave [Rice 1989])
           money 2sO-**for**-OPT-1sS-gave
           'I gave you money.'

Therefore, in those "applicatives" that are most plausibly analyzed as P incorporation, there is reason to say the movement targets the tense node, rather than the verb proper. The P ends up in the same word as the verb on the surface simply because the verb also moves to tense. The fact that P movement targets tense rather than V follows from the PHMG, given that P is functional.

We thus have converging evidence from several different sources that P really is a functional category, as my restrictive theory of the lexical categories requires. Some of the most obvious sources of evidence are a bit equivocal: Ps are fewer in number and poorer in lexical semantic meaning than the average lexical category, but they are also greater in number and richer in meaning than the average functional category, at least in English. But these measures are expected to give only a crude sense of which categories are lexical and which are functional in any case. We do not expect Universal Grammar to have an explicit principle that says a given category must have at most (or at least) n members; neither do we expect to count the semantic features of a word and deduce whether it is lexical or functional. The incorporation patterns sharpen the picture considerably. They provide morphosyntactic evidence that Ps are consistently functional heads, the range of complex words that include P-like elements being systematically different from those that involve lexical heads like verbs.

A.2 The place of adpositions in a typology of categories

While on the topic, I can also say something about the syntactic positions that PPs can occupy, comparing them to what we have learned about the syntax of VPs, APs, and NPs in the course of this study. This comparison makes it clear that the distribution of PPs is most like that of APs, which suggests that they have neither a referential index nor a specifier. We can then place Ps alongside determiners and Preds within a partial typology of functional categories that parallels my (complete) typology of lexical categories.

A.2.1 *PPs are adjuncts*

It is clear on all accounts that PPs make great adjunct-modifiers. They clearly contrast in this respect with NPs, which are the quintessential argument-type category. Back in section 3.7, I presented the contrasts in (15) and (16) to show that NPs cannot be adjoined to a clause unless they bind some gap or pronoun inside that clause. The other side of this coin is that NPs governed by an adpositional element are not subject to this restriction; they can be freely adjoined to a clause in English, Mohawk, and Chichewa.

(15) a Thíkʌ o-nut-á-'ke   yó-hskats   ne okwire'-shú'a. (Mohawk)
        that NsO-hill-Ø-LOC NsO-be.pretty NE tree-PLUR
        'On that hill, the trees are pretty.'
      b *Thíkʌ onúta', yó-hskats   ne okwire'-shú'a.
        that   hill   NsO-be.pretty NE tree-PLUR
        '(As for) that hill, the trees are pretty.'

(16) a Ku San Jose ndi-ma-sung-a   galimoto y-anga m'garaji. (Chichewa)
        at-San Jose IsS-HAB-keep-FV 9.car   9-my in-garage
        'In San Jose, I keep my car in the garage.' (Bresnan 1991)
      b *?Mkango uwu fisi a-na-dy-a   iwo
        lion   this hyena 3sS-PAST-eat-FV it. (Bresnan and Mchombo
                                                      1987: 749)
        'As for this lion, the hyena ate it (something else).'

This difference in syntactic distribution helps to justify analyzing elements like
–'ke in Mohawk and ku- in Chichewa as adpositions, rather than as category
neutral affixes that attach to nouns, as has been claimed by Deering and Delisle
(1976) for Mohawk and by Bresnan (1991) for Chichewa. If one said that
these expressions with locative morphemes were still NPs, there would be no
obvious explanation for why they alone can be freely attached to virtually
any clause. (17) in English further illustrates that most common modifications
cannot be expressed by bare NPs, but only by NPs in adpositional phrases.
This includes locative adjuncts, benefactive adjuncts, instrumental adjuncts,
temporal adjuncts, and purpose adjuncts, among others.[4]

(17)   a John cooked the yams *(in) the kitchen
         b   *(for) Mary
         c   *(with) oil.
         d   ?(on) Tuesday.
         e   *(for) money.

In this respect, the distribution of PPs is quite unlike the distribution of NPs.
It is, however, very much like the distribution of APs, given that adverbs are a
subtype of adjective (section 4.5). This suggests that PPs, like APs, do not bear
a referential index. (These examples also show that the P must have a theta-role
that is coindexed with its NP complement, as is standardly assumed. As a result,
the noun licensing condition is satisfied internal to the PP, and the NP need not
bind any other dependent element in the clause – although in some cases it may,
as discussed below.)

---

[4] There are a few sporadic cases of "bare NP adverbs" such as *John cooked the yams yesterday*, but
this is possible only with a small list of nouns that have inherent locative, temporal, or manner
meanings (Larson 1985). I tentatively adopt the analysis of Bresnan and Grimshaw (1978), who
claim that there is a null preposition governing the noun in these cases.

PPs also appear to varying degrees in the other syntactic environments that I identified in chapter 4 as being characteristic of APs. For example, APs are unique among the lexical categories in acting as resultative secondary predicates, but PPs also make fine resultatives:

(18)   a I cut the bread thin.   (AP)
        b I cut the bread into slices.   (PP)
           I smashed the vase to pieces.

In fact, many languages allow resultatives like (18b) but do not allow resultatives like (18a), including French (Legendre 1997) and Hebrew (Levin and Rappaport-Hovav 1995). Another characteristic position of APs is as attributive modifiers adjoined to NP, and PPs can also be restrictive modifiers of NPs in English:[5]

(19)   a a letter to/for Mary   (compare: a long letter)
        b chicken soup with rice   (compare: hot chicken soup)
        c the box on the table   (compare: the big box)

Finally, APs but not other lexical categories can be complements of degree heads. PPs with idiomatic meanings can also appear in this position (Maling 1983):

(20)   a John is as crazy as Mary is.
        b John is as out to lunch (= crazy) as Mary is.
           John is too in love for his own good.
           (but: *John is as in the kitchen as Mary is.)

As a first approximation, we can say that the difference between the idiomatic PPs and the more literal ones is simply that the idiomatic ones have gradable meanings and the literal ones do not. There are many degrees of being in love, for example, but either you are in the kitchen or you are not. The badness of *John is too in the kitchen*, then, is comparable to the badness of *The number seven is too prime*. Where the semantic requirement of gradability is met, PPs can appear with degree heads, just as APs do. This range of facts thus implies that PPs, like APs, must have no referential index and no theta-marked specifier position.[6]

---

[5] Not all languages allow adnominal PPs; Edo, for example, does not. I do not investigate the nature of this crosslinguistic difference here. Note that As without a complement left-adjoin to NP, whereas PPs (which always have a complement) right-adjoin to NP. This is a subcase of the so-called head-final filter in English (Emonds 1976; Williams 1982; Giorgi and Longobardi 1991: 97–100), which I also do not take up here.

[6] One problem for the view that PPs do not have referential indices comes from the existence of pro-PPs such as *there* in English. Not only do these seem to take PP antecedents, they can even have bound variable readings in sentences like *On every shelf stands the statue that Rodin originally put there*. According to the reasoning of section 3.5, this should imply that PPs do

A.2.2   PPs are not predicates

If PPs are syntactically similar to APs, then they must not be intrinsic predicates, the way verbs are. They should not license specifier positions, and can only be used predicatively by being the complement of Pred or some kind of copular verb that licenses a specifier. The standard generative view has been the opposite, that at least some PPs are predicates and do theta-mark a subject in copular sentences ((21a)) and small clause constructions ((21b) [Stowell 1983]).

(21)   a Chris$_i$ is [t$_i$ in the kitchen].
        b I want [a table in the kitchen].

Some analyses take this view quite far, positing a small clause even in examples like *Chris put the book in the box*. For them, the theme *the book* is analyzed not as the direct object of *put*, but rather as the subject of the PP *in the box* (Hoekstra 1988; Dikken 1995).

Chapter 2 has, however, taught us the importance of looking below the surface of this kind of data to detect the contribution of null Pred heads. African languages like Edo and Chichewa were particularly useful in this connection, because their Preds are spelled out overtly. In fact, PPs in these languages cannot be used as the primary predicate of a matrix clause, even when a copular particle is used, as shown by the ungrammaticality of (22a) and (23a).

(22)   a *Òzó (yé/rè)   vbè òwá.   (Edo: *Pred + PP)
          Ozo PRED   at   house
          'Ozo is in the house.'
        b Òzó rré   òwá.   (locative verb)
          Ozo is.at house
          'Ozo is in the house.'
        c Òzó mùdìá yè esuku.   (posture verb)
          Ozo stand at school
          'Ozo is at school.'

(23)   a *Ukonde ndi   pa-m-chenga   (Chichewa: *Pred + PP)
          net   PRED on-3-beach
          'The net is on the beach.'

have some kind of referential index. I tentatively assume that these PP-binding effects can be captured by attributing referential indices not to the PPs themselves, but to the NPs inside them – perhaps including an abstract nominal in the syntactic representation of *there*. (Note that *there* can sometimes occupy the true subject position, as in *Is there any sugar?*, in contrast to true PPs (see (43d)).) This assumption may play a role also in the ability of some PPs to identify empty categories in subject and object positions; see (41) and (42) below. That PPs seem to undergo A-movement to subject positions in locative inversion sentences like (43a) may be an illusion. Facts like (43c,d) suggest that the PP is really a fronted topic that binds a null subject position.

b Ukonde u-li   pa-m-chenga   (verbal copula + PP)
net   3S-be on-3-beach
'The net is on the beach.'

Instead of a Pred, a true verb of some kind must be present, either a verb with inherent locative meaning ((22b)), a posture verb ((22c)), or the truly verbal copula ((23b)). (24) shows that PPs also cannot be the predicates of simple copular sentences in Japanese or Mohawk; again, an explicit posture verb is needed.

(24)   a *Hanako-ga   heya de da.   (Japanese)
           Hanako-NOM room in PRED
           'Hanako is in the room.'
        b Sak ka-nakt-óku   *(t-ha-ya't-óru)   (Mohawk)
           Sak NsS-bed-under CIS-MsS-body-be.covered
           'Sak is under the bed.'

Stassen's (1997) study of the forms of intransitive predication confirms that this is the normal situation crosslinguistically. He identifies the use of a truly verbal "support" element together with a PP as the characteristic way of encoding locative predications, and observes that other situations are relatively rare. Locative PPs appear to be directly predicable of subjects in at most 52 of the 410 languages he investigated.[7]

These data suggest that PPs do not license specifiers directly. Indeed, it seems that not even a functional head like Pred is enough to create a specifier for a PP in most languages. The reason for this is presumably semantic rather than syntactic: we can say that there is no theme role implicit in the lexical meaning of the adpositions that a Pred can bring out. In Chierchia's (1985) terms, PPs have a denotation that cannot be mapped readily into a propositional function. A clause can thus be formed only if a true verb is present to theta-mark the subject, and the PP is adjoined to the verbal projection as a modifier. If the verb happens to be a rather bland one – a posture verb, for example, or an existential verb – the PP can carry most of the new information of the sentence. Nevertheless, the PP is not the predicate in the structural sense. I conclude that PPs do not license subjects of their own, just as APs do not.[8]

[7] This number includes languages in which PPs can be inflected like verbs (15 languages) and languages in which a PP can be directly juxtaposed with a subject (37 languages), but not languages in which the verbal copular element is omitted only in the unmarked present tense (as in Russian, for example). It also does not include languages in which the only locative elements that can be predicated directly of subjects are "small words" like *here*, *there*, and *where*. I put the sometimes-unique syntax of these deictic items aside.

[8] In Baker (1996b: ch. 9) I argued against the view that PPs can theta-mark a subject on partially different grounds. There I pointed out that PPs never agree with their putative subjects, even in heavily head-marking languages like Mohawk, in which all other categories necessarily agree with all of their arguments. This makes sense if PPs do not in fact take subjects.

A.2.3   PPs are not arguments

The claim that PPs are syntactically comparable to APs also suggests that they should not be able to receive theta-roles the way NPs can, because they do not bear a referential index that could bind such a theta-role. This too runs contrary to most of the generative tradition, which holds that PPs can function as arguments in at least some limited cases. The empirical evidence on this point seems mixed. Some configurations clearly go in the direction I predict: (25) shows that English PPs cannot normally appear in subject positions, object positions, or as the objects of a preposition.

(25)   a *In San Jose pleases me.   (Bresnan 1991)
             (compare: 'It pleases me in San Jose.')
         b *I like in San Jose.
             (compare: 'I like it in San Jose.')
         c *I went to in San Jose.
             (compare: 'I went into San Jose.')

It is unlikely that these examples are out for trivial semantic reasons. If *in San Jose* is referential at all, it should refer to a location (Jackendoff 1983), and it seems reasonable that a location-denoting phrase could satisfy the very general selectional restrictions of the theta-markers in these examples. This is confirmed by the grammaticality of sentences like (25a) and (25b) when the PP is "extraposed" to an adjoined position, with a quasi-argumental pronoun *it* in the argument position. Nor is this resistance toward locative PP arguments peculiar to English. Launey (1981) mentions that locative expressions formed by incorporating a noun into an adposition cannot function as the subject or object of ordinary verbs in Classical Nahuatl:

(26)   a *Ca   cualli in   Mexi'-co.
            PRT good DET Mexico-LOC
            'In Mexico is nice; it is nice in Mexico.'
         b *Ni-qu-itta   in   Mexi'-co.
            1sS-3sO-see DET Mexico-LOC
            'I saw (in) Mexico.'

Locational PPs also cannot serve as subjects or objects in Edo:

(27)   a *Vbè èkì   yèé   Àdésúwà.
            at   market pleases Adesuwa.
            '(Being) at the market pleases Adesuwa.'

The discussion in the text implies that the subject in (21a) is theta-marked by *is* (presumably the otherwise rare *be* of existence) and the object in (21b) is theta-marked by *want*.

b *Àdésúwà khuèmwén vbè èkì.
Adesuwa like   at   market
'Adesuwa likes (it) at the market.'

Chichewa is a particularly interesting case for these issues. Bresnan and Kanerva (1989) and Bresnan (1991) argue that locative-denoting expressions in Chichewa can be categorized as NPs rather than PPs.[9] The most obvious sign of this is the fact that Chichewa's locative prefixes are counted as gender prefixes, equivalent to the noun class prefixes that all nouns in the language begin with. As a result, modifiers can agree with locative elements, just as they agree in gender and number with other, more canonical nouns (Bresnan and Mchombo 1995: 211):

(28) *mu*-dzi *w*-áthú;   *ku*-mu-dzi   *kw*-athu
      3-village 3-our;   at(17)-3-village 17-our
      'our village'   'at our village'

In exactly those cases where Chichewa has location-denoting NPs, those expressions can be used as subjects and objects. The examples in (29) are thus perfectly grammatical, in marked contrast to their English counterparts in (25).

(29) a A-lendo á-ma-pa-kond-a   pa-mu-dzi   w-áthú p-ó-chítítsa
        2-visitor 2S-HAB-16O-love-FV in(16)-3-village 3-our 16-ASSOC-attract
        chi-dwi.
        7-interest
        'Visitors love (it in) our interesting village.' (Bresnan and Mchombo 1995: 220)
      b Ku San Jose kú-ma-ndi-sangaláts-a. (Bresnan 1991)
        At-San Jose 17sS-HAB-1sO-please-FV
        '(Being in) San Jose pleases me.'

Even so, phrases headed by elements that are unambiguously prepositions, such as instrumental *ndi* 'with', cannot be subjects in Chichewa, as shown in (30).

(30)   *Ndi Sam ??-ma-ndi-sangala-ts-a.   (Sam Mchombo, personal communication)
        with Sam ??S-HAB-1sO-be.happy-CAUS-FV
        '(Being) with Sam makes me happy.'

---

[9] Unlike Bresnan and Kanerva, I take the position that locative prefix + noun constituents in Chichewa can be categorized as either PPs or NPs (Baker 1992). Evidence that they can be PPs is that they can be freely adjoined to a clause without being coreferent to a pronoun inside the clause, as shown in (16a). If the locative expression could only be an NP, this example should be ruled out by the NLC. This view also fits with the fact that locative prefixes need not determine the agreement on a modifying expression; the modifier can agree instead with the inherent gender of the noun root, as in *ku-nyanjá y-ánga* (at(17)-9.lake 9-my) 'at my lake' (compare with (28)). This form is exactly what one would expect if the locative prefix can be a simple adposition.

There is then some crosslinguistic variation in which expressions count as NPs and which as PPs, but there seems to be no variation on the point that PPs are excluded from canonical argument positions. (See Baker [1996b: 423] for discussion of similar cases in Mohawk and Nahuatl.)

What, then, are we to make of the evidence that PPs do seem to receive theta-roles from the verb in a few narrowly defined cases? There are two particular cases in which it seems especially plausible to say that the PP is theta-marked. One is verbs of the *put*-class, which can take any locative PP in addition to their direct object NP; the other is verbs like *depend*, which select for one particular preposition. With both types of verbs, sentences become ungrammatical if the PP is omitted, suggesting that the PP is an obligatory argument of the verb:[10]

(31)   a Chris put the book *(on/under/near/in/behind the table).
        b I depend *(on Chris).

The simple fact that a PP is obligatory is not by itself very good evidence that the PP is an argument syntactically, however. It is well known that English has a few verbs that more or less require a manner adverb, including *word* and *behave*:

(32)   a John worded the letter *(carefully).
        b Mary behaved *(badly) at the party.

These contrast with the vast majority of verbs, which can appear with a manner adverb but do not have to. Nevertheless, the morphology and syntax of the adverbs in (32) is no different from that of other manner adverbs; see, for example, Rizzi's (1990: 77–78) discussion of *wh*-extraction effects. It is thus standard to say that these adverbs are still adjunct modifiers. I suggest that the PP in (31a) should be thought of in exactly the same way: *put* and its synonyms in English are verbs that require a PP adjunct. The parallel between the two cases is a close one. Very few verbs require a manner adverb to become meaningful and informative, but then very few require a prepositional phrase. Even verbs that count as translations of *put* in other languages often do not need a PP, as shown by the following examples from Mohawk and Edo:

---

[10] Neeleman (1997) distinguishes three classes of PPs: "PP adjuncts" like (31a); "PP complements" like (31b); and "PP arguments" like the subject of *Under the tree is a nice place for a picnic*. His PP arguments have the syntactic distribution and behavior of NPs, even though there is no obvious noun head. I assume that they are in fact NPs, either because "heavy Ps" like *under* can sometimes be taken as nominals themselves (see note 1 above for a suggestion), or because a noun head is deleted by ellipsis.

(33) Ke-'nerohkw-ʌhaw-í-hne' sok wá'-k-yʌt-'.
      1sS-box-carry-IMPF-PAST then FACT-1sS-put-PUNC
      'I was carrying the box, but then I put it (down).'

(34) Òzó rhié íghó (yè ekpetin).
      Ozo take/put money in box.
      With PP: 'Ozo put the money in the box.'
      Without PP: 'Ozo took the money.'

Obligatory PPs in English do not have a markedly different syntax from optional ones like the PP in *Chris baked bread in the kitchen*. Both required and optional PPs can follow an adverb without being 'heavy,' for example ((35a)). Both can be stranded by *wh*-movement ((35b)), both can be extracted out of a weak island with relative ease (compared to words like *how* or *why*, ((35c))), and both can be carried along by VP-fronting ((35d)).

(35) a Chris put the book carefully in the box.
         Chris cooked the meat slowly in the kitchen.
      b Which box did Chris put the book in?
         Which store did Chris buy the book in?
      c (?)In which container do you know how to put explosives?
         (?)In which country do you know how to buy explosives?
      d I said I'd put the book in the box, and [put the book in the box] I will!
         I said I'd cook the meat in the oven, and [cook the meat in the oven] I will!

This is parallel to the fact that obligatory adverbs do not differ from optional adverbs with respect to word order, extraction, and constituency.

It is also instructive to consider what else can appear in the same syntactic position as an obligatory PP, immediately following the direct object. NP, the quintessential argumental category cannot generally appear here, but APs can:

(36) a Chris put the metal in the furnace.
      b Chris beat the metal flat.
      c *Chris beat the metal a sword.

There are strong semantic affinities between the PP in (36a) and the AP in (36b). Both are types of resultatives: (36a) implies that the metal comes to be in the furnace as a result of the putting, just as (36b) implies that the metal comes to be flat as a result of the beating. If this "second complement" position is a theta position, it is extremely odd that it does not allow phrase types that occur in all other argument positions (NPs) and does allow phrase types that never otherwise appear in argument positions (PPs, APs). A more elegant interpretation is that these "second complements" are not arguments at all, but rather adjoined modifiers of a particular kind.

The view that no PP is an argument does not commit me to saying that there are never any syntactic differences among PPs. Even if all PPs are adjunct modifiers, it is reasonable to suppose that some PPs adjoin to a high position in the clause, whereas others adjoin to a lower position. The lowest possible adjunction site in my theory is the AP that contributes the resulting-state part of the verb's meaning (section 2.9). I assume that resultative PPs appear here, thereby maximizing their parallelism with resultative AP constructions (see section 4.4). Other PPs adjoin to vP (or even higher), giving structures like the one in (37).

(37)

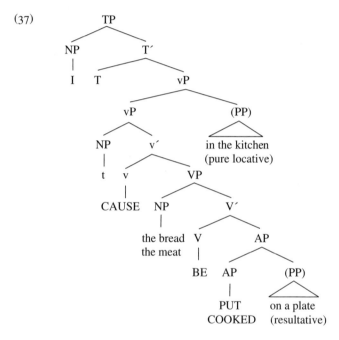

Certain minor syntactic differences can be derived from this structural difference, such as the fact that a resultative PP typically comes before a general location PP in English:

(38) a I put the bread on a plate in the kitchen.
      b #I put the bread in the kitchen on a plate.

This is exactly parallel to the fact that resultative APs come before depictive APs in English (see section 4.4). That *do so* replaces a resultative PP but not necessarily a locative PP (see (39)) also follows from (37) together with the assumption that *do so* is a special kind of vP.

(39)   a ?*I put a box in the kitchen and Chris did so in the living room.
        b I read the newspaper in the kitchen and Chris did so in the living room.

A locative PP can adjoin to *do so*, but *do so* contains no AP inside it that a resultative PP can adjoin to, giving rise to the contrast in (39). The traditional distinction between PP complements and PP adjuncts, familiar from Jackendoff (1977) and others, can thus be recast as a distinction between low-adjoined PPs and high-adjoined PPs.

    The second class of putative PP arguments to consider is those associated with verbs like *depend*, some canonical examples of which are given in (40).

(40)   a Chris depends on the checks from home.
        b You can count on me!
        c They believe in God.

These so-called "PP complements," studied in detail by Neeleman (1997), differ from the PPs associated with verbs like *put* in that the P is fixed and does not have its usual compositional meaning. One cannot depend *in* something, for example, nor can one infer from (40a) that something is on the checks. My remarks about these cases are more tentative, centering on how aspects of Neeleman's analysis of English and Dutch can be recast in my framework.

    I would like to maintain that these "PP complements" are also obligatory adjuncts with respect to the syntax. Unlike the PPs found with *put*-class verbs, however, these govern and identify the content of a nominal empty category that is a true argument of the verb. The structure of (40a) is then roughly (41).

(41)   Chris $[_{VP}$ $[_{VP}$ depends$<\ldots\theta_i>$ e_i] on checks]

That an adjoined PP can play a role in licensing an NP empty category is independently motivated by locative inversion structures like (42) in English (see Stowell [1981]).

(42)   a On the desk stood the trophy that Chris won at the debate tournament.
        b $[_{CP}$ On the desk $[_{CP}$ e Tense $[_{VP}$ stand the trophy ...]]]

The structure in (42b) captures the fact that the preverbal PP behaves like the subject of the clause for some purposes but not others. Like a subject, it undergoes subject-to-subject raising ((43a)), and its extraction gives rise to *that*-trace effects ((43b)) (Bresnan 1994); like a CP-adjunct it cannot appear in

322   *Appendix. Adpositions as functional categories*

certain embedded clauses ((43c)) and it cannot be crossed by subject-auxiliary inversion ((43d)).

(43)   a On the desk seemed to stand a trophy.
         b On which desk do you think (*that) – stood a trophy?
         c *Because on the desk stood a trophy, Chris put the package on the table.
         d *Did on the desk stand a trophy?

The apparent contradiction is resolved by saying that the PP is adjoined to CP but locally controls an NP in subject position, which may itself have (for example) undergone subject raising.

My proposal sketched in (41) is designed to explain the fact that the so-called PP complements show a rather similar mixture of argument and adjunct properties. On the one hand, the PP seems to be in an adjoined position in that it has essentially the same word order properties as more canonical PPs. For example, these PPs can easily be separated from the verb by adverbs, unlike comparable NP complements:

(44)   a Chris depends very much on Pat.
            (contrast: ??Chris trusts very much Pat.)
         b He believes fervently in God.
            (contrast: ??He believes fervently my story.)

PP complements can also be extraposed to the right of the verb in Dutch, like PP adjuncts but unlike NP arguments (Neeleman 1997: 111–12). On the other hand, PP complements seem like arguments of the verb in that any given verb can take at most one of them, according to Neeleman. This is especially striking with verbs like *supply*, which can take two internal arguments. Either one of its arguments can be expressed as a PP, but it is impossible for both to be expressed as PPs simultaneously:

(45)   a Chris supplied medicine to the refugees.
         b Chris supplied the refugees with medicine.
         c *Chris supplied to the refugees with medicine.

This follows if there is only one position – the immediate sister of the verb – that the verb governs in such a way as to license the nominal empty category.[11]

---

[11] Here I am assuming the bipartite theory of licensing empty categories proposed by Rizzi (1986a) and subsequent work. The verb is the formal licenser of the empty category (and therefore there can be only one such element), and the PP is the identifier of its content (and therefore must be present).
      There are both similarities and differences between my proposal and Neeleman's. Neeleman also claims that the restricted distribution of PP complements follows from there being an empty category that requires licensing under government, but for Neeleman this empty category is the

My theory also explains immediately Neeleman's (1997: 117–22) observation that a PP complement cannot be coordinated with an NP, even when the verb can in principle select either type of phrase:

(46)   *Chris believes the Bible and in God.

(46) is bad because it involves coordinating phrases of fundamentally different syntactic and semantic types, one an argumental phrase with a referential index and the other an adjunct phrase with no index. The conjunction of the two cannot be resolved to form either an argument or an adjunct.[12] This proposal leaves a number of important matters to be filled in – such as the exact nature of the empty category in (41) and its relationship to the licensing PP – but it has some positive empirical consequences and is consistent with the claim that PPs are always adjuncts, never arguments in themselves.

I note in passing that it may be reasonable to analyze the PPs that appear with *give* and other dative shifting verbs in this same way. This would involve developing the following analogy: (47d) is to (47c) as (47b) is to (47a).

(47)   a I believe Pat's story.
         b I believe *e* in Pat's honesty.
         c I gave Chris a gift.
         d I gave *e* a gift to Chris.

On this view, verbs like *give* would always be double object verbs, taking two NP complements. This is true on the surface in many languages, including Mohawk and Nupe, which have the equivalent of (47c) but not (47d). In English, however, the first of those objects has the option of being an empty category, identified by a PP headed by the preposition *to*. These *to* phrases are syntactically similar to PP complements in that they cannot be coordinated with noun phrases (**John showed [Mary and to her father] the photographs he took in Kenya*), and they

---

trace of the preposition after it has been incorporated into the verb at LF. I cannot adopt this view, because I believe P is a functional category that cannot incorporate into a verb.

[12] My proposal might also shed some new light on the old mystery of why certain NPs seem to c-command other elements in the structure even though they are embedded in a PP, as shown in (i) (Reinhart 1983: 175–77).

(i)   I spoke e_i to each father$_i$ about his$_i$ child.

Here the first PP identifies a null NP complement of the verb, and it is not surprising that this null NP would have the same c-command domain as an ordinary, unembedded direct object. (This does not explain all the residual problems with c-command and PPs, however.)

My proposal also helps to make sense of the fact that case markers evolve diachronically out of adpositions. It is very natural for children acquiring a language with structures like (41) to reanalyze the adjunct PP that governs a null NP argument as being itself an NP argument with a particle or affix that indicates which argument position it is associated with.

do not co-occur with other PP complements (see (45c)). The facts surrounding dative shift and double object constructions are, of course, notoriously complex, and reassessing the literature on these topics goes beyond what I can do here. For now I am content to leave this as a tentative suggestion about how the *to*-phrases associated with verbs of transfer might fit into the overall typology of PPs.

A.2.4   A fuller typology of categories

If all this is on the right track, then PPs are always adjunct modifiers, never predicates apart from a theta-marking verb or arguments apart from a theta-role receiving null NP. As such, their distribution is much more like that of adjectives than like that of any other lexical category. Ps do, however, select NPs, which they theta-mark. In this respect, they create a fundamental change in the character of the projection. When this is combined with what we saw about Pred and determiner/pronoun in previous chapters, a partial typology of functional categories begins to emerge.

Most previous treatments of functional categories have taken them to be more or less inert categorially; they do not change the inherent nature of the complement that they select. One particularly clear and influential implementation of this intuition is Grimshaw's (1991) notion of "extended projection," in which the functional heads associated with nouns (such as determiner) bear nominal features and the functional heads associated with verbs (tense, complementizer) bear verbal features. The co-occurrence of functional heads and lexical phrases for Grimshaw is then regulated not by selection, but rather by matching categorial features. If I am right, then functional categories are not all of this kind. Rather, Ps select NPs and make them into something like an AP. The functional category P is thus rather like the syntactic equivalent of a derivational morpheme. In the same way, Pred is a functional category that selects an NP or AP and makes it into a phrase that is approximately equivalent to a VP by constructing a theta-role out of its complement. Finally, there are various functional categories that seem to take VP or AP complements and create a phrase that has a referential index and thus can bear thematic roles, stand in argument positions, and enter into anaphoric dependencies. The gerundive morpheme *–ing* in English is a case in point: it takes a fully verbal complement and projects a phrase that has the external syntax of an NP (Abney 1987).[13]

---

[13] Even ordinary complementizers like *that* in English may have something of this quality. Although CPs do not have exactly the same distribution as NPs, they are much more like NPs than smaller verbal projections are. We saw in chapter 3 that CPs can stand in argument positions, can undergo movement, and can be antecedents for pronouns in discourse. This shows that they have some kind of referential index.

(48) a I appreciated Chris's washing the dishes so cheerfully. Pat appreciated it too.

b $[_{DP\{i,j\}}$ Chris 's $[_{ingP\{i,j\}}$ -ing$_{\{i,j\}}$ $[_{vP}$ wash the dishes so cheerfully]]]

Putting all this together, we can discern the outlines of a three-by-three typology of categories. First there are the three lexical categories defined by the two properties of having a referential index and having a specifier. Second, there are three types of functional categories that form extended projections with the corresponding lexical categories in roughly Grimshaw's sense. These can be thought of as functional items whose categorial essence happens to match that of the only lexical category they can combine with for predictable semantic reasons. Determiners and degrees are this kind of functional category, given the analyses in sections 3.3 and 4.3. Finally, there are (at least) three types of category-shifting functional heads. These are functional heads that have the same substantive properties as the various lexical heads, but not the same properties as their complements. They therefore change the distribution of their lexical complements in major ways. This class consists of the various Ps, the various Preds, gerundive elements like *–ing* and perhaps other kinds of syntactic nominalizers. This typology is summarized in (49).

(49)

	Lexical	Functional/Transparent	Functional/Opaque
Licenses specifier	Verb	Aspect, Tense	$Pred_N$, $Pred_A$
Bears Ref. Index	Noun	Det, Number, Case	*-ing*, (*that?*, *-ness?*)
Neither	Adjective	Degree	Adposition

The theory developed in the body of this book for the lexical categories thus also induces an interesting partial typology of the functional categories.

References

Abney, Steven. 1987. The English noun phrase in its sentential aspect. Ph.D dissertation, MIT, Cambridge, Mass.

Adelaar, Willem. 1994. A grammar of Huallaga (Huanuco) Quechua (Weber). *International Journal of American Linguistics* 60: 83–87.

Agheyisi, Rebecca. 1990. A grammar of Edo. ms., UNESCO.

Aissen, Judith. 1987. *Tzotzil clause structure*. Dordrecht: Reidel.

Alexiadou, Artemis and Elena Anagnostopoulou. 1998. Parametrizing AGR: word order, V-movement and EPP-checking. *Natural Language and Linguistic Theory* 16: 491–539.

Allen, Barbara, Donna Gardiner and Donald Frantz. 1984. Noun incorporation in Southern Tiwa. *International Journal of American Linguistics* 50: 292–311.

Alsina, Alex. 1992. On the argument structure of causatives. *Linguistic Inquiry* 23: 517–56.

Alsina, Alex and Sam Mchombo. 1991. Object extraction and the accessibility of thematic information. In *Berkeley Linguistics Society* 17, Berkeley, Calif.

Anderson, John. 1997. *A notional theory of syntactic categories*. Cambridge: Cambridge University Press.

Anderson, Stephen. 1992. *A-morphous morphology*. Cambridge: Cambridge University Press.

Andrews, J. Richard. 1975. *Introduction to Classical Nahuatl*. Austin: University of Texas Press.

Aronoff, Mark. 1994. *Morphology by itself: stems and inflection classes*. Cambridge, Mass.: MIT Press.

Austin, Peter and Joan Bresnan. 1996. Non-configurationality in Australian aboriginal languages. *Natural Language and Linguistic Theory* 14: 215–68.

Baker, Mark. 1988a. *Incorporation: a theory of grammatical function changing*. Chicago: University of Chicago Press.

1988b. Morphological and syntactic objects: a review of A.M. di Sciullo and E. Williams, On the definition of word. *Yearbook of Morphology* 1: 259–83.

1988c. Morphology and syntax: an interlocking independence. In *Morphology and modularity*, ed. Martin Everaert. Dordrecht: Foris.

1991. On some subject/object non-asymmetries in Mohawk. *Natural Language and Linguistic Theory* 9: 537–76.

1992. Thematic conditions on syntactic structures: evidence from locative applicatives. In *Thematic structure: its role in grammar*, ed. I. M. Rocca, 23–46. Berlin: Foris.

1995. On the absence of certain quantifiers in Mohawk. In *Quantification in natural languages*, ed. Emond Bach, Eloise Jelinek, Angelika Kratzer, and Barbara Partee, 21–58. Dordrecht: Kluwer.

1996a. On the structural positions of themes and goals. In *Phrase structure and the lexicon*, ed. Johan Rooryck and Laurie Zauring, 7–34. Dordrecht: Kluwer.

1996b. *The polysynthesis parameter*. New York: Oxford University Press.

1996c. Unaccusativity and the adjective/verb distinction: English and Mohawk evidence. In Eastern States Conference on Linguistics, Saint John, New Brunswick, Cornell University.

1997. Thematic roles and syntactic structure. In *Elements of grammar*, ed. Liliane Haegeman, 73–137. Dordrecht: Kluwer.

2001a. The natures of nonconfigurationality. In *The handbook of syntax*, ed. Mark Baltin and Chris Collins, 407–38. Oxford: Blackwell.

2001b. Phrase structure as a representation of "primitive" grammatical relations. In *Objects and other subjects: grammatical functions, functional categories and configurationality*, ed. William Davies and Stan Dubinsky, 21–52. Dordrecht: Kluwer.

2002. Building and merging, not checking: the nonexistence of (Aux) SVO languages. *Linguistic Inquiry* 33: 321–9.

Baker, Mark and O. T. Stewart. 1996. Unaccusativity and the adjective/verb distinction: Edo evidence. In NELS 27, McGill University, GSLA.

1998. Verb movement, objects, and serialization. In *North East Linguistics Society* 29, 17–32. Newark, Delaware, GSLA.

1999. On double-headedness and the anatomy of the clause. ms., Rutgers University and University of British Columbia, New Brunswick, NJ.

Baker, Mark and Lisa Travis. 1998. Events, times, and Mohawk verbal inflection. *Canadian Journal of Linguistics* 43: 149–203.

Barker, Muhammad. 1967. *A course in Urdu*. Montreal: McGill University Press.

Belletti, Adriana. 1988. The case of unaccusatives. *Linguistic Inquiry* 19: 1–34.

Belletti, Adriana and Luigi Rizzi. 1981. The syntax of *ne*: some theoretical implications. *The Linguistic Review* 1: 117–54.

Benmanmoun, Elabbas. 2000. *The feature structure of functional categories: a comparative study of Arabic dialects*. New York: Oxford University Press.

Bhat, D. N. S. 1994. *The adjectival category: criteria for differentiation and identification*. Amsterdam: John Benjamins.

Bittner, Maria. 1999. Concealed Causatives. *Natural Language Semantics* 7: 1–78.

Bittner, Maria and Kenneth Hale. 1995. Remarks on definiteness in Warlpiri. In *Quantification in natural languages*, ed. Emond Bach, Angelika Kratzer, Eloise Jelinek, and Barbara Partee, 81–105. Dordrecht: Kluwer.

1996. The structural determination of case and agreement. *Linguistic Inquiry* 27: 1–68.

Bobaljik, Jonathan. 1994. What does adjacency do? In *The morphology syntax connection*, ed. Colin Phillips and Heidi Harley. Cambridge, Mass.: MIT Working Papers in Linguistics.

Bolinger, Dwight. 1967. Adjectives in English: attribution and predication. *Lingua* 18: 1–34.

Borer, Hagit. 1988. On the morphological parallelism between compounds and constructs. *Yearbook of Morphology* 1: 45–66.

1990. V + ing: it walks like an adjective, it talks like an adjective. *Linguistic Inquiry* 21: 95–102.

1991. The causative–inchoative alternation: a case study in parallel morphology. *The Linguistic Review* 8.

2000. Exo-skeletal vs. endo-skeletal explanations: syntactic projections and the lexicon. Unpublished ms., University of Southern California, Los Angeles.

Borer, Hagit and Yosef Grodzinsky. 1986. Syntactic cliticization and lexical cliticization: the case of Hebrew dative clitics. In *Syntax and semantics 19: the syntax of pronominal clitics*, ed. Hagit Borer, 175–217. San Diego: Academic Press.

Bowers, John. 1993. The syntax of predication. *Linguistic Inquiry* 24: 591–656.

Bresnan, Joan. 1982. Control and complementation. In *The mental representation of grammatical relations*, ed. Joan Bresnan, 282–390. Cambridge, Mass.: MIT Press.

1991. Locative case vs. locative gender. In *Proceedings of the Berkeley Linguistics Society* 17, 53–68. Berkeley, Calif., BLS.

1994. Locative inversion and the architecture of Universal Grammar. *Language* 70: 72–131.

Bresnan, Joan and Jane Grimshaw. 1978. The syntax of free relatives in English. *Linguistic Inquiry* 9: 331–91.

Bresnan, Joan and Joni Kanerva. 1989. Locative inversion in Chichewa: a case study of factorization in grammar. *Linguistic Inquiry* 20: 1–50.

Bresnan, Joan and Sam Mchombo. 1987. Topic, pronoun, and agreement in Chichewa. *Language* 63: 741–82.

1995. The lexical integrity principle: evidence from Bantu. *Natural Language and Linguistic Theory* 13: 181–254.

Broadwell, George A. 1990. Extending the Binding theory: a Muskogean case study. Ph.D. dissertation, UCLA.

Burzio, Luigi. 1986. *Italian syntax: a government–binding approach*. Dordrecht: Reidel.

Carey, Susan. 1994. Does learning a language require the child to reconceptualize the world? *Lingua* 92: 143–67.

Carey, Susan and Fei Xu. 1999. Sortals and kinds: an appreciation of John Macnamara. In *Language, logic, and concepts*, ed. Ray Jackendoff, 311–36. Cambridge, Mass.: MIT Press.

Carlson, Greg. 1977. Reference to kinds in English. Ph.D. dissertation, University of Massachusetts, Amherst, Mass.

1984. Thematic roles and their role in semantic interpretation. *Linguistics* 22: 259–79.

Carnie, Andrew. 1995. Non-verbal predication and head movement. Ph.D. dissertation, MIT, Cambridge, Mass.

Cheng, Lisa Lai-Shen and Rint Sybesma. 1999. Bare and not-so-bare nouns and the structure of NP. *Linguistic Inquiry* 30: 509–42.

Chierchia, Gennaro. 1985. Formal semantics and the grammar of predication. *Linguistic Inquiry* 16: 417–44.

1998. Reference to kinds across languages. *Natural Language Semantics* 6: 339–405.

Chierchia, Gennaro and Ray Turner. 1988. Semantics and property theory. *Linguistics and Philosophy* 11: 261–302.

Chomsky, Noam. 1957. *Syntactic structures*. The Hague: Mouton.

1970. Remarks on nominalization. In *Readings in English transformational grammar*, ed. R. Jacobs and P. Rosenbaum, 184–221. Waltham, Mass.: Ginn.

1973. Conditions on transformations. In *A festschrift for Morris Halle*, ed. Stephen Anderson and Paul Kiparsky, 222–86. New York: Holt, Rinehart and Winston.

1977. On wh-movement. In *Formal syntax*, ed. Peter Cullcover, Thomas Wasow, and Adrian Akmajian, 71–132. New York: Academic Press.

1980. On binding. *Linguistic Inquiry* 11: 1–46.

1981. *Lectures on government and binding*. Dordrecht: Foris.

1982. *Some concepts and consequences of the theory of government and binding*. Cambridge, Mass.: MIT Press.

1986a. *Barriers*. Cambridge, Mass.: MIT Press.

1986b. *Knowledge of language: its nature, origin, and use*. New York: Praeger.

1991. Some notes on economy of derivation and representation. In *Principles and parameters in comparative grammar*, ed. Robert Freidin, 417–54. Cambridge, Mass.: MIT Press.

1993. A minimalist program for linguistic theory. In *The view from building 20*, ed. Kenneth Hale and Samuel Jay Keyser, 1–52. Cambridge, Mass.: MIT Press.

1994. Bare Phrase Structure, manuscript, MIT, Cambridge, Mass.

1995. *The minimalist program*. Cambridge, Mass.: MIT Press.

Chung, Sandra and James McCloskey. 1987. Government, barriers, and small clauses in Modern Irish. *Linguistic Inquiry* 18: 173–238.

Cinque, Guglielmo. 1990. Ergative adjectives and the lexicalist hypothesis. *Natural Language and Linguistic Theory* 8: 1–40.

1994. On the evidence for partial N-movement in the Romance DP. In *Paths towards Universal Grammar: studies in honor of Richard S. Kayne*, ed. Guglielmo Cinque, Jan Koster, Jean-Yves Pollock, Luigi Rizzi, and Raffaella Zanuttini, 85–110. Washington D.C.: Georgetown University Press.

1999. *Adverbs and functional heads: a cross-linguistic perspective*. New York: Oxford.

Clark, Eve. 1993. *The lexicon in acquisition*. New York: Cambridge University Press.

Cole, Peter. 1985. *Imbabura Quechua*. London: Croom Helm.

Corver, Norbert. 1997. Much-support as a last resort. *Linguistic Inquiry* 28: 119–64.

Craig, Colette and Kenneth Hale. 1988. Relational preverbs in some languages of the Americas. *Language* 64: 312–44.

Croft, William. 1991. *Syntactic categories and grammatical relations*. Chicago: University of Chicago Press.

Daley, Jon. 1985. *Tzutujil grammar*. Berkeley, Calif.: University of California Press.

Davidson, Donald. 1967. The logical form of action sentences. In *The logic of decision and action*, ed. N. Rescher. Pittsburgh: University of Pittsburgh Press.

Davies, William. 1986. *Choctaw verb agreement and universal grammar*. Dordrecht: Reidel.

Davis, Henry. 1999. On nouns and nominalizations in Salish. Unpublished ms., University of British Columbia, Vancouver.

Davis, Henry and Hamida Dermidache. 2000. On lexical verb meanings: evidence from Salish. In *Events as grammatical objects*, ed. Carol Tenny and James Pustejovsky, 97–142. Stanford, Calif.: CSLI Publication.

Davis, Henry, I-Ju Sandra Lai and Lisa Matthewson. 1997. Cedar roots and singing detectives: attributive modification in Salish and English. In *Papers for the 32nd international conference on Salish and neighbouring languages*, 291–316.

Dayal, Veneeta. 2001. Number marking and (in)definiteness in kind terms. Unpublished ms., Rutgers University.

Déchaine, Rose-Marie. 1993. Predicates across categories. Ph.D. dissertation, University of Massachusetts, Amherst, Mass.

Déchaine, Rose-Marie and Mireille Tremblay. 1996. Adverbial PPs and prepositional adverbs in French and English. In *Canadian Linguistics Association Proceedings*. Calgary: University of Calgary Working Papers in Linguistics.

Deering, Nora and Helga Delisle. 1976. *Mohawk: a teaching grammar*. Kahnawake, Quebec: Thunderbird Press.

Dermidache, Hamida and Lisa Matthewson. 1995. On the universality of syntactic categories. In *Proceedings of NELS* 25. GLSA, University of Massachusetts, Amherst, Mass.

Di Sciullo, Anna Maria and Edwin Williams. 1987. *On the definition of word*. Cambridge, Mass.: MIT Press.

Diesing, Molly. 1992. *Indefinites*. Cambridge, Mass.: MIT Press.

Dikken, Marcel den. 1995. *Particles: on the syntax of verb-particle, triadic, and causative constructions*. New York: Oxford University Press.

Dixon, R. M. W. 1977. *Grammar of Yidiɲ*. Cambridge: Cambridge University Press.

    1982. *Where have all the adjectives gone?* Berlin: de Gruyter.

Doetjes, Jenny, Ad Neeleman, and Hans van de Koot. 1998. Degree expressions and the autonomy of syntax. Unpublished ms., University College London.

Donohue, Mark. 1999. Syntactic categories in Tukang Besi. *Revue quebecoise de linguistique* 27: 71–90.

Dowty, David. 1979. *Word meaning and Montague grammar*. Dordrecht: Reidel.

    1991. Thematic proto-roles and argument selection. *Language* 67: 547–619.

Emonds, Joseph. 1976. *A transformational approach to English syntax*. New York: Academic Press.

    1985. *A unified theory of syntactic categories*. Dordrecht: Foris.

Enç, Murvet. 1986. Towards a referential analysis of temporal expressions. *Linguistics and Philosophy* 9: 405–26.

Evans, Nicholas. 1991. A draft grammar of Mayali. Unpublished ms., University of Melbourne.

    1997. Role or cast? Noun incorporation and complex predicates in Mayali. In *Complex Predicates*, ed. Alex Alsina, Joan Bresnan, and Peter Sells, 397–430. Stanford: CSLI.

Everett, Daniel and Barbara Kern. 1997. *Wari: the Pacaas Novos language of western Brazil*. London: Routledge.

Fabb, Nigel. 1988. English suffixation is constrained only by selectional restrictions. *Natural Language and Linguistic Theory* 6: 527–39.

Feldman, Harry. 1986. *A grammar of Awtuw*. Canberra: Australian National University.

Fiengo, Robert and Robert May. 1994. *Indices and identity*. Cambridge, Mass.: MIT Press.

Foley, William. 1991. *The Yimas language of New Guinea*. Stanford, Calif.: Stanford University Press.

Fortescue, Michael. 1984. *West Greenlandic*. London: Croom Helm.

Frank, Paul. 1990. *Ika syntax*. Arlington, Tex.: SIL and University of Texas: Arlington.

Fu, Jingqi, Thomas Roeper and Hagit Borer. 2001. The VP within process nominals: evidence from adverbs and the VP anaphor *do so*. *Natural Language and Linguistic Theory* 19: 549–82.

Fukui, Naoki and Margaret Speas. 1986. Specifiers and projections. *MIT Working Papers in Linguistics* 8: 128–72.

Geach, Peter. 1962. *Reference and generality*. Ithaca, NY: Cornell University Press.

Giorgi, Alessandra and Giuseppe Longobardi. 1991. *The syntax of noun phrases: configuration, parameters and empty categories*. Cambridge: Cambridge University Press.

Givón, Talmy. 1984. *Syntax: a functional-typological introduction*. Amsterdam: John Benjamins.

Gordon, Lynn. 1987. Relative clauses in Western Muskogean. In *Muskogean linguistics*, ed. Pamela Munro, 66–80. Los Angeles: UCLA Department of Linguistics.

Greenberg, Joseph. 1963. *Universals of language*. Cambridge, Mass.: MIT Press.

Grimshaw, Jane. 1981. Form, function, and the language acquisition device. In *The logical problem of language acquisition*, ed. C. L. Baker and John McCarthy. Cambridge, Mass.: MIT Press.

  1991. Extended projection. Unpublished ms., Brandeis University, Waltham, Mass.

Grimshaw, Jane and Armin Mester. 1988. Light verbs and θ-marking. *Linguistic Inquiry* 19: 205–32.

Gupta, Anil. 1980. *The logic of common nouns*. New Haven, Conn.: Yale University Press.

Hale, Kenneth. 1983. Warlpiri and the grammar of nonconfigurational languages. *Natural Language and Linguistic Theory* 1: 5–49.

Hale, Kenneth and Samuel Jay Keyser. 1993. On argument structure and the lexical expression of syntactic relations. In *The view from building 20*, ed. Kenneth Hale and Samuel Jay Keyser, 53–110. Cambridge, Mass.: MIT Press.

  1997. On the complex nature of simple predicators. In *Complex predicates*, ed. Alex Alsina, Joan Bresnan, and Peter Sells, 29–66. Stanford, Calif.: CSLI.

Halle, Morris and Alec Marantz. 1993. Distributed morphology and the pieces of inflection. In *The view from building 20*, ed. Kenneth Hale and Samuel Jay Keyser, 111–76. Cambridge, Mass.: MIT Press.

  1994. Some key features of Distributed Morphology. In *MIT working papers in linguistics 21: papers on phonology and morphology*, ed. Andrew Carnie and Heidi Harley, 275–88. Cambridge, Mass.: MITWPL.

Halle, Morris and Jean-Roger Vergnaud. 1987. *An essay on stress*. Cambridge, Mass.: MIT Press.

Haspelmath, Martin. 1993. *A grammar of Lezgian*. Berlin: Mouton de Gruyter.

Heath, Jeffrey. 1984. *Functional grammar of Nunggubuyu*. Canberra: Australian Institute of Aboriginal Studies.

Heim, Irene. 1982. The semantics of definite and indefinite noun phrases. Ph.D. dissertation, University of Massachusetts, Amherst, Mass.

Heim, Irene and Angelika Kratzer. 1998. *Semantics in generative grammar*. Malden, Mass.: Blackwell.

Hengeveld, Kees. 1992. *Non-verbal predication: theory, typology, diachrony*. Berlin: Mouton de Gruyter.

Higginbotham, James. 1985. On semantics. *Linguistic Inquiry* 16: 547–94.

Hoekstra, Tuen. 1988. Small clause results. *Lingua* 74: 101–39.

1992. Aspect and theta theory. In *Thematic structure and its role in grammar*, ed. I. M. Roca, 145–74. Berlin: Foris.

Hopper, Paul and Sandra Thompson. 1984. The discourse basis for lexical categories in universal grammar. *Language* 60: 703–52.

Ingram, David. 1989. *First language acquisition: method, description, and explanation*. New York: Cambridge University Press.

Jackendoff, Ray. 1976. Toward an explanatory semantic representation. *Linguistic Inquiry* 7: 89–150.

1977. *X-bar syntax*. Cambridge, Mass.: MIT Press.

1983. *Semantics and cognition*. Cambridge, Mass.: MIT Press.

Jacobsen, William. 1979. Noun and verb in Nootkan. In *The Victoria conference on northwestern languages*, ed. Barbara Efrat, 83–155. Victoria: British Columbia Provincial Museum.

Jelinek, Eloise. 1984. Empty categories, case, and configurationality. *Natural Language and Linguistic Theory* 2: 39–76.

Jelinek, Eloise and Richard Demers. 1994. Predicates and pronominal arguments in Straits Salish. *Language* 70: 697–736.

Julien, Marit. 2000. Syntactic heads and word formation. Ph.D. dissertation, University of Tromsoe, Tromsoe.

Kamp, Hans. 1975. Two theories about adjectives. In *Formal semantics of natural language*, ed. Edward Keenan, 123–55. London: Cambridge University Press.

1981. A theory of truth and semantic representation. In *Formal methods in the study of language*, ed. J. Groenendijk. Amsterdam: Mathematical Centre.

Kamp, Hans and Uwe Reyle. 1993. *From discourse to logic*. Dordrecht: Kluwer.

Kayne, Richard. 1975. *French syntax: the transformational cycle*. Cambridge, Mass.: MIT Press.

1984a. *Connectedness and binary branching*. Dordrecht: Foris.

1984b. Principles of particle constructions. In *Grammatical representation*, ed. Jacqueline Guéron, Hans-Georg Obenauer, and Jean-Yves Pollock, 101–40. Dordrecht: Foris.

1989. Null subjects and clitic climbing. In *The Null Subject Parameter*, ed. Oswaldo Jaeggli and Kenneth Safir, 239–61. Kluwer: Dordrecht.

1991. Romance clitics, verb movement, and PRO. *Linguistic Inquiry* 22: 647–86.

1995. *The antisymmetry of syntax*. Cambridge, Mass.: MIT Press.

Kennedy, Christopher. 1999. *Projecting the adjective: the syntax and semantics of gradability and comparison*. New York: Garland.

Kennedy, Christopher and Jason Merchant. 2000. Attributive comparative deletion. *Natural Language and Linguistic Theory* 18: 89–146.

Klamer, Marian. 1994. Kambera: a language of Eastern Indonesia. Ph.D. dissertation, Vrije Universiteit, Amsterdam.

Koopman, Hilda. 1984. *The syntax of verbs*. Dordrecht: Foris.

Kratzer, Angelika. 1989. Stage level and individual level predicates. Unpublished ms., University of Massachusetts, Amherst, Mass.

1996. Severing the external argument from its verb. In *Phrase structure and the lexicon*, ed. Johan Rooryck and Laurie Zaring, 109–38. Dordrecht: Kluwer.

Kuno, Susumu. 1973. *The structure of the Japanese language*. Cambridge, Mass: MIT Press.

Lamontagne, Greg and Lisa Travis. 1987. The syntax of adjacency. In *Proceedings of the west coast conference on formal linguistics* 6, 173–86, Stanford University, Stanford, Calif.

Langacker, Ronald. 1987. *Foundations of cognitive grammar*. Stanford, Calif.: Stanford University Press.

Larson, Richard. 1985. Bare NP adverbs. *Linguistic Inquiry* 16: 595–622.

1988. On the double object construction. *Linguistic Inquiry* 19: 335–92.

Larson, Richard and Gabriel Segal. 1995. *Knowledge of meaning: an introduction to semantic theory*. Cambridge, Mass.: MIT Press.

Lasnik, Howard. 1989. *Essays on anaphora*. Dordrecht: Kluwer.

Lasnik, Howard and Mamoru Saito. 1992. *Move alpha: conditions on its applications and output*. Cambridge, Mass.: MIT Press.

Launey, Michel. 1981. *Introduction à la langue et à la littérature azteques*. Paris: L'Harmattan.

Lebeaux, David. 1988. Language acquisition and the form of the grammar. Ph.D dissertation, University of Massachusetts, Amherst, Mass.

Lechner, Winfried. 1999. Comparatives and DP structure. Ph.D. dissertation, University of Massachusetts, Amherst, Mass.

Lefebvre, Claire. 1998. Multifunctionality and variation among grammars: the case of the determiner in Haitian and Fongbe. *Journal of Pidgin and Creole Languages* 13: 93–150.

Legendre, Géraldine. 1997. Secondary predication and functional projections in French. *Natural Language and Linguistic Theory* 15: 43–87.

Levin, Beth and Malka Rappaport. 1986. The formation of adjectival passives. *Linguistic Inquiry* 17: 623–61.

Levin, Beth and Malka Rappaport-Hovav. 1995. *Unaccusativity: at the syntax-lexical semantics interface*. Cambridge, Mass.: MIT Press.

Li, Charles and Sandra Thompson. 1976. Subject and topic: a new typology. In *Subject and topic*, ed. Charles Li, 457–89. New York: Academic Press.

Li, Yafei. 1990. X^0-binding and verb incorporation. *Linguistic Inquiry* 21: 399–426.

Lieber, Rochelle. 1993. *Deconstructing morphology*. Chicago: University of Chicago Press.

Longobardi, Giuseppe. 1994. Reference and proper nouns. *Linguistic Inquiry* 25: 609–66.

Lounsbury, Floyd. 1953. *Oneida verb morphology*. New Haven, Conn.: Yale University Press.

Macnamara, John. 1982. *Names for things: a study of human learning*. Cambridge, Mass.: MIT Press.

Maling, Joan. 1976. Notes on quantifier postposing. *Linguistic Inquiry* 7: 708–18.

1983. Transitive adjectives: a case of categorial reanalysis. In *Linguistic categories: auxiliaries and related puzzles*, ed. Frank Henry and B. Richards, 253–89. Dordrecht: Reidel.

Manfredi, Victor. 1993. Verb focus in the typology of Kwa/Kru and Haitian. In *Focus and grammatical relations*, ed. Francis Byrne and D. Winfrod, 3–51. Amsterdam: John Benjamins.

Marantz, Alec. 1984. *On the nature of grammatical relations*. Cambridge, Mass.: MIT Press.

1988. Clitics, morphological merger, and the mapping to phonological structure. In *Theoretical morphology*, ed. Michael Hammond and Michael Noonan, 253–70. New York: Academic Press.

1997. No escape from syntax. In *University of Pennsylvania working papers in linguistics*, ed. A. Dimitriadis and I. Siegel, 201–25. Philadelphia: University of Pennsylvania Department of Linguistics.

2000. Reconstructing the lexical domain with a single generative engine. Unpublished ms., MIT, Cambridge, Mass.

Massam, Diane. 2001. Pseudo noun incorporation in Niuean. *Natural Language and Linguistic Theory* 19: 153–97.

Matthewson, Lisa and Henry Davis. 1995. The structure of DP in St'at'imcets (Lillooet Salish). In *Papers for the 30th international conference of Salish and neighbouring languages*, 54–68. University of Victoria.

Mithun, Marianne. 1984. The evolution of noun incorporation. *Language* 60: 847–93.

Miyagawa, Shigeru. 1987. Lexical categories in Japanese. *Lingua* 73: 29–51.

1989. *Syntax and semantics 22: structure and case marking in Japanese*. San Diego: Academic Press.

Mosel, Ulrike and Even Hovdhaugen. 1992. *Samoan reference grammar*. Oslo: Scandinavian University Press.

Munro, Pamela. 1976. *Mojave syntax*. New York: Garland.

Munro, Pamela and Lynn Gordon. 1982. Syntactic relations in Western Muskogean. *Language* 58: 81–115.

Murasugi, Keiko. 1990. Adjectives, nominal adjectives and adjectival verbs in Japanese: their lexical and syntactic status. In *UConn working papers in linguistics*, 55–86. Storrs, Conn.: Department of Linguistics.

Muysken, Pieter. 1988. Affix order and interpretation: Quechua. In *Morphology and modularity*, ed. Martin Everaert, Arnold Evers, Riny Huybregts, and Mieke Trommelen, 259–79. Dordrecht: Foris.

Neeleman, Ad. 1997. PP-complements. *Natural Language and Linguistic Theory* 15: 89–137.

Newman, Paul. 2000. *The Hausa language: an encyclopedic reference grammar.* New Haven, Conn.: Yale University Press.

Newmeyer, Frederick. 1998. *Language form and language function.* Cambridge, Mass.: MIT Press.

Nicklas, Dale. 1972. The elements of Choctaw. Ph.D. dissertation, University of Michigan, Ann Arbor.

Nishiyama, Kunio. 1999. Adjectives and the copulas in Japanese. *Journal of East Asian Languages* 8: 183–222.

O'Herin, Brian. 1995. Case and agreement in Abaza. Ph.D. dissertation, University of California, Santa Cruz, Calif.

Ohkado, Masayuki. 1991. On the status of adjectival nouns in Japanese. *Lingua* 83: 67–82.

Omoruyi, Thomas. 1986. Adjectives and adjectivization processes in Edo. *Studies in African Linguistics* 17: 283–301.

1989. Focus and question formation in Edo. *Studies in African Linguistics* 20: 279–99.

Ormston, Jennifer. 1993. Some aspects of Mohawk: the system of verbal inflectional categories. Master's thesis, McGill University, Montreal, Quebec.

Parsons, Terence. 1990. *Events in the semantics of English: a study in subatomic semantics.* Cambridge, Mass.: MIT Press.

Pensalfini, Robert. 1997. Jingulu grammar, dictionary, and texts. Ph.D. dissertation, MIT, Cambridge, Mass.

Pereltsvaig, Asya. 2000. Syntactic categories are neither primitive nor universal: evidence from short and long adjectives in Russian. Unpublished ms., McGill University.

Perlmutter, David and Paul Postal. 1984. The 1-advancement exclusiveness law. In *Studies in Relational Grammar 2,* ed. David Perlmutter and Carol Rosen, 81–125. Chicago: University of Chicago Press.

Pesetsky, David. 1982. Paths and categories. Ph.D dissertation, MIT, Cambridge, Mass.

1995. *Zero syntax.* Cambridge, Mass.: MIT Press.

Pietroski, Paul. 1998. Actions, adjuncts, and agency. *Mind* 107: 73–111.

Pinker, Steven. 1984. *Language learnability and language development.* Cambridge, Mass.: Harvard University Press.

Pollard, Carl and Ivan Sag. 1994. *Head-driven phrase structure grammar.* Chicago: University of Chicago Press.

Pollock, Jean-Yves. 1989. Verb movement, Universal Grammar, and the structure of IP. *Linguistic Inquiry* 20: 365–424.

Postal, Paul. 1979. *Some syntactic rules of Mohawk.* New York: Garland.

Pylkkänen, Liina. 1997. Stage and individual-level psych verbs in Finnish. In *Events as grammatical objects.* Cornell University.

Quine, W. V. O. 1960. *Word and object.* Cambridge, Mass.: MIT Press.

Rapoport, Tova. 1991. Adjunct-predicate licensing and D-structure. In *Perspectives on phrase structure,* ed. Susan Rothstein, 159–87. San Diego: Academic Press.

1993. Verbs in depictives and resultatives. In *Semantics and the lexicon*, ed. James Pustejovsky, 163–84. Dordrecht: Kluwer.

Reinhart, Tanya. 1976. The syntactic domain of anaphora. Ph.D. dissertation, MIT, Cambridge, Mass.

1983. *Anaphora and semantic interpretation*. Chicago: University of Chicago Press.

1987. Specifier and operator binding. In *The representation of (in)definiteness*, ed. Eric Reuland and Alice TerMeulen, 130–67. Cambridge, Mass.: MIT Press.

Reinhart, Tanya and Eric Reuland. 1993. Reflexivity. *Linguistic Inquiry* 24: 657–720.

Renck, G. L. 1975. *A grammar of Yagaria*. Canberra: Australian National University.

Rice, Keren. 1989. *A grammar of Slave*. Berlin: Mouton de Gruyter.

Ritter, Elizabeth. 1991. Two functional categories in noun phrases: evidence from Modern Hebrew. In *Perspectives on phrase structure* ed. Susan Rothstein, 37–62. San Diego, Calif.: Academic Press.

Rizzi, Luigi. 1982. *Issues in Italian syntax*. Dordrecht: Foris.

1986a. Null objects in Italian and the theory of pro. *Linguistic Inquiry* 17: 501–58.

1986b. On chain formation. In *The syntax of pronominal clitics*, ed. Hagit Borer, 65–97. San Diego: Academic Press.

1990. *Relativized minimality*. Cambridge, Mass.: MIT Press.

Robins, R. H. 1989. *A short history of linguistics*. London: Longman.

Roeper, Thomas. 1988. Compound syntax and head movement. *Yearbook of morphology 1988*: 187–228.

Rosen, Carol. 1997. Auxiliation and serialization: on discerning the difference. In *Complex predicates*, ed. Alex Alsina, Joan Bresnan, and Peter Sells, 175–202. Stanford, Calif.: Center for the Study of Language and Information.

Rothstein, Susan. 1983. The syntactic forms of predication. Ph.D. dissertation, MIT, Cambridge, Mass.

Sadock, Jerrold. 1980. Noun incorporation in Greenlandic. *Language* 56: 300–19.

1985. Autolexical syntax: a proposal for the treatment of noun incorporation and similar phenomena. *Natural Language and Linguistic Theory* 3: 379–440.

1990. Book review: Mark C. Baker, Incorporation: a theory of grammatical function changing. *Natural Language and Linguistic Theory* 8: 129–42.

1991. *Autolexical syntax*. Chicago: University of Chicago Press.

Sag, Ivan and Thomas Wasow. 1999. *Syntactic theory: a formal introduction*. Stanford, Calif.: Center for Study of Language and Information.

Saito, Mamoru. 2000. Predicate raising and theta relations. Unpublished ms., Nanzan University, Nagoya.

Saito, Mamoru and Naoki Fukui. 1998. Order in phrase structure and movement. *Linguistic Inquiry* 29: 439–74.

Saito, Mamoru and Hiroto Hoshi. 1998. Control in complex predicates. In Tsukuba Workshop on Complex Predicates, Tsukuba.

Sakaguchi, Mari. 1987. Adjectives in the Seminole dialect of Creek. In *Muskogean linguistics*, ed. Pamela Munro, 134–45. Los Angeles: UCLA Department of Linguistics.

Sapir, Edward. 1921. *Language*. New York: Harcourt Brace Jovanovich.

Sapir, Edward and Morris Swadesh. 1939. *Nootka texts, tales and ethnological narratives, with grammatical notes and lexical materials.* Philadelphia: Linguistic Society of America.

1946. American Indian grammatical categories. *Word* 2.

Sasse, Hans-Jürgen. 1988. Der Irokesische Sprachtyp. Arbeitspapiere des Institutes für Sprachwissenschaft Universität Zu Köln. Neue Folge 9.

Schachter, Paul. 1985. Parts-of-speech systems. In *Language typology and syntactic description*, ed. Timothy Shopen, 3–61. Cambridge: Cambridge University Press.

Selkirk, Elisabeth. 1982. *The syntax of words.* Cambridge, Mass.: MIT Press.

Siegel, Muffy. 1980. *Capturing the adjective.* New York: Garland.

Simpson, Jane. 1983. Resultatives. In *Papers in lexical-functional grammar*, ed. Lori Levin, Malka Rappaport, and Anne Zaenen, 143–57. Bloomington, Ind.: Indiana University Linguistics Club.

1991. *Warlpiri morpho-syntax: a lexicalist approach.* Dordrecht: Kluwer.

Smeets, Ineke. 1989. A Mapuche grammar. Ph.D. dissertation, University of Leiden, Leiden.

Snyder, William. 2001. On the nature of syntactic variation: evidence from complex predicates and complex word formation. *Language* 77: 324–43.

Speas, Margaret. 1990. *Phrase structure in natural language.* Dordrecht: Kluwer.

Sportiche, Dominique. 1988. A theory of floating quantifiers and its corollaries for constituent structure. *Linguistic Inquiry* 19: 425–50.

Sproat, Richard. 1985. On deriving the lexicon. Ph.D dissertation, MIT, Cambridge, Mass.

Sproat, Richard and Chilin Shih. 1991. The cross-linguistic distribution of adjective ordering restrictions. In *Interdisciplinary approaches to language*, ed. Carol Georgopoulos and Roberta Ishihara, 565–93. Dordrecht: Kluwer.

Sridhar, S. N. 1990. *Kannada.* London: Routledge.

Stassen, Leon. 1997. *Intransitive predication.* Oxford: Oxford University Press.

Stewart, Osamuyimen. 1997. Object agreement and the serial verb construction: some minimalist considerations. In *Objects in Benue-Kwa*, ed. Rose-Marie Dechaine and Victor Manfredi, 153–68. The Hague: Graphics Academic Press.

1998. The serial verb construction parameter. Ph.D. dissertation, McGill University, Montreal, Quebec.

2001. *The serial verb construction parameter.* New York: Garland.

Stowell, Timothy. 1981. Origins of phrase structure. Ph.D. dissertation, MIT, Cambridge, Mass.

1983. Subjects across categories. *The Linguistic Review* 2: 285–312.

1991. Small clause restructuring. In *Principles and parameters in comparative syntax*, ed. Robert Freidin, 182–217. Cambridge, Mass.: MIT Press.

Strawson, P. F. 1959. *Individuals: an essay in descriptive metaphysics.* London: Methuen & Co.

Stuurman, Frits. 1985. *Phrase structure theory in generative grammar.* Dordrecht: Foris.

Swadesh, Morris. 1939. Nootka internal syntax. *International Journal of American Linguistics* 9: 77–102.

Talmy, Leonard. 1985. Lexicalization patterns. In *Language typology and syntactic description*, ed. Timothy Shopen, 57–149. Cambridge: Cambridge University Press.

Tchekhoff, Claude. 1981. *Simple sentences in Tongan*. Canberra: Australian National University.

Thompson, Sandra. 1988. A discourse approach to the category "adjective." In *Explaining language universals*, ed. John Hawkins, 167–85. Oxford: Blackwell.

Travis, Lisa. 1984. Parameters and effects of word order variation. Ph.D. dissertation, MIT, Cambridge, Mass.

van Eijk, Jan and Thom Hess. 1986. Noun and verb in Salish. *Lingua* 69: 319–31.

Vergnaud, Jean-Roger. 1974. French relative clauses. Ph.D. dissertation. MIT, Cambridge, Mass.

Washio, Ryuichi. 1997. Resultatives, compositionality and language variation. *Journal of East Asian Languages* 6: 1–49.

Watanabe, A. 1991. Wh-in-situ, subjacency, and chain formation. Unpublished ms., MIT, Cambridge, Mass.

Watkins, Laurel J. 1984. *A grammar of Kiowa*. Lincoln: University of Nebraska Press.

Weber, David. 1989. *A grammar of Huallaga (Huanuco) Quechua*. Berkeley: University of California Press.

Wetzer, Harrie. 1996. *The typology of adjectival predication*. Berlin: Mouton de Gruyter.

Whorf, Benjamin. 1956. *Language, thought, and reality*. Cambridge, Mass.: MIT Press.

Wiggins, David. 1980. *Sameness and substance*. Cambridge, Mass.: Harvard University Press.

Williams, Edwin. 1980. Predication. *Linguistic Inquiry* 11: 203–38.

   1981. Argument structure and morphology. *The Linguistic Review* 1: 81–114.

   1982. Another argument that passive is transformational. *Linguistic Inquiry* 13: 160–63.

   1989. The anaphoric nature of θ-roles. *Linguistic Inquiry* 20: 425–56.

Williamson, Janis. 1987. An indefiniteness restriction for relative clauses in Lakhota. In *The representation of indefiniteness*, ed. Eric Reuland and Alice TerMeulen. Cambridge, Mass.: MIT Press.

Wojdak, Rachel. 2001. An argument for category neutrality? In *Proceedings of WCCFL* 20, 621–34. Cascadilla Press.

Zepter, Alex. 2001. Mixed head directionality: German and beyond. Unpublished ms., Rutgers University, New Brunswick, NJ.

Index

Abaza
  incorporation in, 309, 310
  tensed nouns and adjectives in, 51, 162, 208n.
Abney, Steven, 1n., 3, 196, 212, 266, 269, 324
acquisition, of lexical categories, 15n., 36,
    296–301
Adelaar, Willem, 181
adjectives, 2n., 107
  acquired late, 298
  and determiners, 111–19, 121–23
  and incorporation, 4, 152, 169n.
  and measure phrases, 106n.
  and morphological causatives, 53–56
  and tense marking, 46–47, 51–52, 52n.
  as attributive modifiers, 183
  as complements, 149
  as expression of degree, 213
  as modifiers of null nouns, 151–52
  as supplanting nouns, 171
  cannot be arguments, 142–44
  compared to PPs, 313, 319
  compared to verbs, 4, 10, 13, 15, 36, 64,
    69–73, 75–76, 91–92
  in decomposition of verbs, 79–83, 275, 320
  definition of, 2, 11, 14, 16, 21, 101, 190,
    213, 270
  derivable into verbs, 162
  morphology of, 277–78
  movement of, 133–36, 138, 140, 141
  nominalization of, 284
  nonintersective readings of, 120n., 259
  not involved in anaphora, 98, 126, 128–29,
    131, 163
  notional core of, 14, 291, 293, 296
  predicate versus attributive, 122, 194–95,
    205–11
  predicative use of, 30–31, 35, 69
  stage level and individual level, 33
  subtypes of, 240–44
  theta-role assignment by, 31n., 41, 43, 62,
    65, 66, 79, 83–85
  universality of, 88
  used as adverbs, 155, 230–37

adjuncts
  as expressions of degree, 212n., 218
  category restrictions on, 155
  PPs as, 312, 315, 319–23
  versus complements, 78n.
  see also adverbs
adpositions, 303–25
  as adjuncts, 78n., 155, 311–25
  as bearers of a referential index, 133n.
  as functional categories, 21, 303–11
  as lexical categories, 1n.
  as making nouns into modifiers, 193, 198,
    246
  contrasted to derivational affixes, 7–8
  covert, in manner adverbs, 235n.
  distinctive features of, 2, 12
  in resultative phrases, 219n., 226
  objects of, 99, 143
  universality of, 6, 11
adverbs, 39
  adjectives used as, 230–37, 243
  as expressions of degree, 196n., 213, 216,
    218, 246
  in derived nominals, 284
  obligatory, 318
  of quantification, 110n.
  pronominal, 130n.
  word order of, 223, 228, 322
affixes
  as triggers of head movement, 48, 49
  selection properties of, 48, 50–51, 58–59
  role in affecting theta-roles, 65
agent
  assigned only by verb, 78, 92
  structure for assignment of, 25–26, 66,
    79–80, 148
Agheyisi, Rebecca, 40
agreement
  as clitic, 188
  as pleonastic, 27
  as sign of category distinctions, 4, 5, 9
  as test for adjectives, 247, 248n.
  as unaccusativity diagnostic, 76

Bhat, D. N. S., 14, 16, 21, 143, 153, 166n.,
171, 176n., 190, 191, 192, 193, 194,
205n., 213, 218, 237, 238, 274, 290, 293
binding theory
as evidence for category differences, 30n.
as evidence for null subjects, 29
predicate-oriented version, 146n.
relationship to theta-role assignment, 145n.
use of indices in, 96
Bittner, Maria, 173, 181, 222, 291, 304
Bobaljik, Jonathan, 276n.
Bolinger, Dwight, 194, 200n., 206, 209
Borer, Hagit, 57n., 65, 72, 73, 77, 141, 193n.,
265–69, 277, 284
Bowers, John, 25, 34–35, 37–39, 68, 69
Bresnan, Joan, 13, 54, 58, 95, 96, 155, 156,
170, 247, 248, 282, 304, 308, 312, 316,
317, 321
Broadwell, George, 251, 252
Burzio, Luigi, 31, 40, 63, 64, 69

canonical structural realizations, 296–97, 300,
301
Carey, Susan, 299
Carlson, Greg, 115, 226
Carnie, Andrew, 45n.
case
and lexical category distinctions, 2n.
as functional head, 181, 304
in nonconfigurational languages, 171, 173
of predicate nominals, 254
on heads of relative clauses, 252
relationship to adpositions, 304, 323n.
Categorial Grammar, 207
causatives, 141, 287
and Pred–verb distinction, 45
category restrictions on, 58, 100, 151, 159,
167n., 186, 249
of adjectives, 243, 251, 284n.
periphrastic, 247
syntactic versus non-syntactic, 282–83
CAUSE operator, 79
c-command, 67n.
among arguments, 80–82
as condition on agreement, 208n.
as condition on binding, 127
as condition on noun licensing, 153
as condition on theta-role assignment, 145
condition on floated quantifiers, 74
condition on possessive interpretation, 72, 74
in attributive constructions, 198n.
in PPs, 323n.
chain formation, 96
Chamorro, 158
Cheng, Lisa, 117

Chichewa
adjective–noun agreement in, 122
adjunct licensing in, 155
adpositions in, 304, 308, 312, 317
applicative in, 58, 309
bare noun phrases in, 113
causative in, 54, 282, 287
lexical categories in, 238, 250
no degree heads in, 218
no zero derivation in, 266n.
nouns replacing adjectives in, 198, 246–48
Pred in, 44–45, 165
resultatives in, 226
Chierchia, Gennaro
on bare noun phrases, 113, 115–21, 123,
144, 268
on type theory, 14, 35, 36, 57, 80, 204, 315
Chinese
bare nouns in, 113, 115–16
compound verbs in, 228
free topics in, 156–57
overt Pred in, 46
zero derivation in, 266n.
Choctaw
adjectives in, 10, 251–54
unaccusativity in, 76
Chomsky, Noam, 48, 49, 80
barriers theory, 67n., 114, 254
government and binding theory, 2n., 29, 66,
96, 123, 127, 133, 134, 137, 154, 197, 267
minimalist program, 2, 20, 25, 26, 28n., 35,
36, 48n., 49, 66, 67n., 79, 83, 86, 96, 97,
134, 196, 197, 199
on *wh*-movement, 136n., 138
"Remarks on nominalization," 1, 3, 11, 77,
85, 190, 238, 304
Chung, Sandra, 45n.
Cinque, Guglielmo, 131, 231, 267, 273, 280
on adjectives, 32, 63–65, 69, 77, 85, 200n.
Clark, Eve, 297, 298n.
classifiers, 119n.
clauses
as bearing a referential index, 98n.
coindexed with topic, 156
marked for definiteness, 125n.
NPs cannot constitute, 99, 157–59
cleft constructions, 136, 140
cliticization, *see* Italian, *ne*-cliticization in
clitics
incorporating verbs as, 308
pronominal, 309
tense as, 188
cognate objects
in predicate clefts, 141
with unergative verbs, 86

Demers, Richard, 181, 185
demonstratives, 182
depictive predicates, 172, 223n.
  compared to resultatives, 219–21
Dermidache, Hamida, 83n., 175, 182–84, 203
desideratives, 58–59, 287
determiners
  and argumenthood, 115, 117–18, 144
  and referential indices, 119n.
  as disguising category distinctions, 188
  as licensers of null nouns, 151
  as selecting only nouns, 112, 120–25, 201,
    179–82
  blocking noun incorporation, 114
  compared to degrees, 217n.
  missing in nonconfigurational languages,
    171
  movement of nouns to, 141
  place in typology of categories, 325
  quantifiers as, 110
  semantics of, 118–19
  see also articles
Di Sciullo, Anna-Maria, 85, 281
Diesing, Molly, 33
Dikken, Marcel den, 67n., 220n., 314
Dionysius Thrax, 1
discourse referents
  introduced by nouns, 115, 153, 157, 163
  not introduced by denominal verbs, 166
Discourse Representation Theory
  definiteness in, 111
  semantics of nouns in, 104–05
  treatment of anaphora, 128
dislocation, 155, 173
distinctive features
  and case assignment, 2n.
  and category distinctions, 1, 12–13, 190,
    239, 241, 303
  as theory of selection, 48, 58, 213
distributed morphology, 52n., 165, 244
  view of categories in, 265–71, 280
Dixon, R. M. W., 14, 166n., 192, 238, 248,
    296, 298
Doetjes, Jenny, 212n., 214n.
domination, 254
Donohue, Mark, 176, 177, 180n., 185, 187,
    192, 256
double object constructions
  incompatible with resultatives, 220, 224,
    228
  relationship to PPs, 323
Dowty, David, 26, 79, 83n., 85
Dutch
  adpositions in, 304, 321, 322
  predicate nominals in, 162n.

economy of representation, 49
Edo
  adjectives in, 120, 210, 223n.
  adverbs in, 232, 237
  arguments in, 143
  articles in, 111, 119–20
  bare nouns in, 113, 116–17
  compounding in, 202
  derivation in, 59n., 161
  existential sentences in, 158
  focus constructions in, 140
  lexical categories in, 10, 121n., 251
  modification in, 192, 198, 200, 201, 203
  no degree heads in, 218
  no zero derivation in, 266n.
  Pred in, 40–44, 165
  prepositions in, 304, 313n., 316, 319
  resultatives in, 219, 222n., 223
  serial verbs in, 227–30
ellipsis, 130, 132
  and fragment NP answers, 157n.
  of NP leaving PP, 318n.
  role in rescuing traces, 138n.
Emonds, Joseph, 205n., 231, 304, 313n.
empty category
  licensed by PP, 321–22
  see also null operators; PRO; traces
Empty Category Principle, 67
  and null nouns, 123
  as account of unaccusativity diagnostics,
    68–69, 88
  regulating head movement, 70, 72
Enc, Murvet, 209
English
  absence of SVCs in, 228
  adjectives in, 120–21, 141, 206, 210
  adjuncts in, 312
  adpositions in, 304, 316
  articles in, 111, 120–21
  attributive modification in, 192, 200, 205n.
  causative affixes in, 56
  compounding in, 202, 271
  copula in, 40
  degree heads in, 123n., 212
  derivational morphemes in, 283–85,
    287–88, 305
  existential sentences in, 158
  gerunds in, 325
  inflection of verbs in, 279
  lexical categories in, 238
  locative inversion in, 321
  null nouns in, 122n.
  optional nouns in, 176
  predicate nominals in, 163, 325
  range of pronominal forms in, 129–32